Hands-on Booting

Learn the Boot Process of Linux, Windows, and Unix

Yogesh Babar

Apress®

Hands-on Booting

Yogesh Babar
Pune, India

ISBN-13 (pbk): 978-1-4842-5889-7 ISBN-13 (electronic): 978-1-4842-5890-3
https://doi.org/10.1007/978-1-4842-5890-3

Managing Director, Apress Media LLC: Welmoed Spahr
Acquisitions Editor: Celestin Suresh John
Development Editor: Matthew Moodie
Coordinating Editor: Aditee Mirashi

Cover designed by eStudioCalamar

Cover image designed by Pixabay

Distributed to the book trade worldwide by Springer Science+Business Media New York, 233 Spring Street, 6th Floor, New York, NY 10013. Phone 1-800-SPRINGER, fax (201) 348-4505, e-mail orders-ny@springer-sbm.com, or visit www.springeronline.com. Apress Media, LLC is a California LLC and the sole member (owner) is Springer Science + Business Media Finance Inc (SSBM Finance Inc). SSBM Finance Inc is a **Delaware** corporation.

For information on translations, please e-mail rights@apress.com, or visit www.apress.com/rights-permissions.

Apress titles may be purchased in bulk for academic, corporate, or promotional use. eBook versions and licenses are also available for most titles. For more information, reference our Print and eBook Bulk Sales web page at www.apress.com/bulk-sales.

Any source code or other supplementary material referenced by the author in this book is available to readers on GitHub via the book's product page, located at www.apress.com/978-1-4842-5889-7. For more detailed information, please visit www.apress.com/source-code.

Printed on acid-free paper

This book is dedicated to Red Hat. Its amazing work culture has proved that sharing is caring.

Table of Contents

About the Author

Yogesh Babar has been with Red Hat for the past ten years. Currently he is a principal technical support engineer in the Linux kernel domain. He specializes in the troubleshooting and performance tuning of Linux enterprise servers. The Linux boot process is his forte, and he regularly speaks at open source conferences and forums. He also conducts workshops on operating systems for engineering students.

About the Technical Reviewer

Marc Sandusky is an embedded software engineer with 28 years' experience in low-level programming. He has worked in industries such as PC BIOS, medical devices, and defense. He is experienced in embedded OSs (Linux, Windows Embedded Compact), RTOS (uCOS/II, FreeRTOS), and bare-metal systems. He currently lives in southern California with his wife and three children. You can reach him at marc_sandusky@outlook.com or www.linkedin.com/in/marc-sandusky-67852b2/.

Acknowledgments

I would like to thank Harald Hoyer for writing dracut and Lennart Poettering for writing systemd. Harald, you had tremendous patience when answering my back-to-back questions.

Thanks also to: Sheetal, Rama and Shoumik, who encouraged me to document the booting procedure; Parth Goswami, who helped me write a brief article about it; Rangan and Raghvendra Pai for asking for regular updates on it; and Gokhale Sir for igniting a spark in me and also for showing me what I am really good at.

To the entire Apress team, especially acquisitions editor Celestine John, project coordinator Aditee Mirashi, and development editor Matthew Moodie who put tremendous efforts into developing this book. Special thanks to Marc Sandusky for technically reviewing the book. With it being my first book, I made a lot of mistakes, but the entire Apress team stood behind me throughout the process.

Last but not the least, thanks to my beautiful, strong, and amazing wife. Darshana, what patience you have shown! Sometimes I wonder how you managed to stay with someone like me who is always chasing some project.

Introduction

I was in the first week at a new job, and I saw one of our customers asking for assistance on a "can't boot" issue. I was new and inexperienced. I wanted to assist, but I could not. The customer was panicked since it brought production down. Every minute was counting for them, because thousands of users were not able to access that system since it was unbootable. Everyone was panicking. Eventually some of our most senior engineers resolved the issue. It took them almost five hours to put the system back in production. Everything turned out well in the end, but that tense situation created something in me, which was a desire to learn. I decided to learn the entire booting sequence.

When I started looking for books and articles on the Internet, I was disappointed. There are thousands of books and countless articles available on operating systems, but I could not find a single book that thoroughly explained the entire booting sequence.

There is a saying in the open source world: if there is something you are looking for and it is not available, then build it. So, I decided to learn the booting sequence on my own. It took me years to understand the entire booting sequence. The best thing I did on my journey was to keep notes and also start teaching what I learned to others. After all, sharing is caring. My booting sessions became popular among engineering students and system administrators. Some of them really pushed me hard to write a proper book on the topic. I contacted Apress, and they liked the idea, so today you have the first book of booting in your hands.

This book has a unique approach. First I discuss why someone should learn about booting. In other words, why is it important? Next I explain how different bootloaders work by installing almost 100+ operating systems on one machine. There is a dedicated chapter on the Linux bootloader. In fact, there are dedicated chapters for every component involved in the booting sequence. Next, I explain the kernel's role in the booting sequence. The kernel plays a vital role along with systemd. Since systemd is the first process started by kernel, eventually it takes care of the entire booting sequence. There are several chapters that cover systemd, so this book is a good resource for those who want to read about systemd. I have also covered the most common "can't boot" scenarios of Linux. This makes the book a great resource for system admins as well. It does not mean this book is for Linux experts only. If you know basics of Linux, then this book is for you. The book is a great bridge between the beginners and experts of Linux. I hope you will like the effort.

There is an old saying: no book is perfect. If you find some bugs in this book or you simply want to get in touch with me, please feel free to write to me at yogeshbabar420@gmail.com.

Thank you,

Yogesh Babar

CHAPTER 1

Introduction

Not everyone knows Fedora. One day, someone asked me a question:

> **Student**: What is Fedora?
>
> **Me**: Fedora is Linux.
>
> **Student**: What is Linux?
>
> **Me**: Linux is an operating system.
>
> **Student**: What is an operating system?
>
> **Me**: It runs computers.
>
> **Student**: What is a computer?
>
> **Me**: Computers help users.
>
> **Student**: What is a user?
>
> **Me**: A user is just like me.
>
> **Student**: Who the hell are you?
>
> **Me**: Well, my name is Yogesh Babar. I have worked at Red Hat for the last ten years, and I love talking about how operating systems boot.

Why?

Everyone knows that an operating system takes approximately 20 to 30 seconds to boot. So, why did I write a 486-page book about a 30-second booting sequence? The answer is simple.

- There is no proper document/article/book available that explains the complete booting sequence. You will find hundreds of good books on operating systems but none on how a system boots.

1

© Yogesh Babar 2020
Y. Babar, *Hands-on Booting*, https://doi.org/10.1007/978-1-4842-5890-3_1

- You can resolve boot issues only if you know how the system boots.

- If you are a sysadmin and attending an interview, the interviewers will ask about how Linux boots.

- "Can't boot" issues are always the highest severity as the entire production system goes down because of them. If the system is slow, the production is still up and running; though it is affected, at least it is still running. A server that has 10,000 users but can't boot means the entire production system is down. That's the importance of booting, and as I said, you cannot solve boot issues if you don't know how a system boots.

- It's fun to understand the booting procedure.

- While learning all of this, you will gain immense happiness.

What?

So, what exactly is booting? In technical terms, the process of copying the kernel from the hard disk to memory and then executing it is called *booting*. But that definition does not really inspire us to learn about booting.

I will put it in my own words: A mother is a superset, and her newborn baby is a subset of her. In the same way, an operating system is a superset, and booting is a subset of it. A subset belongs to its superset.

Now consider this statement: "A child gives birth to a mother."

Technically it is wrong, but imagine that until a woman has a baby, she is a woman; the moment she has a baby, a woman becomes a mother. So, a child gives birth to a mother.

The same happens in computers. Technically booting is part of an operating system, and the operating system should give birth to booting, but it's the other way around. It's booting that gives birth to the operating system. Hence, we can say that *booting* is the procedure that gives birth to an operating system.

The Focus of This Book

The book explains the booting procedure of an x86 architecture–based desktop or server system, and it covers the booting procedure of various operating systems. The primary focus is on the in-depth analysis of the Linux booting procedure, with a secondary focus on other popular operating systems such as Windows and UNIX. As you know, there are a huge number of Linux distributions. Some are for desktop users, some are for enterprise customers, some are solely for gaming purposes, and some are available for users who prefer to follow a do-it-yourself approach. It is almost impossible to cover each and every distribution's booting sequence. Hence, I have decided to choose the Linux distribution that is the first choice for enterprise customers, and that is Red Hat Enterprise Linux (RHEL).

RHEL is based on Fedora Linux. Fedora is fast moving (a six-month release cycle), whereas RHEL is a slow-moving distribution (a two- to three-year release cycle). This means Fedora adopts the latest developments as soon as the QE (Quality Engineering) team gives them the green light. Since Fedora is a testing bed of popular enterprise Linux distributions, whatever is available in Fedora eventually becomes part of RHEL. systemd is the best example of this. That's why I have chosen Fedora Linux to explain the Linux booting sequence.

Power Supply

It all starts when you hit the power button. When you press the power button, the power supply goes to the motherboard. The motherboard sends a signal to your power supply (SMPS/PSU), which returns a good power supply, and as a result, the motherboard tries to start the CPU.

CPU

When the x86 architecture–based CPU starts, it clears the old data from all the registers and starts with this:

```
IP              0xfff0
CS selector     0xf000
CS base         0xffff0000
```

0xffff0000 + 0xfff0 = 0xfffffff0. This is the memory location at which the CPU expects to find the first instruction to execute. At this location, it contains a jump instruction that points to a BIOS entry point. In other words, this is how the BIOS starts or the CPU lands at the BIOS/firmware.

After this, the firmware and bootloader are the next stage of a booting procedure. It's the job of the firmware to launch the bootloader of an operating system. In the next chapter, I will discuss what happens in the firmware and how it executes the bootloader.

CHAPTER 2

Multiboot

Understanding the bootloader and firmware is complex. It is not necessarily difficult, but the topic can be complicated. To make it easy to digest for the readers of this book, I will use three test systems.

System Number	System Name	Purpose
1	BIOS	To demonstrate the BIOS
2	UEFI	To demonstrate UEFI
3	Jarvis	For a 100+ OS multiboot project

Since the bootloaders and firmware work closely together, I will start by installing a specific list of operating systems on each system and while doing that explain the relationship between the bootloader and the firmware. This approach will make complex topics easier to understand, more interesting, and a lot of fun. In short, I will explain the bootloader and firmware (BIOS/UEFI) together though they are different concepts.

Note The BIOS-based multiboot part of this chapter was inspired by Mr Vijay Gokhale Sir's workshop on the subject. I thank him for the inspiration.

List of Operating Systems

We will be installing the following operating systems on our first BIOS system, which means on a system that has the BIOS firmware installed:

- Sun OpenSolaris 2009
- Fedora Linux 15
- PC-BSD 9.0

5

© Yogesh Babar 2020
Y. Babar, *Hands-on Booting*, https://doi.org/10.1007/978-1-4842-5890-3_2

- Windows 7

- Red Hat Enterprise Linux 6.0

- Windows Server 2003 (2k3)

- Windows XP

I know these operating systems are quite old, but I have chosen them for a reason.

See, the BIOS itself is an outdated firmware, so if you want to understand the BIOS, you have to use old operating systems only. Remember, you can understand UEFI (the current firmware) only if you understand the BIOS. It's like you will understand Java better if you know C well. Also, using these old operating systems will give me a chance to touch upon the Windows and Unix bootloaders as well. In addition, it will provide me with the opportunity to explain the GRUB legacy bootloader of Linux.

The idea is to multiboot our BIOS system with all the operating systems mentioned earlier. To do that, we need to follow every operating system's rules and regulations.

OS	Rules
Unix	Unix operating systems (OpenSolaris and BSD) have to be installed on a primary partition only.
Linux	Linux does not have any installation rules. It can be installed on any primary or logical partition.
Windows	The Windows operating system can be installed on any partition (primary or logical), but the predecessor of the Windows family has to be present on the first primary. That means you can install Windows 7 on a logical partition, but its predecessor, which is XP or win2k3, has to be present on the first primary partition. Also, you cannot break the Windows operating system sequence of installation. For example, one cannot install Windows 7 first and then the older win2k3 or XP. It has to be in this sequence: 98, then 2000, and then XP.

Take some time and try to prepare your OS installation sequence. Verify your booting sequence now.

The final sequence of the operating system is as shown here:

1) Windows XP

2) Sun OpenSolaris 2008

3)   PC-BSD 9.0

4)   Windows Server 2003

5)   Windows 7

6)   Red Hat Enterprise Linux 6

7)   Fedora 15

Installing the Operating Systems

Now we'll talk about installing the operating systems.

Primary/Logical Partitions

With the BIOS, we can create only four partitions. But of course you probably have seen more partitions used than that. So, let me change my statement a bit. On a BIOS-based system, you can create only four *primary* partitions on your disk. If you want more than that, then you need to make the fourth primary partition a *secondary* (also called an *extended*) partition. The extended partition will work as a container, and inside this container you can create as many *logical* partitions as you want. Why are these partitions called logical partitions, because they are not visible to BIOS? Also, why can the BIOS make only four primary partitions? These questions will be answered when we discuss the master boot record.

Partitioning

Let's partition the BIOS system's hard disk first. We will use the GParted live CD for this. GParted is a tool from the GNU community. It's a free, open source, Debian Linux-based live ISO image. Figure 2-1 shows our BIOS system's partition layout.

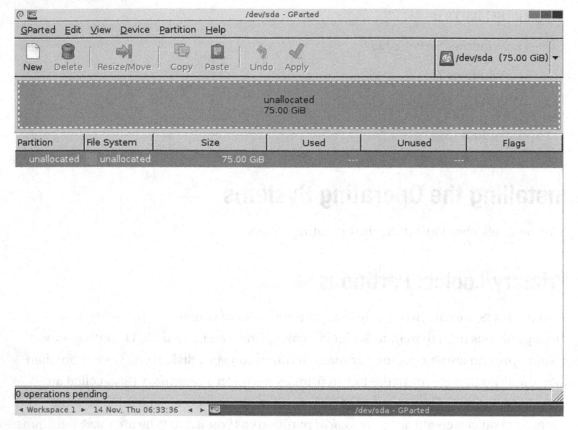

Figure 2-1. *The partition layout of the BIOS in GParted*

The GParted operation to partition a hard disk is straightforward. We will create the
partition layout shown in Figure 2-2 on the 75 GB of disk space.

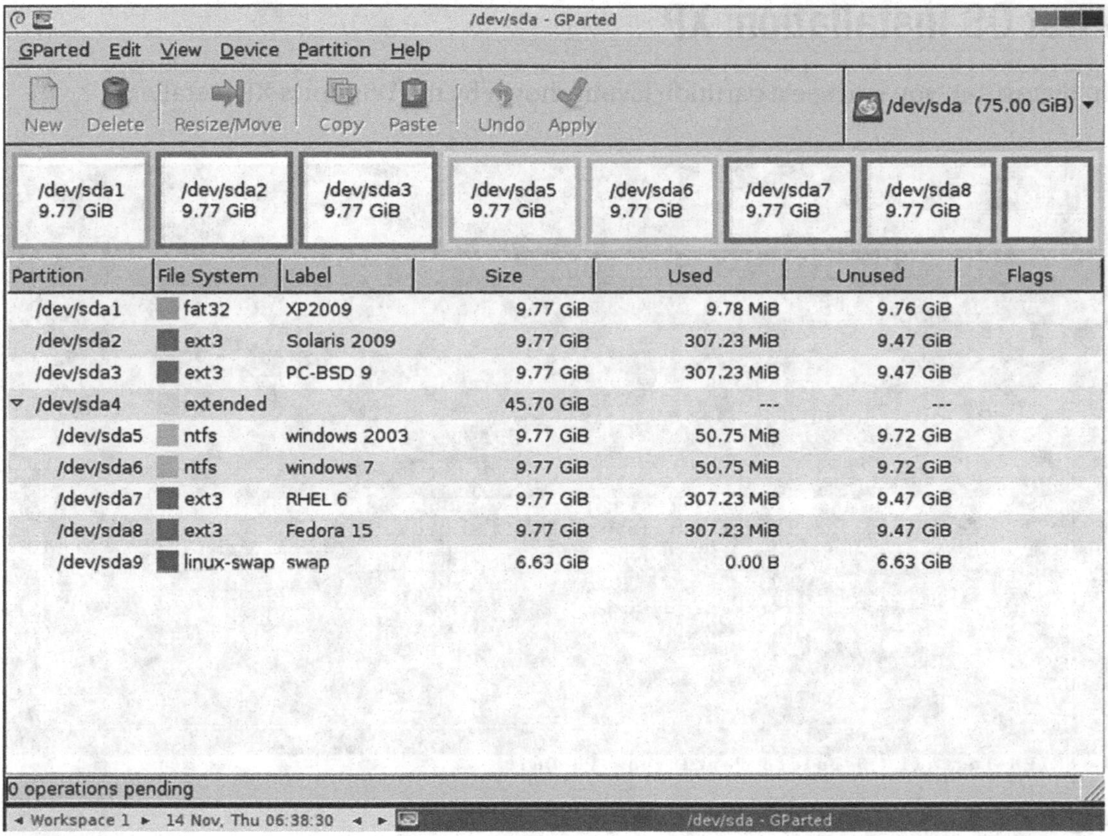

Figure 2-2. *GParted-made partition layout*

For more information on how to use GParted to partition your hard drive, please refer to the GParted documentation at `https://gparted.org/articles.php`.

In Figure 2-3, you can see the disk name, partition size, used filesystem, and associated flags (if any).

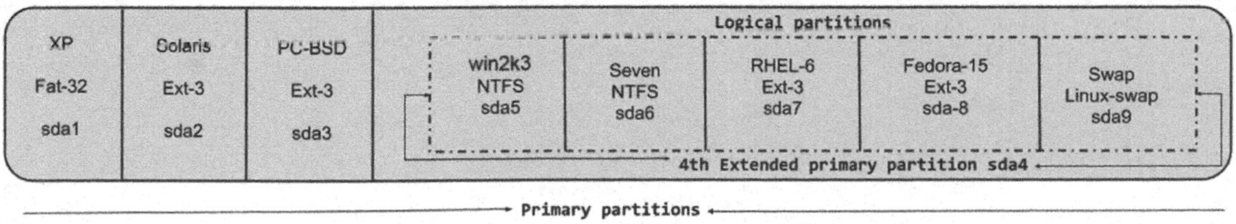

Figure 2-3. *GParted-made filesystem layout*

Let's install our first operating system on our first primary partition.

First OS Installation: XP

In Figure 2-4, you can see a partition layout shown by the Windows XP installer.

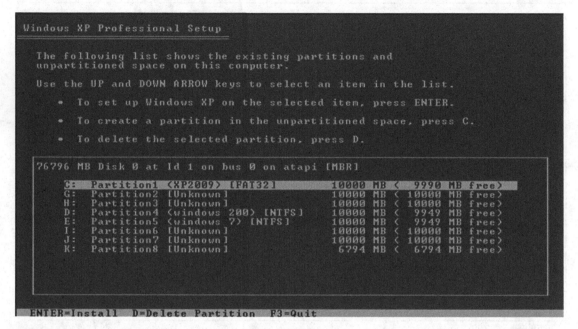

Figure 2-4. *Partition layout shown by XP's installer*

We are installing XP on the first primary partition. In terms of Windows, it is a C: drive, as shown in Figure 2-4. After finishing the installation and rebooting the system, we get Windows XP on our screen (Figure 2-5).

Figure 2-5. *XP after successful installation*

It's time to understand how Windows XP has been booted, but before that, we need to understand the boot sector. The *boot sector* is every HDD's first sector (512 bytes) plus 31 KB of space; in other words, it's the first 63 sectors on the boot medium (0 to 62). Or, you can consider under the boot sector that some space (512 bytes + 31 KB) of every partition will be reserved to store the bootloader-related information. This space (again, 512 bytes + 31 KB) will not be shown by the OS to users. The actual data storage in a partition starts after this reserved space. Refer to Figure 2-6 for a better understanding of this.

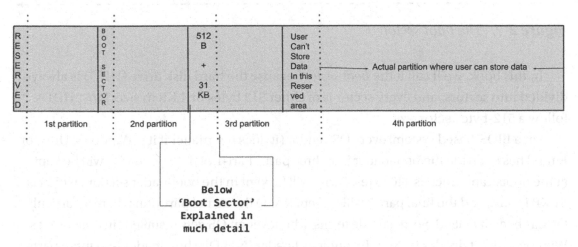

Figure 2-6. *The disk layout on a BIOS-based system*

Boot Sector

There is one amazing saying in Sanskrit that goes like this: "एकम सत विप्रा: बहुधा: वदन्ति सत्य". This means there is only one truth but various ways to reach it. As shown in Figure 2-7, the boot sector is called by different names, but ultimately the concept remains the same. People refer this structure with the following names:

- Master boot record (MBR)

- Boot record

- Boot sector

- Bootloader

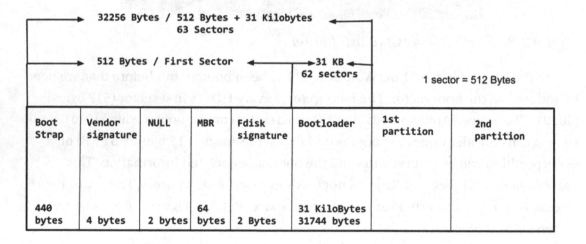

Figure 2-7. *The boot sector*

In this book, we'll call it the *boot sector* because the hard disk drive (HDD) is always divided into sectors, and every sector is of either 512 bytes or 4 KB in size. Most HDDs follow a 512-byte sector size.

On a BIOS-based system, every OS vendor (it does not matter if it is Windows, Unix, or Linux) has to divide the bootloader into three parts. Part-1 of the bootloader will be kept at the bootstrap, which is 440 bytes. Part-2 will be kept in the bootloader section, which is 31 KB in size, and the final part-3 will be kept inside the actual partition where a particular OS has been installed. So, in simple terms, whenever an OS gets installed (in our case it's Windows XP), it divides its New Technology Loader (NTLDR) bootloader into three parts.

Location	Size	Part	Information
Bootstrap	440 bytes	NTLDR part-1	The tiniest part
Bootloader	31 KB	NTLDR part-2	Bigger compared to part-1
Inside an actual OS partition	No size limitation	NTLDR part-3	The biggest part

But why is the bootloader divided into three parts?

It is because of historical reasons. The BIOS has technical limitations in that it cannot access more than 512 bytes or cannot read beyond the first sector. So, it is obvious that when BIOS finishes its task, it jumps on the entire HDD's first 512 bytes and whoever is there simply runs that program. Fortunately, that program will be our bootstrap (440 bytes). Since the bootstrap is tiny in size, it does only one thing, which is to jump on a bigger space, which is the part-2 bootloader. It is 31 KB in size. This 31 KB is again very tiny, and it has to find an even bigger size. This bootloader will jump to part-3, which is inside a partition. This part-3 file will be at the C: drive with the file name NTLDR. The part-3 file of XP's bootloader is visible in Figure 2-8.

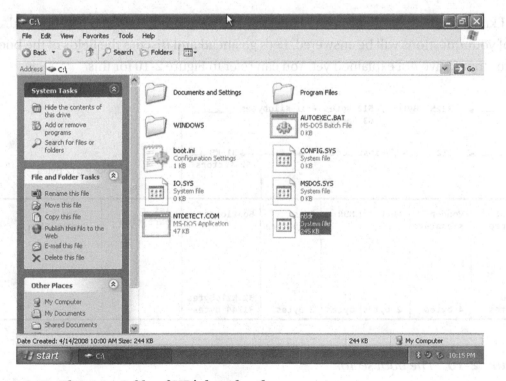

Figure 2-8. *The part-3 file of XP's bootloader*

As you can see, the file is much bigger in size (245 KB). This file will do the heavy lifting of the bootloader's actual job, which is copying the kernel of Windows XP called `winload.exe` (this file knows where XP's kernel is) from `C:\windows` in memory. Once the kernel is copied into memory, the bootloader's job is done, and it goes away. Remember, `OS==kernel==OS`. Once the kernel is in memory, it will take care of the rest of the booting sequence. You can see XP's boot sequence in Figure 2-9.

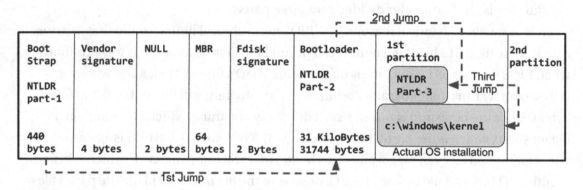

Figure 2-9. *The boot sequence of Windows XP*

I know there are probably a lot of questions in your mind. But keep reading, and all of your questions will be answered. Let's go ahead and discuss the fields of the boot sector that I have not explained yet. You can refer to Figure 2-10 for this.

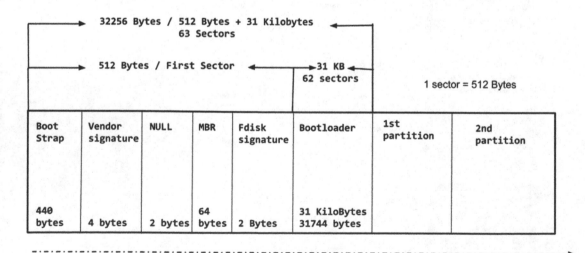

Figure 2-10. *The boot sector*

The vendor signature field is for HDD vendors. The data that is mentioned here tells us which vendor has manufactured this HDD, such as Seagate, Western Digital, Samsung, etc. So, basically it holds the HDD manufacturer information.

NULL has only 2 bytes of space. The NULL means NULL. If this is not NULL, then the BIOS will consider this HDD as faulty/corrupted at the time of the POST routine, and booting will be halted. So, it has to be NULL. Whenever the OS abruptly reboots or when the OS or HDD itself detects the bad sector or some sort of serious corruption, this field will be marked as non-NULL.

The MBR field could be the most popular section of all of these fields. MBR stands for "master boot record," and it is 64 bytes in size. The MBR is further divided into four parts. Each part is 16 bytes in size, and every part holds one partition's information.

Size	Parts	Stores
16 bytes	Part-1	First partition's information
16 bytes	Part-2	Second partition's information
16 bytes	Part-3	Third partition's information
16 bytes	Part-4	Fourth partition's information

This means 64 bytes of the MBR can hold only four entries of the partition, and this is the reason why you can make only four primary partitions on a BIOS-based system.

The fdisk signature is also called the *boot flag*; some people simply call it *, or in Windows style, it is also called an *active/inactive flag*. The fdisk is important in the case of multibooting different operating systems, which we will not talk about now. For now, I want you to remember these two rules:

- The logical partition cannot be active.

- The OS cannot boot from the logical partition.

As of now, these two rules will not make any sense to you, but we will discuss them at the right time. Figure 2-11 shows the complete booting sequence of Windows XP.

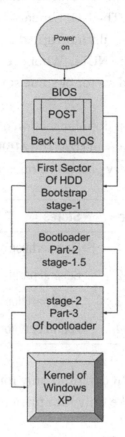

Figure 2-11. *The boot sequence of Windows XP*

We will install and boot a new OS now, namely, OpenSolaris 2008.

OpenSolaris 2008

Figure 2-12 shows the screen when booting with an OpenSolaris 2008 installation medium.

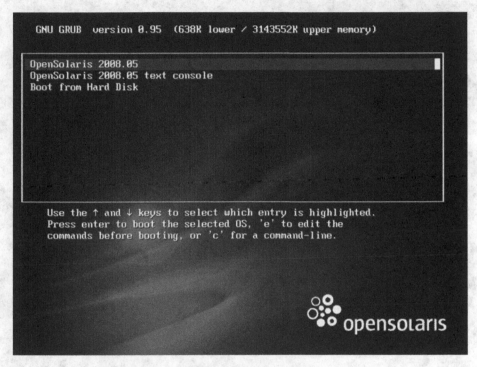

Figure 2-12. *The welcome screen of the OpenSolaris 2008 installation medium*

We need to install OpenSolaris on the second partition. You can see in Figure 2-13 that we have chosen the second primary partition for the installation.

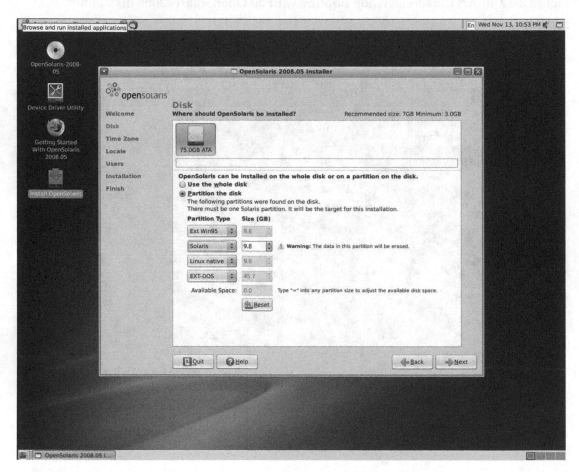

Figure 2-13. *Disk layout shown by the OpenSolaris 2008 installer*

But as you can see in Figure 2-14, the installation fails with some error messages.

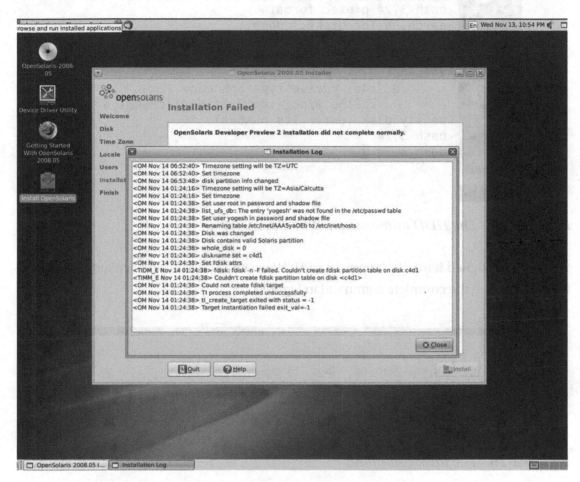

Figure 2-14. *The installation fails with some error messages.*

The error messages are related to the filesystem. So, we will prepare the filesystem manually by using the fdisk utility; however, before that, you should know what hard disk name has been assigned by OpenSolaris. The pfexec format command output (shown in Figure 2-15) will provide us with the HDD name.

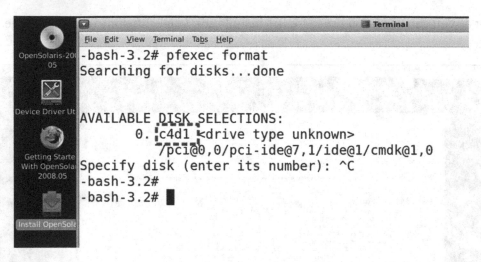

Figure 2-15. *The HDD name assigned by OpenSolaris*

So, the assigned hard disk's name is c4d1. We need to pass this device name to the fdisk utility. See the complete command in Figure 2-16.

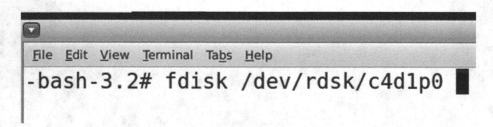

Figure 2-16. *The fdisk command*

The disk name indicates controller number 4, disk number 1, and partition number 0. Through the fdisk utility, we first deleted the second partition (which was ext3/Linux native) and created a new partition with a Solaris2 filesystem. The new partition becomes partition number 4. Also, it automatically becomes the active partition (refer to Figure 2-17). We have not yet talked about the "active or fdisk signature" part, but we will talk about it soon.

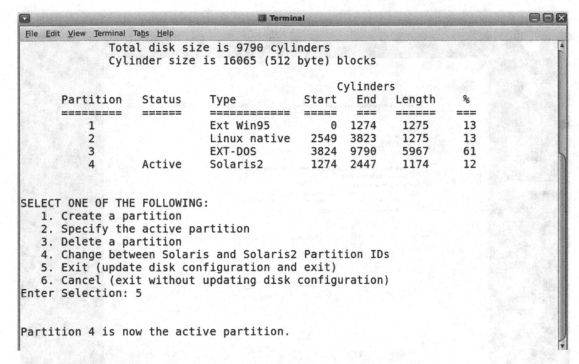

Figure 2-17. *The changes made through the fdisk command*

Returning to our installation, let's restart the installation, and as you can see in Figure 2-18, this time we have chosen the OpenSolaris filesystem–formatted partition to install our OpenSolaris 2008.

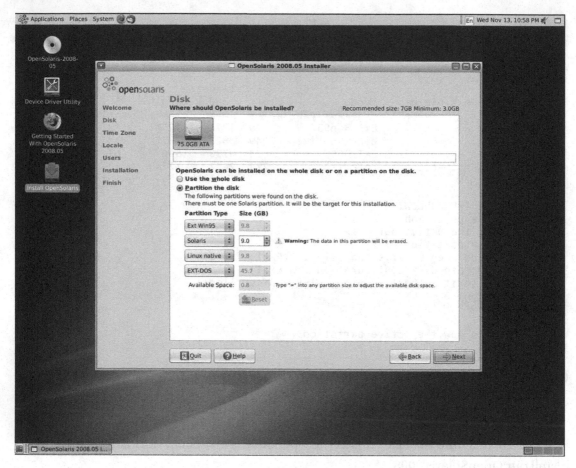

Figure 2-18. *Installing OpenSolaris on the OpenSolaris filesystem partition*

This time, the installation will not fail (refer to Figure 2-19), and OpenSolaris 2008 will be installed.

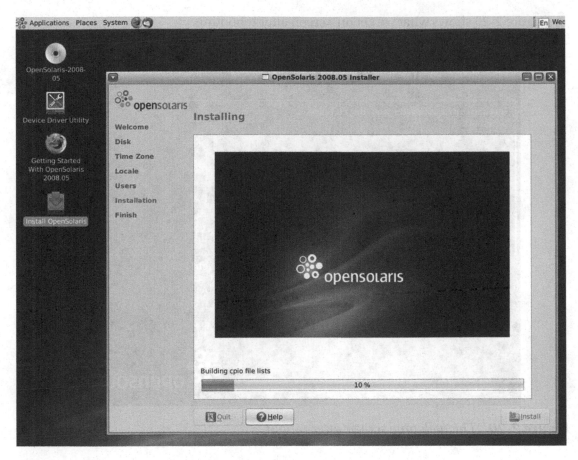

Figure 2-19. *The installer will not fail*

After the installation, we will reboot our BIOS system. What OS do you think will boot?

- – Windows XP?

- – OpenSolaris?

- – XP and OpenSolaris together?

- – None?

Take a while and think before continuing....

Figure 2-20 shows what we get on-screen after rebooting.

Figure 2-20. *The welcome screen after reboot*

So, the OS that is booting here is OpenSolaris, and it is giving us an option to boot XP as well. Let's shed some light on what happened in the background. OpenSolaris saw that it was getting installed in its own partition (the second partition), but there is another OS available in the first partition, which is Windows (or at least a "non-Unix OS").

But how did OpenSolaris come to know there is another OS installed on the first primary partition?

When OpenSolaris was installed in its own partition, it saw that the fdisk signature was set on the first primary partition. (Again, the fdisk signature is also called the *active flag* or simply the * flag.) As we saw earlier in our boot sector specification diagram (Figure 2-21), every partition has 512 bytes + 31 KB of space reserved for booting purposes, and this space is hidden from the user.

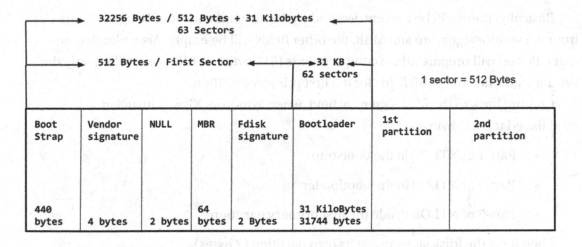

Figure 2-21. *The boot sector*

In other words, when we created a partition layout through GParted, the tool made the following compartments for every partition:

1) Bootstrap

2) Vendor signature

3) NULL

4) MBR

5) Fdisk signature

6) Bootloader

But it filled data only in the vendor signature and MBR fields. The vendor signature field will have data as per the vendor of the HDD, whereas in the case of the MBR field, the data will be as follows:

- The start and end of the first primary partition

- The start and end of the second primary partition

- The start and end of the third primary partition

- The start and end of the fourth primary partition

Basically, there will be four entries, and each entry will consume 16 bytes. Apart from the vendor signature and MBR, the other fields will be empty. Also, please note that GParted will prepare all the compartments (512 bytes + 31 KB) but will fill only the vendor signature and MBR fields for the first primary partition.

Coming back to the fdisk signature field, when Windows XP was installed, it established the following:

- Part-1 of NTLDR in the bootstrap

- Part-2 of NTLDR in the bootloader

- Part-3 of NTLDR inside the first primary partition

Then it set the fdisk signature in its own partition (2 bytes).
So, the disk layout will be something like shown in Figure 2-22.

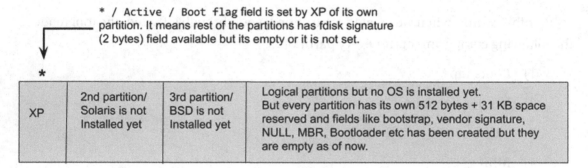

Figure 2-22. *The disk layout after XP's installation*

OpenSolaris found this disk layout. When the OpenSolaris installation was complete and it wanted to install its bootloader (GRUB), it saw an asterisk (*) on the first primary partition, and that is when it realized there is a Windows OS already installed. Now GRUB (the OpenSolaris bootloader) has two options.

- Install part-1 (bootstrap) and part-2 (bootloader) of Grand Unified Bootloader (GRUB) in the first primary partition, and install part-3 of GRUB in its own partition (the second partition where OpenSolaris has been installed).

- Or install part-1 (bootloader) in its own partition's first 512 bytes, part-2 in its own partition's 31 KB, and part-3 also in its own partition; then put * on its own second partition (refer to Figure 2-23).

Partition	File System	Label	Size	Used	Unused	Flags
/dev/sda1	fat32		9.77 GiB	2.97 GiB	6.79 GiB	lba
/dev/sda4 ⚠	ext3	Solaris 2009	8.99 GiB	---	---	boot
unallocated	unallocated		790.86 MiB	---	---	
/dev/sda2	ext3	PC-BSD 9	9.77 GiB	307.23 MiB	9.47 GiB	
▽ /dev/sda3	extended		45.70 GiB	---	---	
/dev/sda5	ntfs	windows 2003	9.77 GiB	50.78 MiB	9.72 GiB	
/dev/sda6	ntfs	windows 7	9.77 GiB	50.78 MiB	9.72 GiB	
/dev/sda7	ext3	RHEL 6	9.77 GiB	307.23 MiB	9.47 GiB	
/dev/sda8	ext3	Fedora 15	9.77 GiB	307.23 MiB	9.47 GiB	
/dev/sda9	linux-swap	swap	6.63 GiB	0.00 B	6.63 GiB	

Figure 2-23. *The disk layout in GParted after OpenSolaris installation*

Please note that the boot flag is back to the OpenSolaris partition. Also, GParted does not understand the Solaris2 partition; hence, it shows ext3 as a filesystem name.

If OpenSolaris chooses option 1, then OpenSolaris has to clear Windows XP's part-1 and part-2 of the bootloader. It also means only OpenSolaris will boot, and XP will never be able to boot. Hence, OpenSolaris chooses option-2, giving equal opportunity to boot Windows XP. OpenSolaris also makes a Windows XP entry in one of its own files (we will talk about this file later in the chapter). Whenever OpenSolaris starts booting up, GRUB will refer to that file, and it will find the Windows entry in it, which will be shown on-screen. Figure 2-24 shows the OpenSolaris welcome screen.

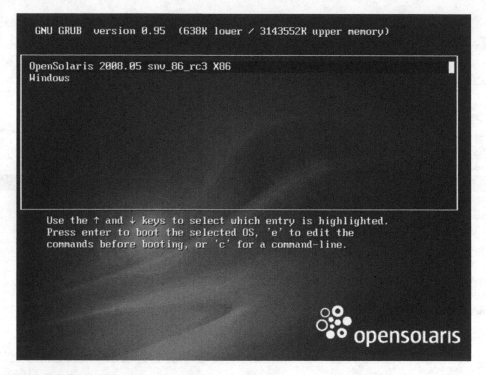

Figure 2-24. *The OpenSolaris welcome screen*

So, the complete booting sequence of OpenSolaris is as follows:

1. Power on the system.

2. The CPU jumps to the BIOS.

3. The BIOS runs the POST routine.

4. We go back to the BIOS.

5. The BIOS is kind of dumb; it will check the boot priority set by the user.

    -   When I say *boot priority*, I means the device through which system will boot.

    -   It could be CDROM, USB, HDD, PXE, etc.

6. The BIOS will jump to the entire HDD's first 512 bytes or on the first sector of the boot device.

    -   The boot device could be anything, but as of now we are considering an HDD.

7. The BIOS will hand over control to whichever binary is present in the bootstrap.

    - Who do you think is there? The Windows bootloader (NTLDR) or OpenSolaris (GRUB)? Think for a while and then continue.

    - The boot sector stored in the first 512 bytes is NTLDR of Windows XP.

    - You must have noticed the 440 bytes of the bootstrap space is very tiny, and no code can boot an OS from it. Hence, part-1 of NTLDR (bootstrap) just jumps to the bigger space, which is part-2 (bootloader/31 KB/virtual boot record). Part-2 checks the MBR (64 bytes) and finds four entries in it. This means the disk has four primary partitions. But there is an issue here: out of four primary partitions, which partition has the OS? You might say, of course, it's the first and second partitions, but how will the bootloader know where the OS is? And which one should it boot? This is a genuine question, and to solve this problem, the fdisk signature field has been created. Whichever partition has these 2 bytes filled or set, that partition has an OS. So, when Windows XP or OpenSolaris was getting installed, it's a duty of that OS to fill the 2 bytes of the fdisk signature field or set the * on its own partition so that the bootloader will know which partition has the OS. In our case, the * is on its second partition (OpenSolaris kept it while it was getting installed). This is how part-2 of NTLDR will know that it has to jump to the second partition.

8. Part-2 of NTLDR jumps to the second partition, which means it simply jumps to part-1 of the GRUB bootloader in the second partition (bootstrap).

9. Part-1 of GRUB (bootstrap/440 bytes) is again tiny, so it will again jump to a bigger space, which is part-2 of GRUB (bootloader).

10. Part-2 knows where part-3 is. The location of part-3 will be hard-
     coded in part-2, so it will simply jump to part-3. Part-3 will read
     the text file `/rpool/boot/grub/menu.lst` (see Figure 2-25); this is
     the same file that was created by OpenSolaris when it detected XP
     on the first primary.

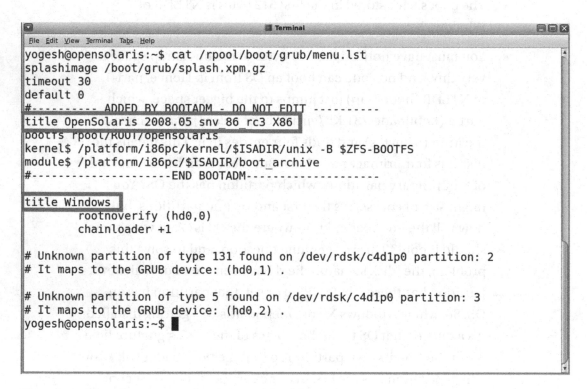

```
yogesh@opensolaris:~$ cat /rpool/boot/grub/menu.lst
splashimage /boot/grub/splash.xpm.gz
timeout 30
default 0
#--------- ADDED BY BOOTADM - DO NOT EDIT ----------
title OpenSolaris 2008.05 snv_86_rc3 X86
bootfs rpool/ROOT/opensolaris
kernel$ /platform/i86pc/kernel/$ISADIR/unix -B $ZFS-BOOTFS
module$ /platform/i86pc/$ISADIR/boot_archive
#--------------------END BOOTADM--------------------

title Windows
        rootnoverify (hd0,0)
        chainloader +1

# Unknown partition of type 131 found on /dev/rdsk/c4d1p0 partition: 2
# It maps to the GRUB device: (hd0,1) .

# Unknown partition of type 5 found on /dev/rdsk/c4d1p0 partition: 3
# It maps to the GRUB device: (hd0,2) .
yogesh@opensolaris:~$
```

Figure 2-25. *The OpenSolaris menu.lst file*

11. Part-3 of GRUB will read this text file and print whatever is written after the 'title variable, and that is how we reach the screen shown in Figure 2-26.

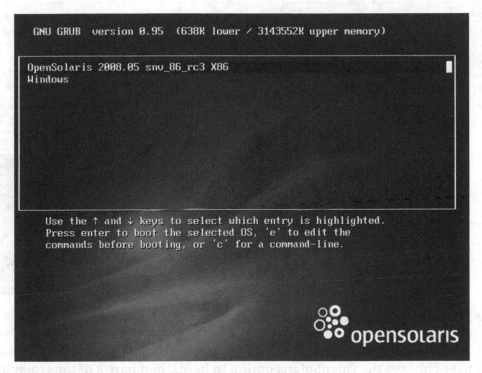

Figure 2-26. *The OpenSolaris welcome screen*

Figure 2-27 shows the complete booting sequence of OpenSolaris.

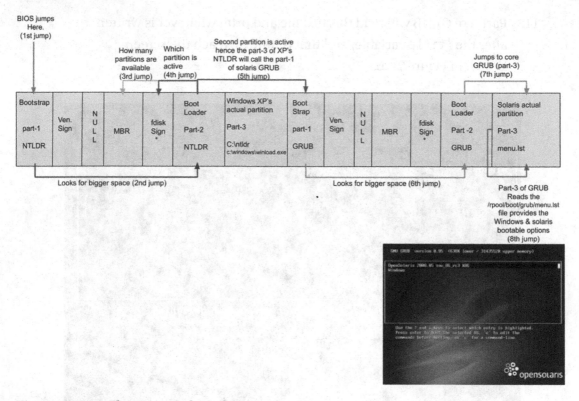

Figure 2-27. *The OpenSolaris booting sequence*

If a user chooses the OpenSolaris option to boot, then part-3 of the OpenSolaris GRUB knows where the kernel of OpenSolaris is, which is in the /boot directory. GRUB will copy the kernel from /boot to memory and give control to the kernel. This is where the GRUB bootloader's task ends, and it goes away. Now the kernel of OpenSolaris will take care of the rest of the booting sequence. We will talk about the kernel in Chapter 4.

If a user chooses the Windows XP option to boot, then part-3 of the OpenSolaris GRUB will jump back to part-1 of NTLDR (bootstrap). Part-1 of NTLDR will jump to part-2 of NTLDR. Part-2 will jump to part-3. Part-3 of NTLDR will load winload.exe in memory. The winload.exe file knows where the kernel of XP is. It will eventually be copied or loaded into memory by NTLDR. Once the kernel is in memory, NTLDR's job is done (remember, kernel=OS=kernel). Since XP's kernel is in memory, it will take care of the rest of the booting sequence.

PC-BSD 9.0

The * or the boot flag is on the OpenSolaris partition, so now we will install PC-BSD 9.0.
In Figure 2-28, the installer of PC-BSD shows the number of partitions on which PC-BSD
9.0 can be installed.

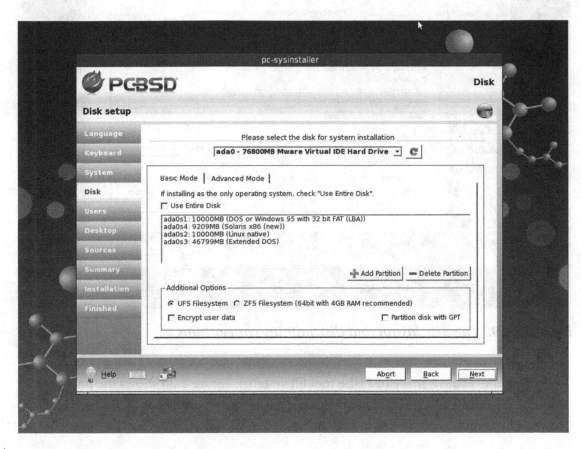

Figure 2-28. *The number of partitions*

As you can see, the hard disk naming convention is different in BSD compared to
earlier OSs. We need to install BSD on the third partition, which is ada0s2. It stands for
"Adapter number zero and slice number 2." The slice can be considered as a partition.
Figure 2-29 shows the disk layout and disk naming conventions.

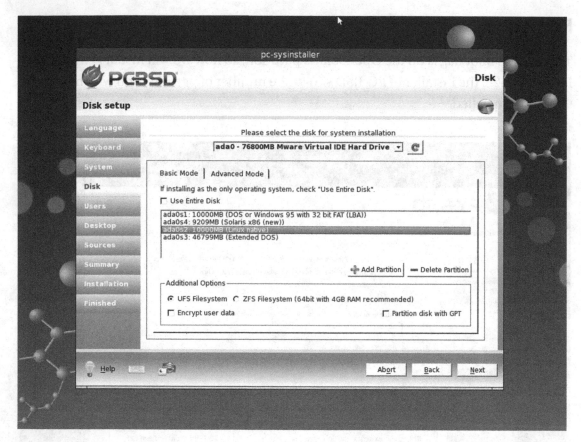

Figure 2-29. *The disk layout and disk naming conventions*

Assign the `ada0s2` space to / (the root filesystem). Figure 2-30 shows the partition layout of PC-BSD 9.0. You will also notice that the filesystem of BSD is UFS, which is the Unix File System.

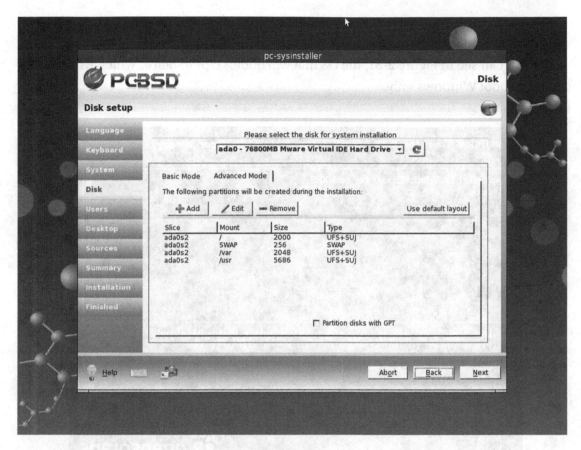

Figure 2-30. *The partition layout of PC-BSD 9.0*

After the installation, the system will restart. Now take some time and think about which OS will boot.

Which of the following will it be?

- OpenSolaris, which would give it a chance to boot Windows and BSD

- Will it be PC-BSD, which would give it chance to boot the other two OSs?

- Will it be PC-BSD alone?

- Will it be Windows XP alone?

- Will it be OpenSolaris alone?

- Or will none of the OSs boot?

Please visit the booting flowcharts of earlier operating systems and try to come up with your own booting sequence.

As you can see in Figure 2-31, the OS that will boot is OpenSolaris, which will create a chance to boot Windows only.

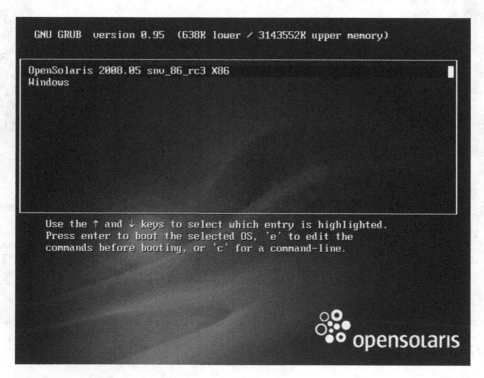

Figure 2-31. *PC-BSD is not booting.*

PC-BSD is not booting. Before going to the next page, again take some time and think about what happened

You are right—there is a chance that PC-BSD might have not kept the */boot flag/ fdisk signature on its own partition. Let's see if that is the case. We will boot with GParted (Figure 2-32) and verify our theory.

Figure 2-32. *The GParted welcome screen*

As you can see in Figure 2-33, PC-BSD does not have * set on its own partition.

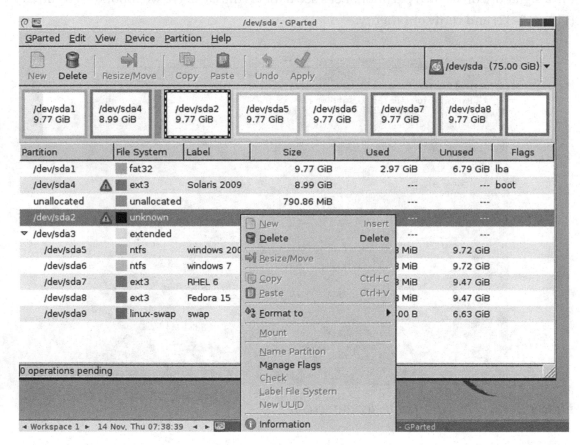

Figure 2-33. *The disk layout on GParted*

So, the booting sequence looks like Figure 2-34.

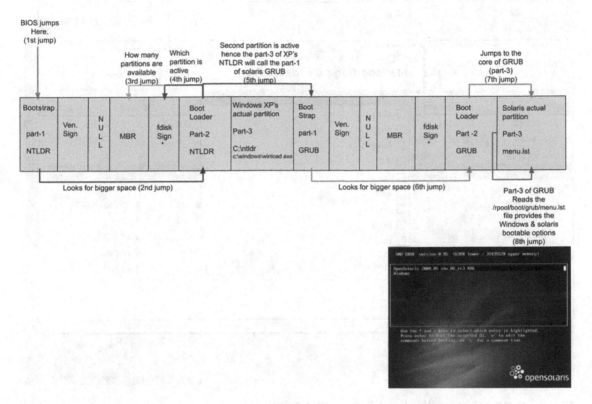

Figure 2-34. *The boot sequence and why PC-BSD is not able to boot*

This means OpenSolaris does not know BSD is installed on the third partition. Hence, the PC-BSD entry is not with OpenSolaris. What if we keep the boot flag on BSD's partition? Will it boot? But how do we keep the boot flag on the third partition? It's simple—GParted gives us that option. Right-click the third partition and select the boot flag, as shown in Figure 2-35.

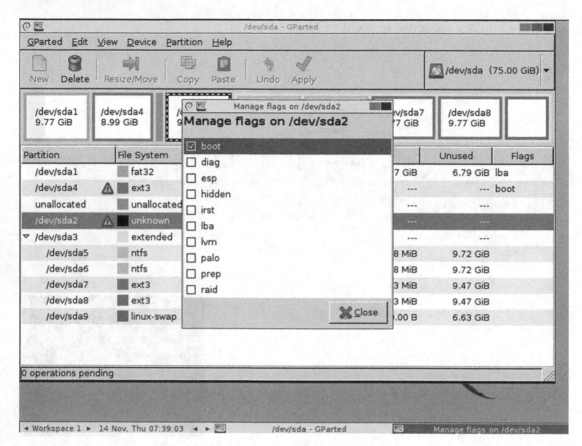

Figure 2-35. *Setting the boot flag on PC-BSD*

Figure 2-36 shows how the disk layout looks after setting the boot flag on BSD's third partition.

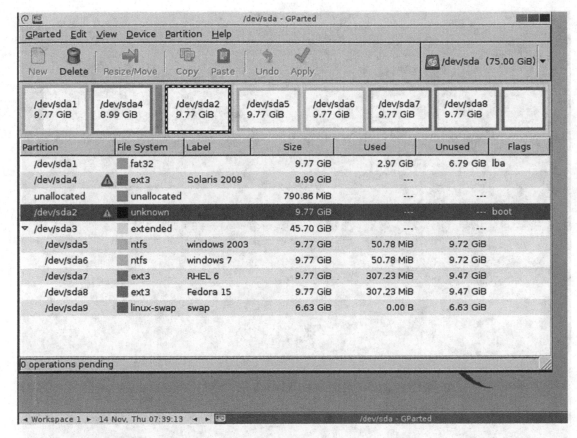

Figure 2-36. *The disk layout*

Now which OS do you think will boot?

- PC-BSD alone?

- PC-BSD, which would give the chance to boot every other OS?

- Again OpenSolaris, which would create an option to boot Windows?

- OpenSolaris alone?

- Windows XP alone?

Figure 2-37 shows the answer; after reboot, it's only PC-BSD that is booting, and it is not giving an option to boot any other OS.

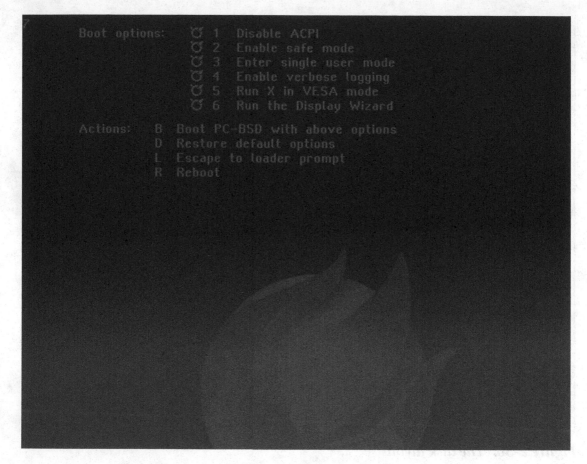

Figure 2-37. *The welcome screen of PC-BSD*

Let's try to understand how PC-BSD managed to boot.

1. Power on the system.

2. The BIOS executes the POST routine. The POST checks the hardware health and gives a healthy beep if everything is good and goes back to the BIOS.

3. The BIOS is dumb, and it simply jumps to the first sector of the entire HDD, which is a bootstrap of Windows XP.

4. XP's part-1 (NTLDR) jumps to a bigger space, which is part-2 of NTLDR (the bootloader). The bootloader checks the MBR and finds there are four primary partitions, but which one is active? To check that, the bootloader checks the first primary partition's fdisk signature, which is not set, so it checks the second partition's boot

flag, which is also not set. Hence, it jumps to the third partition where it finds the boot flag set. The bootloader (part-2) of NTLDR jumps to BSD's partition and runs the bootstrap of BSD's bootloader. The bootloader of BSD is BTX, which stands for Boot Extended. BTX jumps to its second part and eventually to the third part. The third part of BTX knows where the kernel of BSD is. Part-3 of BTX copies the kernel image of BSD in memory, and this is where BTX stops and PC-BSD starts booting and shows us a welcome screen. Figure 2-38 shows the flowchart of the booting sequence of PC-BSD.

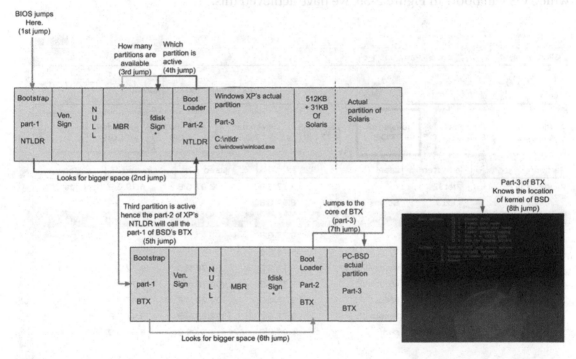

Figure 2-38. *The boot sequence of PC-BSD*

The interesting part of BSD booting is that when PC-BSD was getting installed, it found the boot flag on the second partition, which is the OpenSolaris partition. Now BSD has three options.

a. Keep the boot flag on its own third partition.

b. Keep the boot flag on its own third partition and make a OpenSolaris entry in some of its files.

c. Keep the boot flag as it is on the second partition.

If BSD chooses the first option (a), then only BSD would be able to boot, and that would be an injustice to the other installed operating systems. We want BSD to choose the second option (b) since it gives justice to boot every other OS, but BTX is an old bootloader, and it does not have the ability to multiboot other operating systems. Hence, BSD chooses the third option (c). Therefore, it's only OpenSolaris that is booting, and it provides the option to boot XP. Remember, XP is not booting. It's only OpenSolaris that is booting, and by reading the menu.lst file, it is giving the option to boot XP. It also means BSD itself chose not to boot.

What if we go back and keep the boot flag on the first partition of Windows XP? Then which OS will boot? In Figure 2-39, we have achieved this.

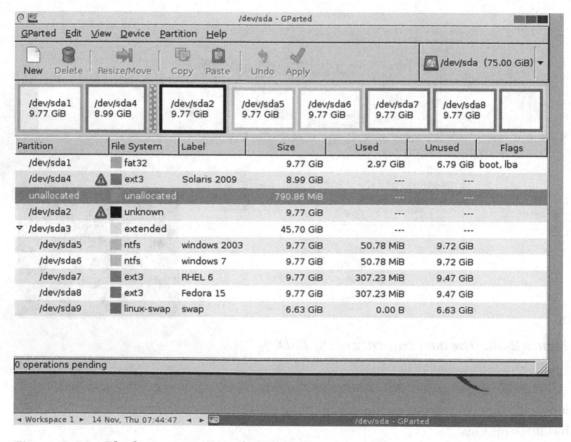

Figure 2-39. *The boot sequence of PC-BSD*

It's Windows XP alone that will boot, and the booting sequence is simple. Figure 2-40 explains how Windows XP is able to boot.

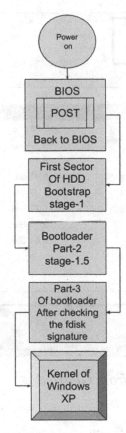

Figure 2-40. *The boot sequence of Windows XP*

Before installing the new OS, we need to move the boot flag from BSD's third partition to OpenSolaris' second partition. Figure 2-41 shows the changed boot flag from XP's partition to the OpenSolaris partition.

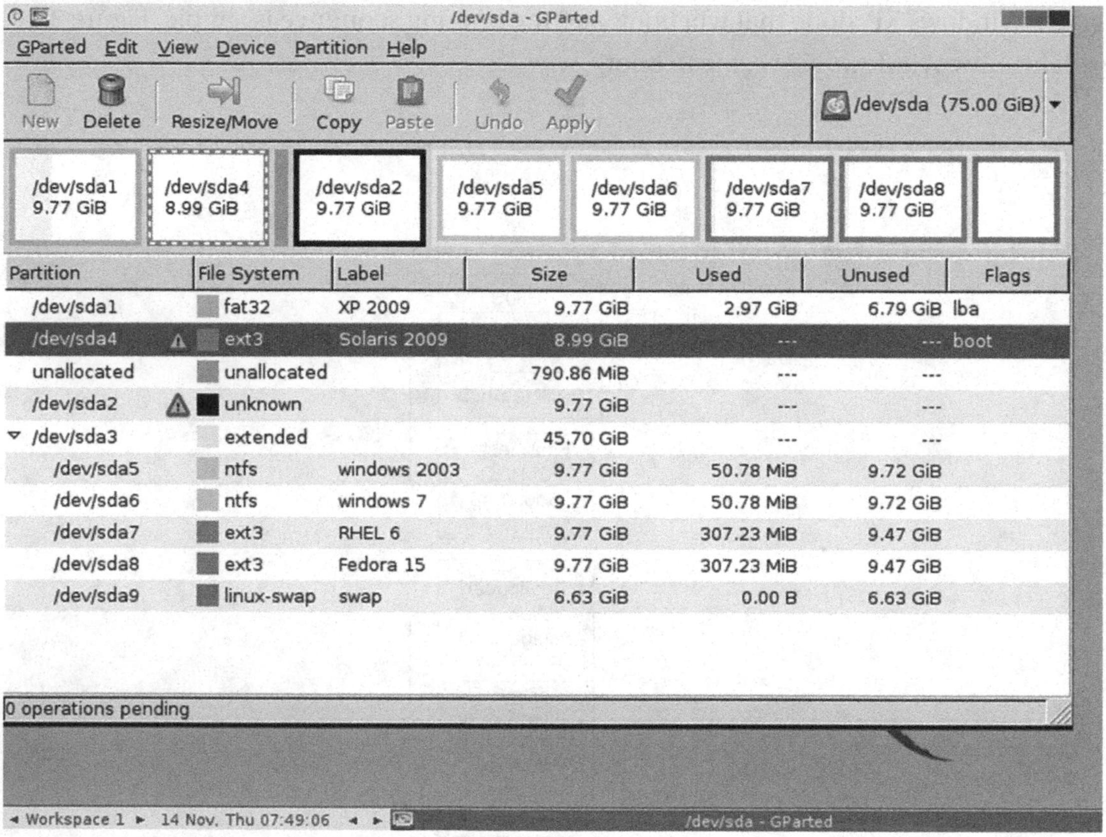
/dev/sda - GParted
GParted Edit View Device Partition Help
New Delete Resize/Move Copy Paste Undo Apply
/dev/sda (75.00 GiB)
/dev/sda1 9.77 GiB
/dev/sda4 8.99 GiB
/dev/sda2 9.77 GiB
/dev/sda5 9.77 GiB
/dev/sda6 9.77 GiB
/dev/sda7 9.77 GiB
/dev/sda8 9.77 GiB
Partition File System Label Size Used Unused Flags
/dev/sda1 fat32 XP 2009 9.77 GiB 2.97 GiB 6.79 GiB lba
/dev/sda4 ext3 Solaris 2009 8.99 GiB --- --- boot
unallocated unallocated 790.86 MiB --- ---
/dev/sda2 unknown 9.77 GiB --- ---
/dev/sda3 extended 45.70 GiB --- ---
/dev/sda5 ntfs windows 2003 9.77 GiB 50.78 MiB 9.72 GiB
/dev/sda6 ntfs windows 7 9.77 GiB 50.78 MiB 9.72 GiB
/dev/sda7 ext3 RHEL 6 9.77 GiB 307.23 MiB 9.47 GiB
/dev/sda8 ext3 Fedora 15 9.77 GiB 307.23 MiB 9.47 GiB
/dev/sda9 linux-swap swap 6.63 GiB 0.00 B 6.63 GiB
0 operations pending
Workspace 1 14 Nov, Thu 07:49:06
/dev/sda - GParted

Figure 2-41. *The disk layout from GParted*

With this change, OpenSolaris will start booting, and along with that, Windows XP will also boot, but BSD will not be able to boot. So, does this mean that every time we boot BSD we have to put the boot flag back to BSD's partition? As of now, yes, but we will automate all of this with the help of bootloaders.

Windows Server 2003

As you can see in Figure 2-42, we will install Windows Server 2003 (win2k3) on the first logical partition. For win2k3, it is a D: drive.

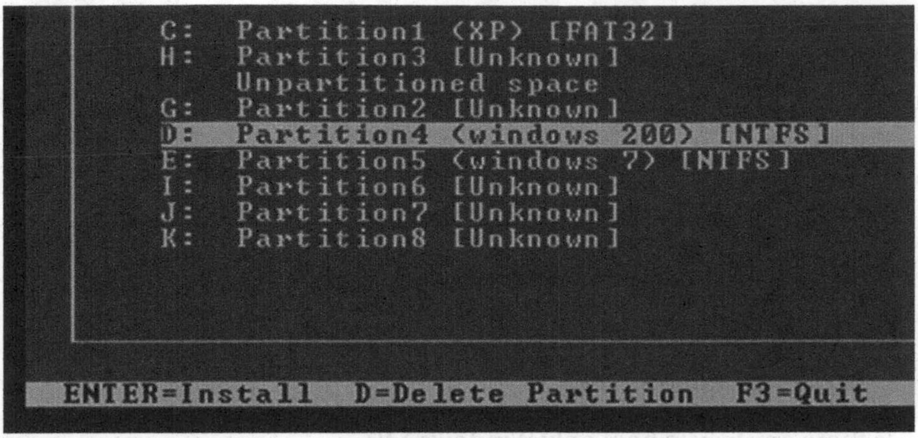

```
C:    Partition1 (XP) [FAT32]
H:    Partition3 [Unknown]
      Unpartitioned space
G:    Partition2 [Unknown]
D:    Partition4 (windows 200) [NTFS]
E:    Partition5 (windows 7) [NTFS]
I:    Partition6 [Unknown]
J:    Partition7 [Unknown]
K:    Partition8 [Unknown]


  ENTER=Install   D=Delete Partition   F3=Quit
```

Figure 2-42. *The disk layout shown by the win2k3 installer*

After the installation, which OS do you think will boot?

- win2k3 alone?

- Will win2k3 provide an option to boot every other OS?

- win2k3 and OpenSolaris together?

- PC-BSD?

- XP alone?

- win2k3 and XP?

Before continuing, think for a while and come up with your own answer.

As you can see in Figure 2-43, the OS that will boot is win2k3.

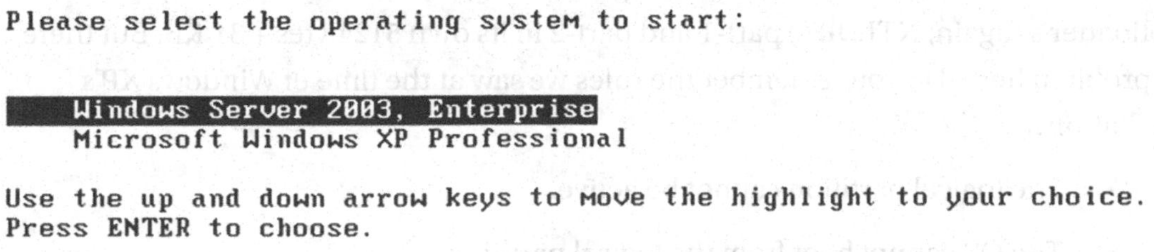

```
Please select the operating system to start:

  Windows Server 2003, Enterprise
  Microsoft Windows XP Professional

Use the up and down arrow keys to move the highlight to your choice.
Press ENTER to choose.
```

Figure 2-43. *win2k3's welcome screen after reboot*

And win2k3 is giving the option to boot Windows XP. This means only the Windows family of operating systems is booting. Also, here are some questions that we should consider:

- Where is the boot flag now?

- Which OS will boot if we keep the boot flag on the second partition?

- Which OS will boot if we keep the boot flag on the third partition?

- Which OS will boot if we keep the boot flag on the logical partition (win2k3's partition)?

- Is there any way to boot only Windows XP?

You will receive all the answers to these questions in the following discussion.

One thing is clear here: win2k3 is the only OS that is booting. Before discussing how it is able to boot, we need to check what scenario it has created on the disk to boot successfully.

When win2k3 was getting installed, it saw that it was getting installed on a logical partition and that the boot flag is on the OpenSolaris partition (refer to Figure 2-44).

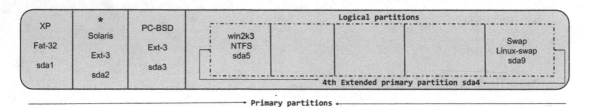

Figure 2-44. *The disk layout when win2k3 was getting installed*

To boot, win2k3 has to put the boot flag on its own partition by installing its bootloader's (again, NTLDR's) part-1 and part-2 in its own 512 bytes + 31 KB. But there is a problem here. Do you remember the rules we saw at the time of Windows XP's installation?

- The logical partition cannot be active.

- The OS cannot boot from the logical partition.

Because of these two rules, win2k3 cannot keep the boot flag on its own partition, and ultimately it cannot boot from the logical partition. Figure 2-45 shows the boot sequence of why win2k3 cannot boot from the logical partition. But what is the reason for such rules?

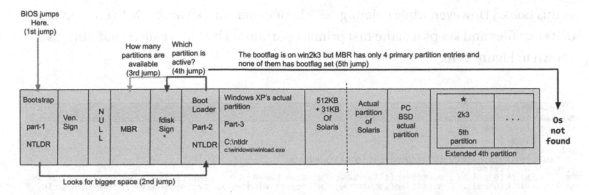

Figure 2-45. *win2k3's boot sequence if it tries to boot from the logical partition*

It's simple: MBR has only four entries, which are as follows:

- First primary = sda1

- Second primary = sda2

- Third primary = sda3

- Fourth primary = extended partition (not logical partition) = sda4

The win2k3 partition is sda5. In other words, it is SATA disk a (first) and partition number 5. Since the MBR does not have an entry for a logical partition, part-2 of XP's NTLDR does not know that there is a fifth partition available. So, even if win2k3 keeps the boot flag on its own partition, XP's NTLDR cannot see it. Hence, win2k3 will never boot. Now, why can the MBR not have more than five entries? It's because 64 bytes can store only four entries. Why not increase the size of the MBR? Actually, even if the developers want to increase the size of the MBR, they simply can't. You will understand the reason when we talk about the UEFI firmware later in this chapter.

Now this has become a chicken-and-egg problem for win2k3. It wants to boot, but for that it has to keep the boot flag on its own partition, but if it does that, then the BIOS cannot see that partition. How do we resolve this problem?

Some amazing developers have resolved this problem, and whoever came up with this idea is simply a legend. win2k3 transfers its NTLDR bootloader on the first primary, which means part-1, part-2, and part-3. It also means win2k3 will delete all the XP NTLDR's parts since the space (512 bytes + 31 KB) is tiny and both the bootloaders can't fit there. (There is one sweet spot here, which is called VBR, which is beyond the scope of this book.) However, while deleting, XP's bootloader win2k3 makes XP's entry in one of its text files and keeps it at the first primary partition. The file is called boot.ini, as shown in Figure 2-46.

Figure 2-46. *The boot.ini file*

While doing this, win2k3 keeps the boot flag on the first primary partition only. So, this is how win2k3 is booting:

1. Power on the system.

2. The CPU goes to the BIOS. The BIOS runs the POST.

3. POST checks, and the hardware gives the healthy beep and goes back to the BIOS.

4. The BIOS jumps to the first primary partition's first 512 bytes.

5. The bootstrap will start, which is win2k3's part-1 of NTLDR.

6. Part-1 will look for part-2 of NTLDR.

7. Part-2 will check the MBR and check the fdisk signature.

8. The fdisk signature is set on the first primary, which means part-2 will jump inside XP's first primary partition and will run part-3 of win2k3's NTLDR. To just give you an idea, part-3 is new and not XP's old NTLDR. Here I provide two images.

    •   Note the size of NTLDR (part-3) in Figure 2-47. This is when we installed Windows XP.

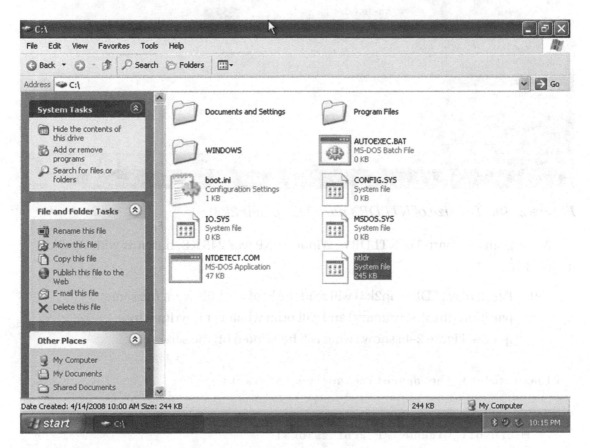

Figure 2-47. *The size of NTLDR's part-3 file of Windows XP*

    •   In Figure 2-48, note the size of NTLDR (part-3) after the installation of win2k3.

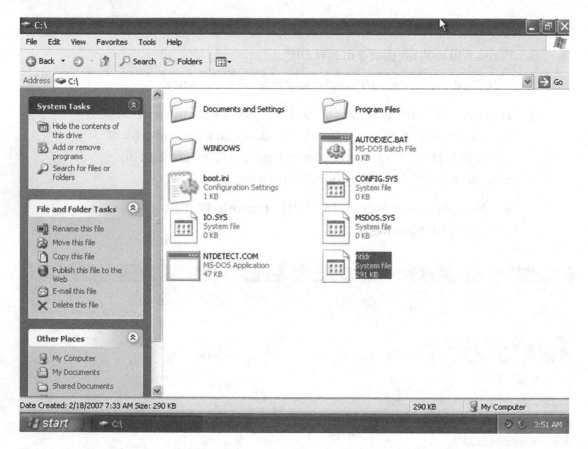

Figure 2-48. *The size of NTLDR's part-3 file of win2k3*

As you can see, part-3 of NTLDR of Windows XP was 245 KB, but now with win2k3 it's 291 KB.

9. Part-3 of NTLDR (win2k3) will read the boot.ini file from the same partition (the first primary) and will print whatever is written in quotes. Figure 2-49 shows what will be printed on the screen.

```
Please select the operating system to start:

    Windows Server 2003, Enterprise
    Microsoft Windows XP Professional

Use the up and down arrow keys to move the highlight to your choice.
Press ENTER to choose.
```

Figure 2-49. *The welcome screen shown by win2k3*

10. If a user chooses the Windows Server 2003, Enterprise option, then part-3 of win2k3's NTLDR knows where the kernel of win2k3 is. This is in the fifth partition where win2k3 has been installed. It copies the kernel in memory, and NTLDR of win2k3 goes away.

11. If a user chooses the Microsoft Windows XP Professional option, then part-3 of NTLDR also knows where the kernel of Windows XP is. This is in the first primary partition. First it starts `winload.exe`; eventually `winload.exe` copies XP's kernel in memory, and NTLDR goes away. Figure 2-50 shows the complete boot sequence of Windows XP.

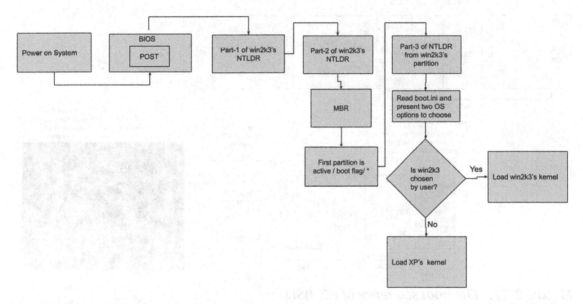

Figure 2-50. *The boot sequence of Windows XP*

So, this is how Windows XP and win2k3 are able to boot. Let's return to our fdisk signatures discussion; since only win2k3 is booting and the other OSs are not able to boot, I have some questions to ask:

- Can we boot only Windows XP?
- What if we keep the boot flag on OpenSolaris?
- What if we keep the boot flag on PC-BSD?
- What if we don't keep the boot flag anywhere?

Take your time, think, revisit the flowcharts, and come up with your answer.

Ready? We cannot boot only Windows XP. It's just not possible since in the Windows XP bootloaders all the parts have been replaced by win2k's NTLDR. Also, only win2k3 knows now where XP is, and only win2k3 can boot Windows XP. This also means if win2k3's bootloader's part-1 is corrupted or deleted, we will lose XP forever. But if we keep the boot flag on PC-BSD, then it will boot as usual. Figure 2-51 shows the boot sequence of PC-BSD.

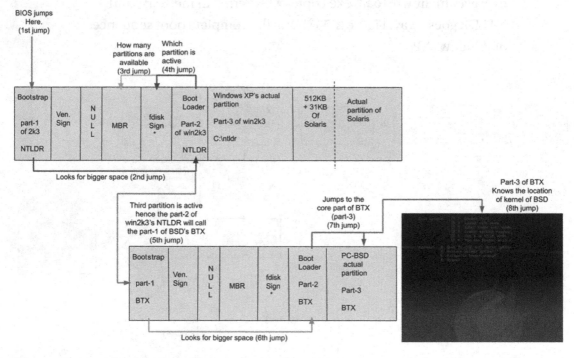

Figure 2-51. *The boot sequence of PC-BSD*

If we don't keep the boot flag on any of the partitions, then it simply won't boot. This is similar to the situation that we discussed when talking about what would happen if the boot flag was set on the logical partition. Figure 2-52 shows the boot sequence to explain why none of the OSs is able to boot.

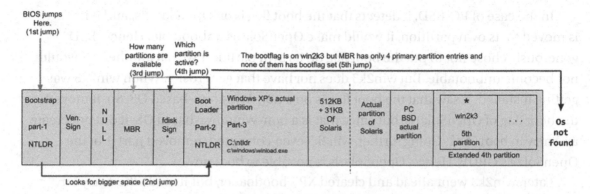

Figure 2-52. *The boot sequence to show why none of the OSs is able to boot*

Setting up a boot flag on the logical partition is as good as not setting up a boot flag anywhere.

Now, the main question is, what if we keep the boot flag on the OpenSolaris partition? OpenSolaris will fail to boot. The OpenSolaris bootloader, which is GRUB, will throw the error message shown in Figure 2-53.

```
Minimal BASH-like line editing is supported. For the first word,
TAB lists possible command completions. Anywhere else TAB lists
possible device or file completions. ESC at any time exits.

grub> _
```

Figure 2-53. *GRUB dropped on prompt*

But why? It should boot, right? Nothing has been changed in OpenSolaris (512 bytes + 31 KB). It's just that win2k3 has moved the boot flag from the OpenSolaris partition to the first primary. So, ideally, it should boot, but it won't, and the reason is win2k3's behavior. When win2k3 was getting installed, it faced a similar situation that OpenSolaris and PC-BSD faced. In other words, the boot flag is on a different partition, and that partition has another OS. What OpenSolaris did in that situation was move the boot flag from XP's partition to its own second partition, but since this will make XP unbootable, it generously made an entry for XP in its own file (menu.lst). OpenSolaris reads this file every time and gives an equal chance to XP to boot.

In the case of PC-BSD, it detects that the boot flag is on OpenSolaris, and if it is moved to its own partition, it would make OpenSolaris unbootable. Hence, BSD generously chose not to put the boot flag on its own partition so that another OS would not become unbootable. But win2k3 does not have that generosity. When win2k3 was getting installed, it saw that the boot flag is on a non-Windows-based OS. So, it moved the boot flag of OpenSolaris, but since that is a non-Windows-based OS, it did not create an entry in boot.ini. Going further, win2k3 even corrupted/removed part-1 of the OpenSolaris GRUB. Hence, OpenSolaris is not able to boot now.

Later, win2k3 went ahead and cleared XP's bootloader, but it made the entry for XP in boot.ini since it is a Windows operating system. That's why I said win2k3 does not have the same generosity that is shown by OpenSolaris and PC-BSD. But we will fix OpenSolaris in the "Tweaking GRUB" section of this chapter.

Windows 7

As you can see in Figure 2-54, we are installing Windows 7 in the fifth partition.

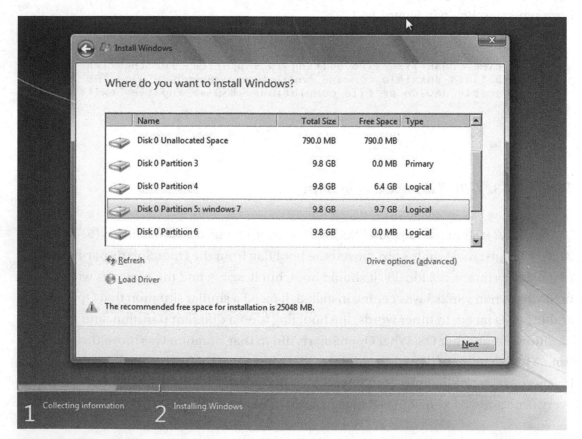

Figure 2-54. *The disk layout shown by the Windows 7 installer*

Windows does not show an extended partition to avoid confusion for simple desktop users.

1st = XP   **2nd** = Solaris   **3rd** = PC-BSD   **4th** = win2k3   **5th** = 7

After the installation, which OS do you think will boot? As usual, take your time and come up with your answer before continuing to Figure 2-55.

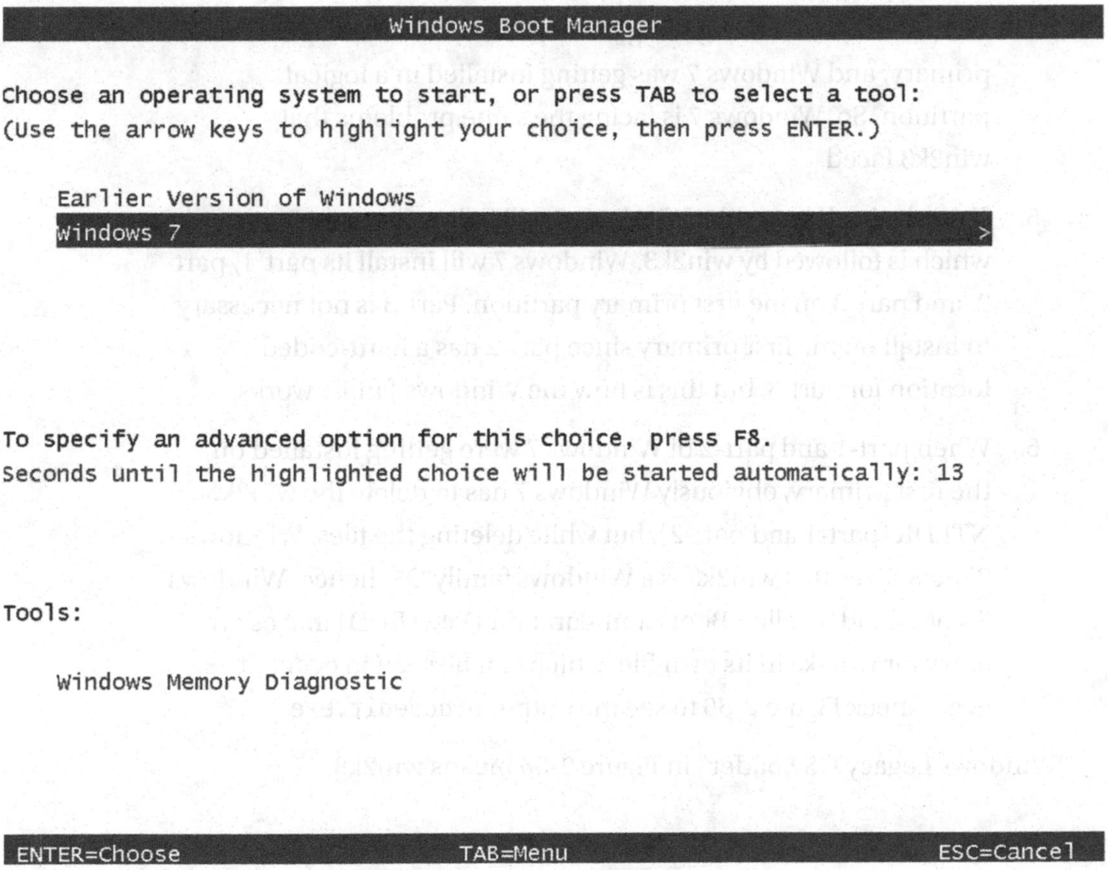

```
                              Windows Boot Manager

Choose an operating system to start, or press TAB to select a tool:
(Use the arrow keys to highlight your choice, then press ENTER.)

    Earlier Version of Windows
    Windows 7                                                               >




To specify an advanced option for this choice, press F8.
Seconds until the highlighted choice will be started automatically: 13




Tools:

    Windows Memory Diagnostic




 ENTER=Choose                    TAB=Menu                         ESC=Cancel
```

Figure 2-55. *The welcome screen shown by Windows 7*

You guessed right: Windows 7 will boot. The following is the complete booting sequence of Windows 7:

1. Power on the system.

2. The CPU will jump to the BIOS.

3. After the POST routine, the BIOS will jump to the entire HDD's first sector.

4. When Windows 7 was getting installed, the * was on the first primary, and Windows 7 was getting installed in a logical partition. So, Windows 7 is facing the same problems that win2k3 faced.

5. To make itself bootable, Windows 7 will follow the same path, which is followed by win2k3. Windows 7 will install its part-1, part-2, and part-3 on the first primary partition. Part-3 is not necessary to install on the first primary since part-2 has a hard-coded location for part-3, but this is how the Windows family works.

6. When part-1 and part-2 of Windows 7 were getting installed on the first primary, obviously Windows 7 has to delete the win2k3 NTLDR (part-1 and part-2), but while deleting the files, Windows 7 recognizes that win2k3 is a Windows family OS; hence, Windows 7's bootloader called Boot Configuration Data (BCD) makes an entry for win2k3 in its own file, which can be seen in bcdedit.exe. Check Figure 2-56 to see the output of bcdedit.exe.

"Windows Legacy OS Loader" in Figure 2-56 means win2k3.

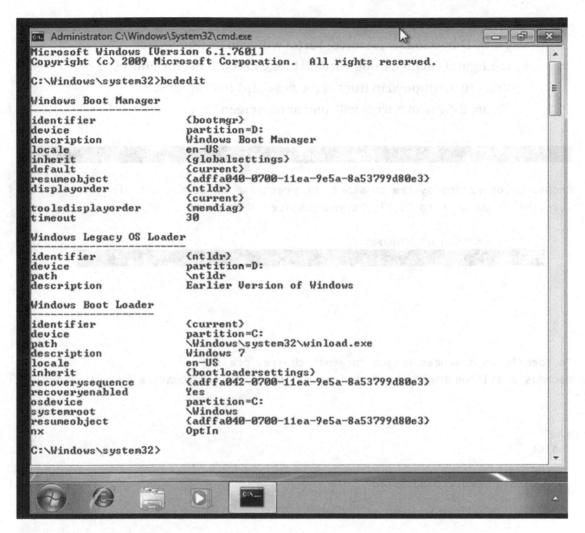

Figure 2-56. *The output of bcdedit.exe*

7. So, coming back to booting sequence, it looks like this: BIOS ➤ POST ➤ BIOS ➤ first sector of HDD.

8. The first 440 bytes of the bootstrap is part-1 of Window 7's BCD bootloader. It will look for a bigger space, which is part-2 of BCD.

9. Part-2 of BCD will read the MBR and will come to know that on this HDD there are four primary partitions, but to check which one is active, it will start checking the fdisk signature of every partition, but it will find the first primary itself is active.

10. Part-2 will jump inside the first primary where part-3 of Window 7's BCD bootloader is stored. Part-3 will read its bootloader configuration file through `bcdedit.exe` and will list the entries that are mentioned in front of the `description` variable. Figure 2-57 shows what will appear on-screen.

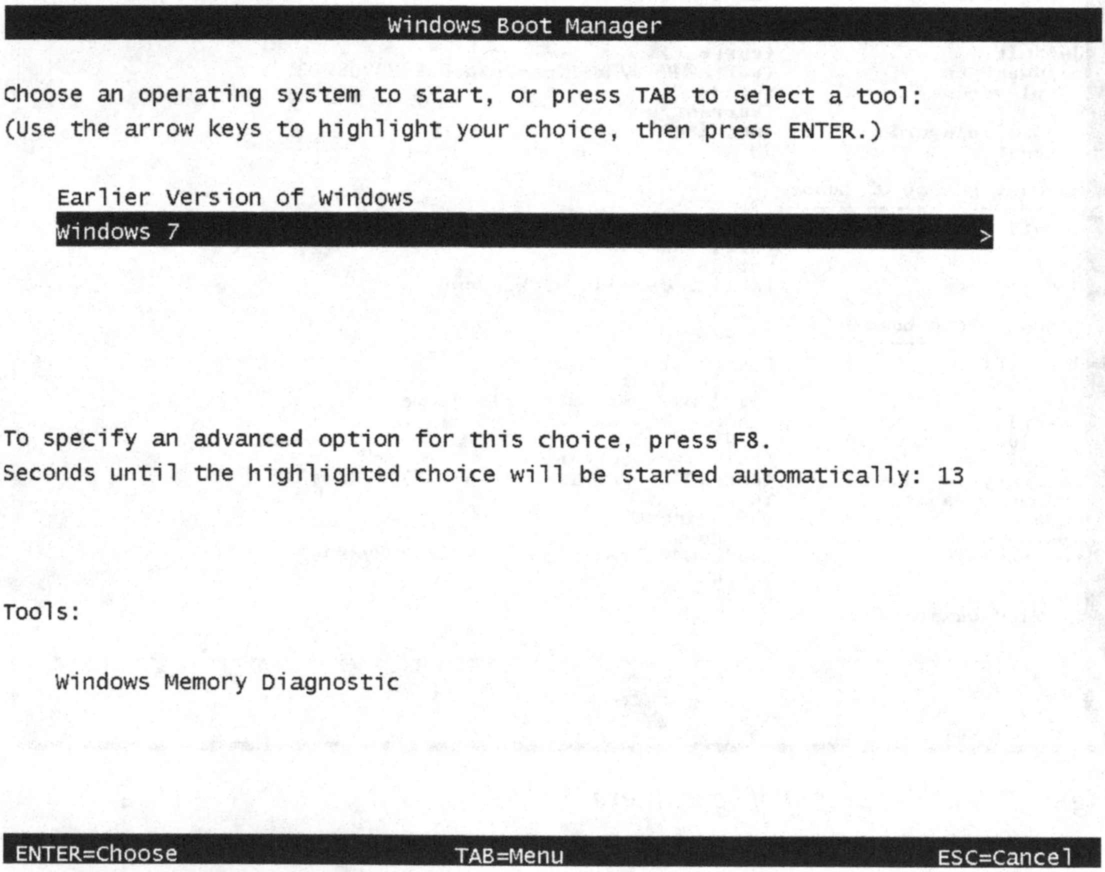

```
                         Windows Boot Manager

Choose an operating system to start, or press TAB to select a tool:
(Use the arrow keys to highlight your choice, then press ENTER.)

    Earlier Version of Windows
    Windows 7                                                          >




To specify an advanced option for this choice, press F8.
Seconds until the highlighted choice will be started automatically: 13


Tools:

    Windows Memory Diagnostic




ENTER=Choose                    TAB=Menu                    ESC=Cancel
```

Figure 2-57. *Welcome screen shown by Windows 7*

11. If a user chooses Windows 7, then as you can see in `bcdedit.exe`, part-3 of BCD will call `winload.exe` from `C:\windows\systemd32`. Remember, here C: means Windows 7's partition, which is the sixth logical partition.

12. The `winload.exe` file knows the location of Windows 7's kernel.
     It will start loading the kernel in memory, and once it is done,
     Windows 7's kernel will take care of the rest of the booting
     sequence. You can see the animation shown by Windows 7 once it
     starts its booting sequence in Figure 2-58.

Figure 2-58. *The animation shown by Windows 7 during the booting sequence*

Figure 2-59 shows the complete flowchart of Windows 7's booting sequence.

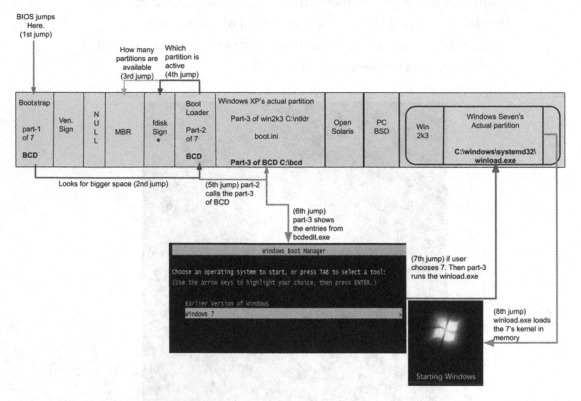

Figure 2-59. *The booting sequence of Windows 7*

13. If the user chooses Earlier Version of Windows, then BCD's part-3 will call part-3 of NTLDR, which is on the first primary partition only, and the booting sequence will continue, which we saw with win2k3. Figure 2-60 explains the boot sequence of win2k3 and XP.

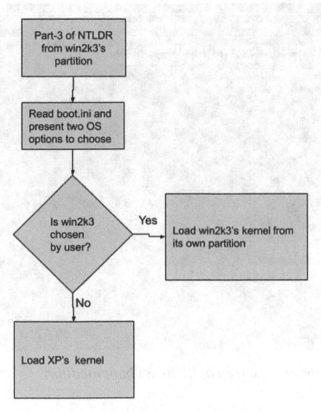

Figure 2-60. *The boot sequence of win2k3 and XP*

Red Hat Enterprise Linux 6 (RHEL 6)

The RHEL installer's name is Anaconda. The Anaconda installer is used by all the Fedora-based distributions. In Figure 2-61, we have started installing RHEL 6.

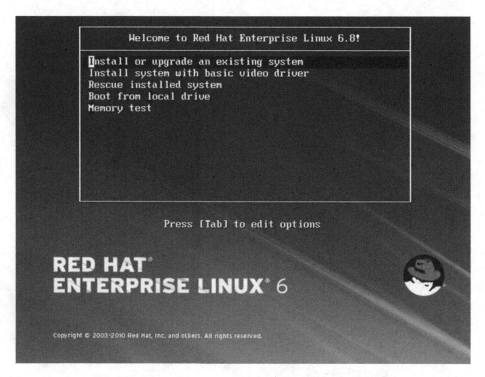

Figure 2-61. *The welcome screen of RHEL 6's boot medium*

Figure 2-62 shows our current partition layout.

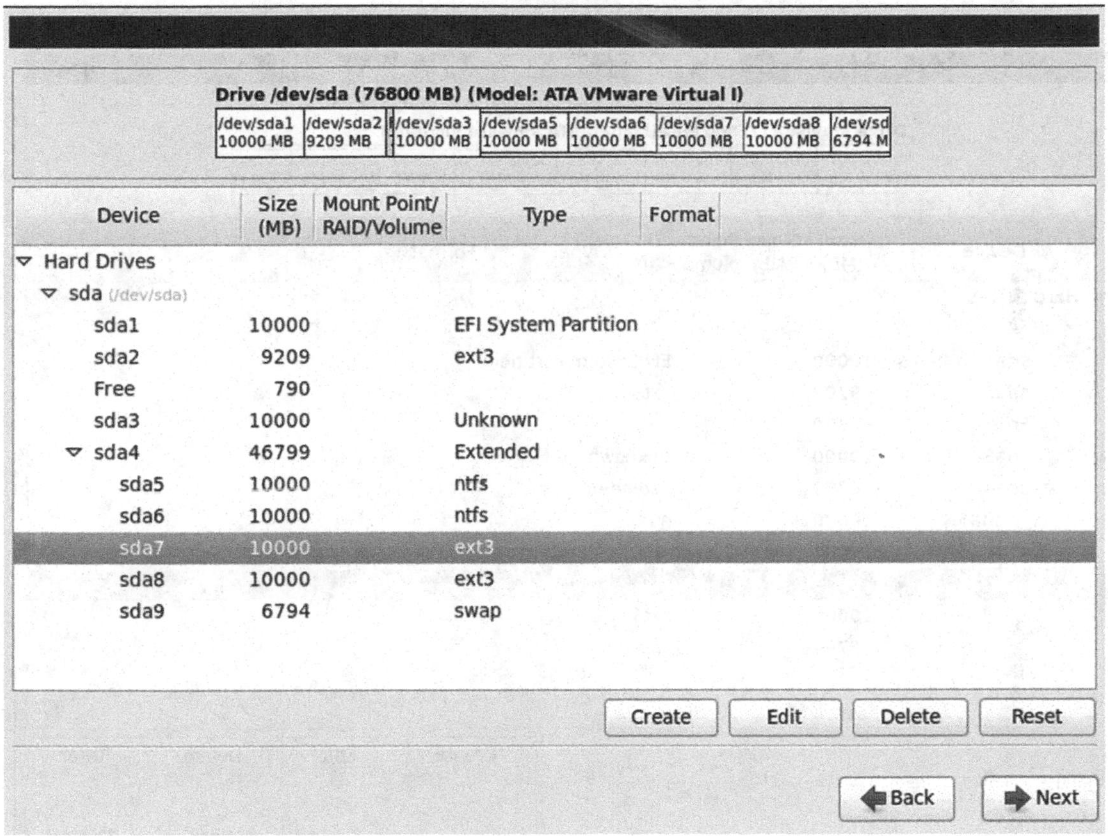

Drive /dev/sda (76800 MB) (Model: ATA VMware Virtual I)							
/dev/sda1 10000 MB	/dev/sda2 9209 MB	/dev/sda3 10000 MB	/dev/sda5 10000 MB	/dev/sda6 10000 MB	/dev/sda7 10000 MB	/dev/sda8 10000 MB	/dev/sd 6794 M

Device	Size (MB)	Mount Point/ RAID/Volume	Type	Format
▽ Hard Drives				
▽ sda (/dev/sda)				
sda1	10000		EFI System Partition	
sda2	9209		ext3	
Free	790			
sda3	10000		Unknown	
▽ sda4	46799		Extended	
sda5	10000		ntfs	
sda6	10000		ntfs	
sda7	10000		ext3	
sda8	10000		ext3	
sda9	6794		swap	

Create   Edit   Delete   Reset

◀ Back   ▶ Next

Figure 2-62. *Partition layout shown by the Anaconda installer*

As shown in Figure 2-63, we need to assign root (/) to the sda7 partition and reformat it with ext4, which is the default filesystem choice of RHEL 6.

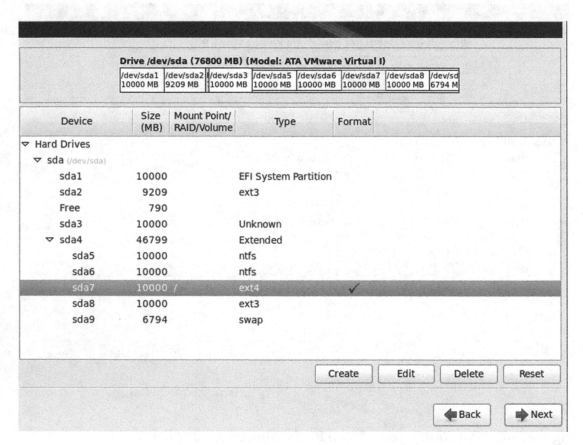

Figure 2-63. *The partition scheme that Anaconda will implement*

As visible in Figure 2-64, RHEL 6 (or Anaconda) has detected some OS, and it is trying to give equal opportunity to the other OS to boot (specified as Other). There are two OS entries, which RHEL 6's bootloader (GRUB) will show at the time of the boot.

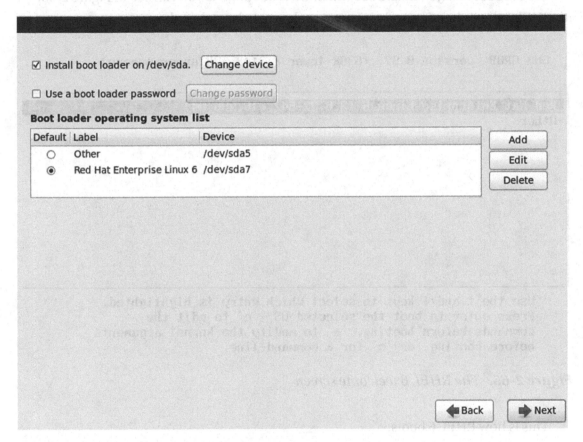

Figure 2-64. *Anaconda detecting another OS*

As per RHEL 6, the other OS will boot from sda5. This means the following:

```
sda1 = XP
sda2 = Solaris
sda3 = PC BSD
sda4 = Extended partition
sda5 = Win win2k3    <<<-----------
```

At the time of the boot, if a user chooses the Other option, win2k3 is supposed to boot. Which OS will boot after choosing the Other option? Take your time and come up with your own booting sequence.

Let's reboot the system and see which OS is booting. As you can see in Figure 2-65, it's RHEL 6 that is booting and giving you a chance to boot the other OS.

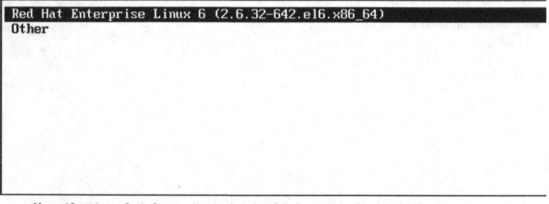

Figure 2-65. *The RHEL 6 welcome screen*

This is how RHEL 6 boots:

1. When the system is powered on, it goes to the BIOS, then from the BIOS to POST, and from POST back to the BIOS.

2. The BIOS ultimately lands in the entire HDD's first sector and runs the bootstrap.

3. When RHEL 6 was getting installed, the * was on the first primary partition.

4. The problem that was faced by win2k3 and Windows 7 is faced by RHEL 6 also. RHEL 6 is getting installed in a logical partition that the BIOS cannot reach or see. So, to tackle this issue, RHEL 6 has to shift its part-1 and part-2 of the bootloader (GRUB) to the first

primary partition. Remember, Windows shifted part-3 as well to the first primary, but RHEL (and in general any Linux OS) will shift only the first two parts to the first primary partition, and part-3 of GRUB will be kept in its own partition; in our case, this is sda-7.

5. While replacing the first primary partition's part-1 and part-2, RHEL noticed that there is already some other OS installed, and to give it an equal chance to boot, it made an entry for it in its own partition's /boot/grub/grub.conf named configuration file. Figure 2-66 shows the grub.conf file.

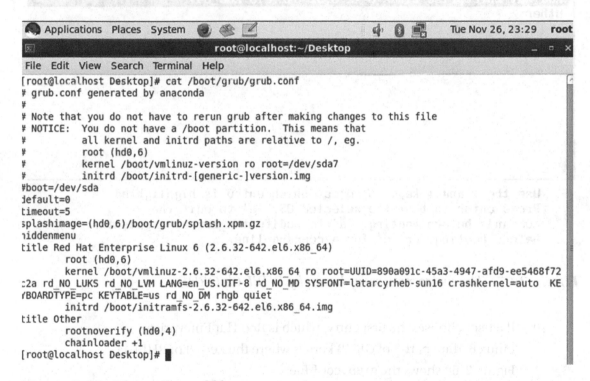

Figure 2-66. *The grub.conf file*

As you can see, whatever is written after the title variable will be printed on the screen.

6. Returning to the boot sequence, the bootstrap that is in the first primary partition is from RHEL.

7. Part-1 of RHEL's GRUB will jump to part-2.

8. Part-2 of GRUB has a hard-coded location for part-3 of GRUB. Part-3 of GRUB is on RHEL's partition, which is sda7.

9. Part-3 of GRUB will read the `grub.conf` file from the `/boot/grub` directory, and whatever is written after `title` will be printed on the screen. Figure 2-67 shows this.

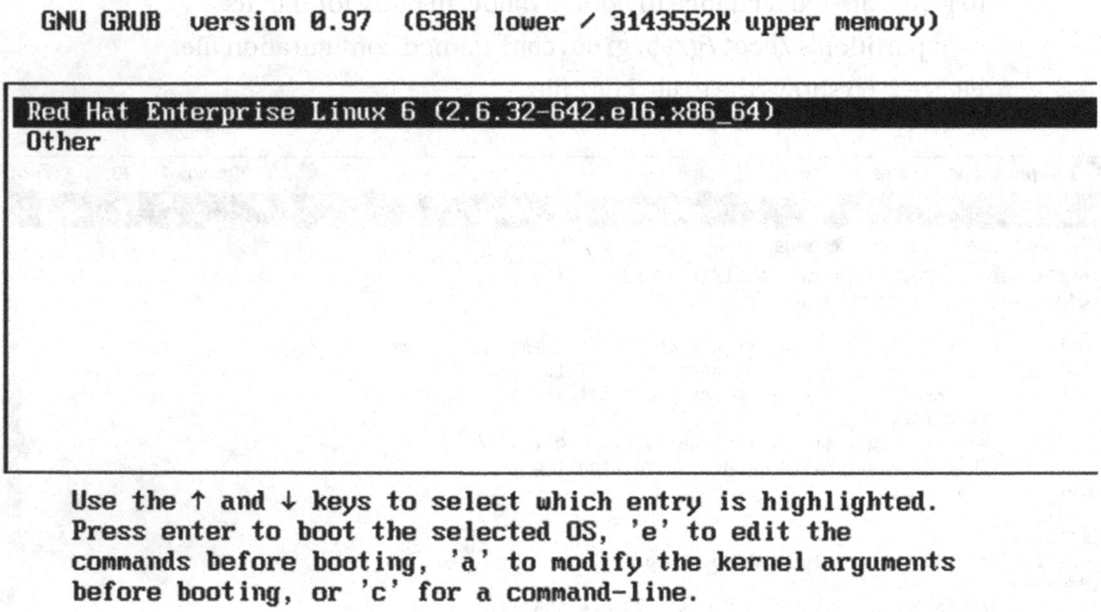

```
GNU GRUB  version 0.97  (638K lower / 3143552K upper memory)

Red Hat Enterprise Linux 6 (2.6.32-642.e16.x86_64)
Other

      Use the ↑ and ↓ keys to select which entry is highlighted.
      Press enter to boot the selected OS, 'e' to edit the
      commands before booting, 'a' to modify the kernel arguments
      before booting, or 'c' for a command-line.
```

Figure 2-67. *The welcome screen shown by RHEL 6's GRUB*

10. If a user chooses the first entry, which is Red Hat Enterprise Linux 6, then part-3 of GRUB knows where the kernel of RHEL is. Figure 2-68 shows the `grub.conf` file.

```
------------
:itle Red Hat Enterprise Linux 6 (2.6.32-642.el6.x86_64)
      root (hd0,6)
      kernel /boot/vmlinuz-2.6.32-642.el6.x86_64 ro root=UUID=890a091c-45a3-4947-afd9-ee5468f72
:2a rd_NO_LUKS rd_NO_LVM LANG=en_US.UTF-8 rd_NO_MD SYSFONT=latarcyrheb-sun16 crashkernel=auto  KE
'BOARDTYPE=pc KEYTABLE=us rd_NO_DM rhgb quiet
      initrd /boot/initramfs-2.6.32-642.el6.x86_64.img
```

Figure 2-68. *The grub.conf file of RHEL 6*

11. The kernel binary file will be at /boot/vmlinuz. (Notice the
     kernel variable from Figure 2-68.) Basically, the same grub.conf
     file will tell the location of the kernel to part-3 of GRUB. It will
     copy the kernel (vmlinuz) in memory, and the GRUB bootloader's
     job is done. RHEL's kernel will take care of the rest of the booting
     sequence. Meanwhile, when the system is booting, a nice
     animation, as shown in Figure 2-69, will appear on the screen.

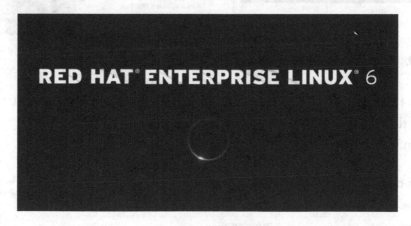

Figure 2-69. *The animation to hide the complicated log messages*

Figure 2-70 shows the flowchart of the complete booting sequence of RHEL 6.

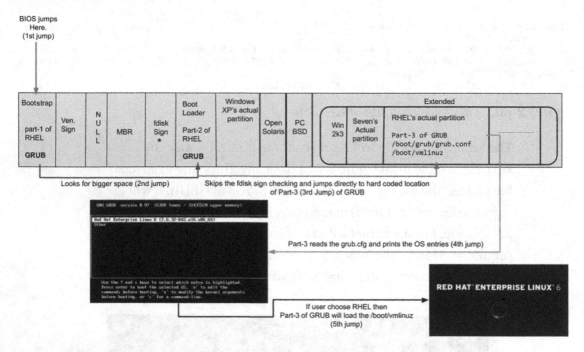

Figure 2-70. *The boot sequence of RHEL 6*

12. If a user chooses Other instead, then it will call whatever is present on the sda5 partition. As you can see in Figure 2-71, sda5 is on win2k3's partition.

Boot loader operating system list		
Default	Label	Device
○	Other	/dev/sda5
◉	Red Hat Enterprise Linux 6	/dev/sda7

Figure 2-71. *The other OS is on partition 5*

13. When win2k3 was installed, it shifted all of its bootloader's parts to the first primary. This means win2k3's partition does not have a bootloader present, so of course no OS will boot. Figure 2-72 shows the error message thrown on-screen if you try to boot the other OS.

```
NTLDR is missing
```

Figure 2-72. *The error message*

Now, I have a couple of questions to ask:

- Where is the * now?

- If I keep the * on the second partition, which OS will boot?

- If I keep the * on the third partition, which OS will boot?

- If I keep the * on the fifth (logical) partition, which OS will boot?

- If I do not keep the * on any of the partition, which OS will boot?

In all of these scenarios, only one OS will boot, and that will be RHEL 6 (Figure 2-73).

Figure 2-73. *The RHEL 6 desktop screen*

No matter where you keep the * or even if you don't keep the * on any partition, it's only the RHEL that will be booting all the time. The reason is simple, but it changes the booting sequence altogether. The Red Hat Enterprise Linux bootloader, which is GRUB, does not follow the *, and it does not check which partition is active before calling part-3 of its bootloader. In fact, none of the Linux OSs bothers to check the active partition. They simply skip that step. So, the booting sequence becomes the following:

1. First the system goes to the BIOS, then POST, then back to the BIOS, and finally to the first primary partition's bootstrap.

2. RHEL's part-1 of GRUB jumps to part-2 of GRUB, which (after skipping the fdisk signature part) jumps to part-3 of GRUB.

3. Part-3 of GRUB goes to /boot/grub.conf, which prints the OS entries.

4. If a user chooses RHEL, then the kernel loads from /boot/vmlinuz in memory.

5. The kernel will take care of the rest of the OS booting, which has been extensively explained in the rest of the book.

This also means there is only one OS currently booting, and that is RHEL 6. That's bad! Hence, we need to tweak GRUB to boot the rest of the operating systems.

Tweaking GRUB

The best feature of GRUB is that it can boot any other OS, regardless of whether it is Linux based or not. The trick to boot another OS used by GRUB is simple but amazing. For any bootloader to boot OS, you need to do nothing more than load the respective OS's kernel in memory. GRUB knows where the kernel of a Linux OS is (/boot/vmlinuz). But GRUB does not know where the kernel of Windows or PC-BSD is. The trick is that these operating systems' respective bootloaders know the location of their respective kernels. So, GRUB just calls their respective bootloaders; for example, if GRUB wants to boot BSD, it is at the third primary partition. Refer to Figure 2-74, which shows the partition layout, for a better understanding of this.

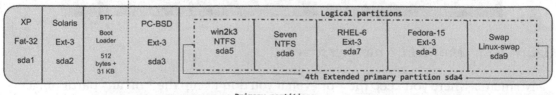

Figure 2-74. *The partition layout of the BIOS*

BSD installed its bootloader on its own partition's reserved 512 bytes + 31 KB. So, GRUB will call part-1 of BTX. This is called *chainloading*. The GRUB bootloader's part-3 will chainload part-1 of BTX. BTX's part-1 knows what to do next, which is to look for part-2. Part-2 will jump to part-3, and it will load BSD's kernel in memory so BSD will start booting up. To achieve this chainloading, we need to tell GRUB the location of part-1 of BTX through the grub.conf file. The location will be hard disk number 1 and partition number 3, but GRUB starts its count from 0 so the location will be hard disk number 0 and partition number 2. The entry in /boot/grub.conf is as follows:

```
title pc-bsd            <<<---- the os entry title
rootnoverify (hd0,2)    <<<---- location of BTX
chainloader +1          <<<---- grub will chainload the BTX
```

As you can see in Figure 2-75, the other operating system entries are similar to BSD; only the partition number will change.

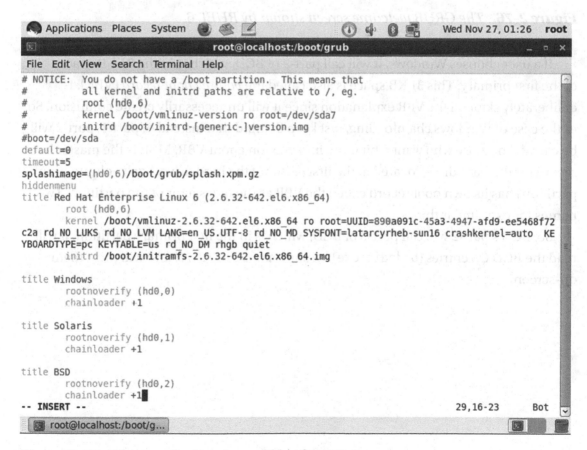

Figure 2-75. The tweaked grub.conf file of RHEL 6

After rebooting, GRUB will show the mentioned `title` entries. See Figure 2-76.

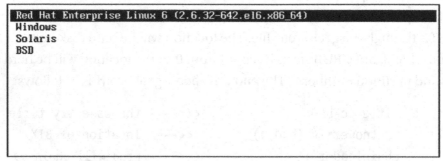

```
GNU GRUB  version 0.97  (638K lower / 3143552K upper memory)

 Red Hat Enterprise Linux 6 (2.6.32-642.el6.x86_64)
 Windows
 Solaris
 BSD




      Use the ↑ and ↓ keys to select which entry is highlighted.
      Press enter to boot the selected OS, 'e' to edit the
      commands before booting, 'a' to modify the kernel arguments
      before booting, or 'c' for a command-line.
```

Figure 2-76. *The GRUB welcome screen shown by RHEL 6*

If a user chooses Windows, it will call part-2 of BCD, which is in the 31 KB space of the first primary. This 31 KB space is also called the *volume boot record* (VBR). I deliberately skipped the VBR explanation since it will unnecessarily create confusion. So, in the case of Windows chainloading, just keep in mind that instead of part-1, part-2 will be called. For those who want a bit more information about VBR, MBR is the master boot record for the hard drive, located at the first sector of the hard drive. Each volume (think partition) has its own boot record called the VBR as the first sector of the partition. Two names for two similar things.

So, BCD's part-2 will call part-3 of BCD, which is in the first primary partition. It will read the BCD OS entries (`bcdedit.exe`), as shown in Figure 2-77, and will print them on-screen.

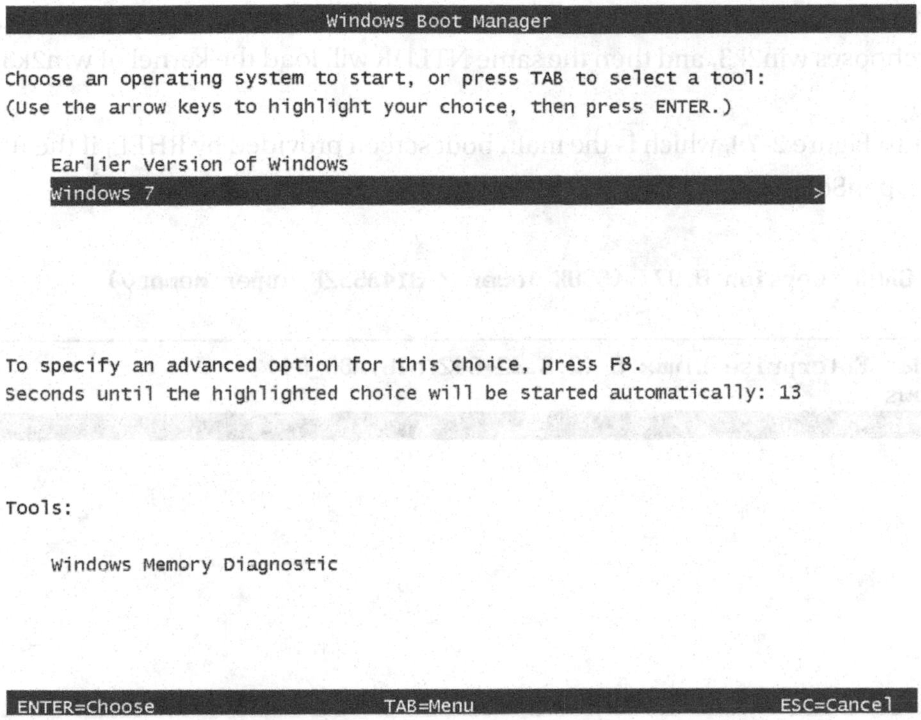

```
                        Windows Boot Manager

Choose an operating system to start, or press TAB to select a tool:
(Use the arrow keys to highlight your choice, then press ENTER.)

    Earlier Version of Windows
    Windows 7                                                        >




To specify an advanced option for this choice, press F8.
Seconds until the highlighted choice will be started automatically: 13




Tools:

    Windows Memory Diagnostic




 ENTER=Choose                 TAB=Menu                    ESC=Cancel
```

Figure 2-77. *The OS entries shown by the BCD bootloader*

If a user chooses the Earlier Version of Windows, as we saw earlier (during Windows 7's booting sequence), it will run part-3 of NTLDR, which is again on the first primary partition. As shown in Figure 2-78, NTLDR will read the boot.ini file from the C drive and will print the OS entries.

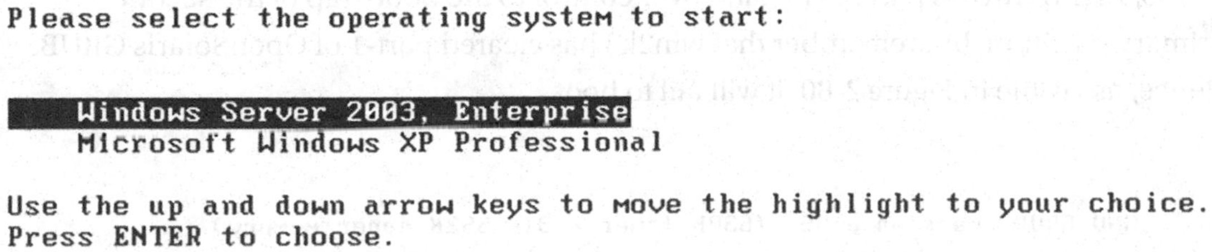

```
Please select the operating system to start:

  Windows Server 2003, Enterprise
  Microsoft Windows XP Professional

Use the up and down arrow keys to move the highlight to your choice.
Press ENTER to choose.
```

Figure 2-78. *The OS entries shown by win2k3's NTLDR*

If a user chooses XP, part-3 of NTLDR knows where the kernel of XP is. Instead, the user chooses win2k3, and then the same NTLDR will load the kernel of win2k3 in memory.

Refer to Figure 2-79, which is the main boot screen provided by RHEL, if the user chooses OpenSolaris.

```
GNU GRUB  version 0.97  (638K lower / 3143552K upper memory)

 ┌──────────────────────────────────────────────────────────────────┐
 │ Red Hat Enterprise Linux 6 (2.6.32-642.el6.x86_64)                 │
 │ Windows                                                            │
 │ Solaris                                                            │
 │ BSD                                                                │
 │                                                                    │
 │                                                                    │
 │                                                                    │
 │                                                                    │
 │                                                                    │
 │                                                                    │
 └──────────────────────────────────────────────────────────────────┘
```

Figure 2-79. *The OS entries shown by RHEL*

The following are the instructions that will be followed by GRUB:

```
title Solaris
     rootnoverify (hd0,1)
     chainloader  +1
```

So, RHEL GRUB's part-3 will hand over control to the bootstrap of the second primary partition, but remember that win2k3 has cleared part-1 of OpenSolaris GRUB. Hence, as visible in Figure 2-80, it will fail to boot.

```
   GNU GRUB  version 0.95  (638K lower / 3143552K upper memory)

 [ Minimal BASH-like line editing is supported.  For the first word, TAB
   lists possible command completions.  Anywhere else TAB lists the possible
   completions of a device/filename. ]

 grub>
```

Figure 2-80. *OpenSolaris failed to boot*

This means we need to fix the OpenSolaris bootloader first. To fix it, we need to boot from the OpenSolaris live CD image, which we used to install OpenSolaris and, once it was booted, installed part-1 and part-2 (part-2 is not necessary but good to reinstall) of GRUB from the live CD to the OpenSolaris partition's reserved 512 bytes + 31 KB. The command that we will use is installgrub. As the name suggests, the command will copy part-1 (stage1) and part-2 (stage2) of GRUB from the live image and place them in the OpenSolaris partition's 512 bytes + 31 KB space. Figure 2-81 shows the command in action.

#installgrub   /boot/grub/stage1   /boot/grub/stage2   /dev/rdsk/c4d1s0

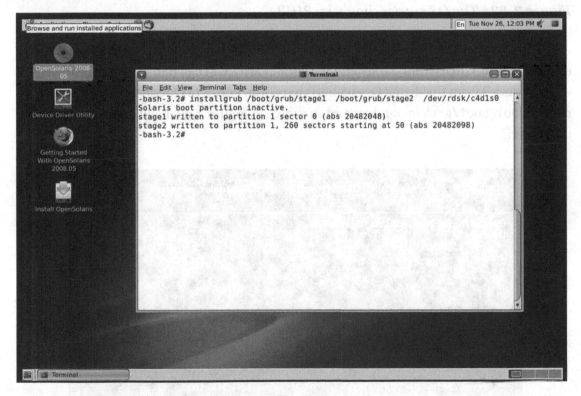

Figure 2-81. *The installgrub command*

After rebooting, RHEL will again show the same OS entries (Figure 2-82) since for RHEL nothing has changed.

```
GNU GRUB  version 0.97  (638K lower / 3143552K upper memory)

┌──────────────────────────────────────────────────────────────────────┐
│ Red Hat Enterprise Linux 6 (2.6.32-642.el6.x86_64)                     │
│ Windows                                                                │
│▓Solaris▓▓▓▓▓▓▓▓▓▓▓▓▓▓▓▓▓▓▓▓▓▓▓▓▓▓▓▓▓▓▓▓▓▓▓▓▓▓▓▓▓▓▓▓▓▓▓▓▓▓▓▓▓▓▓▓▓▓▓▓▓▓▓▓│
│ BSD                                                                    │
│                                                                        │
│                                                                        │
│                                                                        │
│                                                                        │
│                                                                        │
│                                                                        │
└──────────────────────────────────────────────────────────────────────┘
```

Figure 2-82. *The OS entries shown by RHEL*

If this time we choose OpenSolaris, then RHEL GRUB's part-3 will chainload part-1 of OpenSolaris GRUB from the second partition. Part-1 will call part-2, and eventually it will call part-3 from the actual OpenSolaris partition. Part-3 of OpenSolaris GRUB will read /rpool/boot/grub/menu.lst, and as shown in Figure 2-83, it will print the titles on the screen.

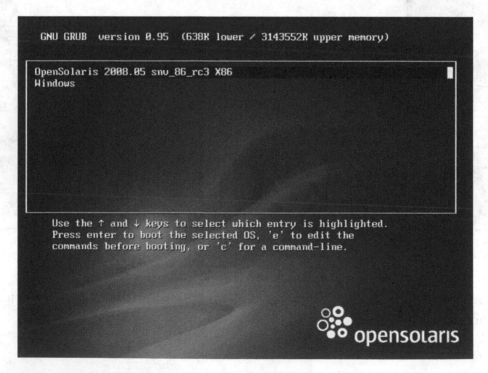

Figure 2-83. *The OS entries shown by OpenSolaris*

If a user chooses OpenSolaris, then part-3 of OpenSolaris GRUB will load the kernel from /boot. If the user chooses Windows, then part-3 of OpenSolaris GRUB will follow these instructions from /rpool/boot/grub/menu.lst:

```
title Solaris
     rootnoverify (hd0,1)
     chainloader  +1
```

We know now what is going to appear on-screen (refer to Figure 2-84).

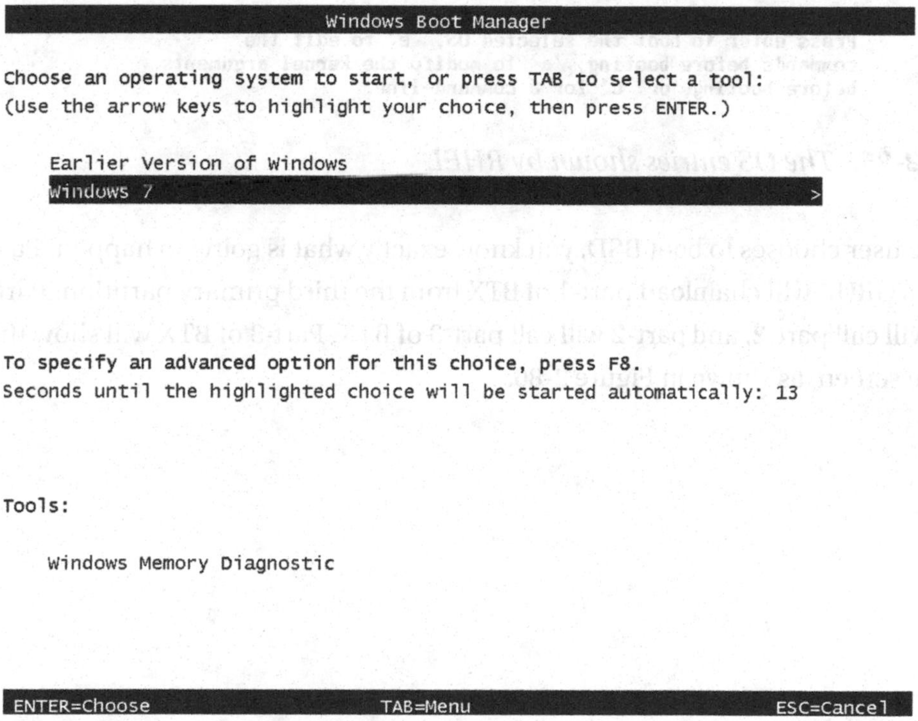

Figure 2-84. *The OS entries shown by BCD*

The story will continue if the user chooses Earlier Version of Windows, which we have already discussed. Going back to the original OS list, Figure 2-85 shows what is presented by RHEL's GRUB.

81

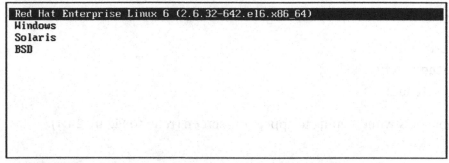

GNU GRUB version 0.97 (638K lower / 3143552K upper memory)

```
Red Hat Enterprise Linux 6 (2.6.32-642.el6.x86_64)
Windows
Solaris
BSD
```

Use the ↑ and ↓ keys to select which entry is highlighted.
Press enter to boot the selected OS, 'e' to edit the
commands before booting, 'a' to modify the kernel arguments
before booting, or 'c' for a command-line.

Figure 2-85. *The OS entries shown by RHEL*

If the user chooses to boot BSD, you know exactly what is going to happen. Part-3 of RHEL's GRUB will chainload part-1 of BTX from the third primary partition. Part-1 of BTX will call part-2, and part-2 will call part-3 of BTX. Part-3 of BTX will show the welcome screen, as shown in Figure 2-86.

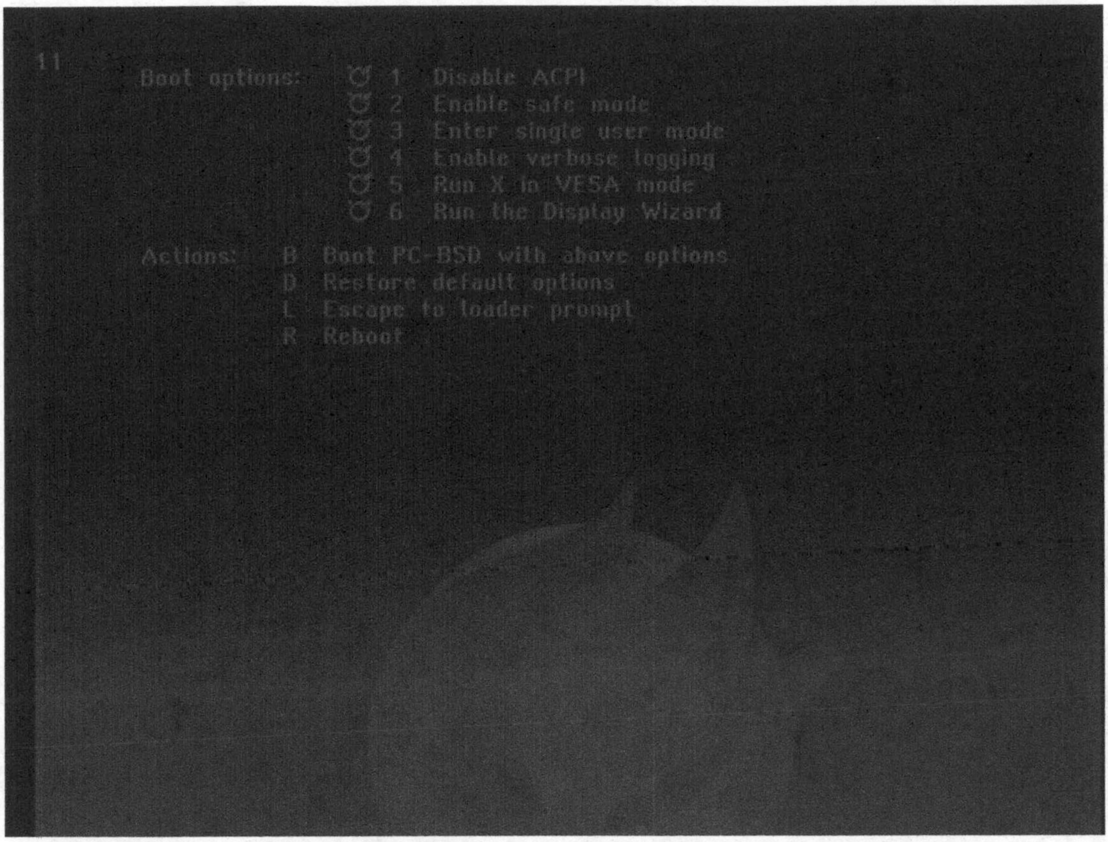

Figure 2-86. *PC-BSD's welcome screen*

Once chosen to boot, part-3 of BTX will load the kernel of BSD Unix in memory. So, all the operating systems, whichever we installed so far, are able to boot now, and it does not matter which partition is active. But can we hack the Windows bootloaders and force them to boot the Linux and Unix operating systems from our list? We can, and that's what we will do now.

Hacking the Windows Bootloaders

It's actually pretty easy to trick the Windows bootloaders. As we saw earlier, bootloaders do chainloading; for example, part-1 calls part-2 of its bootloader and so on. To understand the trick, let's take BSD as an example. Part-1 of BCD is calling its part-2 of BCD, but if we tell BCD's part-1 to chainload part-1 of RHEL, then part-1 of RHEL will run, and it will eventually follow its own booting sequence. Part-1 of GRUB (RHEL) will call part-2 of GRUB, and it will eventually chainload part-3 of GRUB since part-3's block address is hard-coded in part-2. This means once part-1 of any bootloader runs, it will start following its own boot sequence, and we will take advantage of this behavior.

To achieve this, we need to get part-1 of every non-Windows-based bootloader and place it into the Windows filesystem. So, the filesystem could be FAT32 or NTFS. Obviously, placing part-1 of every non-Windows-based bootloader on the first primary has the most advantages since every Windows operating system has installed their respective bootloaders on the first primary partition. So, through the dd command, we will copy the first 512 bytes (even the first 440 bytes is enough) of every non-Windows-based OS and place them in XP's partition. Let's mount the first primary partition, as shown in Figure 2-87.

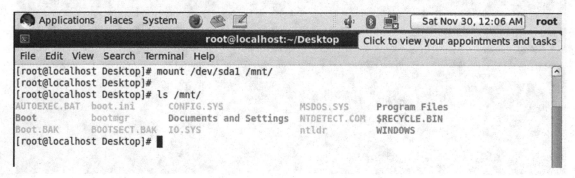

Figure 2-87. *The mount command*

Let's copy the first 512 bytes and place them on the sda1 partition. Refer to Figure 2-88 for this.

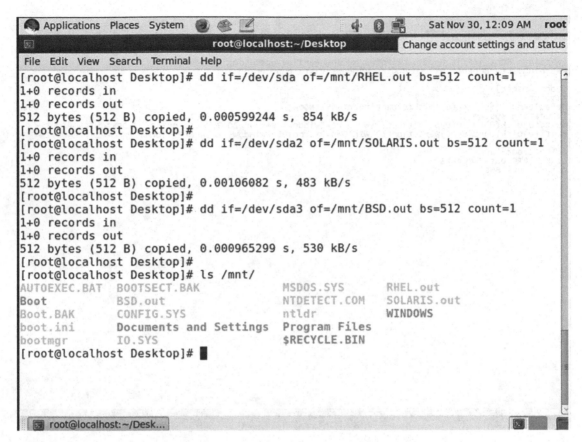

Figure 2-88. Transferring the first 512 bytes to the first primary

Now we will boot back in XP, and as shown in Figure 2-89, we will add the part-1 files entries in the boot.ini file. The boot.ini file is read by both Windows bootloaders, which are BCD and win2k3's NTLDR.

Figure 2-89. Adding the entries in the boot.ini file

The following are the entries that we have added:

c:\RHEL.out="RHEL"

c:\SOLARIS.out = "SOLARIS"

c:\BSD.out="BSD"

Just like the grub.conf file, whatever is written in double quotes in boot.ini will be considered the title of the OS entry. Now let's reboot the system and choose the Windows OS entry from the RHEL OS list (refer to Figure 2-90).

```
 GNU GRUB  version 0.97  (638K lower / 3143552K upper memory)

┌─────────────────────────────────────────────────────────────────────┐
│ Red Hat Enterprise Linux 6 (2.6.32-642.el6.x86_64)                    │
│ Windows                                                               │
│ Solaris                                                               │
│ BSD                                                                   │
│                                                                       │
│                                                                       │
│                                                                       │
│                                                                       │
│                                                                       │
│                                                                       │
│                                                                       │
│                                                                       │
└─────────────────────────────────────────────────────────────────────┘
```

Figure 2-90. *The OS list shown by RHEL*

How we reached this screen is easy to understand.

1. The system goes first to the BIOS, then to POST, then to the BIOS, then to the first 512 bytes, and then to the bootstrap (part-1) of RHEL (GRUB).

2. Then comes part-1 of GRUB, which jumps to part-2 of GRUB, which jumps to part-3 of GRUB, which goes to /boot/grub.conf, which prints the OS titles.

3. The user has chosen Windows, so next comes part-1 of BCD from the first primary partition and then part-2 of BCD.

4. Finally, it goes to part-3, then bcd.exe, and it will read the boot.ini file and whatever is written into the double quotes will be printed on screen.

The OS list is visible in Figure 2-91.

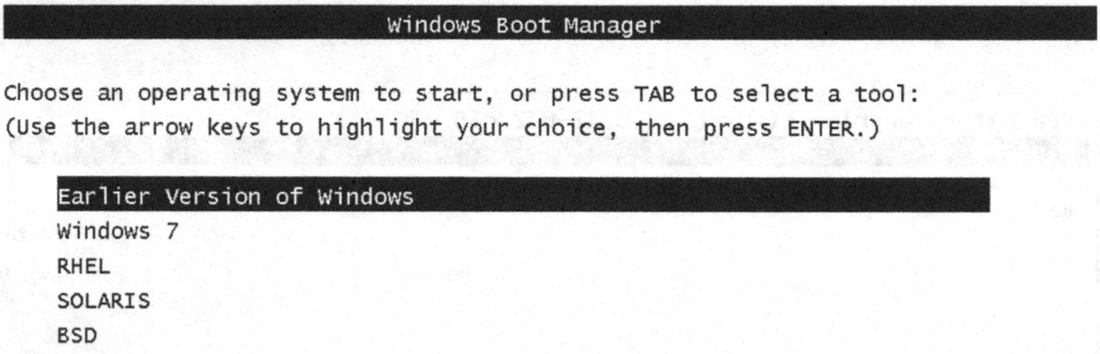

```
Windows Boot Manager
```

```
Choose an operating system to start, or press TAB to select a tool:
(Use the arrow keys to highlight your choice, then press ENTER.)

    Earlier Version of Windows
    Windows 7
    RHEL
    SOLARIS
    BSD
```

Figure 2-91. *The OS entries shown by Windows 7 (BCD)*

If the user chooses Earlier Version of Windows, then BCD's part-3 will call part-3 of win2k3's NTLDR. NTLDR will again read the boot.ini file and print the OS list, as shown in Figure 2-92.

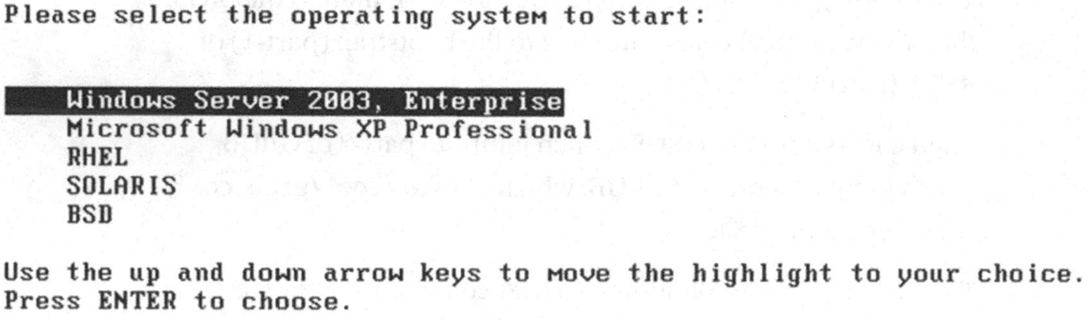

```
Please select the operating system to start:

    Windows Server 2003, Enterprise
    Microsoft Windows XP Professional
    RHEL
    SOLARIS
    BSD

Use the up and down arrow keys to move the highlight to your choice.
Press ENTER to choose.
```

Figure 2-92. *The OS entries shown by win2k3's NTLDR*

If a user chooses OpenSolaris, then part-3 of NTLDR will run the Solaris.out file from C: (the first primary partition). The Solaris.out file is nothing but part-1 of the OpenSolaris bootloader from the second partition. Part-1 of the OpenSolaris bootloader will call part-2 and eventually part-3 of GRUB. It will read the menu.lst file and will print the OS list (Figure 2-93).

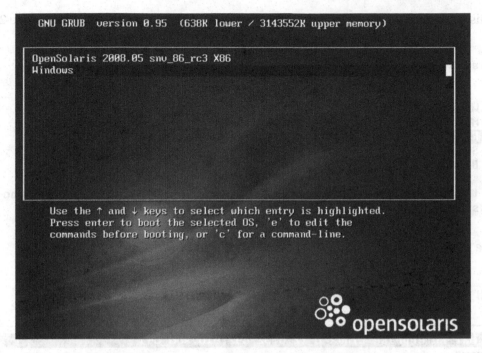

Figure 2-93. *The OS entries shown by OpenSolaris GRUB*

If the user again chooses Windows, then part-3 of OpenSolaris will call part-2 of BCD from the first primary partition (`rootnoverify (hd0,0)`). (Part-2 of BCD will be in the VBR section of the first primary partition. We will not cover the VBR in this book.) BCD's part-2 will call part-3 of BCD. It will read the OS entries through `bcdedit.exe` and from `boot.ini` and print the OS entries. The OS entries printed on the screen are visible in Figure 2-94.

```
                        Windows Boot Manager

Choose an operating system to start, or press TAB to select a tool:
(Use the arrow keys to highlight your choice, then press ENTER.)

 Earlier Version of Windows
 Windows 7
 RHEL
 SOLARIS
 BSD
```

Figure 2-94. *The OS entries shown by Windows 7 (BCD)*

This is how we have created a bootloader's loop (refer to Figure 2-95 and Figure 2-96).

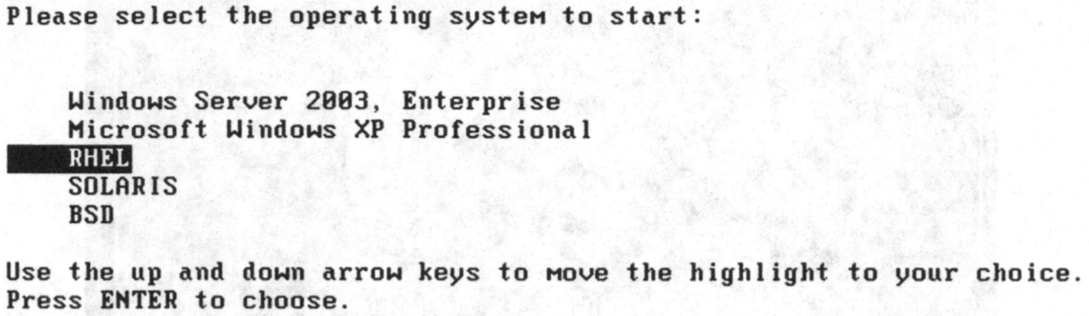

```
Please select the operating system to start:

    Windows Server 2003, Enterprise
    Microsoft Windows XP Professional
    RHEL
    SOLARIS
    BSD

Use the up and down arrow keys to move the highlight to your choice.
Press ENTER to choose.
```

Figure 2-95. *The RHEL entry has been chosen to boot*

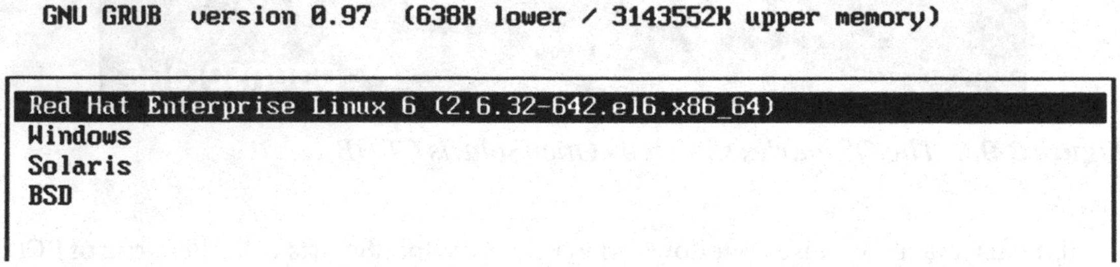

```
 GNU GRUB  version 0.97  (638K lower / 3143552K upper memory)

┌──────────────────────────────────────────────────────────────┐
│ Red Hat Enterprise Linux 6 (2.6.32-642.el6.x86_64)            │
│ Windows                                                        │
│ Solaris                                                        │
│ BSD                                                            │
│                                                                │
│                                                                │
└──────────────────────────────────────────────────────────────┘
```

Figure 2-96. *The OS entries shown by RHEL's GRUB*

As you can see, Linux is booting Windows, Linux is booting Unix, Unix is booting Windows, Windows is booting Windows, and Windows is booting Linux, but one thing is still missing, and that is Linux is booting Linux. For that, we will install the final OS from our list, and that is Fedora 15.

Fedora 15

As shown in Figure 2-97, we are installing Fedora 15 on sda8.

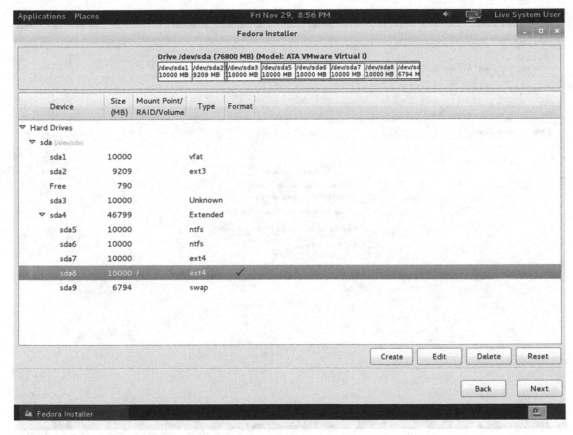

Figure 2-97. *The Fedora installer*

By default Fedora will try to install its bootloader on the first primary, but if we allow that, then again we need to add the entry of every other OS in its grub.conf. Instead, we will follow a different approach. We will install the bootloader of Fedora (GRUB) on its own partition (sda8) instead of sda1. See Figure 2-98.

Figure 2-98. *The bootloader device selection*

This means after rebooting Fedora will never be able to boot since RHEL's GRUB does not know about this new OS, so we need to add Fedora's entry into grub.conf of RHEL. To do that, let's mount sda8, as shown in Figure 2-99.

Figure 2-99. *The mounting of Fedora's partition*

Copy Fedora's entries (see Figure 2-100) from Fedora GRUB's grub.conf file: /mnt/boot/grub.conf.

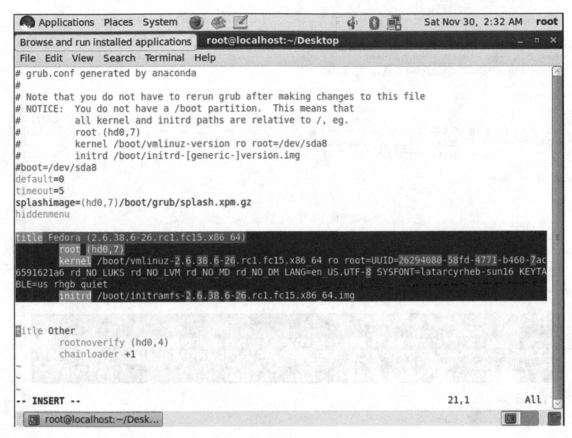

Figure 2-100. *The grub.conf file of Fedora 15*

The entries are simple. Whenever part-3 of Fedora is called, it will load the kernel of Fedora from /boot/vmlinuz-2.6.38.6-26.rc1.fc15.x86_64 into the memory. After that, it will load initramfs from /boot/initramfs-2.6.38.6-26.rc1.fc15.x86_64.img into the memory.

Figure 2-101 shows RHEL's /etc/grub.conf file after copying the entry of Fedora from /mnt/etc/grub.conf.

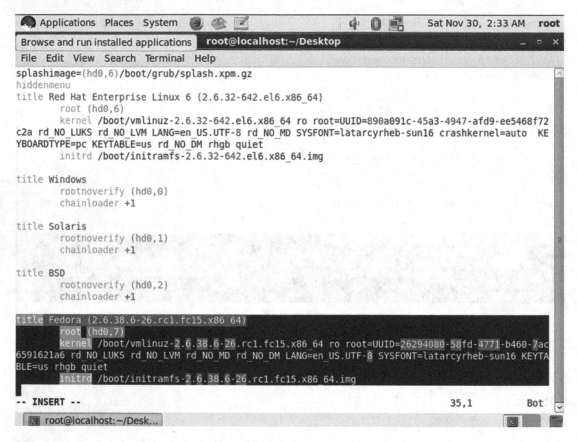

Figure 2-101. *The grub.conf file of RHEL*

After reboot, we will get the Fedora entry (Figure 2-102).

```
GNU GRUB  version 0.97  (638K lower / 3143552K upper memory)
```

```
Red Hat Enterprise Linux 6 (2.6.32-642.el6.x86_64)
Windows
Solaris
BSD
Fedora (2.6.38.6-26.rc1.fc15.x86_64)
```

Figure 2-102. *The OS entries shown by RHEL*

When the user chooses Fedora to boot, as per the entry in RHEL's `grub.conf` file, part-3 of RHEL's GRUB will load the kernel from the eighth partition (sda8 of Fedora) and will also load initramfs from the same location (we will talk about initramfs in Chapter 5), and the bootloader will go away.

Complete Flowchart

Figure 2-103 shows the complete flowchart of every OS that we have installed so far.

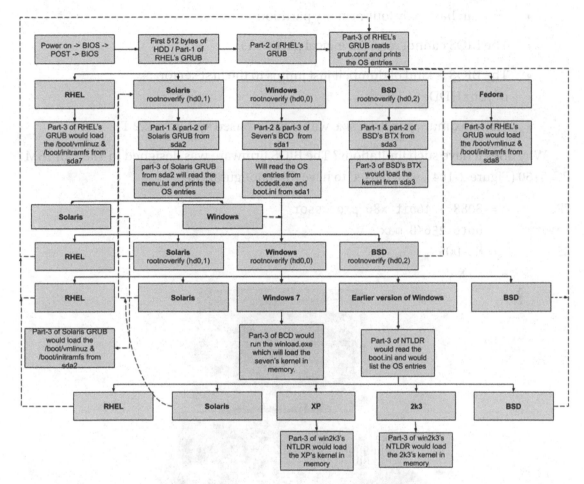

Figure 2-103. *The complete flowchart of all the operating systems*

I hope you now understand the way bootloaders boot the operating systems on a BIOS-based system. Now it's time to understand the new firmware, which is Unified Extensible Firmware Interface (UEFI).

Unified Extensible Firmware Interface (UEFI)

Here are the BIOS limitations you have observed so far:

- You can have only four primary partitions.

- The BIOS cannot read the logical partitions.

- The BIOS is kind of dumb; it just jumps to the first sector of your HDD.

- The maximum partition size with a BIOS-based system is 2.2 TB.

Why does it have such limitations? The BIOS firmware was designed in 1982 for IBM PC-5150 (Figure 2-104), which used to have this configuration:

```
CPU      = 8088 - 16bit x86 processor
Memory   = upto 256KB max
OS       = MS-DOS
```

Figure 2-104. *IBM PC-5150*

As you can see, the BIOS was designed for this PC 38 years ago. In these three decades, operating systems grew from floppy disks to NVME disks and from text mode to shiny GUIs. The hardware devices went from drivers to plug and play, but the BIOS remained the same, which initially had a 16-bit instruction set, and in later stages it started using a 32-bit instruction set. Nowadays we have 64-bit CPUs, but the BIOS is still made from 32-bit instructions. The reason we did not upgrade the BIOS to 64-bit is because of historical reasons. When everything is working, why rewrite something? That's the philosophy the computer industry has adopted anyway. When the CPU went from 16-bit (8088) to 64-bit (i9), the BIOS remained either on 16-bit or on 32-bit, because at the time of the early stages of booting, it was not necessary to have a 64-bit CPU, and this is the reason we have CPU modes (real, protected, and long).

In real mode, the CPU will be restricted to 16 bits. In this mode, programs like the old BIOS that have 16-bit instructions will run. These programs cannot run in any other mode. Later, the CPU will switch from real mode to protected mode. The protected mode is 32 bits, and programs these days, like the BIOS, that have 32-bit instructions sets will run under this mode, and later the CPU will be placed in long mode, which is 64 bits. Remember, these modes are not implemented by the CPU; rather, they are implemented by firmware like the BIOS. This means if we remove the same CPU from a real mode-enabled system and place it on a system that does not have real mode, then the same CPU will directly start in protected mode. We will talk about these modes again in Chapter 4.

Since the BIOS runs in protected mode, the address space that is available for the BIOS is only 4 GB. If the system has 20 GB of memory, the BIOS will only be able to address up to 4 GB. Though the system has a 64-bit I9 processor, the BIOS will still be able to use only 32 bits of it. Because of these hardware challenges, the BIOS has limitations.

BIOS Limitations

These are some limitations of the BIOS:

- BIOS will only be able to jump to the first sector, which is 512 bytes.

    - The MBR, which is 64 bytes in size, is part of the first boot sector. If we increase the size of the MBR, it will go beyond the 512 bytes; hence, we cannot increase the size of the MBR, which is the reason why the BIOS can provide only four primary partitions.

- BIOS cannot generate good graphics/GUIs.

    - Now this is a generic statement, and it is used in comparison with UEFI. There are some BIOS vendors that have implemented web browsers outside of the OS, but such implementations are rare to see on normal desktop hardware.

- Also, at Phoenix, some of the BIOS implementations has a FAT32 driver in it through which it manages to show icons inside a setup.

- You cannot use a mouse in the BIOS.

  - There are many BIOS vendors that have mouse support, but again it is rare to find in normal desktop systems.

- The maximum partition size is 2.2 TB.

  - The BIOS uses and supports an MS-DOS partition table, which is quite old, and it has its own drawbacks like 2.2 TB of maximum partition size.

- The BIOS is dumb because it does not understand the bootloader or the OS.

- It is slow because of the hardware limitations.

  - In terms of booting speed, the BIOS is slow since it takes time to initialize the hardware.

  - The BIOS takes almost 30 seconds to start the actual OS-level booting.

- It struggles to initialize the new-generation hardware devices.

- BIOS has limited preboot tools.

  - Compared to the UEFI firmware, the BIOS has very few preboot tools such as remote hardware diagnostics, etc.

So, to overcome all these BIOS limitations, Intel started an initiative in 1998 called Intel Boot Initiative (IBI); later it became Extensible Firmware Interface (EFI). Intel was joined by every other possible OS and hardware vendor (HP/Apple/Dell/Microsoft/ IBM/Asus/AMD/American Megatrends /Phoenix Technologies). They made an open source forum for this project, and finally it became Unified Extensible Interface (UEFI).

The open source code is signed under the BSD license, but Intel's base code is still proprietary. UEFI is basically an open source framework, and vendors build their applications on top of it based on the specification provided by UEFI.org. For example, American Megatrends built APTIO, and Phoenix Technologies built the SecureCore UEFI firmware. Apple was the first that dared to launch systems with UEFI firmware in it. All the drawbacks that the BIOS has are because of its 16-bit instruction set. Since this 16-bit instruction set limits BIOS hardware usage to 1 MB of address space, UEFI targeted and resolved that limitation.

UEFI Advantages

UEFI supports 64-bit processors; hence, it does not face any of the hardware limitations that the BIOS faces.

- UEFI can use the full CPU. Unlike the BIOS (which is stuck with 16 bits of processor), UEFI can access up to 64 bits.

- UEFI can use a full RAM module. Unlike 1 MB of address space of the BIOS, UEFI can support and use terabytes of RAM.

- Instead of 64 bytes of a tiny MBR, UEFI uses the GPT (GUID) partition table, which will provide an infinite number of partitions, and all will be primary partitions. In fact, there is no concept of primary and logical partitions.

- A maximum partition size is 8 zettabytes.

- UEFI has enterprise management tools.

    a) You will be able to fix the computer remotely.

    b) You will be able to browse the Internet inside the UEFI firmware.

    c) You will be able to change the UEFI firmware behavior/ settings from OS.

        i) To change the settings of BIOS, we have to reboot the system since OS runs in long mode, whereas BIOS runs in real mode, and real mode can only be possible at the time of boot.

- UEFI is a small OS.

    a) You will have full access to audio and video devices.

    b) You will be able to connect to WiFi.

    c) You will be able to use the mouse.

d) In terms of the GUI, UEFI will provide a rich graphics
    interface.

e) UEFI will have its own app store like we have for Android and
    Apple phones.

f) You will be able to download and use the applications from
    the UEFI app store, just like with Android and Apple phones.
    Hundreds of apps are available such as calendars, email
    clients, browser, games, shells, etc.

g) UEFI is able to run any binary that has an EFI executable
    format.

h) It boots operating systems securely with the help of the Secure
    Boot feature. We will discuss the Secure Boot feature in depth
    later in this book.

i) UEFI is backward compatible, meaning it will support the
    "BIOS way" of booting. In other words, operating systems that
    do not have UEFI support will also be able to boot with UEFI.

The GUI of UEFI

Figure 2-105 shows the GUI implementation of ASUS.

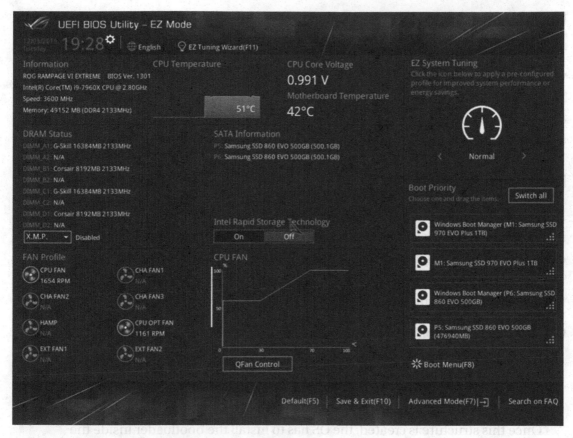

Figure 2-105. *ASUS UEFI implementation*

Here are some things to notice:

- The rich GUI

- Mouse pointer

- Icons, buttons, scroll options, animations, graphs, drop-down options, etc.

Of course, you need to get an expensive motherboard to get such a rich UEFI implementation, but even the basic UEFI implementations are much better than the BIOS implementations.

UEFI Implementation

The UEFI forum releases the UEFI specification. The current UEFI specification when writing this book was 2.8 and can be downloaded from `https://uefi.org/specifications`. The current specification is 2,551 pages long, and every vendor (motherboard, OS, UEFI developer, etc.) has to agree to it. The specification forces regulations that every vendor has to follow. The following are some of the major UEFI regulations.

EFI System Partition (ESP)

Every OS vendor has to create one EPS partition, and the bootloader has to be installed in this partition only. It is not necessary to create ESP as a first partition; it could be created anywhere, but the ESP should have the FAT16/32 (preferably FAT32) filesystem. The recommended ESP size is a minimum of 256 MB. The OS vendor has to create the following directory structure in ESP:

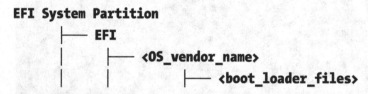

Once this structure is created, the OS has to install the bootloader inside the `/EFI/<os_vendor_name>/` location only. Figure 2-106 shows you the UEFI structure.

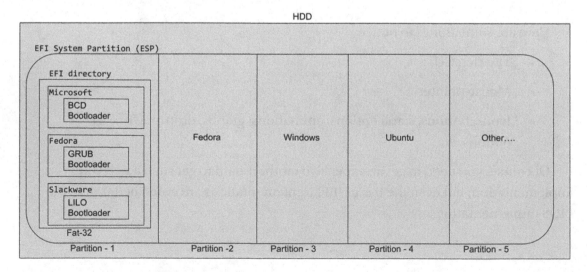

Figure 2-106. *The UEFI structure*

This means, like the 512 bytes + 31 KB space reserved for bootloaders, in the same way we have a 256 MB minimum dedicated space for bootloaders in UEFI. The ESP partition will be mounted in Linux under the mount point `/boot/efi`.

EFI

It's compulsory for every OS vendor to write bootloader files in the EFI executable format. Also, the files should have the `.efi` extension.

Secure Boot

One of the best features UEFI provides is Secure Boot. The feature was proposed by Microsoft and later added in the UEFI specification. Microsoft first used the Secure Boot feature in Windows 8. We will talk about Secure Boot in detail once we get familiarized with how UEFI works.

Partition Table

The recommended partition table is GPT, which is a GUID partition table, whereas the BIOS uses an MS-DOS partition table.

For a better understanding of UEFI, we will use the same approach that we used with the BIOS. We will use a new system named UEFI, which has the UEFI firmware on it, and we will install a couple of OSs in it.

List of Operating Systems

As you know, UEFI uses a GPT partition table; hence, there is no primary or secondary/logical partition concept. This also means there is no particular priority to the installations of operating systems. You can install operating systems in any way you want. We will install the OSs in this order:

1) Ubuntu 18

2) Windows 10

3) Fedora 31

Ubuntu 18.04 LTS

We have almost 64.4 GB of HDD. It is not necessary to use a GParted-like tool to create the partition layout like we used with the BIOS. We will use a Ubuntu-provided default disk utility instead. See Figure 2-107.

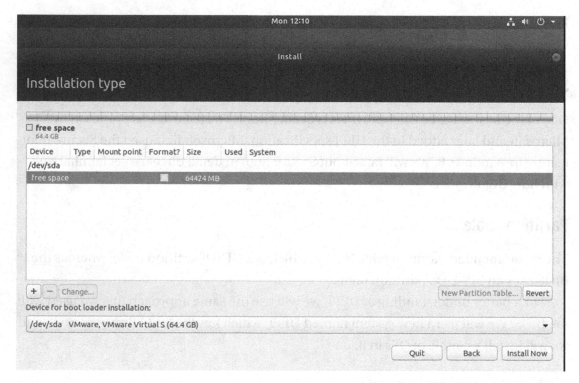

Figure 2-107. *The disk layout provided by Ubuntu*

As shown in Figure 2-108, we will create a 3 GB ESP partition first.

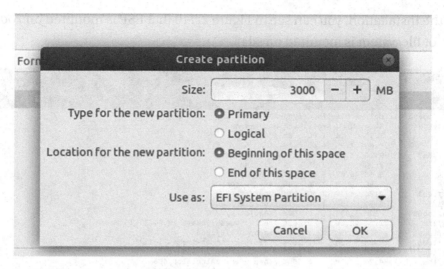

Figure 2-108. *Creating the ESP partition*

Once ESP is created, we will make one more partition (10 GB) for Ubuntu's root filesystem. Figure 2-109 shows the final partition layout of Ubuntu.

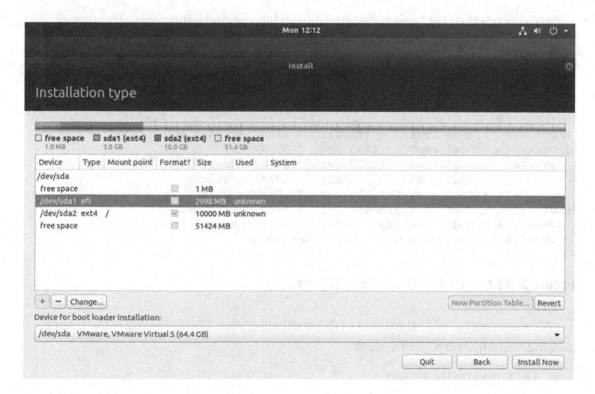

Figure 2-109. *The partition layout of Ubuntu*

105

After the installation, you can see in Figure 2-110 that ESP is mounted on /boot/efi and the root filesystem is mounted on sda2.

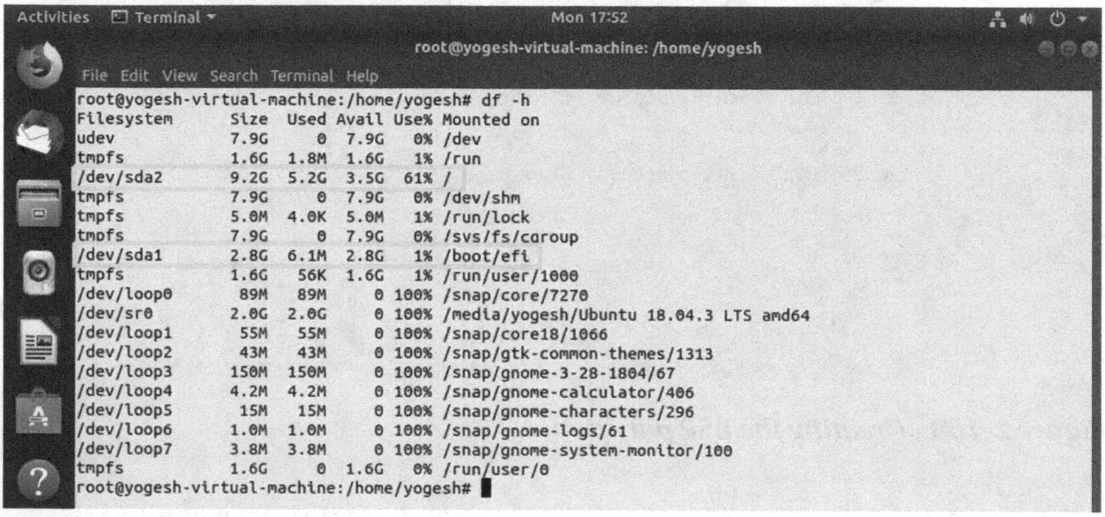

Figure 2-110. *The mount points*

Also, as per the UEFI specification, Ubuntu has created a directory structure of /EFI/ubuntu in the /boot/efi (sda1) mount point and installed the GRUB bootloader in it. See Figure 2-111.

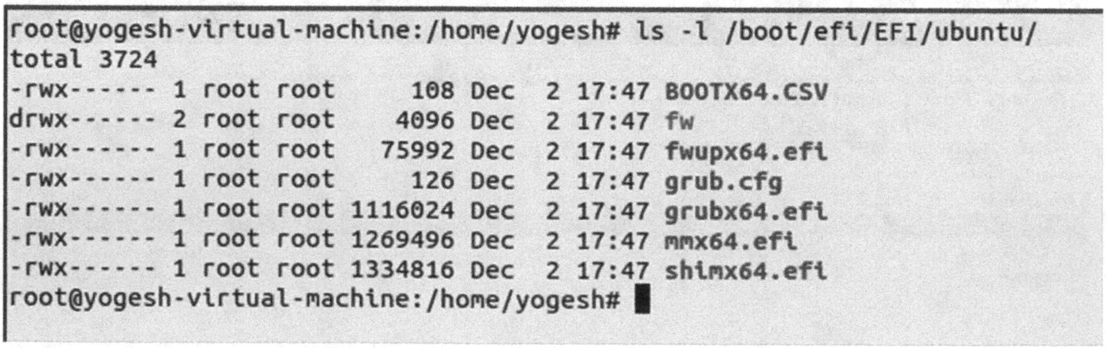

Figure 2-111. *The EFI directory of Ubuntu*

Also notice the .efi extensions to the bootloader files. The following is the Ubuntu booting sequence on a UEFI system:

1) Power on the system.

2) It goes to the UEFI firmware. UEFI launches POST.

3) POST checks the hardware and gives a healthy beep if everything is good.

4) POST goes back to UEFI.

5) UEFI is smart; instead of jumping to the first 512 bytes, UEFI finds the ESP partition.

6) It jumps inside ESP. Again, UEFI is smart, and it understands the bootloader. It lists the bootloader's name on the screen. In Ubuntu's case, it sees the grubx64.efi file; hence, it lists the Ubuntu name in the boot priority of UEFI. Please refer to Figure 2-112, where you can see the ubuntu entry inside UEFI's boot priority menu.

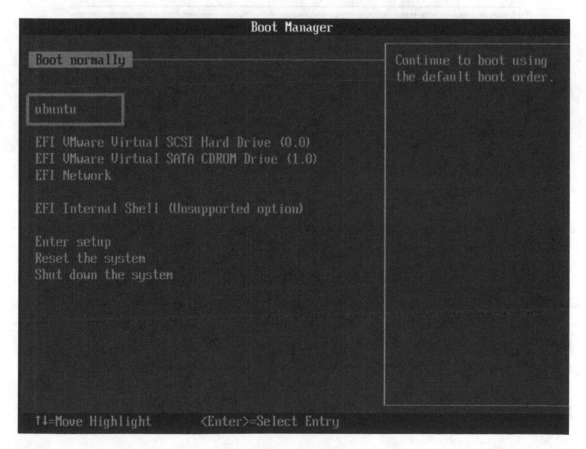

Figure 2-112. *The boot priority window of UEFI*

7) Remember, the bootloader has not yet been called or started by UEFI. The BIOS used to show you only the available boot device names like CD-ROM, HDD, and PXE, but UEFI goes inside the device to check for the ESP partition and shows the OS name directly.

8) The moment the user chooses the Ubuntu option, UEFI will run `grubx64.efi` from the ESP partition. The absolute path will be `/boot/efi/EFI/ubuntu/grubx64.efi` Next, `grubx64.efi` will read `grub.cfg`, which is present in the same directory, and as shown in Figure 2-113, it will print the title entries.

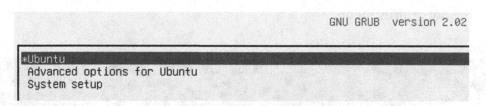

Figure 2-113. *The welcome screen of Ubuntu*

With the BIOS, there used to be jumps like this:

a) Go to the fdisk signature, go to part-1 of the bootloader, and go to part-2 of the bootloader.

b) Go to part-3 of the bootloader and then go to the bootloader configuration file like `menu.lst` or `grub.cfg`.

c) Print the titles.

With UEFI, the (a) jump is skipped. UEFI directly jumps to (b). The BIOS used to have a bootloader divided into three parts because of space constraints, but UEFI does not have any space limitations. Hence, the entire bootloader is available in just one single binary. For example, in the case of Ubuntu, `grubx64.efi` has one, two, and three parts all added in a single binary, which is `grubx64.efi`.

The grubx64.efi file will eventually load the kernel (vmlinuz) and initramfs from / boot into the memory, and then Ubuntu's GRUB bootloaders job is done. Figure 2-114 shows the flowchart of Ubuntu's boot sequence.

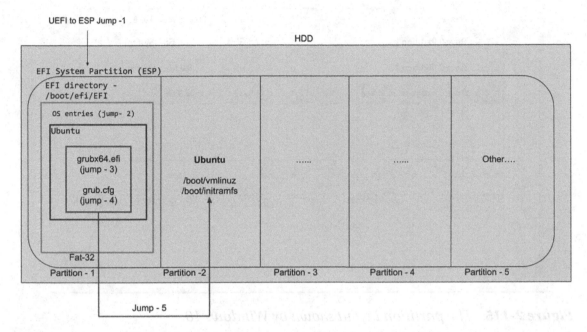

Figure 2-114. *Ubuntu's boot sequence*

Windows 10

As you can see in Figure 2-115, partition 1 is ESP, and partition 2 is the root (/) of Ubuntu.

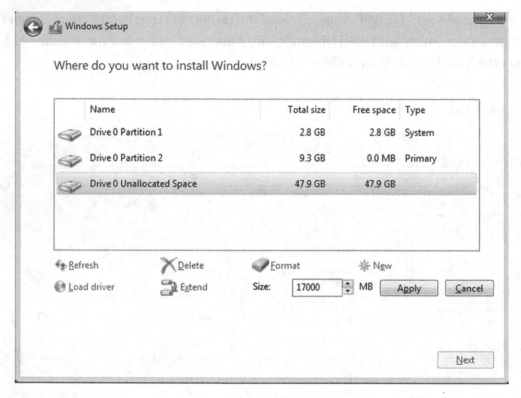

Figure 2-115. *The partition layout shown by Windows 10*

Now we will create a new partition for Windows. While creating a new partition, Windows will reserve some space for the Windows recovery tool called MSR (Microsoft Recovery, partition 3). See Figure 2-116.

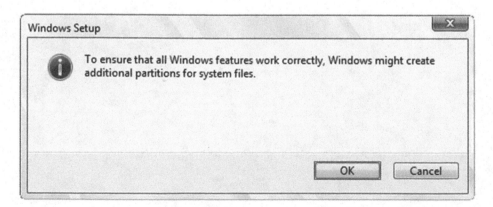

Figure 2-116. *The MSR space reservation*

As shown in Figure 2-117, on the newly created partition 4, we will install Windows 10.

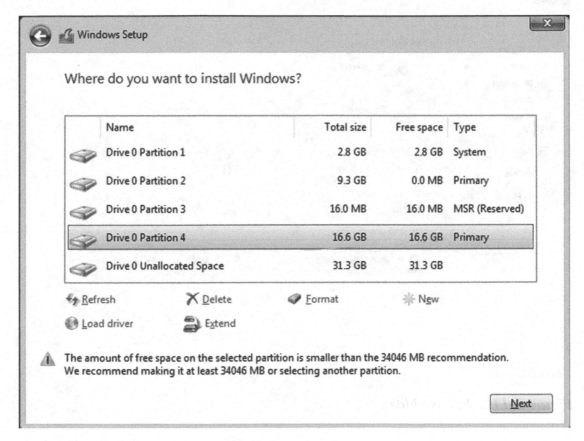

Figure 2-117. *Installing Windows 10 on partition 4*

Windows will by default detect the ESP partition, and by following the UEFI specification, it will create a directory named `Microsoft` in it and will install its bootloader (BCD) in it. If Windows does not find ESP, then it will create one for us. Since Windows is mainly for desktop users, it will not show us the ESP partition (refer to Figure 2-118) the way Ubuntu shows it.

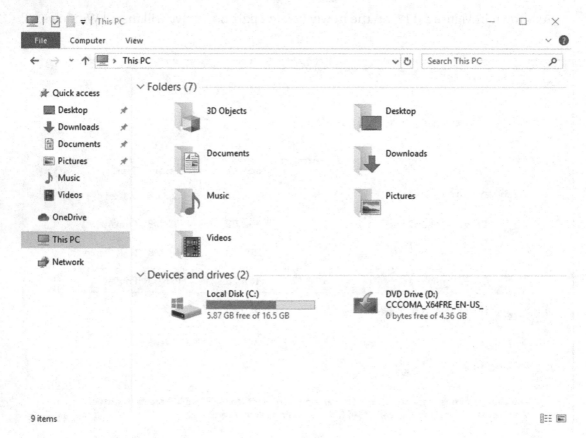

Figure 2-118. *ESP is hidden*

This is how Windows 10 will boot on a UEFI-based system:

1) Power on the system: first UEFI, then POST, then UEFI, and then ESP.

2) As visible in Figure 2-119, print the OS entries as per the directories found in ESP (/boot/efi/EFI).

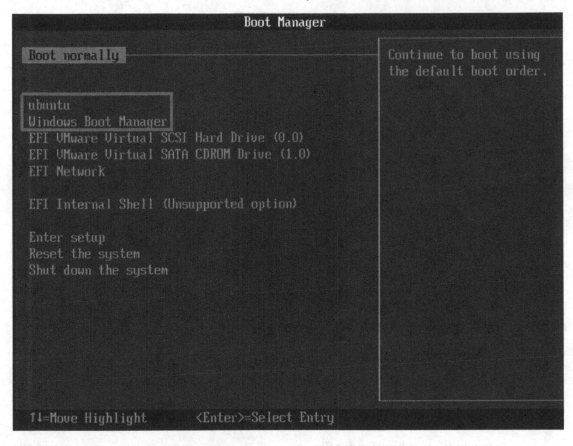

Figure 2-119. *The OS entries inside UEFI*

3)   The moment the user chooses Windows Boot Manager, UEFI will launch the `bootmgfw.efi` file from the `EFI/Microsoft` directory. On a Linux-based system, the same file's absolute path will be `/boot/efi/EFI/Microsoft/bootmgfw.efi`.

4)   `bootmgfw.efi` will eventually load the kernel of Windows from `C:\windows\system32\`.

5)   The Windows kernel will take care of the rest of the booting, and while doing that, a famous animation, shown in Figure 2-120, will be shown to users.

Figure 2-120. *The famous Windows loading screen*

6) As you can see from Figure 2-121, as of now, only one OS is booting, and that is Windows 10. But don't worry, because Windows 10 is bound to follow the UEFI specification, so it has not touched Ubuntu's directory and of course has not added Ubuntu's entry in its own bootloader file.

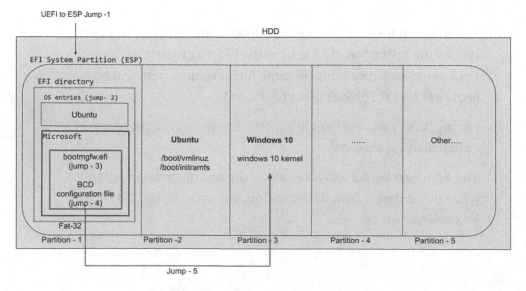

Figure 2-121. *The boot sequence of Windows 10*

Fedora 31

The final OS that we will install is Fedora 31. As shown in Figure 2-122, we will again create a standard partition, which is sda5, and we will mount /dev/sda1 (ESP) on /boot/efi.

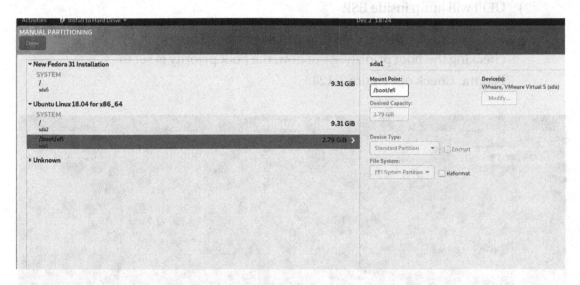

Figure 2-122. *The Fedora installation*

Remember, do not format sda1, which is ESP. Losing ESP means losing the bootloaders of Windows and Ubuntu. After installation, Fedora's GRUB will present us with the OS list (Figure 2-123).

```
Fedora (5.3.7-301.fc31.x86_64) 31 (Thirty One)
Fedora (0-rescue-280526b3bc5e4c49ac83c8e5fbdfdb2e) 31 (Thirty One)
Windows Boot Manager (on /dev/sda1)
Ubuntu 18.04.3 LTS (18.04) (on /dev/sda2)
Advanced options for Ubuntu 18.04.3 LTS (18.04) (on /dev/sda2)
System setup
```

Figure 2-123. *The OS entries shown by Fedora*

While installing GRUB, the Fedora installer Anaconda detected other operating systems from ESP. To give them an equal chance to boot, Fedora added Ubuntu and Windows entries in grub.cfg. The following is the booting sequence of Fedora:

1) Power on the system: first UEFI, then POST, then UEFI.

2) UEFI will jump inside ESP.

3) It will go inside an ESP directory and choose the OS to boot by checking the boot priority. As of now, the boot priority is set to Fedora. Check out Figure 2-124.

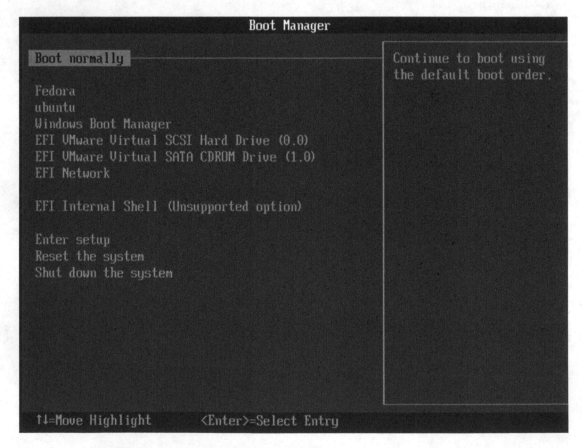

Figure 2-124. *The Fedora entry inside UEFI*

4) Since the boot priority is set to Fedora, UEFI will go inside the / boot/efi/EFI/fedora directory (refer Figure 2-125) and will launch the file grubx64.efi.

```
[root@localhost yogesh]# ls -l /boot/efi/EFI/fedora/
total 14836
-rwx------. 1 root root     112 Oct  2  2018 BOOTIA32.CSV
-rwx------. 1 root root     110 Oct  2  2018 BOOTX64.CSV
drwx------. 2 root root    4096 Oct 23 18:14 fonts
-rwx------. 1 root root 1468744 Oct 10 02:26 gcdia32.efi
-rwx------. 1 root root 2271560 Oct 10 02:26 gcdx64.efi
-rwx------. 1 root root   10801 Dec  2 08:02 grub.cfg
-rwx------. 1 root root    1024 Dec  2 08:02 grubenv
-rwx------. 1 root root 1468744 Oct 10 02:26 grubia32.efi
-rwx------. 1 root root 2271560 Oct 10 02:26 grubx64.efi
-rwx------. 1 root root  927824 Oct  2  2018 mmia32.efi
-rwx------. 1 root root 1159560 Oct  2  2018 mmx64.efi
-rwx------. 1 root root 1210776 Oct  2  2018 shim.efi
-rwx------. 1 root root  975536 Oct  2  2018 shimia32.efi
-rwx------. 1 root root  969264 Oct  2  2018 shimia32-fedora.efi
-rwx------. 1 root root 1210776 Oct  2  2018 shimx64.efi
-rwx------. 1 root root 1204496 Oct  2  2018 shimx64-fedora.efi
[root@localhost yogesh]#
```

Figure 2-125. *The Fedora EFI directory*

5)   grubx64.efi will read the file grub.cfg and print the OS entries
     on-screen. Figure 2-126 shows this.

```
Fedora (5.3.7-301.fc31.x86_64) 31 (Thirty One)
Fedora (0-rescue-280526b3bc5e4c49ac83c8e5fbdfdb2e) 31 (Thirty One)
Windows Boot Manager (on /dev/sda1)
Ubuntu 18.04.3 LTS (18.04) (on /dev/sda2)
Advanced options for Ubuntu 18.04.3 LTS (18.04) (on /dev/sda2)
System setup
```

Figure 2-126. *The OS entries shown by Fedora*

6)   The moment the user chooses Fedora, the same grubx64.efi
     will load vmlinuz and initramfs of Fedora from /boot (sda4)
     into memory. The Fedora kernel will take care of the rest of the
     booting sequence. Check out Figure 2-127 for the flowchart. The
     steps taken by the kernel will be discussed in much more detail in
     Chapter 4.

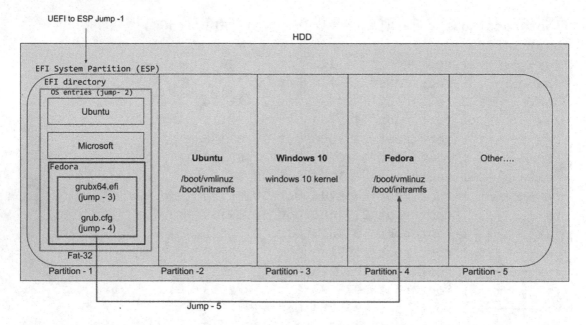

Figure 2-127. *The boot sequence of Fedora*

UEFI Shell

UEFI is a small operating system. Like normal operating systems, UEFI provides a required environment to run the applications. Of course, UEFI will not be able to run every binary, but the binaries that are built in the EFI executable format will easily be able to run. One of the best apps (application/binary) provided by UEFI is the shell. As shown in Figure 2-128, you can find it mostly in boot priority settings of UEFI.

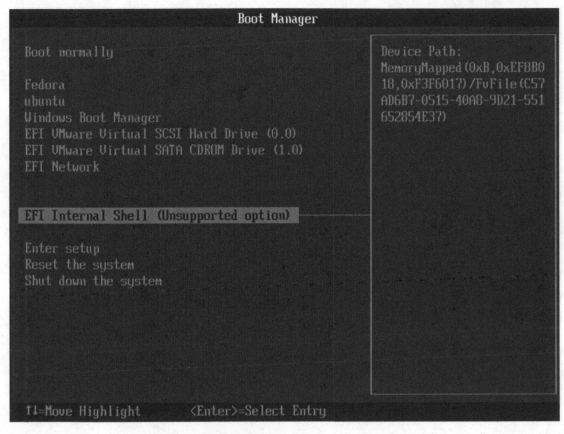

Figure 2-128. *The built-in UEFI shell*

If your system's UEFI implementation does not provide the shell, then you can download the shell app from the TianoCore project site or from its EDK-II GitHub page.

```
https://www.tianocore.org/
```
```
https://github.com/tianocore/edk2/blob/UDK2018/ShellBinPkg/UefiShell/
X64/Shell.efi
```

Format the USB device with the FAT32 filesystem and place the downloaded `Shell.efi` file in it. Boot back with the same USB device, and UEFI will present you a UEFI shell through its boot priority window. See Figure 2-129.

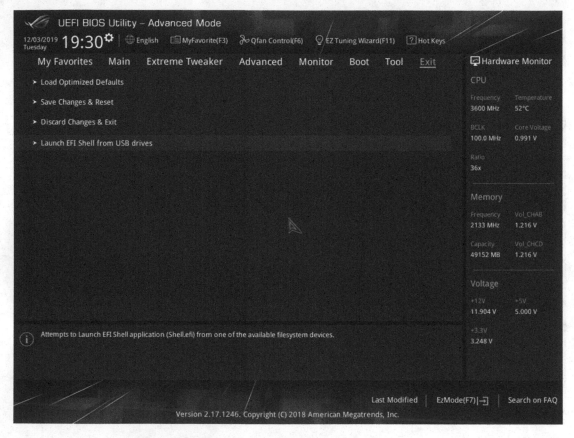

Figure 2-129. *The UEFI shell loaded from USB*

The amazing thing to notice here is that UEFI did not show that the system has a USB device connected. Rather, UEFI went inside the USB device and saw the FAT32 filesystem. It saw the `shell.efi` file and realized this is not a normal EFI app; rather, it will provide the shell to the user. If it had been a BIOS, it would have only shown that system as USB disk connected, but here UEFI is showing you have a shell inside a USB-connected disk.

The moment you choose the option Launch EFI Shell from USB drives, it will execute the `shell.efi` file and will present you with a shell (Figure 2-130) when an OS is not present. That is remarkable.

```
  blk3    :HardDisk - Alias (null)
          PciRoot(0x0)/Pci(0x11,0x0)/Pci(0x4,0x0)/Sata(0x1,0x0,0x0)/HD(2,MBR,0x
6F869649,0xAC,0x54D4)
  blk4    :CDRom - Alias (null)
          PciRoot(0x0)/Pci(0x11,0x0)/Pci(0x4,0x0)/Sata(0x1,0x0,0x0)/CDROM(0x0,0
x41D4,0x4)
  blk5    :BlockDevice - Alias (null)
          PciRoot(0x0)/Pci(0x11,0x0)/Pci(0x4,0x0)/Sata(0x1,0x0,0x0)
  blk6    :Removable HardDisk - Alias (null)
          PciRoot(0x0)/Pci(0x15,0x0)/Pci(0x0,0x0)/Scsi(0x0,0x0)/HD(2,GPT,B49BD5
62-70F9-4477-A0D3-0143F07E89E6,0x596800,0x12A0800)
  blk7    :Removable HardDisk - Alias (null)
          PciRoot(0x0)/Pci(0x15,0x0)/Pci(0x0,0x0)/Scsi(0x0,0x0)/HD(3,GPT,4FB8AC
07-CA42-41C9-910B-E323BCBD82FD,0x1837000,0x8000)
  blk8    :Removable HardDisk - Alias (null)
          PciRoot(0x0)/Pci(0x15,0x0)/Pci(0x0,0x0)/Scsi(0x0,0x0)/HD(4,GPT,BE7E9E
01-B172-42F5-B95D-6E378E6A2C93,0x183F000,0x212C000)
  blk9    :Removable HardDisk - Alias (null)
          PciRoot(0x0)/Pci(0x15,0x0)/Pci(0x0,0x0)/Scsi(0x0,0x0)/HD(5,GPT,A500E8
3E-8702-4CB6-A00B-85EC28F59F47,0x396B000,0x12A0000)
  blkA    :Removable BlockDevice - Alias (null)
          PciRoot(0x0)/Pci(0x15,0x0)/Pci(0x0,0x0)/Scsi(0x0,0x0)

Press ESC in 3 seconds to skip startup.nsh, any other key to continue.
Shell> _
```

Figure 2-130. *The UEFI shell*

The blk* entries are the device names, whereas fs* is a filesystem naming convention. Since the UEFI shell is able to read the FAT32 filesystem (ESP partition), we can browse the ESP directory, as shown in Figure 2-131.

```
Shell> fs0:

fs0:\> ls
Directory of: fs0:\

    10/23/19  11:21p <DIR>              2,048
              0 File(s)        0 bytes
              1 Dir(s)


fs0:\> cd EFI

fs0:\EFI> ls
Directory of: fs0:\EFI

    10/23/19  11:21p <DIR>              2,048  .
    10/23/19  11:21p <DIR>                  0  ..
    10/23/19  11:21p <DIR>              2,048
              0 File(s)        0 bytes
              3 Dir(s)


fs0:\EFI> cd BOOT

fs0:\EFI\BOOT> _
```

Figure 2-131. *Browsing the EFI directory*

The fs0 stands for file system number 0. It is shell's internal command that we can use to change the partition. As you can see in Figure 2-132 and in Figure 2-133, fs2 is our ESP.

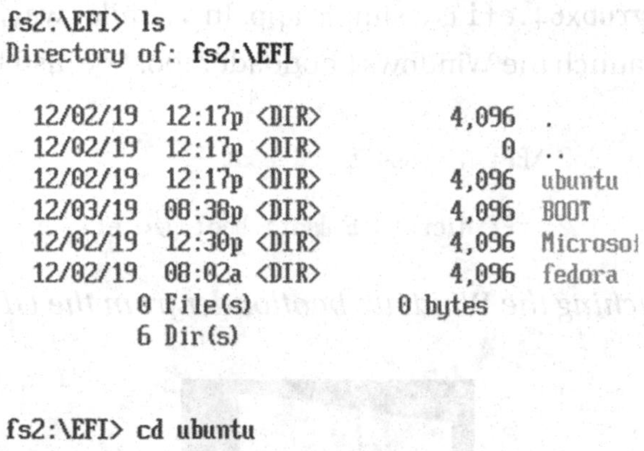

```
fs2:\EFI> ls
Directory of: fs2:\EFI

12/02/19  12:17p <DIR>        4,096 .
12/02/19  12:17p <DIR>            0 ..
12/02/19  12:17p <DIR>        4,096 ubuntu
12/03/19  08:38p <DIR>        4,096 BOOT
12/02/19  12:30p <DIR>        4,096 Microsoi
12/02/19  08:02a <DIR>        4,096 fedora
         0 File(s)            0 bytes
         6 Dir(s)


fs2:\EFI> cd ubuntu
```

Figure 2-132. *The EFI directory*

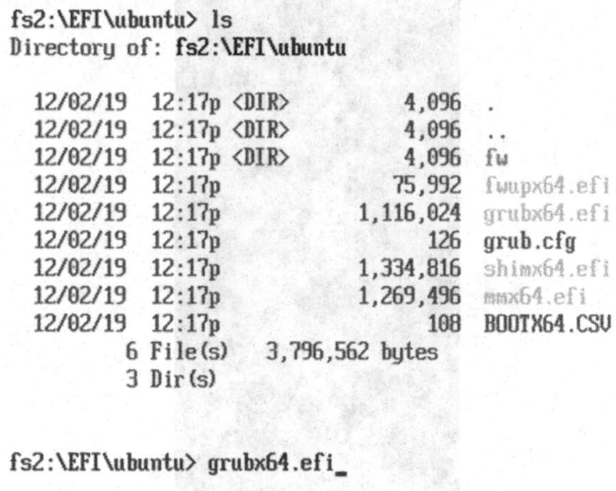

```
fs2:\EFI\ubuntu> ls
Directory of: fs2:\EFI\ubuntu

12/02/19  12:17p <DIR>          4,096 .
12/02/19  12:17p <DIR>          4,096 ..
12/02/19  12:17p <DIR>          4,096 fw
12/02/19  12:17p             75,992 fwupx64.efi
12/02/19  12:17p          1,116,024 grubx64.efi
12/02/19  12:17p                126 grub.cfg
12/02/19  12:17p          1,334,816 shimx64.efi
12/02/19  12:17p          1,269,496 mmx64.efi
12/02/19  12:17p                108 BOOTX64.CSV
         6 File(s)    3,796,562 bytes
         3 Dir(s)


fs2:\EFI\ubuntu> grubx64.efi_
```

Figure 2-133. *Ubuntu's bootloader directory*

We can simply run the grubx64.efi file through the shell, and GRUB will appear on-screen. See Figure 2-134.

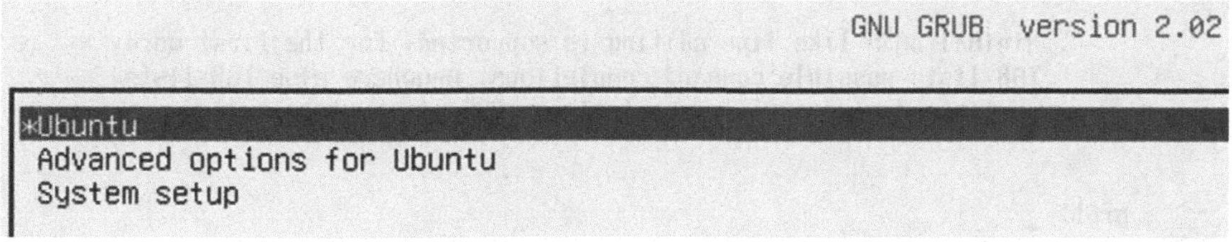

```
                                        GNU GRUB  version 2.02

*Ubuntu
 Advanced options for Ubuntu
 System setup
```

Figure 2-134. *The GRUB of Ubuntu*

For a UEFI shell, `grubx64.efi` is a simple app. In a similar way, as shown in Figure 2-135 we can launch the Windows bootloader too. See also Figure 2-136.

```
fs2:\EFI\Microsoft> cd Boot

fs2:\EFI\Microsoft\Boot> bootmgfw.efi_
```

Figure 2-135. *Launching the Windows bootloader from the UEFI shell*

Figure 2-136. *The famous Windows animation*

The shell can be useful in resolving the "can't boot" scenarios. Consider the scenario shown in Figure 2-137 where the system is throwing an error on a GRUB prompt.

```
Minimal BASH-like line editing is supported. For the first word,
TAB lists possible command completions. Anywhere else TAB lists
possible device or file completions. ESC at any time exits.


grub> _
```

Figure 2-137. *The system is unable to boot*

By using a UEFI shell, we are able to check whether GRUB-related files are present or not.

Misconceptions About UEFI

The following are some misconceptions about UEFI.

Misconception 1: UEFI Is a New BIOS or UEFI Is a BIOS

People keep saying that UEFI is a new BIOS. In fact, when you go inside the UEFI firmware, the firmware itself says it is a UEFI BIOS. Check out Figure 2-138.

No, UEFI is not a BIOS nor is it a new BIOS. UEFI is here to replace the BIOS. UEFI is a completely new firmware, and you cannot have a BIOS and UEFI on the same system. You have either UEFI or a BIOS.

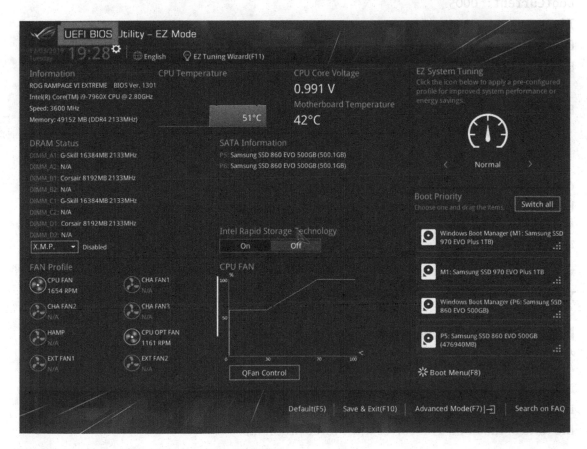

Figure 2-138. *The UEFI is not a BIOS*

It is pretty simple to identify whether you have a BIOS or UEFI. If you can use a mouse inside the firmware, then you have UEFI, and if you see a rich GUI, then you have UEFI. The correct way to check is by using an efibootmgr-like command.

 # efibootmgr -v

```
Fatal: Couldn't open either sysfs or procfs directories for accessing EFI
variables.
Try 'modprobe efivars' as root.
```

If you get output like this from the efibootmgr command on a Linux system, then you have a BIOS. If you get something like this, then you have UEFI:

 # efibootmgr -v

```
BootCurrent: 0005
Timeout: 2 seconds
BootOrder: 0005,0004,0003,0000,0001,0002,0006,0007,000A
Boot0000* EFI VMware Virtual SCSI Hard Drive (0.0)
     PciRoot(0x0)/Pci(0x15,0x0)/Pci(0x0,0x0)/SCSI(0,0)
Boot0001* EFI VMware Virtual SATA CDROM Drive (1.0)
     PciRoot(0x0)/Pci(0x11,0x0)/Pci(0x4,0x0)/Sata(1,0,0)
```

This is the correct way of identifying what firmware your system has. Returning to our UEFI BIOS discussion, the vendors are using the UEFI and BIOS terms together because most users will not understand the term UEFI. For example, an article saying "change the parameters in your UEFI" might be confusing for most users, but saying "change the parameters in your BIOS" will be well understood by everyone. Hence, vendors are using the term UEFI/BIOS just for the sake of understanding, but remember you can have only one firmware at a time, not both.

Misconception 2: Microsoft Is Evil

As we have seen, UEFI is a forum, and operating system vendors are part of it, including Microsoft. To make the booting more secure, Microsoft proposed a Secure Boot feature in UEFI. Secure Boot will stop the execution of unauthorized or compromised binaries at the time of the boot. This solves these three problems:

- It guarantees that `grubx64.efi`, which is about to run, is from an authentic source.

- It guarantees that BCD does not have any backdoor in it.

- It stops something from executing if it is unauthorized.

This is how Secure Boot works:

1) Microsoft will generate a key pair (public and private key).

2) Microsoft will digitally sign its bootloader or its files with the private key.

3) The public key of Microsoft will be kept inside the UEFI firmware.

4) The digital signature that was generated in step 2 will be regenerated by the public key of Microsoft, which is present inside the UEFI.

5) If the digital signature matches, then only UEFI will allow the `*.efi` file's execution.

6) If the digital signature does not match, then UEFI will consider that a harmful program, or at least it is not shipped by Microsoft, UEFI will halt the execution.

Pretty nice implementation by Microsoft, right? Yes, it is. But the problem will arise when the Secure Boot feature is enabled and you choose Linux to boot. UEFI will take out Microsoft's public key and will generate the digital signature of `grubx64.efi`. The generated digital signature will not, of course, match with Microsoft's bootloader files, so it will be considered an unauthorized program, and UEFI will stop the execution. In other words, Linux or any non-Windows OS will never be able to boot. So, what's the resolution to this? Simple: UEFI should provide an option to disable the Secure Boot feature, which it does. See Figure 2-139. In fact, the option to disable the Secure Boot feature has to be present in UEFI firmware. This is imposed in the UEFI specification.

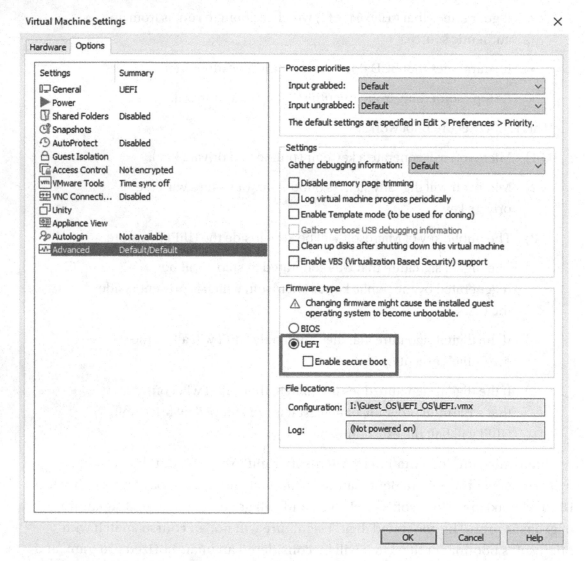

Figure 2-139. *Disabling the Secure Boot feature*

But Microsoft has clearly called out that the only systems that will be certified are ones that have Secure Boot enabled. This means if you are hardware vendor and want your system to be certified for Windows, then it has to have Secure Boot enabled. This move was considered "evil" by some of industry leaders since non-Windows-based operating systems will not be able to boot on the same hardware. We will return to the discussion of whether Microsoft is evil or not later, but first let's see what options non-Windows OSs have.

Linux Vendors Should Make Their Own Key Pair

Yes, every Linux OS vendor should make their own key pair and then sign their bootloaders with their private key and keep the public key in the UEFI firmware. Whenever a user chooses Windows to boot, UEFI will use the Windows public key, and whenever the user chooses Linux to boot, UEFI will use the Linux public key to regenerate the digital signature of the Linux bootloader's files. This seems to be an easy resolution, but this will not work. There are almost 200+ active Linux distributions on the market, and they generally have new versions released every six months. This means almost every six months you will have a newer version of Linux distro on the market. This means roughly that Linux vendors will have almost 400 keys a year, so obviously you cannot fit this many keys in UEFI. Even if you could, this will hamper one of the main mottos of UEFI design, which is speedy booting. So, in short, this cannot be a resolution.

All Linux Vendors Should Make Only One Key Pair

This also cannot be a resolution. There are 200+ active Linux distributions, and their offices are spread over the world. If all Linux vendors came together and made only one key pair, then this key pair would have to be shipped throughout the internet to the developers throughout the world. It would be a security nightmare. So in short, it would be difficult to maintain; hence, this is not a resolution.

Disable UEFI's Secure Boot Feature

This seems to be the only workable approach. UEFI does provide a facility to disable the Secure Boot feature, and Microsoft has no objection on providing such a facility. For example, say you have a dual-boot system, which has Windows 10 and Fedora 31 installed. If you want to boot Windows, then Secure Boot has to be enabled in UEFI, and if next time you want to boot Linux, then you have to go inside UEFI and change the enabled Secure Boot to a disabled state. You can consider this a workaround, but this is not practical; hence, it cannot be considered as a resolution.

So, how can Linux take advantage of Secure Boot? There is only one resolution, and that is to use Microsoft's private key to digitally sign the Linux bootloader files, and guess what, Microsoft has agreed to this. So, at this stage, Linux is able to secure boot by using Microsoft's key pair, and hence Microsoft is certainly not evil. It just wanted to make its boot sequence secure.

But there is one problem in this arrangement; GRUB development will be dependent on Microsoft's key pair. If any new change is committed to GRUB, we need to re-sign it by using Microsoft's key. Ubuntu resolved this problem first by introducing a smaller bootloader called shim. This bootloader is supposed to get signed by Microsoft's key, and then this bootloader's job is to call the actual bootloader, which is GRUB. With this approach, the Linux world has broken Microsoft's signing dependency. Since shim will never change (at least it would be rare), GRUB development will continue the way it has.

So, if Secure Boot is enabled, then the boot sequence of Linux will be as follows:

1. Power on the system: first UEFI, then POST, and then UEFI.

2. ESP lists the operating systems and available bootable devices.

3. If the user chooses Linux, the boot process regenerates the digital signature of the shim.efi file by using Microsoft's public key.

4. If the digital signature matches, then allow execution of shim.efi.

5. shim.efi will call the original bootloader, which is grubx64.efi.

6. grubx64.efi will read the grub.cfg file from ESP and will present the available OS list.

7. If the user again chooses Linux, then the same grubx64.efi file will start loading the kernel and initramfs in memory.

Refer to Figure 2-140 to see the list of files involved in this boot sequence.

```
[root@localhost yogesh]# ls -l /boot/efi/EFI/fedora/
total 14836
-rwx------. 1 root root      112 Oct  2  2018 BOOTIA32.CSV
-rwx------. 1 root root      110 Oct  2  2018 BOOTX64.CSV
drwx------. 2 root root     4096 Oct 23 18:14 fonts
-rwx------. 1 root root  1468744 Oct 10 02:26 gcdia32.efi
-rwx------. 1 root root  2271560 Oct 10 02:26 gcdx64.efi
-rwx------. 1 root root    10801 Dec  2 08:02 grub.cfg
-rwx------. 1 root root     1024 Dec  2 08:02 grubenv
-rwx------. 1 root root  1468744 Oct 10 02:26 grubia32.efi
-rwx------. 1 root root  2271560 Oct 10 02:26 grubx64.efi
-rwx------. 1 root root   927824 Oct  2  2018 mmia32.efi
-rwx------. 1 root root  1159560 Oct  2  2018 mmx64.efi
-rwx------. 1 root root  1210776 Oct  2  2018 shim.efi
-rwx------. 1 root root   975536 Oct  2  2018 shimia32.efi
-rwx------. 1 root root   969264 Oct  2  2018 shimia32-fedora.efi
-rwx------. 1 root root  1210776 Oct  2  2018 shimx64.efi
-rwx------. 1 root root  1204496 Oct  2  2018 shimx64-fedora.efi
[root@localhost yogesh]#
```

Figure 2-140. *The files involved in the described boot sequence*

Misconception 3: Disable the UEFI

One of the biggest misconceptions is that you can disable UEFI and start the BIOS. No, you cannot disable the firmware of your system; also, you cannot have two firmware on one system. You have either UEFI or the BIOS. When people say "disable UEFI," it means they would like to say, let UEFI boot with the BIOS or in a legacy way. One of the biggest features of UEFI is that it is backward compatible, meaning it does understand the BIOS way of booting, which is the 512 bytes + 31KB approach. So, when you change the UEFI settings from the UEFI way to the legacy way, it only means that UEFI will not follow the ESP way of booting. Rather, the firmware will follow the BIOS way of booting, but this does not mean you are disabling the UEFI firmware. When you boot a UEFI system the BIOS way, then you lose all the features that UEFI provides.

Since you now have a better understanding of firmware and the way bootloaders work, it is the right time to dive deeper into the GRUB bootloader.

Figure 2-12.

Misallocation — Disable the HP?

CHAPTER 3

GRUB Bootloader

The bootloader that Linux systems use these days is GRUB version 2. The first stable release of GRUB 2 was in 2012, but it started appearing in enterprise-level Linux in 2014 with Centos 7 and RHEL 7. After 2015, it saw wide adoption in almost every popular Linux distribution. Usually when users file bugs or ask for new features, developers listen to the feedback, prioritize the work, and eventually launch a new version of code. However, in the case of GRUB, it worked another way. The developers decided to change the entire structure of GRUB 2 when users were happy with GRUB Legacy (version 1).

> "GRUB Legacy has become unmaintainable, due to messy code and design failures. We received many feature requests, and extended GRUB beyond the original scope, without redesigning the framework. This resulted in the state that it was impossible to extend GRUB any further without rethinking everything from the ground."
>
> —GNU GRUB FAQ (`https://www.gnu.org/software/grub/grub-faq.html`)

Here are some of the features that GRUB 2 provides or are in development:

- Full USB support.

- Linux Unified Setup Key (LUKS) support. LUKS is the standard for Linux hard disk encryption.

- A fancy menu implementation that will have animations, colorful effects, style sheets, etc.

- A "parted" tool will be added inside the bootloader. When this is added, users will be able to edit the disk configuration at the time of boot.

© Yogesh Babar 2020
Y. Babar, *Hands-on Booting*, https://doi.org/10.1007/978-1-4842-5890-3_3

This chapter will cover the following:

- How GRUB 2 is implemented for the BIOS and UEFI firmware

- The firmware-specific structural changes in GRUB 2

- The Bootloader Specification feature of GRUB 2

- The Secure Boot feature of UEFI and how it is implemented in GRUB 2

- Several bootloader-related issues and how we can fix them

GRUB 2 Implementation

As we have seen so far, GRUB takes control of the firmware. This means it has to deal with UEFI as well as the BIOS. Let's see how GRUB 2 has been implemented on BIOS-based systems first.

GRUB 2 on BIOS-Based Systems

GRUB 2 on a BIOS-based system keeps all of its files in three different locations.

- /boot/grub2/

- /etc/default/grub

- /etc/grub.d/

In the case of Ubuntu, version 2 is not used in GRUB's name, so it will be /boot/grub/ instead of /boot/grub2/, grub-install instead of grub2-install, or grub-mkconfig instead of grub2-mkconfig.

Let's discuss the locations and their contents.

/boot/grub2

This is the location where GRUB 2 will be installed. As you can see in Figure 3-1, the directory holds the bootloader's core files.

```
[root@localhost yogeshbabar]# ls /boot/grub2/ -l
total 32
-rw-r--r--. 1 root root    64 Dec  6 20:10 device.map
lrwxr-xr-x. 2 root root  4096 Dec  6 20:10 fonts
-rw-r--r--. 1 root root  5814 Dec  6 20:10 grub.cfg
lrwxrwxrwx. 1 root root    25 Oct 10 12:56 grubenv -> ../efi/EFI/fedora/grubenv
lrwxr-xr-x. 2 root root 12288 Dec  6 20:10 i386-pc
lrwxr-xr-x. 3 root root  4096 Oct 24 04:42 themes
[root@localhost yogeshbabar]#
```

Figure 3-1. The files present in /boot/grub2

Device.map

GRUB does not understand disk names like sda or vda since these disk naming conventions were created by the SCSI drivers of operating systems. It is obvious that GRUB runs when the OS is not present, so it has its own disk naming convention. The following are GRUB's disk naming conventions:

GRUB Version	Disk Naming Convention	Meaning
2	hd0, msdos1	Hard disk number 0 and partition number 1, which has an MS-DOS partition table
2	hd1, msdos3	Hard disk number 2 and partition number 3, which has an MS-DOS partition table
2	hd2, gpt1	Hard disk number 3 and partition number 1, which has a GPT partition table
1	hd0, 0	Hard disk number 0 and partition number 1

In GRUB, the hard disk starts at 0, and the partition numbers start at 1, whereas the OS naming conventions of disks and partitions start at 1. Since the OS and GRUB disk naming conventions are different, there has to be a mapping for the users, and that is why the device.map file was created.

 # cat /boot/grub2/device.map
```
    # this device map was generated by anaconda
    (hd0)       /dev/sda
```

The device.map file will be used by the grub2-install like commands to understand on which disk GRUB's core files are installed. Here's an example of this file:

```
# strace -o delete_it.txt  grub2-install  /dev/sda
      Installing for i386-pc platform.
      Installation finished. No error reported.
```

```
# cat delete_it.txt | grep -i 'device.map'
      openat(AT_FDCWD, "/boot/grub2/device.map", O_RDONLY) = 3
      read(3, "# this device map was generated "..., 4096) = 64
      openat(AT_FDCWD, "/boot/grub2/device.map", O_RDONLY) = 3
      read(3, "# this device map was generated "..., 4096) = 64
```

The grub2-install command will take input in the form of the OS disk naming conventions since users are not aware of the GRUB disk naming conventions. During the execution, grub2-install will convert the SCSI disk naming conventions to the GRUB disk naming conventions by reading the device.map file.

grub.cfg

This is the main configuration file of GRUB. As you can see in Figure 3-2, it's a huge script file that is generated by referring to some other script files, which we will discuss soon. It is highly advisable not to change the contents of grub.cfg as doing so might make your Linux version unbootable. This is the file from which GRUB part-3 takes instructions like the following:

- Location of the kernel and initramfs

    - /boot/vmlinuz-<version>

    - /boot/initramfs-<version>

- Kernel command-line parameters

    - Root filesystem name and its location, etc.

```
     if [ x$grub_platform = xxen ]; then insmod xzio; insmod lzopio; fi
     insmod part_msdos
     insmod ext2
     set root='hd0,msdos1'
     if [ x$feature_platform_search_hint = xy ]; then
         search --no-floppy --fs-uuid --set=root --hint-bios=hd0,msdos1 --hint-efi=hd0,msdos1 --hint-baremetal=ahci0,msdos1  6feb8fc4-3f57-4843-8a47-a245ff76443e
     else
         search --no-floppy --fs-uuid --set=root 6feb8fc4-3f57-4843-8a47-a245ff76443e
     fi
     linux    /boot/vmlinuz-5.0.0-23-generic root=UUID=6feb8fc4-3f57-4843-8a47-a245ff76443e ro find_preseed=/preseed.cfg auto noprompt priority=critical locale=en_US quiet
     initrd   /boot/initrd.img-5.0.0-23-generic
}
submenu 'Advanced options for Ubuntu' $menuentry_id_option 'gnulinux-advanced-6feb8fc4-3f57-4843-8a47-a245ff76443e' {
     menuentry 'Ubuntu, with Linux 5.0.0-23-generic' --class ubuntu --class gnu-linux --class gnu --class os $menuentry_id_option 'gnulinux-5.0.0-23-generic-advanced-6feb8fc4
-3f57-4843-8a47-a245ff76443e' {
         recordfail
         load_video
         gfxmode $linux_gfx_mode
         insmod gzio
         if [ x$grub_platform = xxen ]; then insmod xzio; insmod lzopio; fi
         insmod part_msdos
         insmod ext2
         set root='hd0,msdos1'
         if [ x$feature_platform_search_hint = xy ]; then
             search --no-floppy --fs-uuid --set=root --hint-bios=hd0,msdos1 --hint-efi=hd0,msdos1 --hint-baremetal=ahci0,msdos1  6feb8fc4-3f57-4843-8a47-a245ff76443e
         else
             search --no-floppy --fs-uuid --set=root 6feb8fc4-3f57-4843-8a47-a245ff76443e
         fi
         echo    'Loading Linux 5.0.0-23-generic ...'
         linux   /boot/vmlinuz-5.0.0-23-generic root=UUID=6feb8fc4-3f57-4843-8a47-a245ff76443e ro find_preseed=/preseed.cfg auto noprompt priority=critical locale=en_US q
uiet
         echo    'Loading initial ramdisk ...'
         initrd  /boot/initrd.img-5.0.0-23-generic
     }
     menuentry 'Ubuntu, with Linux 5.0.0-23-generic (recovery mode)' --class ubuntu --class gnu-linux --class gnu --class os $menuentry_id_option 'gnulinux-5.0.0-23-generic-r
ecovery-6feb8fc4-3f57-4843-8a47-a245ff76443e' {
         recordfail
         load_video
         insmod gzio
         if [ x$grub_platform = xxen ]; then insmod xzio; insmod lzopio; fi
         insmod part_msdos
         insmod ext2
         set root='hd0,msdos1'
```

Figure 3-2. The grub.cfg file

GRUB has its own set of commands, as you can see here:

GRUB Command	Purpose
menuentry	This will print the title on-screen.
set root	This will provide the disk and partition names where the kernel and initramfs are stored.
linux	The absolute path of the Linux kernel file
initrd	The absolute path of the initramfs file of Linux

So, the booting sequence of GRUB 2 on a BIOS-based system of Fedora is as follows:

1. Power on a system: first BIOS, then POST, then BIOS, and then the first sector.

2. First is the bootstrap (part-1 of GRUB), then part-2 of GRUB, and then part-3 of GRUB.

3. Part-3 of GRUB will read the previously shown grub.cfg from / boot/grub2/ (in the case of Ubuntu, it will be /boot/grub/) and will print the welcome screen, as shown in Figure 3-3.

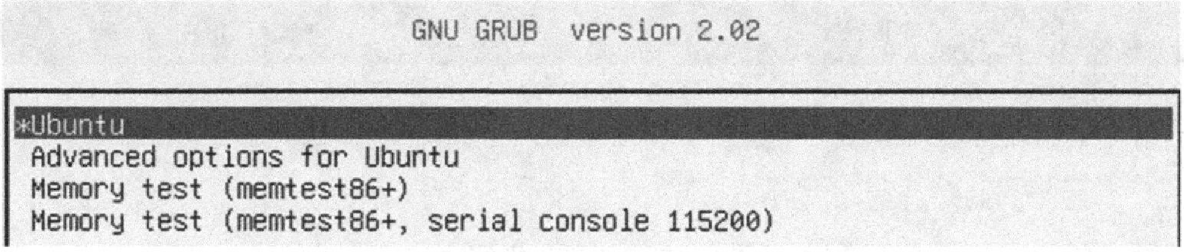

```
                    GNU GRUB   version 2.02

 *Ubuntu
  Advanced options for Ubuntu
  Memory test (memtest86+)
  Memory test (memtest86+, serial console 115200)
```

Figure 3-3. *The welcome screen*

4. The moment the user chooses the Ubuntu menuentry, it will run
   the set root, linux, and initrd commands and will start loading
   the kernel and initramfs in memory.

5. In Fedora-like Linux distributions, you will find a different
   approach. There will be a grub.cfg file, but the menuentry, set
   root, linux, and initrd commands will not be available in grub.
   cfg. There has been a new development in a GRUB upstream
   project called BLS. We will cover that later in this chapter.

i386-pc

This directory has all the GRUB-supported filesystem modules (drivers) in it (please refer
to Figure 3-4). All the *.mod files are the modules. By using these modules, GRUB can
load the kernel and initramfs files in memory. For example, the /boot of this system has
an ext4 filesystem, so obviously when exploring and loading the vmlinuz and initramfs
files from /boot, GRUB needs the ext4 module, which it gets from the ext4.mod file. It's
similar to /boot on the XFS or UFS filesystem; hence, the xfs.mod and ufs.mod files are
present in /boot/grub2/i386-pc. At the same time, you will find modules like http.mod
and pxe.mod. This means GRUB 2's part-3 can load the kernel and initramfs files from
the http and pxe devices. In general, the *.mod files add features, not just devices. The
features may include device support, filesystem support, or protocol support.

Earlier, /boot under LVM was not possible, and the reason was simple. GRUB had
to understand the LVM devices. To understand and assemble the LVM device, GRUB
would need the LVM module as well as LVM binaries such as vgscan, vgchange, pvs,
lvscan, etc. It would increase the size of GRUB as a package; hence, the enterprise Linux
system vendors have always avoided /boot under LVM devices. But since UEFI has been
introduced, GRUB has started supporting /boot on LVM devices.

```
[root@fedorab yogesh]# ls /boot/grub2/i386-pc/
acpi.mod                    gcry_twofish.mod            pata.mod
adler32.mod                 gcry_whirlpool.mod          pbkdf2.mod
affs.mod                    gdb.mod                     pbkdf2_test.mod
afs.mod                     geli.mod                    pcidump.mod
ahci.mod                    gettext.mod                 pci.mod
all_video.mod               gfxmenu.mod                 plan9.mod
aout.mod                    gfxterm_background.mod      play.mod
archelp.mod                 gfxterm_menu.mod            png.mod
ata.mod                     gfxterm.mod                 priority_queue.mod
at_keyboard.mod             gptsync.mod                 probe.mod
backtrace.mod               gzio.mod                    procfs.mod
bfs.mod                     halt.mod                    progress.mod
biosdisk.mod                hashsum.mod                 pxechain.mod
bitmap.mod                  hdparm.mod                  pxe.mod
bitmap_scale.mod            hello.mod                   raid5rec.mod
blocklist.mod               help.mod                    raid6rec.mod
blscfg.mod                  hexdump.mod                 random.mod
boot.img                    hfs.mod                     read.mod
boot.mod                    hfspluscomp.mod             reboot.mod
bsd.mod                     hfsplus.mod                 regexp.mod
bswap_test.mod              http.mod                    reiserfs.mod
btrfs.mod                   increment.mod               relocator.mod
bufio.mod                   iorw.mod                    romfs.mod
cat.mod                     iso9660.mod                 scsi.mod
cbfs.mod                    jfs.mod                     search_fs_file.mod
cbls.mod                    jpeg.mod                    search_fs_uuid.mod
cbmemc.mod                  keylayouts.mod              search_label.mod
cbtable.mod                 keystatus.mod               search.mod
cbtime.mod                  ldm.mod                     sendkey.mod
chain.mod                   legacycfg.mod               serial.mod
cmdline_cat_test.mod        legacy_password_test.mod    setjmp.mod
cmosdump.mod                linux.mod                   setjmp_test.mod
cmostest.mod                loadenv.mod                 setpci.mod
cmp.mod                     loopback.mod                sfs.mod
cmp_test.mod                lsacpi.mod                  shift_test.mod
command.lst                 lsapm.mod                   signature_test.mod
configfile.mod              lsmmap.mod                  sleep.mod
core.img                    ls.mod                      sleep_test.mod
cpio_be.mod                 lspci.mod                   spkmodem.mod
cpio.mod                    luks.mod                    squash4.mod
cpuid.mod                   lvm.mod                     strtoull_test.mod
crc64.mod                   lzopio.mod                  syslinuxcfg.mod
```

Figure 3-4. *The .mod* files from /boot/grub2/i386-pc*

```
cryptodisk.mod          macbless.mod            tar.mod
crypto.lst              macho.mod               terminal.lst
crypto.mod              mda_text.mod            terminal.mod
cs5536.mod              mdraid09_be.mod         terminfo.mod
ctz_test.mod            mdraid09.mod            test_blockarg.mod
datehook.mod            mdraid1x.mod            testload.mod
date.mod                memdisk.mod             test.mod
datetime.mod            memrw.mod               testspeed.mod
diskfilter.mod          minicmd.mod             tftp.mod
disk.mod                minix2_be.mod           tga.mod
div.mod                 minix2.mod              time.mod
div_test.mod            minix3_be.mod           trig.mod
dm_nv.mod               minix3.mod              tr.mod
drivemap.mod            minix_be.mod            truecrypt.mod
echo.mod                minix.mod               true.mod
efiemu.mod              mmap.mod                udf.mod
ehci.mod                moddep.lst              ufs1_be.mod
elf.mod                 modinfo.sh              ufs1.mod
eval.mod                morse.mod               ufs2.mod
exfat.mod               mpi.mod                 uhci.mod
exfctest.mod            msdospart.mod           usb_keyboard.mod
ext2.mod                mul_test.mod            usb.mod
extcmd.mod              multiboot2.mod          usbms.mod
f2fs.mod                multiboot.mod           usbserial_common.mod
fat.mod                 nativedisk.mod          usbserial_ftdi.mod
file.mod                net.mod                 usbserial_pl2303.mod
font.mod                newc.mod                usbserial_usbdebug.mod
freedos.mod             nilfs2.mod              usbtest.mod
fshelp.mod              normal.mod              vbe.mod
fs.lst                  ntfscomp.mod            verify.mod
functional_test.mod     ntfs.mod                version.mod
gcry_arcfour.mod        ntldr.mod               vga.mod
gcry_blowfish.mod       odc.mod                 vga_text.mod
gcry_camellia.mod       offsetio.mod            video_bochs.mod
gcry_cast5.mod          ohci.mod                video_cirrus.mod
gcry_crc.mod            part_acorn.mod          video_colors.mod
gcry_des.mod            part_amiga.mod          video_fb.mod
gcry_dsa.mod            part_apple.mod          videoinfo.mod
gcry_idea.mod           part_bsd.mod            video.lst
gcry_md4.mod            part_dfly.mod           video.mod
gcry_md5.mod            part_dvh.mod            videotest_checksum.mod
gcry_rfc2268.mod        part_gpt.mod            videotest.mod
gcry_rijndael.mod       partmap.lst             xfs.mod
gcry_rmd160.mod         part_msdos.mod          xnu.mod
```

Figure 3-4. *(continued)*

140

```
gcry_rsa.mod              part_plan.mod             xnu_uuid.mod
gcry_seed.mod             part_sun.mod              xnu_uuid_test.mod
gcry_serpent.mod          part_sunpc.mod            xzio.mod
gcry_sha1.mod             parttool.lst              zfscrypt.mod
gcry_sha256.mod           parttool.mod              zfsinfo.mod
gcry_sha512.mod           password.mod              zfs.mod
gcry_tiger.mod            password_pbkdf2.mod
[root@fedorab yogesh]# []
```

Figure 3-4. *(continued)*

As you can see in Figure 3-5, along with these *.mod files, you will find a couple of other files in the /boot/grub2/i386-pc/ location.

```
[root@localhost yogeshbabar]# ls -lhS /boot/grub2/i386-pc/ | grep -v mod
total 3.0M
-rw-r--r--. 1 root root  30K Dec  7 11:35 core.img
-rw-r--r--. 1 root root 4.0K Dec  7 11:35 command.lst
-rw-r--r--. 1 root root  936 Dec  7 11:35 crypto.lst
-rw-r--r--. 1 root root  512 Dec  7 11:35 boot.img
-rw-r--r--. 1 root root  219 Dec  7 11:35 fs.lst
-rw-r--r--. 1 root root  202 Dec  7 11:35 terminal.lst
-rw-r--r--. 1 root root  111 Dec  7 11:35 partmap.lst
-rw-r--r--. 1 root root   33 Dec  7 11:35 video.lst
-rw-r--r--. 1 root root   17 Dec  7 11:35 parttool.lst
[root@localhost yogeshbabar]# █
```

Figure 3-5. *The files in addition to *.mod*

The core.img file is part-3 of GRUB 2. So, the Linux booting sequence becomes as follows:

```
-> Power on -> BIOS -> POST -> BIOS ->
-> part-1 of GRUB2 -> Part-2 of GRUB2 -> core3.img -> grub.cfg ->
-> if /boot is on an xfs filesystem -> /boot/grub2/i386-pc/xfs.mod ->
-> load vmlinuz & initramfs in main memory.
```

Once the kernel is in memory, GRUB 2's job is done. The rest of the booting sequence will be carried out by the kernel, which we will discuss in Chapter 4.

/etc/default/grub

Another important file is, of course, /etc/default/grub. Please see Figure 3-6.

```
[root@localhost yogeshbabar]#
[root@localhost yogeshbabar]# ls /etc/default/ -l
total 8
-rw-r--r--. 1 root root 363 Dec  6 20:10 grub
-rw-r--r--. 1 root root 119 Sep  2 19:20 useradd
[root@localhost yogeshbabar]#
```

Figure 3-6. *The contents of the /etc/default directory*

This file is used by GRUB to accept the cosmetic and kernel command-line changes from the user.

$ cat /etc/default/grub
```
GRUB_TIMEOUT=10
GRUB_DISTRIBUTOR="$(sed 's, release .*$,,g' /etc/system-release)"
GRUB_DEFAULT=saved
GRUB_DISABLE_SUBMENU=true
GRUB_TERMINAL_OUTPUT="console"
GRUB_CMDLINE_LINUX="resume=/dev/mapper/root_vg-swap rd.lvm.lv=root_vg/root
rd.lvm.lv=root_vg/swap console=ttyS0,115200 console=tty0"
GRUB_DISABLE_RECOVERY="true"
GRUB_ENABLE_BLSCFG=true
```

As you can see, in this file, we can change the default timeout of the GRUB welcome screen, the font, the submenus, and the default kernel command-line parameters like the root device name, the swap device name, etc.

/etc/grub.d/

Now this is where things get really interesting about GRUB 2.

GRUB 2 has a command called grub2-mkconfig. The name of command suggests that it will make the GRUB configuration file grub.cfg, which will be referred by part-3 of GRUB to show the welcome screen. The grub2-mkconfig file will first take the cosmetic and kernel command-line parameter inputs from /etc/default/grub and run the script files listed in Figure 3-7 from the /etc/grub.d/ directory.

```
[root@localhost yogeshbabar]#
[root@localhost yogeshbabar]# ls /etc/grub.d/ -l
total 88
-rwxr-xr-x. 1 root root  9346 Oct 10 12:56 00_header
-rwxr-xr-x. 1 root root   236 Oct 10 12:56 01_users
-rwxr-xr-x. 1 root root   835 Oct 10 12:56 08_fallback_counting
-rwxr-xr-x. 1 root root 13797 Oct 10 12:56 10_linux
-rwxr-xr-x. 1 root root   762 Oct 10 12:56 10_reset_boot_success
-rwxr-xr-x. 1 root root   892 Oct 10 12:56 12_menu_auto_hide
-rwxr-xr-x. 1 root root 11699 Oct 10 12:56 20_linux_xen
-rwxr-xr-x. 1 root root  2562 Oct 10 12:56 20_ppc_terminfo
-rwxr-xr-x. 1 root root 10673 Oct 10 12:56 30_os-prober
-rwxr-xr-x. 1 root root  1415 Oct 10 12:56 30_uefi-firmware
-rwxr-xr-x. 1 root root   218 Oct 10 12:56 40_custom
-rwxr-xr-x. 1 root root   220 Oct 10 12:56 41_custom
-rw-r--r--. 1 root root   483 Oct 10 12:56 README
[root@localhost yogeshbabar]# █
```

Figure 3-7. *The contents of the /etc/grub.d/ directory*

As you can see, the files have numbers assigned with them. This means they will run in order.

The 00_header, 01_users, 08_fallback_counting, 10_reset_boot_success, and 12_menu_auto_hide script files do the housekeeping work. For instance, the 00_header script file is responsible for adding a header to the grub.cfg file. For example, on Fedora Linux, the following header will be added in grub.cfg after running the grub2-mkconfig file:

```
### BEGIN /etc/grub.d/00_header ###
set pager=1

if [ -f ${config_directory}/grubenv ]; then
  load_env -f ${config_directory}/grubenv
elif [ -s $prefix/grubenv ]; then
  load_env
fi
if [ "${next_entry}" ] ; then
   set default="${next_entry}"
   set next_entry=
```

```
    save_env next_entry
    set boot_once=true
else
    set default="${saved_entry}"
fi

if [ x"${feature_menuentry_id}" = xy ]; then
  menuentry_id_option="--id"
else
  menuentry_id_option=""
fi

export menuentry_id_option

if [ "${prev_saved_entry}" ]; then
  set saved_entry="${prev_saved_entry}"
  save_env saved_entry
  set prev_saved_entry=
  save_env prev_saved_entry
  set boot_once=true
fi
function savedefault {
  if [ -z "${boot_once}" ]; then
    saved_entry="${chosen}"
    save_env saved_entry
  fi
}

function load_video {
  if [ x$feature_all_video_module = xy ]; then
    insmod all_video
  else
    insmod efi_gop
    insmod efi_uga
    insmod ieee1275_fb
    insmod vbe
    insmod vga
```

```
    insmod video_bochs
    insmod video_cirrus
  fi
}

terminal_output console
if [ x$feature_timeout_style = xy ] ; then
  set timeout_style=menu
  set timeout=5
# Fallback normal timeout code in case the timeout_style feature is
# unavailable.
else
  set timeout=5
fi
### END /etc/grub.d/00_header ###
```

The 08_fallback_counting script file will add the following contents in grub.cfg:

```
### BEGIN /etc/grub.d/08_fallback_counting ###
insmod increment
# Check if boot_counter exists and boot_success=0 to activate this
behaviour.
if [ -n "${boot_counter}" -a "${boot_success}" = "0" ]; then
  # if countdown has ended, choose to boot rollback deployment,
  # i.e. default=1 on OSTree-based systems.
  if  [ "${boot_counter}" = "0" -o "${boot_counter}" = "-1" ]; then
    set default=1
    set boot_counter=-1
  # otherwise decrement boot_counter
  else
    decrement boot_counter
  fi
  save_env boot_counter
fi
### END /etc/grub.d/08_fallback_counting ###
```

As you can see, the file adds the code that will watch the default timeout value of a GRUB's welcome screen, the same way the rest of the files (`10_reset_boot_success` and `menu_auto_hide`) will do the housekeeping work for GRUB. Let's look at the script files that make GRUB 2 one of the best bootloaders for multibooting.

10_linux

This file contains almost 500 lines of a bash script file. Whenever a user executes the `grub2-mkconfig` command, it will run this script. The `10_linux` file will find out what other Linux distributions you have installed on your system. It will literally go partition by partition and find all the other Linux versions that have been installed on your system. If there are any others, then it will make a `menuentry` of it in `grub.cfg`. Along with `menuentry`, it will add the respective kernel and initramfs entries. Isn't that amazing?

Consider you installed Ubuntu first and then Fedora; now you don't have to add the entries of Ubuntu manually into Fedora's `grub.cfg`. You have to just run `grub2-mkconfig`. The command will run `10_linux` for us, and it will eventually find out that Ubuntu is installed and will add the appropriate entry for it.

20_linux_xen

After `grub2-mkconfig`, this script file will find out whether your system has the XEN kernel installed. If it does, then it will add the appropriate entry for it in `grub.cfg`. Most of the Linux distributors ship XEN as a separate kernel package. XEN is mostly used by hypervisors.

20_ppc_terminfo

If your system has PPC or a PowerPC architecture from IBM, then this script file will find the respective kernel for it and will add the appropriate entry into `grub.cfg`.

30_os_prober

If you have any non-Linux-based OS installed on your HDD, then this script file will find that OS and will make the appropriate entry for it. In other words, if you have Windows installed on your system, it will automatically find that out and will make an appropriate entry for it in `grub.cfg`. This is the reason that, after installing our third OS (Fedora 31) on a UEFI system, we got the list of operating systems without doing anything. You can see the welcome screen presented by Fedora 31 in Figure 3-8.

```
Fedora (5.3.7-301.fc31.x86_64) 31 (Thirty One)
Fedora (0-rescue-280526b3bc5e4c49ac83c8e5fbdfdb2e) 31 (Thirty One)
Windows Boot Manager (on /dev/sda1)
Ubuntu 18.04.3 LTS (18.04) (on /dev/sda2)
Advanced options for Ubuntu 18.04.3 LTS (18.04) (on /dev/sda2)
System setup
```

Figure 3-8. *The welcome screen*

After the Fedora installation, Anaconda ran `grub2-mkconfig` in the background, which eventually ran `30_os_prober`, and it found the Windows installation and made the appropriate entry for it in `grub.cfg`.

30_uefi-firmware

This script will run successfully only if you have a UEFI system. The job of this script file is to add the appropriate entries of UEFI firmware in `grub.cfg`. As you can see in Figure 3-8, the `System setup` entry has been added by the `30_uefi-firmware` script file.

```
### BEGIN /etc/grub.d/30_uefi-firmware ###
menuentry 'System setup' $menuentry_id_option 'uefi-firmware' {
        fwsetup
}
### END /etc/grub.d/30_uefi-firmware ###
```

If the user chooses the "System setup" option, then it will boot back to the UEFI firmware. You can see the UEFI firmware interface in Figure 3-9.

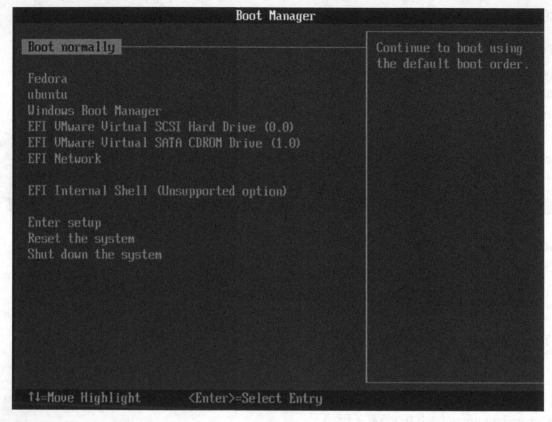

Figure 3-9. *The UEFI firmware*

40_custom and 41_custom

These are given to the user in case the user wants to add some custom entries to grub.
cfg. For example, if grub2-mkconfig fails to add any of the installed OS as entries, then
users can add a custom entry to these two custom files. You can make your own custom
files, but you need to make sure each has a number assigned to it and has executable
permission.

GRUB 2 on UEFI-Based System

Again, there are three locations where GRUB 2 stores its files. Figure 3-10 shows the
directories and its files.

```
[root@localhost yogesh]# ls /boot/grub2/
grubenv  themes
[root@localhost yogesh]# ls /boot/efi/EFI/fedora/
BOOTIA32.CSV  fonts      gcdx64.efi  grubenv     grubx64.efi  mmx64.efi  shimia32.efi        shimx64.efi
BOOTX64.CSV  gcdia32.efi  grub.cfg   grubia32.efi  mmia32.efi   shim.efi   shimia32-fedora.efi  shimx64-fedora.efi
[root@localhost yogesh]# ls /etc/default/grub
/etc/default/grub
[root@localhost yogesh]# 
```

Figure 3-10. *The GRUB 2 locations on a UEFI-based system*

The grub.cfg file that was shown earlier in /boot/grub2/ has been shifted inside ESP (/boot/efi/EFI/fedora/). Also, as you can see, there is no i386-pc directory. This is because of the rich device and filesystem support provided by EFI. Inside ESP, you will find a couple of *.efi files, including our shim.efi and grubx64.efi binaries. The etc/default/grub file, which is responsible for GRUB's cosmetic changes and for kernel command-line parameters, is still at the same location. The device.map file is not available since the grub2-install command does not have significance on a UEFI system. We will talk about this command later in the chapter.

Boot Loader Specification (BLS)

The BLS is a new development on GRUB upstream projects that hasn't been adopted by many mainstream distributions yet. Specifically, this scheme has been adopted by Fedora-based operating systems such as RHEL, Fedora, Centos, Oracle Linux, etc., but not by Debian-based distributions such as Ubuntu, Mint, etc.

On BIOS-based systems, whichever OS has control of the first 512 bytes has control of all the operating systems' booting sequences, which is why every OS tries to get hold of the first 512 bytes. This situation arises because the BIOS always lands in the first 512 bytes of the HDD and calls part-1 of the bootloader (bootstrap). The part-1 to part-2 and part-2 to part-3 transitions happen later, and then at the end part-3 reads the bootloader-specific configuration file (bcdedit in the case of Windows, grub.cfg in the case of Linux). If that configuration file has the entries for other installed OSs, then they will get a chance to boot. So, long story short: whoever has control of the first 512 bytes controls the entire booting sequence. But with ESP, every OS gets an equal chance to boot because UEFI checks the ESP directories and lists all the available OS entries. Developers started wondering if they could get something like this in a BIOS-based system, and they came up with BLS.

In BLS, a new location (the fifth one) has been introduced to store the bootloader-related files, and that is /boot/loader/. So, we have now five locations where GRUB will store its files.

- /boot/grub2/

- /etc/default/grub

- /etc/grub.d

- /boot/efi/EFI/<OS_vendor>/ (in the case of UEFI only)

- /boot/loader/ (BLS files will be stored here)

The idea is that after the new kernel installation, the kernel itself with its post-scripts (something like the kernel-core package in the case of Fedora) will create an entry for a new kernel in the /boot/loader/ directory. For example, we have this kernel package installed:

 # rpm -q kernel

Kernel-5.3.7-301.fc31.x86_64

This is the same package that will provide the /boot/vmlinuz and /boot/initramfs files. Once this kernel is installed, it prepares the following file:

 # cat /boot/loader/entries/36543031048348f9965e3e12e48bd2b1-5.3.7-301.fc31.x86_64.conf

```
title Fedora (5.3.7-301.fc31.x86_64) 31 (Thirty One)
version 5.3.7-301.fc31.x86_64
linux /vmlinuz-5.3.7-301.fc31.x86_64
initrd /initramfs-5.3.7-301.fc31.x86_64.img
options $kernelopts
grub_users $grub_users
grub_arg --unrestricted
grub_class kernel
```

As you can see, the file has four entries.

- The title that will be printed by part-3 of GRUB

- The location and name of the kernel file

- The location and name of the initramfs file

- The $kernelopts variable that has been declared in the /boot/
  grub2/grubenv file

cat /boot/grub2/grubenv

```
# GRUB Environment Block
saved_entry=2058a9f13f9e489dba29c477a8ae2493-5.3.7-301.fc31.x86_64
menu_auto_hide=1
boot_success=0
kernelopts=root=/dev/mapper/fedora_localhost--live-root ro resume=/dev/
mapper/fedora_localhost--live-swap rd.lvm.lv=fedora_localhost-live/root
rd.lvm.lv=fedora_localhost-live/swap rhgb quiet
boot_indeterminate=0
```

Basically, kernelopts provides the kernel command-line parameters like the name of the root filesystem (/dev/mapper/fedora_localhost--live-root) and in which mode it has to be mounted (ro - read only).

So, the booting sequence becomes like this:

1) BIOS -> POST -> BIOS

2) Part-1 of GRUB -> part-2 of GRUB -> part-3 of GRUB

3) Part-3 of GRUB -> read grub.cfg

4) Part-3 of GRUB -> reads /boot/loader/entries/*

5) Prints all the file titles that are present in /boot/loader/entries

For an example, consider a new OS has been installed or a new kernel has been installed. It has to generate its own entry file and place it in the first primary partition's /boot/loader/entries/ directory. This way, every time the first primary OS's GRUB part-3 reads the entry, the other OS will have a chance to boot. The entry file can be created by using Fedora's kernel-install command.

kernel-install add 5.3.7-301.fc31.x86_64 /lib/modules/5.3.7-301.fc31. x86_64/vmlinuz

The command will make the appropriate entry for kernel-5.3.7-301.fc31.x86_64 in /boot/loader/entries/, as shown here:

 # ls /boot/loader/entries/ -l
```
total 8
-rw-r--r--. 1 root root 329 Dec  9 10:18 2058a9f13f9e489dba29c477a8ae2493-
0-rescue.conf
-rw-r--r--. 1 root root 249 Oct 22 01:04
2058a9f13f9e489dba29c477a8ae2493-5.3.7-301.fc31.x86_64.conf
```

The number associated with the *.conf file is unique. The BLS has its own advantages and disadvantages.

Here are the advantages:

- Every OS will get an equal chance to boot.

- It works irrespective of the BIOS and UEFI firmware.

- In the case of the BIOS, the latest Linux installation removes part-1 and part-2 of the earlier installed operating system, which has become obsolete since the latest Linux installation will make its own entry through the kernel-install command on earlier OSs.

Here are the disadvantages:

- The BLS is not completely implemented yet. If the second OS wants to make its entry in the first OS, then /boot of the first OS has to be shared. That is not the case as of now. So, I consider this as a half-implementation.

- The BLS unnecessarily complicates the booting sequence since we have two configuration files to refer to: grub.conf and <uniq_no><kernel_version>.conf from /boot/loader/entries/. The BLS especially makes life difficult in the case of resolving the "can't boot" issues.

- Except Fedora-based distros, no one has adopted the BLS yet, which seems to be a wise decision. It looks like Fedora is the most committed to the upstream project; hence, the BLS has been implemented in Fedora.

Common Bootloader Issues

Based on this knowledge, let's try to resolve some of the most common bootloader-related "can't boot" issues.

"Can't Boot" Issue 1 (Bootloader)

Issue: After powering up the system, it is dropping you on the GRUB prompt, as shown in Figure 3-11.

```
Minimal BASH-like line editing is supported. For the first word,
TAB lists possible command completions. Anywhere else TAB lists
possible device or file completions. ESC at any time exits.

grub> _
```

Figure 3-11. *The GRUB 2 prompt*

This is what you see on your screen. You must have encountered this error at least once in your life. Let's try to resolve it.

1) You will be able to resolve the issue only if you know what the issue is all about. Right now, though, we have no idea what the problem is since we just started the system and this is what we get.

2) The screen is called a GRUB prompt. When this is called a prompt, it means you can execute commands at it. Remember, this is a GRUB command prompt, which means it can accept only GRUB commands.

3) By looking at Figure 3-11, out of three parts of GRUB, which part of GRUB has provided us with the GRUB prompt?

4) Of course, it must be part-3 because part-1 and part-2 have very little space, so they cannot fit such functionality. So, we have successfully reached part-3 of GRUB, and most important, it does not matter whether this system has UEFI or the BIOS. Since we have reached part-3, it means we have left the firmware environment. That's the crucial input. Now we cannot concentrate on part-3 only.

153

5) What is the purpose of part-3 of GRUB? Simple. It reads grub.cfg, and from there it gets the kernel and initramfs locations. If it is a BLS-enabled system, then it gets the kernel and initramfs names from the /boot/loader/entries/ directories. For this example, we will assume this system is not BLS-aware. Part-3 then loads vmlinuz and initramfs in memory.

6) Since part-3 has provided us with the GRUB prompt but failed to load the OS, it means either the kernel and initramfs files are not present or the grub.cfg file is not pointing out the correct location of these files.

7) So, in such a situation we can try to boot Fedora manually. Manually means we will provide the kernel and initramfs files with absolute paths by using the GRUB prompt. This is how it can be done.

8) linux is a GRUB command through which we need to give the absolute path of the kernel (vmlinuz) file. As we know, the vmlinuz file is at /boot, and GRUB follows its own disk naming convention. So, the path of /boot will be hard disk number 0 and partition number 1. Of course, you might not be aware on which HDD or partition /boot has been stored. In that case, you can get the help of the autocomplete feature of GRUB. You can press Tab twice, and GRUB will prompt you for the available options. Let's find out the HDD and partition number of /boot. Please refer to Figure 3-12.

```
      possible device or file completions. ESC at any time exits.

grub> linux (hd0,
Possible partitions are:

        Partition hd0,msdos1: Filesystem type ext* - Last modification time
2019-12-08 05:35:35 Sunday, UUID 223c49e4-f1ae-4f6d-a7a0-ea8aacf6308e -
Partition start at 1024KiB - Total size 1048576KiB
        Partition hd0,msdos2: No known filesystem detected - Partition start at
1049600KiB - Total size 25164800KiB
```

Figure 3-12. *The available partitions on hard disk number 0*

The first tab after hd0 showed us that there are two partitions available under the hard disk number 0. The second partition is not readable to GRUB, so of course the second partition cannot be /boot. Hence, we will choose the msdos1 partition. Then, as shown in Figure 3-13, we will start looking for the vmlinuz file in it with the help of autocomplete.

```
grub> linux (hd0,msdos1)/vmli
Possible files are:

vmlinuz-5.3.7-301.fc31.x86_64
vmlinuz-0-rescue-3654303104834
8f9965e3e12e48bd2b1
```

Figure 3-13. *The vmlinuz file*

As you can see inside HDD number 0 and partition number 1, we found two vmlinuz files; one is of a rescue kernel, and another one is the normal kernel file of Fedora 31. As shown in Figure 3-14, we will choose the normal kernel and will provide the root filesystem name to it. If you are unaware of the root filesystem name of your system, then you can boot the system with the rescue or live image and check the /etc/fstab entries. We will talk about the rescue mode in Chapter 10.

```
            possible device or file completions. ESC at any time exits.

grub> linux (hd0,
Possible partitions are:

        Partition hd0,msdos1: Filesystem type ext* - Last modification time
2019-12-08 05:35:35 Sunday, UUID 223c49e4-f1ae-4f6d-a7a0-ea8aacf6308e -
Partition start at 1024KiB - Total size 1048576KiB
        Partition hd0,msdos2: No known filesystem detected - Partition start at
1049600KiB - Total size 25164800KiB

grub> linux (hd0,msdos1)/vmli
Possible files are:

 vmlinuz-5.3.7-301.fc31.x86_64
vmlinuz-0-rescue-3654303104834
8f9965e3e12e48bd2b1
grub> linux (hd0,msdos1)/vmlinuz-5.3.7-301.fc31.x86_64 ro root=/dev/mapper/fedor
a_localhost--live-root
grub> initrd
Possible commands are:

 initrd initrd16
grub>
```

Figure 3-14. *The root filesystem name and the ro flag*

The absolute path of the vmlinuz file is (hd0,msdos1)/
vmlinuz-5.3.7-301.fc31.x86_64. Next to it is the ro kernel
command-line parameter, which stands for "read-only." After ro,
we have a root kernel command-line parameter to which we have
passed our system's root filesystem name, which is - /dev/mapper/
fedora_localhost--live-root. It's an lvm device.

grub> **linux (hd0,msdos1)/vmlinuz-5.3.7-301.fc31.x86_64 ro**
        root=/dev/mapper/fedora_localhost--live-root

After successfully executing the linux command, we need to pass
on the initramfs name. We have two commands available that we
can use: initrd and initrd16. Please refer to Figure 3-15.

grub> **initrd (hd0,msdos1)/initramfs-5.3.7-301.fc31.x86_64.img**

```
2019-12-08 05:35:35 Sunday, UUID 223c49e4-f1ae-4f6d-a7a0-ea8aacf6308e -
Partition start at 1024KiB - Total size 1048576KiB
        Partition hd0,msdos2: No known filesystem detected - Partition start at
1049600KiB - Total size 25164800KiB

grub> linux (hd0,msdos1)/vmli
Possible files are:

 vmlinuz-5.3.7-301.fc31.x86_64
vmlinuz-0-rescue-3654303104834
8f9965e3e12e48bd2b1
grub> linux (hd0,msdos1)/vmlinuz-5.3.7-301.fc31.x86_64 ro root=/dev/mapper/fedor
a_localhost--live-root
grub> initrd
Possible commands are:

 initrd initrd16
grub> initrd (hd0,msdos1)/initramfs
Possible files are:

 initramfs-5.3.7-301.fc31.x86_64.img
initramfs-0-rescue-36543031048348f99
65e3e12e48bd2b1.img
grub> initrd (hd0,msdos1)/initramfs-5.3.7-301.fc31.x86_64.img
grub> boot_
```

Figure 3-15. *The linux, initrd, and boot commands in action*

9)   The moment you execute the boot command, as shown
      in Figure 3-16 and in Figure 3-17, GRUB's part-3 will take
      these inputs and load /boot/vmlinuz-5.3.7-301.fc31.
      x86_64 from sda1 (hd0,msdos1). Then it will load /boot/
      initramfs-5.3.7-301.fc31.x86_64.img and give control to the
      kernel. The kernel will eventually mount the root (/) filesystem
      from /dev/mapper/fedora_locahost--live-root on the
      / directory and will show the login screen.

```
[  OK  ] Started dnf makecache --timer.
[  OK  ] Started Updates mlocate database every day.
[  OK  ] Started Daily Cleanup of Temporary Directories.
[  OK  ] Started daily update of the root trust anchor for DNSSEC.
[  OK  ] Reached target Paths.
[  OK  ] Reached target Timers.
[  OK  ] Listening on Avahi mDNS/DNS-SD Stack Activation Socket.
[  OK  ] Listening on CUPS Scheduler.
[  OK  ] Listening on D-Bus System Message Bus Socket.
[  OK  ] Listening on Open-iSCSI iscsid Socket.
[  OK  ] Listening on Open-iSCSI iscsiuio Socket.
[  OK  ] Listening on Libvirt local socket.
[  OK  ] Listening on Libvirt admin socket.
[  OK  ] Listening on Libvirt local read-only socket.
[  OK  ] Listening on SSSD Kerberos Cache Manager responder socket.
[  OK  ] Listening on Virtual machine lock manager socket.
[  OK  ] Listening on Virtual machine log manager socket.
[  OK  ] Reached target Sockets.
[  OK  ] Reached target Basic System.
         Starting Modem Manager...
         Starting Avahi mDNS/DNS-SD Stack...
         Starting Bluetooth service...
         Starting firewalld - dynamic firewall daemon...
         Starting GSSAPI Proxy Daemon...
         Starting LSB: Init script for live image....
[  OK  ] Started Machine Check Exception Logging Daemon.
[  OK  ] Started Hardware RNG Entropy Gatherer Daemon.
         Starting RealtimeKit Scheduling Policy Service...
         Starting System Security Services Daemon...
         Starting Switcheroo Control Proxy service...
         Starting Virtual Machine and Container Registration Service...
         Starting Disk Manager...
[  OK  ] Started VGAuth Service for open-vm-tools.
[  OK  ] Started Service for virtual machines hosted on VMware.
[  OK  ] Started LSB: Init script for live image..
         Starting ABRT Automated Bug Reporting Tool...
```

Figure 3-16. *The console messages while booting*

Figure 3-17. *The login screen*

10) In the case of Ubuntu 18, the commands are slightly different. On Fedora 31, we gave the /boot partition's address directly to the linux command, whereas in Ubuntu we have a separate GRUB command called set root for it.

As you can see in Figure 3-18, the root filesystem name of the Ubuntu 18 system is / dev/sda1. It's a standard partition unlike the lvm device of Fedora 31.

```
grub> set root='hd0,msdos1'
grub> linux /boot/vmlinuz-5.0.0-23-generic ro root=/dev/sda1
grub> initrd /boot/initrd.img-5.0.0-23-generic
grub> boot_
```

Figure 3-18. *Ubuntu has a slightly different approach*

As soon as we provide the proper inputs to GRUB 2, it leads us to the login screen. You can see the login screen of Ubuntu in Figure 3-19.

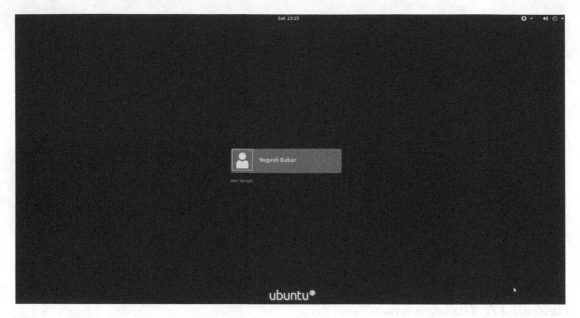

Figure 3-19. *The login screen presented by Ubuntu*

11) Coming back to our Fedora system, since it has been booted now, we can regenerate the grub.cfg file by using the grub2-mkconfig command, as shown in Figure 3-20.

```
[root@localhost yogeshbabar]# grub2-mkconfig -o /boot/grub2/grub.cfg
Generating grub configuration file ...
done
[root@localhost yogeshbabar]#
```

Figure 3-20. *grub2-mkconfig command*

We can execute grub-mkconfig in case of Ubuntu. Please refer to Figure 3-21.

```
root@ubuntu:/home/yogesh# grub-mkconfig -o /boot/grub/grub.cfg
Sourcing file `/etc/default/grub'
Generating grub configuration file ...
Found linux image: /boot/vmlinuz-5.0.0-23-generic
Found initrd image: /boot/initrd.img-5.0.0-23-generic
Found memtest86+ image: /boot/memtest86+.elf
Found memtest86+ image: /boot/memtest86+.bin
done
root@ubuntu:/home/yogesh#
```

Figure 3-21. The grub-mkconfig command of Ubuntu

But if it is a UEFI system and you want to regenerate grub.cfg, then, as shown in Figure 3-22, the location of grub.cfg would be ESP.

```
[root@localhost yogesh]# grub2-mkconfig -o /boot/efi/EFI/fedora/grub.cfg
Generating grub configuration file ...
Found Windows Boot Manager on /dev/sda1@/EFI/Microsoft/Boot/bootmgfw.efi
Found Ubuntu 18.04.3 LTS (18.04) on /dev/sda2
Adding boot menu entry for EFI firmware configuration
done
[root@localhost yogesh]# █
```

Figure 3-22. grub2-mkconfig on a UEFI-based system

12) Once grub.cfg is generated, we need to regenerate the BLS entries for Fedora.

#kernel-install add 5.3.7-301.fc31.x86_64 /lib/modules/5.3.7-301.fc31.x86_64/vmlinuz

The command will make the appropriate entry for kernel-5.3.7-301.fc31.x86_64 in /boot/loader/entries/.

 # ls /boot/loader/entries/ -l
```
total 8
-rw-r--r--. 1 root root 329 Dec  9 10:18
2058a9f13f9e489dba29c477a8ae2493-0-rescue.conf
-rw-r--r--. 1 root root 249 Oct 22 01:04
2058a9f13f9e489dba29c477a8ae2493-5.3.7-301.fc31.x86_64.conf
```

161

13) If Fedora is on a UEFI system, then the BLS step remains the same.

14) After rebooting, Fedora is able to boot smoothly, and the "can't boot" issue has been fixed.

"Can't Boot" Issue 2 (Bootloader)

Issue: After powering on the system, it passes the firmware stage, but after that, as you can see in Figure 3-23, there is nothing on the screen.

Figure 3-23. *The blank screen*

Resolution for a BIOS-Based System

Here are the steps to solve this:

1. Since the BIOS firmware stage has been passed, it means something is wrong at the bootloader level.

2. Since we are not getting anything on the screen, it means part-1 or part-2 of GRUB is missing or at least they are corrupted (512 bytes + 31 KB). If it had reached part-3, then we would have gotten at least the GRUB prompt. So, the issue has been isolated, and the plan of action is to replace part-1 and part-2 of GRUB.

3. This can be done with the `grub2-install` command. First either boot with live medium of the same Linux distro or, if available, boot in rescue mode. The live image and rescue mode will be explained in Chapter 10.

As you can see in Figure 3-24, grub2-install takes the device name as an input. Please note that the device name should not be a partition number; rather, it should be a disk name. This is because part-1 and part-2 of GRUB has to be installed on the first 512 bytes + 31 KB of a disk, not inside a partition. You need to replace sda with your disk name.

```
[root@localhost yogeshbabar]# grub2-install /dev/sda
Installing for i386-pc platform.
Installation finished. No error reported.
[root@localhost yogeshbabar]#
```

Figure 3-24.   The grub2-install command

Along with part-1 and part-2 of the bootloader files, grub2-install repairs or re-installs the i386-pc directory, which has all the modules of the GRUB 2 bootloader. We can cross-verify this by installing the modules in a custom directory. Please see Figure 3-25.

```
[root@localhost yogeshbabar]# grub2-install --boot-directory=temp /dev/sda
Installing for i386-pc platform.
Installation finished. No error reported.
[root@localhost yogeshbabar]#
```

Figure 3-25.   Installing grub2 in a temporary directory

You can see that all the GRUB 2 files have been restored along with GRUB's module files.

```
# ls temp/grub2/
    fonts   grubenv   i386-pc
# ls -l temp/grub2/i386-pc/ | wc -l
    279
```

After rebooting, Fedora should boot normally, and the "can't boot" issue should have been fixed. If GRUB drops you on a command prompt, then you need to follow the steps mentioned for issue 1 since grub2-install repairs the binaries, but it does not regenerate the grub.cfg file.

But what if you face a similar problem on a UEFI-based system?

Resolution for a UEFI-Based System

Here are the steps:

1. As you might have guessed, we have to just change the passed device name of the `grub2-install` command, as shown in Figure 3-26. The device name should be ESP.

```
root@yogesh:/home/yogesh# grub-install --efi-directory=/boot/efi/
Installing for x86_64-efi platform.
Installation finished. No error reported.
root@yogesh:/home/yogesh# █
```

Figure 3-26. *The grub-install command on a UEFI-based system*

"Can't Boot" Issue 3 (Bootloader + Kernel)

Issue: The complete /boot is missing.

Resolution for BIOS-Based Systems

Here are the steps:

1. Recovering the lost /boot is not possible (or at least it's outside the scope of this book).

2. Boot in rescue mode or boot with a live image and mount our "can't boot" system's root filesystem. The rescue mode and how it works are discussed in Chapter 10.

3. First make a new /boot directory and set the proper permissions on it.

    *   **#mkdir /boot**

    *   **#chmod 555 /boot**

    *   **#chown root:root /boot**

    *   If /boot is supposed to be a separate partition, then mount it with the correct partition.

4. As we know, /boot is where we store the files of the bootloader, kernel, and initramfs. Since /boot is missing, we need to create every file for it.

    - **#dnf reinstall kernel**

        - This is for a Fedora-based system. If it is a Debian-based system, then you can use the apt-get command and can reinstall the kernel.

        - This will install the vmlinuz file and will also regenerate the initramfs file for it.

5. Now we need to install GRUB.

    - **#grub2-install /dev/<disk_name>**

        - In our case, the command is #grub2-install /dev/sda.

    - This will repair GRUB's part-1 , part-2, and i386-pc directory from /boot/grub2.

    - To repair part-3 of GRUB and to have some GRUB-provided tools, we need to install two packages on a Fedora-based system.

        - **#dnf reinstall grub2 grub2-tools**

        - As the name suggests, the grub2 package will provide part-3 of GRUB, and grub2-tools will provide some of the tools like grub2-install.

    - Now it's time to regenerate the GRUB configuration file.

        - **#grub2-mkconfig -o /boot/grub2/grub.cfg**

    - Finally, fix the BLS.

        - **#kernel-install add 5.3.7-301.fc31.x86_64 /lib/ modules/5.3.7-301.fc31.x86_64/vmlinuz**

Resolution for UEFI-Based Systems

Here are the steps:

- /boot and /boot/efi/ are separate mount points.

  - **# mkdir /boot**

  - **# chmod 555 /boot**

  - **# chown root:root /boot**

  - **# yum reinstall kernel**

- Now we need to create an ESP partition, and as we know, it has to be a VFAT partition. Then assign an ESP partition type to it.

  - **#mkdir /boot/efi**

  - **#mount /dev/sda2 /boot/efi**

    - In our case, the partition that I have created for ESP is sda2.

  - **#grub2-install --efi-directory=/boot/efi**

    - This will install the grubx64.efi file in ESP.

  - The rest of the required files are provided by the grub2-efi, shim, and grub2-tools packages.

    - **#yum reinstall grub2-efi shim grub2-tools**

  - Regenerate the configuration files.

    - **#grub2-mkconfig -o /boot/efi/EFI/redhat/grub.cfg**

    - **#kernel-install add 5.3.7-301.fc31.x86_64 /lib/ modules/5.3.7-301.fc31.x86_64/vmlinuz**

After rebooting the system, it is able to boot without any issue.

Now it's time to shed some more light on UEFI's Secure Boot environment.

Secure Boot Feature of UEFI

Secure Boot is an amazing feature of UEFI. It makes sure no untrusted binary will run while booting. So far, we have seen the following:

- The digital signature is a unique string.

  - The digital signature of any file will be generated from a private key.

  - The same digital signature can be regenerated from the public key.

  - If the file is not altered, then the digital signature should match.

- Microsoft made its key pair (public and private keys).

- Microsoft digitally signed its bootloader-related files (BCD) with its private key.

- Microsoft's public key is present inside UEFI.

- While booting, UEFI will regenerate the digital signature of the bootloader by using the available public key. If the digital signatures do not match, then UEFI will discard the execution of .efi files.

- To use this feature in the Linux environment, a new bootloader has been created called shim, and it has been signed by Microsoft's private key so that UEFI will allow the shim.efi execution.

- Shim.efi's job is to call the actual GRUB file, which is grubx64.efi.

But Secure Boot does not stop here. Because there is a possibility that grubx64.efi itself has been compromised, or in fact any code that runs after the bootloader could have been compromised, securing the booting environment up to the bootloader level only is not sufficient; hence, these days the Secure Boot feature secures the entire booting procedure of Linux. This is how it works:

1. Fedora will prepare its own key pair and will sign the GRUB files with Fedora's private key.

2. The public key of Fedora will be kept inside the shim.efi file.

3. As the booting sequence continues, GRUB's digital signature will be regenerated by using the public key that is inside `shim.efi`.

4. If the signature matches then `grubx64.efi` and other bootloader files will be allowed to run by UEFI.

5. GRUB's ultimate job is to load the kernel (`/boot/vmlinuz`).

6. This `vmlinuz` file can also be compromised, so to avoid that, the kernel will be signed by the same private key that was used to sign GRUB.

7. `Vmlinuz`'s digital signature will be regenerated by using the public key that is inside `shim.efi`.

8. Once the digital signature matches, the kernel takes control of the booting sequence.

9. But the kernel uses a lot of modules/drivers that are eventually inserted inside the kernel. So, these modules that are again binaries could be compromised, and since they are going to become part of kernel/`vmlinuz`, then eventually the kernel itself will be compromised.

10. So, the kernel as a package will prepare its own key pair. All the modules will be signed by this kernel's private key, and the public key will be shipped with the kernel package itself. The private key of a kernel package will be destroyed later.

11. At the time of the booting, while inserting the modules in the kernel, the digital signature of the module will be regenerated by using the public key, which is with the kernel.

12. By following the steps mentioned, the Secure Boot feature makes sure that only binaries from trusted parties are executed.

The block diagrams shown Figure 3-27 will simplify the booting procedure even more.

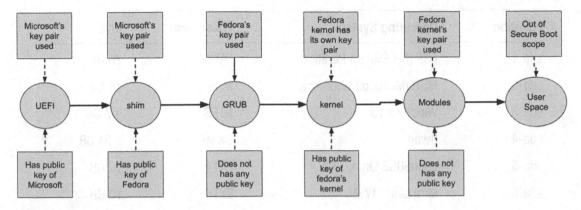

Figure 3-27. *The Secure Boot procedure*

100 OS Multiboot Project

One of my students asked me a question: how many operating systems can we install on one system and multiboot them with one bootloader? I didn't know the answer, but I decided to try to find out. I decided that I would use a GRUB 2 bootloader to boot every operating system that I have installed. I have been installing and multibooting the operating systems for almost two years now. I have installed 106 operating systems so far. This is our third system, which I named Jarvis. Here are the hardware and software details of Jarvis:

- UEFI firmware.

- Two disks attached (sda and sdb).

- The booting method is UEFI.

- sda is formatted with an MS-DOS partition table.

- sdb is formatted with a GPT partition table.

- All the operating systems are identified and booted by the GRUB 2 bootloader.

The operating systems that are installed on the sda disk were installed by setting the booting method to UEFI, and it has all the new operating systems. The operating systems that are on sdb were installed by setting the booting method of the firmware to legacy. sdb hosts most of the old-generation operating systems or at least those operating systems that do not have UEFI support. Here are the details:

Partition	Operating System	Filesystem	Size
sda-1	ESP (EFI System Partition)	FAT32	20 GB
sda-2	MSR (Microsoft Recovery)	MSR	16 MB
sda-3	Windows 10	NTFS	9.7 GB
sda-4	Swap	Swap	2.01 GB
sda-5	openSUSE Linux 13.2	EXT4	10 GB
sda-6	Mint Linux 17.2	EXT4	10 GB
sda-7	Oracle OpenSolaris 11.2	ZFS	10 GB
sda-8	Sabayon Linux 15.06	EXT4	10 GB
sda-9	Some random free space	N/A	8.4 MB
sda-10	Kali Linux 2.0	EXT4	10 GB
sda-11	Arch Linux 2015-8.1	EXT4	10 GB
sda-12	Debian Linux 8.1	EXT4	10 GB
sda-13	Semplice Linux 7.0.1	EXT4	10 GB
sda-14	Slackware 14.1 Linux	EXT4	10 GB
sda-15	Openmandriva 2014.2	EXT4	10 GB
sda-16	Mate Ubuntu Linux15.04	EXT4	10 GB
sda-17	Steam OS beta	EXT4	10 GB
sda-18	Manjaro Linux 0.8.13.1	EXT4	10 GB
sda-19	Netrunner Linux 16	EXT4	10 GB
sda-20	Windows 8	NTFS	10 GB
sda-21	Korora Linux 22	EXT4	10 GB
sda-22	KaOS Linux 2015.08	EXT4	10 GB
sda-23	Lubuntu Linux 15.04	EXT4	10 GB
sda-24	Sonar Linux 2015.2	EXT4	10 GB
sda-25	Antergos Linux 2015.08.18	EXT4	10 GB
sda-26	Mythbuntu Linux 14.04.2	EXT4	10 GB

(continued)

Partition	Operating System	Filesystem	Size
sda-27	Rosa Linux fresh R5	EXT4	10 GB
sda-28	SparkyLinux 4.0	EXT4	10 GB
sda-29	Vinux Linux 4.0	EXT4	10 GB
sda-30	Xubuntu Linux 14.04.3	EXT4	10 GB
sda-31	Ubuntu Studio 14.04.3	EXT4	10 GB
sda-32	Suse Enterprise 12	EXT4	10 GB
sda-33	Ubuntu Linux 14.04	EXT4	10 GB
sda-34	Ubuntu Linux 15.04	EXT4	10 GB
sda-35	Scientific Linux 7	EXT4	10 GB
sda-36	CentOS Linux 7	EXT4	10 GB
sda-37	Solus Linux Daily	EXT4	10 GB
sda-38	Ubuntu Server 14 Linux	EXT4	10 GB
sda-39	Fedora 21 Linux	EXT4	10 GB
sda-40	Fedora 22 Linux	EXT4	10 GB
sda-41	BlackArch 2015.07.31	EXT4	10 GB
sda-42	Gentoo Linux multilib 20140826	EXT4	10 GB
sda-43	Calculate Linux 14.16.2	EXT4	10 GB
sda-44	Fedora 20 Linux	EXT4	10 GB
sda-45	Fedora 23 Linux	EXT4	10 GB
sda-46	Manjaro Linux 15-0.9	EXT4	10 GB
sda-47	Ubuntu Linux 16.04	EXT4	10 GB
sda-48	chapeau Linux 23	EXT4	10 GB
sda-49	Arquetype Linux 22	EXT4	10 GB
sda-50	Fx64 Linux 22	EXT4	10 GB
sda-51	Viperr Linux 7	EXT4	10 GB
sda-52	Hanthana Linux 21	EXT4	10 GB

(*continued*)

Partition	Operating System	Filesystem	Size
sda-53	Qubes R3.1 Linux	EXT4	10 GB
sda-54	Fedora 24	EXT4	10 GB
sda-55	Korora-23	EXT4	10 GB
sda-56	sabayon-16	EXT4	10 GB
sda-57	Korora-24	EXT4	10 GB
sda-58	Sonar 16 Linux	EXT4	10 GB
sda-59	Viper 9 Linux	EXT4	10 GB
sda-60	Arquetype Linux 23	EXT4	10 GB
sda-61	Manjaro Linux 16	EXT4	10 GB
sda-62	Manjaro Linux Gaming 16	EXT4	10 GB
sda-63	Calculate Linux 15	EXT4	10 GB

So, the total number of UEFI OS installations on the sda disk is 59 since four partitions are reserved for ESP- and MSR-like stuff. The following are the sdb disk installations details:

Partition	Operating System	Filesystem	Size
sdb-1	PCBSD 10.1.2	ZFS	10 GB
sdb-2	Magia 2 Linux	EXT4	10 GB
sdb-3	Magia 3 Linux	EXt4	10 GB
sdb-4	Extended/secondary	N/A	970 GB approximately
sdb-5	Q4OS Linux 1.2.8	EXT4	10 GB
sdb-6	Qubes R2 Linux	EXT4	10 GB
sdb-7	Pardus Linux 2013	EXT4	10 GB
sdb-8	GoboLinux 015	EXT4	10 GB
sdb-9	Crux Linux 3.1	EXT4	10 GB
sdb-10	Point Linux 3.0	EXT4	10 GB

(continued)

Partition	Operating System	Filesystem	Size
sdb-11	Extix Linux 15.3	EXT4	10 GB
sdb-12	Bodhi Linux 3.0	EXT4	10 GB
sdb-13	Debian Linux 7.0	EXT4	10 GB
sdb-14	Debian Linux 6.0	EXT4	10 GB
sdb-15	BOSS Linux 6.1	EXT4	10 GB
sdb-16	CrunchBang rc1 Linux	EXT4	10 GB
sdb-17	Handy Linux 2.1	EXT4	10 GB
sdb-18	Lite Linux 2.4	EXT4	10 GB
sdb-19	WattOS Linux R9	EXT4	10 GB
sdb-20	PinGuy OS 14.04.3 Linux	EXT4	10 GB
sdb-21	SuperX 3.0 Linux	EXT4	10 GB
sdb-22	JuLinux 10X Rev 3.1 Linux	EXT4	10 GB
sdb-23	Black Lab Linux 2015.7	EXT4	10 GB
sdb-24	Hamara Linux 1.0.3	EXT4	10 GB
sdb-25	Peppermint LInux 20150518	EXT4	10 GB
sdb-26	Ubuntu 13.10 Linux	EXT4	10 GB
sdb-27	LinuxMint 13 mate	EXT4	10 GB
sdb-28	Linux Mint 14.1 cinnamon	EXT4	10 GB
sdb-29	LinuxMint 15 xfce	EXT4	10 GB
sdb-30	LinuxMint 16 KDE	EXT4	10 GB
sdb-31	Peppermint 4 20131113	EXT4	10 GB
sdb-32	Peppermint 5 20140623	EXT4	10 GB
sdb-33	Fedora 12	EXT4	10 GB
sdb-34	Trisquel 7 Linux	EXT4	10 GB
sdb-35	Oracle Linux 7.1	EXT4	10 GB
sdb-36	Fedora 14 Linux	EXT4	10 GB

(continued)

Partition	Operating System	Filesystem	Size
sdb-37	Fedora 15 Linux	EXT4	10 GB
sdb-38	Fedora 17 Linux	EXT4	10 GB
sdb-39	Fedora 19 Linux	EXT4	10 GB
sdb-40	RHEL 6.5 Linux	EXT4	10 GB
sdb-41	SolydX 201506	EXT4	10 GB
sdb-42	Oracle Linux 6.7	EXT4	10 GB
sdb-43	OpenSuse 11.3	EXT4	10 GB
sdb-44	LMDE (Linux Mint 2 Debian edition)	EXT4	10 GB
sdb-45	Centrych Linux 12.04	EXT4	10 GB
sdb-46	Elementary OS 2013	EXT4	10 GB
sdb-47	Elementary OS 2015	EXT4	10 GB
sdb-48	Sabayon 13.08 Linux	EXT4	10 GB
sdb-49	Deepin 2013 Linux	EXT4	10 GB
sdb-50	Deepin 15.1 Linux	EXT4	10 GB

The total number of operating systems booting the BIOS way on the sdb disks is 50 – 2 = 48.

Two partitions are reserved for swap and the extended partition.

So, the total number of installations on the Jarvis system is 106, and as you can see in Figure 3-28, all of these OSs are multibooted by using the GRUB 2 bootloader. With this project I have realized that there is no end to this. The GRUB 2 and UEFI combination can handle *n* number of operating systems.

Figure 3-28. *The 106 operating systems listed by GRUB 2*

How did I manage to install this many operating systems? Simple. I fired the grub-mkconfig command after every new OS installation, which found all the operating systems from all the attached disks.

time grub-mkconfig -o multiboot_grub.cfg

The previous command is used after installing Ubuntu 18, which was the 106th OS in the list.

As you can see in Figure 3-29, when I installed the 106th OS, grub-mkconfig took almost one hour to complete, and the resulting GRUB configuration file had 5,500 lines in it.

```
Adding boot menu entry for EFI firmware configuration
done

real    52m51.508s
user    0m51.640s
sys     4m25.944s
root@yogesh-desktop:/home/yogesh# 
```

Figure 3-29. *The time taken by the grub-mkconfig command*

A Dummy Small Bootloader

We know that the BIOS jumps to the first 512 bytes and calls the GRUB 2 bootloader. To understand how exactly BIOS calls the bootloader, we will make our own bootloader. Our bootloader will be very tiny compared to GRUB 2. Our bootloader will just print ! on the screen. But with this example, you will be able to understand how the BIOS jumps to the bootloaders as with GRUB 2, as shown here:

#cat boot.nasm

```
;
; Note: this example is written in Intel Assembly syntax
;
 [BITS 16]
 [ORG 0x7c00]

boot:
    mov al, '!'        <<-- Character for interrupt
    mov ah, 0x0e       <<-- Display character
    mov bh, 0x00       <<-- Set video mode
    mov bl, 0x07       <<-- Clear/Scroll screen down
    int 0x10           <<--- BIOS interrupt 10 which is taking inputs
                            from al, ah, bh, bl
    jmp $
    times 510-($-$$) db 0      <<--- Out of 512 bytes first 510 bytes
                                 are filled  with 0's.
                                 In the real world it will be filled with
                                 grub's boot strap.
    db 0x55            <<-- &
    db 0xaa            <<-- | tells BIOS that this is the device which
                            is active/fdisk sign/boot flag.
```

#nasm -f bin boot.nasm && qemu-system-x86_64 boot

This will make a boot disk (disk image) from the boot.nasm file, and it will be an input to qemu, which will execute it. As you can see in Figure 3-30, you will see ! printed on the screen.

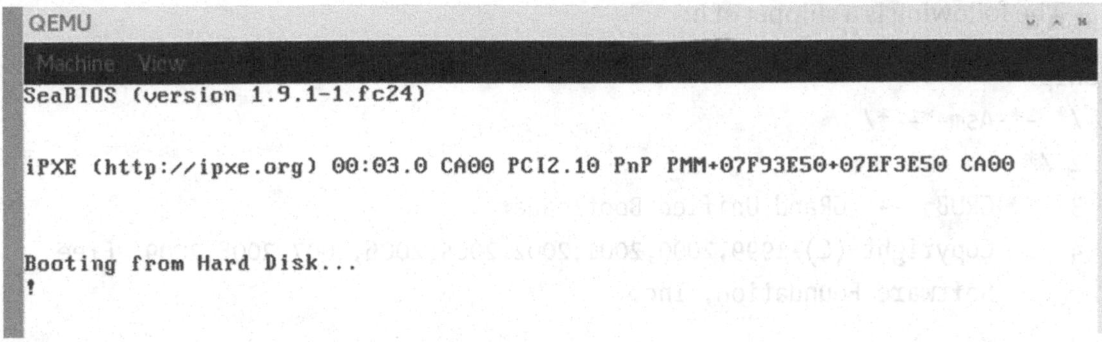

Figure 3-30. *Our small tiny bootloader*

Basically, the qemu machine is considering boot as a disk, and whenever the qemu machine finishes its BIOS stage, the BIOS drops at the first 512 bytes of the boot disk. Here you will find that the first 510 bytes are written as 0 and the in last 2 bytes we have ! (the bootloader), and it will be printed on our screen.

So far, we have gotten a good overview of GRUB 2; now going further in the next section, we will discuss what really happens inside GRUB 2.

GRUB 2 at a Low level

While writing this book, the latest available source code of GRUB was GRUB 2.04, which I have been using here. The bootstrap binary (if the system is BIOS based) from the first 440 bytes of 512 bytes is called boot.img, which is available at /usr/lib/grub/i386-pc/ boot.img.

 # ls -lh /usr/lib/grub/i386-pc/boot.img
-rw-r--r--. 1 root root 512 Mar 28 2019 /usr/lib/grub/i386-pc/boot.img

 # file /usr/lib/grub/i386-pc/boot.img
/usr/lib/grub/i386-pc/boot.img: DOS/MBR boot sector

The boot.img file is created from the source code written in the file /GRUB 2.04/ grub-core/boot/i386/pc/boot.S.

The following is a snippet of it:

```
<snip>
 1 /* -*-Asm-*- */
   2 /*
   3  *   GRUB   --   GRand Unified Bootloader
   4  *   Copyright (C) 1999,2000,2001,2002,2005,2006,2007,2008,2009   Free
         Software Foundation, Inc.
   5  *
   6  *   GRUB is free software: you can redistribute it and/or modify
   7  *   it under the terms of the GNU General Public License as published by
   8  *   the Free Software Foundation, either version 3 of the License, or
   9  *   (at your option) any later version.
  10  *
  11  *   GRUB is distributed in the hope that it will be useful,
  12  *   but WITHOUT ANY WARRANTY; without even the implied warranty of
  13  *   MERCHANTABILITY or FITNESS FOR A PARTICULAR PURPOSE.  See the
  14  *   GNU General Public License for more details.
  15  *
  16  *   You should have received a copy of the GNU General Public License
  17  *   along with GRUB.  If not, see <http://www.gnu.org/licenses/>.
  18  */
  19
  20 #include <grub/symbol.h>
  21 #include <grub/machine/boot.h>
  22
  23 /*
  24  *   defines for the code go here
  25  */
  26
  27          /* Print message string */
  28 #define MSG(x)   movw $x, %si; call LOCAL(message)
  29 #define ERR(x)   movw $x, %si; jmp LOCAL(error_message)
  30
```

```
31          .macro floppy
32 part_start:
33
34 LOCAL(probe_values):
35          .byte    36, 18, 15, 9, 0
36
37 LOCAL(floppy_probe):
38          pushw    %dx
39 /*
40  * Perform floppy probe.
41  */
42 #ifdef __APPLE__
43          LOCAL(probe_values_minus_one) = LOCAL(probe_values) - 1
44          movw     MACRO_DOLLAR(LOCAL(probe_values_minus_one)), %si
45 #else
46          movw     MACRO_DOLLAR(LOCAL(probe_values)) - 1, %si
47 #endif
48
49 LOCAL(probe_loop):
50          /* reset floppy controller INT 13h AH=0 */
51          xorw     %ax, %ax
52          int      MACRO_DOLLAR(0x13)
</snip>
```

You can consider boot.img as a first stage of the bootloader or part-1 of GRUB. This boot.img file transfers control to diskboot.img, which is part-2 of GRUB.

 # ls -lh /usr/lib/grub/i386-pc/diskboot.img

```
-rw-r--r--. 1 root root 512 Mar 28  2019 /usr/lib/grub/i386-pc/diskboot.img
```

 # file /usr/lib/grub/i386-pc/diskboot.img

```
/usr/lib/grub/i386-pc/diskboot.img: data
```

The diskboot.img file is made from the source code of grub-2.04/grub-core/boot/ i386/pc/diskboot.S. The following is a snippet of it:

```
<snip>
 1 /*
 2  *   GRUB   --   GRand Unified Bootloader
 3  * Copyright (C) 1999,2000,2001,2002,2006,2007,2009,2010 Free Software
      Foundation, Inc.
 4  *
 5  *  GRUB is free software: you can redistribute it and/or modify
 6  *  it under the terms of the GNU General Public License as published by
 7  *  the Free Software Foundation, either version 3 of the License, or
 8  *  (at your option) any later version.
 9  *
10  *  GRUB is distributed in the hope that it will be useful,
11  *  but WITHOUT ANY WARRANTY; without even the implied warranty of
12  *  MERCHANTABILITY or FITNESS FOR A PARTICULAR PURPOSE.  See the
13  *  GNU General Public License for more details.
14  *
15  *  You should have received a copy of the GNU General Public License
16  *  along with GRUB.  If not, see <http://www.gnu.org/licenses/>.
17  */
18
19 #include <grub/symbol.h>
20 #include <grub/machine/boot.h>
21
22 /*
23  *  defines for the code go here
24  */
25
26 #define MSG(x)   movw $x, %si; call LOCAL(message)
27
28         .file    "diskboot.S"
29
30         .text
31
```

```
32          /* Tell GAS to generate 16-bit instructions so that this code
            works
33             in real mode. */
34          .code16
35
36          .globl  start, _start
37 start:
38 _start:
39          /*
40          * _start is loaded at 0x8000 and is jumped to with
41          * CS:IP 0:0x8000 in kernel.
42          */
</snip>
```

The diskboot.img file then loads the actual core part of GRUB 2, which is part-3 of GRUB. You can also consider that part-3 of GRUB is a kernel of the bootloader. At this stage, GRUB 2 will be capable of reading the filesystem.

 # ls /boot/grub2/i386-pc/core.img -lh
-rw-r--r--. 1 root root 30K Dec 9 10:18 /boot/grub2/i386-pc/core.img

From /GRUB 2.00/grub-core/kern/main.c, GRUB 2 sets the root device name, reads grub.cfg, and at the end shows the operating system list to choose.

I hope you understand how GRUB 2 works now. The following is a quick summary of what we have discussed so far:

a. The bootloader is the first code that runs after the firmware.

b. The bootloader/GRUB copies the kernel in memory.

c. The bootloader loads the initramfs image in memory and gives the kernel a pointer to it.

d. The bootloader hand overs control to the kernel.

CHAPTER 4

Kernel

This chapter will cover the kernel.

Loading the Kernel in Memory

This is an interesting chapter. So far, we have seen that up to this stage GRUB 2 had full control of the booting procedure. Now it has to hand over control to the kernel. In this chapter, we will see how and where the bootloader loads the kernel. In other words, how is the kernel extracted? Then we will see the booting-related tasks achieved by the Linux kernel and at the end how the kernel starts systemd.

Note   The source code of the kernel that is used in this chapter is version `kernel-5.4.4`. When I was writing this book, that was the latest stable code available; see `https://www.kernel.org/`. An excellent resource on this subject is the *Inside Linux* book, written by 0xAX. I have learned a lot from it, and I'm sure you will too. You can find the book at `https://0xax.gitbooks.io/linux-insides/`.

To hand over the control to the kernel, the bootloader has to achieve two major things.

- Load the kernel into memory
- Set some of the fields of the kernel as per the boot protocol

© Yogesh Babar 2020
Y. Babar, *Hands-on Booting*, https://doi.org/10.1007/978-1-4842-5890-3_4

The complete boot protocol is available at `https://www.kernel.org/doc/Documentation/x86/boot.txt`. The original boot protocol was defined by none other than Linus Torvalds.

```
         ~                                 ~
         | Protected-mode kernel           |
 100000  +--------------------------------+
         | I/O memory hole                 |
 0A0000  +--------------------------------+
         | Reserved for BIOS               | Leave as much as possible unused
         ~                                 ~
         | Command line                    | (Can also be below the X+10000
                                             mark)
X+10000  +--------------------------------+
         | Stack/heap                      | For use by the kernel real-mode
                                             code.
X+08000  +--------------------------------+
         | Kernel setup                    | The kernel real-mode code.
         | Kernel boot sector              | The kernel legacy boot sector.
      X  +--------------------------------+
         | Boot loader                     | <- Boot sector entry point
                                             0000:7C00. You will see the same
         |                                 | address location at our boot.asm
                                             file which we created above.
 001000  +--------------------------------+
         | Reserved for MBR/BIOS           |
 000800  +--------------------------------+
         | Typically used by MBR           |
 000600  +--------------------------------+
         | BIOS use only                   |
 000000  +--------------------------------+
```

As per the boot protocol, it's the duty of a bootloader to pass on or set some of the fields of the kernel header. The fields are the root device name, mount options like ro or rw, the initramfs name, the initramfs size, etc. These same fields are called *kernel command-line parameters*, and we already know that the kernel command-line parameters are passed by GRUB/the bootloader to the kernel.

GRUB will not load the kernel (/boot/vmlinuz) at any random location; it will always be loaded at a special location. The special location will vary as per the Linux distribution and version you are using and as per the CPU architecture of the system. vmlinuz is an archive file, and the archive is made from three parts.

Vmlinuz (bZimage) = Header   + kernel setup code + vmlinux (actual compressed kernel)

                         (part-1)   (part-2)   (part-3)

After Loading the Kernel in Memory

We need to imagine here that GRUB 2 has loaded the kernel in memory at the special location. Here are the initial-level steps carried out by the kernel archive file vmlinuz as soon as it loaded in memory:

1) As soon as the bootloader loads the kernel in memory at a specific location, the binary made from the file arch/x86/boot/header.S runs.

2) Confusion occurs if vmlinuz is an archive and the bootloader has not extracted it yet. The bootloader has just loaded the kernel at a specific location. Then why is the code that is inside the vmlinuz archive file able to run?

3) We will see the short answer first, and the long answer will be discussed in the "What Extracts vmlinuz?" section of this chapter. So, the short answer is a binary made from the arch/x86/boot/header.S file is not in the archive; rather, it is part of a header that does a kernel_setup task. The header is outside of an archive.

Vmlinuz (bZimage) = Header + kernel setup code + vmlinux (actual compressed kernel)
                --->Outside of archive<--- + -------->Inside archive<----
                --->header.s file is here<---

4) Let's consider for now that vmlinuz has been extracted, and let's continue our booting sequence. So far, we have seen that GRUB has loaded the kernel in memory at a special location and runs the binary made from arch/x86/boot/header.S. This binary is responsible for the Kernel_setup part. The kernel_setup file does the following tasks:

a) Align the segment registers

b) Set up the stack and BSS

In every chapter, a flowchart will give us a clear idea about what we have learned and, in terms of booting, where we have reached. Figure 4-1 shows the start of the flowchart that we will build in this chapter as we progress. It shows the actions performed by the kernel_setup code of header.s.

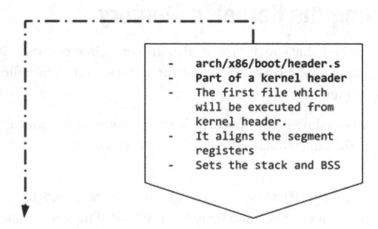

Figure 4-1. *Steps taken by kernel_setup*

5) Then it jumps to the main() function at arch/x86/boot/main.c.
    The main.c file is also part of a kernel header, and the header is
    outside the actual archive.

Vmlinuz (bZimage) = Header + kernel setup code + vmlinux (actual compressed kernel)
```
        --->Outside of archive<--- + -------->Inside archive<---------
        --->main.c file is here<---
```

```
#vim arch/x86/boot/main.c
<snip>
134 void main(void)
135 {
136         /* First, copy the boot header into the "zeropage" */
137         copy_boot_params();
138
139         /* Initialize the early-boot console */
140         console_init();
141         if (cmdline_find_option_bool("debug"))
142                 puts("early console in setup code\n");
143
144         /* End of heap check */
145         init_heap();
146
147         /* Make sure we have all the proper CPU support */
148         if (validate_cpu()) {
149                 puts("Unable to boot - please use a kernel
                            appropriate "
150                      "for your CPU.\n");
151             die();
152         }
153
154         /* Tell the BIOS what CPU mode we intend to run in. */
155         set_bios_mode();
156
```

```
157            /* Detect memory layout */
158            detect_memory();
159
160            /* Set keyboard repeat rate (why?) and query the lock
               flags */
161            keyboard_init();
162
163            /* Query Intel SpeedStep (IST) information */
164            query_ist();
165
166            /* Query APM information */
167 #if defined(CONFIG_APM) || defined(CONFIG_APM_MODULE)
168            query_apm_bios();
169 #endif
170
171            /* Query EDD information */
172 #if defined(CONFIG_EDD) || defined(CONFIG_EDD_MODULE)
173            query_edd();
174 #endif
175
176            /* Set the video mode */
177            set_video();
178
179            /* Do the last things and invoke protected mode */
180            go_to_protected_mode();
181 }
</snip>
```

As you can see, the main.c source code is responsible for the following:

1) It copies the boot parameters (the kernel command-line
   parameters) from the bootloader. The copy_boot_params function
   will be used to copy the following boot parameters passed by the
   bootloader:

   debug, earlyprintk, ro, root, ramdisk_image, ramdisk_size etc.

2) It initializes the console and checks whether the debug-like kernel
command-line parameter has been passed by the user. If it has,
the kernel will show the verbose-level messages on the screen.

3) It initializes the heap.

4) If the CPU cannot be validated, then it throws an error message
through the `validate_cpu()` function. Distributions like Fedora
and Ubuntu customize the error message, from `'unable to
boot - please use the kernel appropriate for your cpu'` to
something like `'The CPU is not supported'`. The customization
will also panic the kernel, and the booting will be halted.

5) Then it detects the memory layout and prints it on-screen at an
early stage of booting. The same memory layout messages can be
seen after the boot by using the `'dmesg'` command, as shown here:

```
[    0.000000] BIOS-provided physical RAM map:
[    0.000000] BIOS-e820: [mem 0x0000000000000000-0x0000000000057fff] usable
[    0.000000] BIOS-e820: [mem 0x0000000000058000-0x0000000000058fff] reserved
[    0.000000] BIOS-e820: [mem 0x0000000000059000-0x000000000009cfff] usable
[    0.000000] BIOS-e820: [mem 0x000000000009d000-0x00000000000fffff] reserved
[    0.000000] BIOS-e820: [mem 0x0000000000100000-0x000000007e5f7fff] usable
[    0.000000] BIOS-e820: [mem 0x000000007e5f8000-0x000000007e5f8fff] ACPI NVS
[    0.000000] BIOS-e820: [mem 0x000000007e5f9000-0x000000007e5f9fff] reserved
[    0.000000] BIOS-e820: [mem 0x000000007e5fa000-0x0000000087f62fff] usable
[    0.000000] BIOS-e820: [mem 0x0000000087f63000-0x000000008952bfff] reserved
[    0.000000] BIOS-e820: [mem 0x000000008952c000-0x0000000089599fff] ACPI NVS
[    0.000000] BIOS-e820: [mem 0x000000008959a000-0x00000000895fefff] ACPI data
[    0.000000] BIOS-e820: [mem 0x00000000895ff000-0x00000000895fffff] usable
[    0.000000] BIOS-e820: [mem 0x0000000089600000-0x000000008f7fffff] reserved
[    0.000000] BIOS-e820: [mem 0x00000000f0000000-0x00000000f7ffffff] reserved
[    0.000000] BIOS-e820: [mem 0x00000000fe010000-0x00000000fe010fff] reserved
[    0.000000] BIOS-e820: [mem 0x0000000100000000-0x000000086e7fffff] usable
```

6) Initialize the keyboard and its layout.

7) Set the basic video mode.

8) Jump to the protected mode through the `go_to_protected_mode()` function. Please refer to Figure 4-2 for a better understanding.

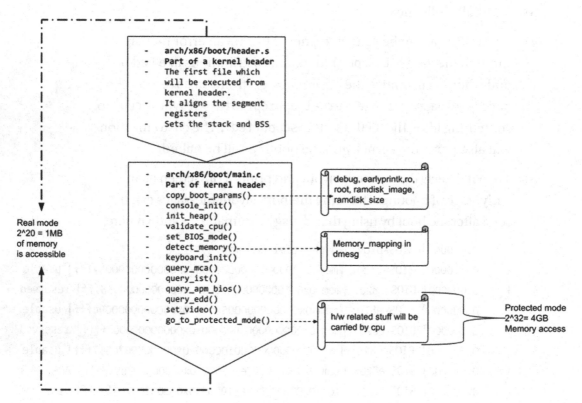

Figure 4-2. *The flowchart*

Protected Mode

Up to this point, we have worked in real mode, which has 20-bit address limitations because of that we can access up to 1 MB of memory. With the `go_to_protected_mode()` function, the kernel has switched the CPU from real mode to the protected mode. Protected mode has a 32-bit address limitation, so the CPU can access up to 4 GB of memory. In simple terms, in real mode only those programs will run that have a 16-bit instruction set, for example, the BIOS. In protected mode, only the 32-bit programs will run. The kernel does some hardware-related tasks in protected mode and then launches a CPU in long mode.

Please note that this book follows Intel's X86 architecture, and the real, protected, and long mode discussions are based on Intel's 64-bit architecture.

Long Mode

Long mode does not put any memory restrictions on the CPU. It can use all the installed memory. Placing the CPU in long mode will be achieved by the head_64.S file from arch/x86/boot/compressed/head_64.S. It is responsible for the following:

1) Preparing for long mode means it will check whether it supports long mode or not.

2) Enter into long mode.

3) Decompress the kernel.

The following are functions that get called from the head_64.S assembly file:

```
$ cat arch/x86/boot/compressed/head_64.S | grep -i call
    call      1f
    call      verify_cpu
    call      get_sev_encryption_bit
    call      1f
    call      1f
    call      .Ladjust_got
     * this function call.
    call      paging_prepare
     * this function call.
    call      cleanup_trampoline
    call      1f
    call      .Ladjust_got
    call      1f
     * Relocate efi_config->call().
    call      make_boot_params
    call      1f
     * Relocate efi_config->call().
    call      efi_main
    call      extract_kernel   /* returns kernel location in %rax */
    .quad     efi_call
```

Function	Working
verify_cpu	This will make sure the CPU has a long mode.
make_boot_params	This will take care of the bootloader-passed boot-time parameters.
efi_main	UEFI firmware-related stuff.
extract_kernel	The function is defined in arch/x86/boot/compressed_misc.c. This is the function that will decompress vmlinux from vmlinuz.

For a better understanding, please refer to the flowchart shown in Figure 4-3.

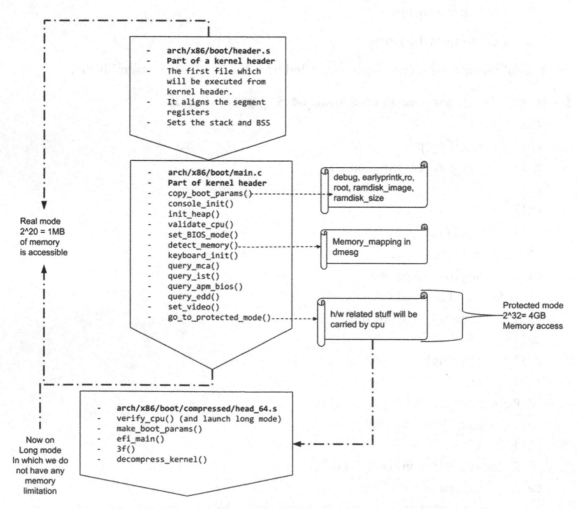

Figure 4-3. *The flowchart, updated*

Wait a minute: if the kernel is not yet decompressed, then how come we proceed at this point? Here comes the long answer.

What Extracts vmlinuz?

So far, we understand that it's GRUB that loads the kernel in memory, but at the same time, we noticed that the vmlinuz image is an archive. So, what extracts this image? Is it GRUB?

No, it is not GRUB. Rather, it's the kernel that extracts itself. Yes, I said it's the kernel that extracts the kernel. The vmlinuz could be the operating system world's only file that extracts itself. But how is it possible to extract yourself? To understand this, let's get some more insight about vmlinuz first.

The "vm" of vmlinuz stands for "virtual memory." In the earlier stages of Linux development, the virtual memory concept was not yet developed, so when it was added, the "vm" characters were added to the name of the Linux kernel. The "z" stands for a zipped file.

```
$ file vmlinuz-5.0.9-301.fc30.x86_64
```

```
vmlinuz-5.0.9-301.fc30.x86_64: Linux kernel x86 boot executable bzImage,
version 5.0.9-301.fc30.x86_64 (mockbuild@bkernel04.phx2.fedoraproject.org)
#1 SMP Tue Apr 23 23:57:35 U, RO-rootFS, swap_dev 0x8, Normal VGA
```

As you can see, vmlinuz is bzImage (bzImage stands for "big zimage"). vmlinuz is a compressed file of the actual kernel's binary vmlinux. You cannot decompress this file with gunzip/bunzip or even with tar. The easiest way to extract vmlinuz and to get the vmlinux file is to use the extract-vmlinux script file provided by the kernel-devel package (in the case of Fedora). The file will be present at /usr/src/kernels/<kernel_version>/scripts/extract-vmlinux.

```
# ./extract-vmlinux /boot/vmlinuz-5.3.7-301.fc31.x86_64 >> /boot/temp/
    vmlinux
```

```
# file /boot/temp/*
/boot/temp/vmlinux: ELF 64-bit LSB executable, x86-64, version 1 (SYSV),
statically linked, BuildID[sha1]=ec96b29d8e4079950644230c0b7868942bb70366,
stripped
```

There are various ways to open the vmlinux and vmlinuz kernel files.

```
$ xxd vmlinux | less
$ objdump vmlinux | less
$ objdump vmlinux -D | less
$ hexdump vmlinux | less
$ od vmlinux | less
```

We will use the od command with some of the switches to open the vmlinuz file.

```
$ od -A d -t x1 vmlinuz-5.0.9-301.fc30.x86_64 | less
<snip>
0000000 4d 5a ea 07 00 c0 07 8c c8 8e d8 8e c0 8e d0 31
0000016 e4 fb fc be 40 00 ac 20 c0 74 09 b4 0e bb 07 00
0000032 cd 10 eb f2 31 c0 cd 16 cd 19 ea f0 ff 00 f0 00
0000048 00 00 00 00 00 00 00 00 00 00 00 00 82 00 00 00
0000064 55 73 65 20 61 20 62 6f 6f 74 20 6c 6f 61 64 65
0000080 72 2e 0d 0a 0a 52 65 6d 6f 76 65 20 64 69 73 6b
0000096 20 61 6e 64 20 70 72 65 73 73 20 61 6e 79 20 6b
0000112 65 79 20 74 6f 20 72 65 62 6f 6f 74 2e 2e 2e 0d
0000128 0a 00 50 45 00 00 64 86 04 00 00 00 00 00 00 00
0000144 00 00 01 00 00 00 a0 00 06 02 0b 02 02 14 80 37
0000160 8e 00 00 00 00 00 80 86 26 02 f0 48 00 00 00 02
0000176 00 00 00 00 00 00 00 00 00 00 20 00 00 00 20 00
0000192 00 00 00 00 00 00 00 00 00 00 00 00 00 00 00 00
0000208 00 00 00 c0 b4 02 00 02 00 00 00 00 00 00 0a 00
0000224 00 00 00 00 00 00 00 00 00 00 00 00 00 00 00 00
*
0000256 00 00 00 00 00 00 06 00 00 00 00 00 00 00 00 00
0000272 00 00 00 00 00 00 00 00 00 00 00 00 00 00 00 00
0000288 00 00 00 00 00 00 00 00 00 00 80 39 8e 00 48 09
0000304 00 00 00 00 00 00 00 00 00 00 2e 73 65 74 75 70
0000320 00 00 e0 43 00 00 00 02 00 00 e0 43 00 00 00 02
0000336 00 00 00 00 00 00 00 00 00 00 00 00 00 00 20 00
0000352 50 60 2e 72 65 6c 6f 63 00 00 20 00 00 00 e0 45
0000368 00 00 20 00 00 00 e0 45 00 00 00 00 00 00 00 00
0000384 00 00 00 00 00 00 40 00 10 42 2e 74 65 78 74 00
```

```
0000400 00 00 80 f3 8d 00 00 46 00 00 80 f3 8d 00 00 46
0000416 00 00 00 00 00 00 00 00 00 00 00 00 00 00 20 00
0000432 50 60 2e 62 73 73 00 00 00 00 80 86 26 02 80 39
0000448 8e 00 00 00 00 00 00 00 00 00 00 00 00 00 00 00
0000464 00 00 00 00 00 00 80 00 00 c8 00 00 00 00 00 00
0000480 00 00 00 00 00 00 00 00 00 00 00 00 00 00 00 ff
0000496 ff 22 01 00 38 df 08 00 00 00 ff ff 00 00 55 aa
0000512 eb 66 48 64 72 53 0d 02 00 00 00 00 00 10 c0 37
0000528 00 01 00 80 00 00 10 00 00 00 00 00 00 00 00 00
0000544 00 00 00 00 50 5a 00 00 00 00 00 00 ff ff ff 7f
0000560 00 00 00 01 01 15 3f 00 ff 07 00 00 00 00 00 00
0000576 00 00 00 00 00 00 00 00 b1 03 00 00 11 f3 89 00
0000592 00 00 00 00 00 00 00 00 00 00 00 00 01 00 00 00 00
0000608 00 c0 b4 02 90 01 00 00 8c d8 8e c0 fc 8c d2 39
0000624 c2 89 e2 74 16 ba 50 58 f6 06 11 02 80 74 04 8b
</snip>
```

```
# od -A d -t x1 /boot/vmlinuz-5.3.7-301.fc31.x86_64 | grep -i '1f 8b 08 00'
0018864 8f 1f 8b 08 00 00 00 00 00 02 03 ec fd 79 7c 54
```

So, on 0018864, the actual kernel (vmlinux) starts, whereas the vmlinuz file starts at 0000000. This means from 0000000 to 0018864, what we have is the header of the file, such as header.S, misc.c, etc. This will extract the actual kernel (vmlinux) from vmlinuz. You can consider a header to be like a cap on a vmlinux binary, and when this cap is available, it becomes vmlinuz. In the following sections, we will see how the kernel routine extracts vmlinuz.

extract_kernel

Let's get back to the extract_kernel function from arch/x86/boot/compressed/misc.c.

```
asmlinkage __visible void *extract_kernel(void *rmode, memptr heap,
                                          unsigned char *input_data,
                                          unsigned long input_len,
                                          unsigned char *output,
                                          unsigned long output_len)
```

As you can see, the function will accept seven arguments.

Argument	Purpose
rmode	A pointer to the boot_params structure that is filled by the bootloader
heap	A pointer to the boot_heap file that represents the start address of the early boot heap
input_data	A pointer to the start of the compressed kernel or in other words a pointer to arch/x86/boot/compressed/vmlinux.bin.bz2
input_len	The size of the compressed kernel
output	The start address of the future decompressed kernel
output_len	The size of decompressed kernel
run_size	The amount of space needed to run the kernel including .bss and .brk sections

Along with the kernel, the bootloader will also load initramfs in memory. We will talk about initramfs in Chapter 5. So, before extracting the kernel image, the header or the kernel routine has to take care that the vmlinuz extraction will not overwrite or overlap the already loaded initramfs image. So, the extract_kernel function will also take care of calculating the initramfs address space and will adjust the kernel image decompression accordingly. Once we get the correct address where the header can decompress vmlinuz, it will extract the kernel there.

```
340 asmlinkage __visible void *extract_kernel(void *rmode, memptr heap,
341                                 unsigned char *input_data,
342                                 unsigned long input_len,
343                                 unsigned char *output,
344                                 unsigned long output_len)
345 {
346         const unsigned long kernel_total_size = VO__end - VO__text;
347         unsigned long virt_addr = LOAD_PHYSICAL_ADDR;
348         unsigned long needed_size;
349
350         /* Retain x86 boot parameters pointer passed from
           startup_32/64. */
351         boot_params = rmode;
```

```
352
353        /* Clear flags intended for solely in-kernel use. */
354        boot_params->hdr.loadflags &= ~KASLR_FLAG;
355
356        sanitize_boot_params(boot_params);
357
358        if (boot_params->screen_info.orig_video_mode == 7) {
359                vidmem = (char *) 0xb0000;
360                vidport = 0x3b4;
361        } else {
362                vidmem = (char *) 0xb8000;
363                vidport = 0x3d4;
364        }
365
366        lines = boot_params->screen_info.orig_video_lines;
367        cols = boot_params->screen_info.orig_video_cols;
368
369        console_init();
370
371        /*
372         * Save RSDP address for later use. Have this after console_
                init()
373         * so that early debugging output from the RSDP parsing code
                can be
374         * collected.
375         */
376        boot_params->acpi_rsdp_addr = get_rsdp_addr();
377
378        debug_putstr("early console in extract_kernel\n");
379
380        free_mem_ptr     = heap;         /* Heap */
381        free_mem_end_ptr = heap + BOOT_HEAP_SIZE;
382
383        /*
```

```
384                 * The memory hole needed for the kernel is the larger of
                      either
385             * the entire decompressed kernel plus relocation table, or the
386             * entire decompressed kernel plus .bss and .brk sections.
387             *
388             * On X86_64, the memory is mapped with PMD pages. Round the
389             * size up so that the full extent of PMD pages mapped is
390             * included in the check against the valid memory table
391             * entries. This ensures the full mapped area is usable RAM
392             * and doesnt include any reserved areas.
393             */
394            needed_size = max(output_len, kernel_total_size);
395  #ifdef CONFIG_X86_64
396            needed_size = ALIGN(needed_size, MIN_KERNEL_ALIGN);
397  #endif
398
399           /* Report initial kernel position details. */
400           debug_putaddr(input_data);
401           debug_putaddr(input_len);
402           debug_putaddr(output);
403           debug_putaddr(output_len);
404           debug_putaddr(kernel_total_size);
405           debug_putaddr(needed_size);
406
407  #ifdef CONFIG_X86_64
408           /* Report address of 32-bit trampoline */
409           debug_putaddr(trampoline_32bit);
410  #endif
411
412           choose_random_location((unsigned long)input_data, input_len,
413                                  (unsigned long *)&output,
414                                  needed_size,
415                                  &virt_addr);
416
417           /* Validate memory location choices. */
```

```
418          if ((unsigned long)output & (MIN_KERNEL_ALIGN - 1))
419                  error("Destination physical address inappropriately
                         aligned");
420          if (virt_addr & (MIN_KERNEL_ALIGN - 1))
421                  error("Destination virtual address inappropriately
                         aligned");
422 #ifdef CONFIG_X86_64
423          if (heap > 0x3fffffffffffUL)
424                  error("Destination address too large");
425          if (virt_addr + max(output_len, kernel_total_size) > KERNEL_
             IMAGE_SIZE)
426                  error("Destination virtual address is beyond the kernel
                         mapping area");
427 #else
428          if (heap > ((-__PAGE_OFFSET-(128<<20)-1) & 0x7fffffff))
429                  error("Destination address too large");
430 #endif
431 #ifndef CONFIG_RELOCATABLE
432          if ((unsigned long)output != LOAD_PHYSICAL_ADDR)
433                  error("Destination address does not match LOAD_
                         PHYSICAL_ADDR");
434          if (virt_addr != LOAD_PHYSICAL_ADDR)
435                  error("Destination virtual address changed when not
                         relocatable");
436 #endif
437
438          debug_putstr("\nDecompressing Linux... ");
439          __decompress(input_data, input_len, NULL, NULL, output, output_len,
440                          NULL, error);
441          parse_elf(output);
442          handle_relocations(output, output_len, virt_addr);
443          debug_putstr("done.\nBooting the kernel.\n");
444          return output;
445 }
```

The decompression method will be chosen according to the compression algorithm used at the time of kernel compilation. The decompression methods can be seen in the same misc.c file.

```
        <snip from misc.c>
57 #ifdef CONFIG_KERNEL_GZIP
58 #include "../../../../lib/decompress_inflate.c"
59 #endif
60
61 #ifdef CONFIG_KERNEL_BZIP2
62 #include "../../../../lib/decompress_bunzip2.c"
63 #endif
64
65 #ifdef CONFIG_KERNEL_LZMA
66 #include "../../../../lib/decompress_unlzma.c"
67 #endif
68
69 #ifdef CONFIG_KERNEL_XZ
70 #include "../../../../lib/decompress_unxz.c"
71 #endif
72
73 #ifdef CONFIG_KERNEL_LZO
74 #include "../../../../lib/decompress_unlzo.c"
75 #endif
    </snip>
```

Once the kernel is decompressed in memory, the entry point of the extracted kernel will be obtained from the extract_kernel function, and the CPU will jump inside a kernel.

Inside the Kernel

The kernel does numerous things, but I will list what is of most interest to you as someone learning about booting.

- The kernel will set the kernel stack size to 16 KB if the architecture is 64-bit. This means every new process will get its own kernel stack which will be 16 KB in size.

- `page_size` will be set to 4 KB, which is the default page size on an Intel 64-bit architecture.

- The kernel will prepare the interrupt and exception handling mechanism also called the *interrupt descriptor table* (IDT).

- The kernel will set the page fault handling mechanism.

- The kernel will collect the initramfs file details such as file name, size, address, relocation address, major and minor numbers of a new root device, etc., from `/arch/x86/kernel/setup.c`.

- Then it extracts initramfs from the source code file `init/initramfs.c`.

- Finally, it launches systemd by using the `start_kernel` function of `init/main.c`.

You will notice that this is the first time we came outside of the `arch` directory. That means we can consider this code as architecture independent. Once the kernel is launched, it does numerous things, and it is almost impossible to cover all of it in this book. In terms of booting, the kernel's motto is to launch systemd from initramfs. Since initramfs has already been loaded in memory by the bootloader, extracting the initramfs kernel requires the initramfs file details, which the kernel will get from `/arch/x86/kernel/setup.c`.

```
Initramfs file name,
Initramfs file size,
Initramfs files address,
Initramfs files relocation address,
Major and minor numbers on which initramfs will be mounted.
```

Once the kernel receives the details of the initramfs file, it will extract the initramfs archive from the `init/initramfs.c` file. We will discuss how exactly the kernel extracts initramfs in memory in Chapter 5. To mount initramfs as a root device, it needs virtual filesystems like `proc`, `sys`, `dev`, etc., so the kernel accordingly prepares them.

```
err = register_filesystem(&proc_fs_type);
    if (err)
    return;
```

The kernel will later mount the extracted initramfs as a root with the help of the do_ mount_root function of init/do_mounts.c. Once the initramfs is mounted in memory, the kernel will launch systemd from it. systemd will be launched through the same start_kernel function of an init/main.c file.

```
asmlinkage void __init start_kernel(void)
```

Basically, once the root filesystem is ready, it will get inside the root filesystem and will create two threads: PID 1 is a systemd process, and PID 2 is a kthread. For better understanding, please refer to the flowchart shown in Figure 4-4.

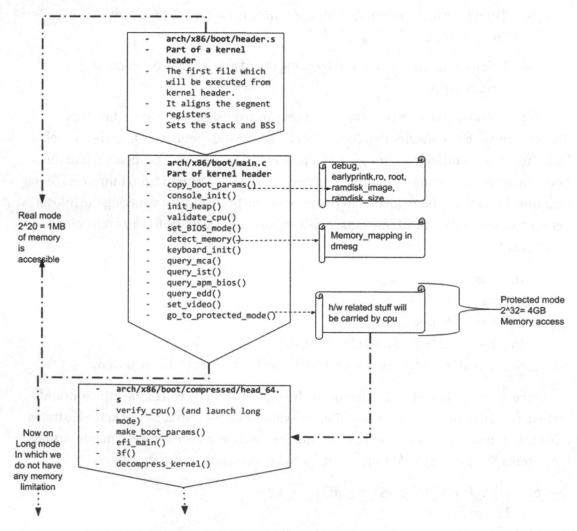

Figure 4-4. *The flowchart, updated again*

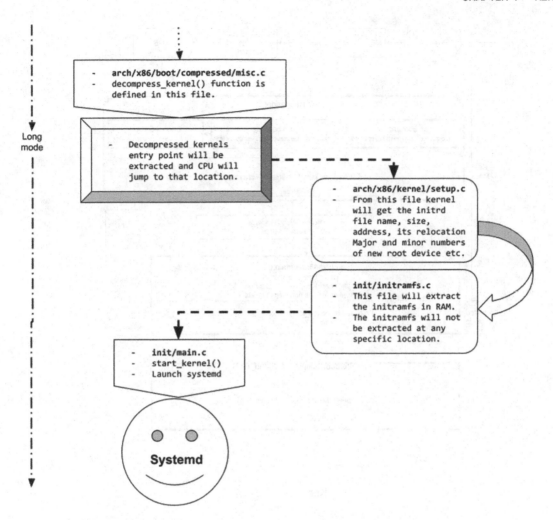

Figure 4.4. *(continued)*

Figure 4-5 shows the complete boot sequence that we have discussed so far.

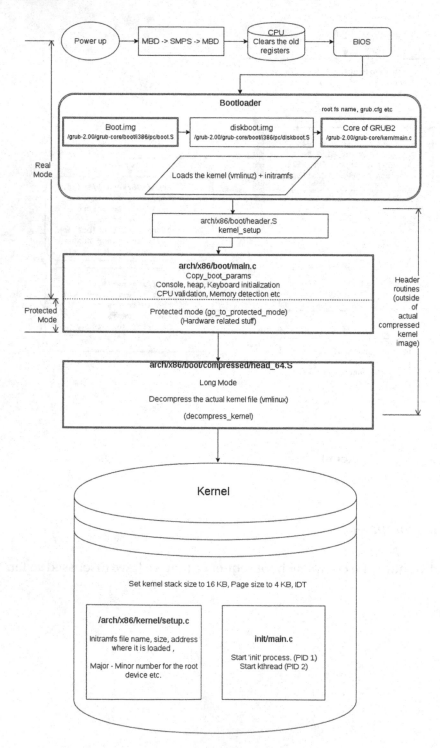

Figure 4-5. *The boot sequence in a block diagram*

Before we continue and look at how the kernel extracts initramfs and runs systemd from it, we need to understand the basics of initramfs such as why we need it, what its structure is, etc. Once we understand the importance and basics of initramfs, we will continue our booting sequence with systemd's role in the boot sequence.

CHAPTER 5

initramfs

In this chapter, we will discuss why we really need initramfs and why it's important in the booting procedure. We know that initramfs is loaded into memory by the bootloader, but we haven't discussed yet how initramfs is extracted. This chapter will address that. We will also see the steps to extract, rebuild, and customize initramfs. Later, we will see the structure of initramfs as well as the booting sequence of a system inside initramfs.

Why initramfs?

The aim of the booting procedure is to present the user with their own files that reside in the root filesystem. In other words, it is the kernel's duty to find, mount, and present the user's root filesystem to the user. To achieve this goal, the kernel has to run the systemd binary, which again resides in the user's root filesystem. Now this has become a chicken-and-egg problem. To run a systemd process, first we have to mount the root filesystem, and to mount the root filesystem, we have to run systemd from the root filesystem. Also, along with the actual root filesystem, users might have files on some other filesystems such as NFS, CIFS, etc., and that list of other filesystems is also inside the root filesystem (/etc/fstab).

So, to solve this chicken-and-egg problem, the developers came up with a resolution called initramfs (which means "initial RAM filesystem"). initramfs is a temporary root filesystem (inside the main memory) that will be used to mount the actual root filesystem (from the hard disk or network). So, the whole purpose of initramfs is to mount the user's root filesystem from the HDD/network. Ideally, the kernel is capable enough to mount the root filesystem from disk on its own without initramfs, but these days a user's root filesystem could be anywhere. It could be on RAID, on an LVM, or on a multipath device. It could be on n number of filesystem types like XFS, BTRFS, ext4, ext3, NFS, etc. It could even be on an encrypted filesystem like LUKS. So, it is almost

© Yogesh Babar 2020
Y. Babar, *Hands-on Booting*, https://doi.org/10.1007/978-1-4842-5890-3_5

impossible for a kernel to incorporate all these scenarios in its own `vmlinux` binary. Let me provide some real-life scenarios in this section.

Let's say the root file system is on NFS and there is no initramfs concept. That means the kernel has to mount the user's root filesystem from NFS on its own. In such a case, the kernel has to achieve the following tasks:

1. Bring up the primary network interface.

2. Invoke a DHCP client and get an IP address from the DHCP server.

3. Find the NFS share and associated NFS server.

4. Mount the NFS share (the root filesystem).

To achieve these steps, the kernel needs to have the following binaries: `NetworkManager`, `dhclient`, `mount`, etc.

Now let's say the root filesystem is on a software RAID device. Then the kernel has to do the following tasks:

1. Find the RAID disks first with `mdadm --examine --scan`.

2. Once the underlying disks on which the software RAID is spanned are identified, it has to assemble the RAID with `mdadm --assemble --scan`.

3. To achieve this, the kernel needs to have the `mount` and `mdadm` binaries and some configuration files of the software RAID devices.

Now let's say the root file system is on a logical volume. Then the kernel has to finish the following tasks on its own:

1. Find the physical volumes with `pvs`.

2. Find the volume group with `vgscan` and then activate it with `vgchange`.

3. Scan the LVS with `lvscan`.

4. Finally, once the `root lv` is populated, mount it as a root filesystem.

5. To achieve this, the kernel needs to have `pvscan`, `pvs`, `lvscan`, `vgscan`, `lvs`, and `vgchange`-like binaries.

Let's say the root filesystem is on an encrypted block device. Then the kernel has to complete the following tasks:

1. Collect a password from the user and/or insert a hardware token (such as a smart card or a USB security dongle).

2. Create a decryption target with the device mapper.

To achieve all of this, the kernel needs LUKS-related binaries.

For a kernel, it is not possible to incorporate all of these root filesystem possibilities; hence, developers have come up with the initramfs concept whose sole purpose is to mount the root filesystem.

The kernel can still perform all of the steps we have discussed. For example, if you build a simple command-line Linux system from LFS (`www.linuxfromscratch.org/`), you don't need initramfs to mount a root filesystem, as the kernel itself is capable enough to mount the root filesystem. But the moment you try to add a GUI into it through BLFS, you need initramfs.

So, the conclusion is that the kernel can mount the root filesystem on its own, but for that, the kernel has to keep all of the discussed binaries, supportive libraries, configuration files, etc., in the `vmlinuz` file. This will create a lot of issues.

- It will spoil the main motive of the kernel binary.

- The kernel binary will be huge in size. The bigger size of the binary will be difficult to maintain.

- The huge binary is difficult to manage, upgrade, share, and handle on servers (in terms of RPM packages).

- The approach won't be as per the KISS rule (keep it simple, stupid).

Infrastructure

To understand the initramfs structure, we need to first understand three different filesystems.

ramfs

For ease of understanding, we will compare ramfs to the kernel's caching mechanism. Linux has a unique feature called a *page cache*. Whenever you perform any I/O transactions, it caches those transactions in pages. Caching pages in memory is always good. This will save our future I/O transactions. And whenever the system encounters a low-memory situation, the kernel just discards these cached pages from memory. ramfs is just like our cache memory. But the issue with ramfs is that it does not have backing storage; hence, it cannot swap out the pages (swap is again a storage device). So, obviously, the kernel will not be able to free this memory as there is no place to save these pages. Hence, ramfs will keep growing, and you cannot really put a limit on its size. What we can do is allow only root users to write into ramfs to ease the situation.

tmpfs

tmpfs is just like ramfs but with a few additions. We can put a limit on the size of tmpfs, which we were not able to do in ramfs. Also, tmpfs pages can use swap space.

rootfs

rootfs is a tmpfs that is an instance of ramfs. The advantage of rootfs is you cannot unmount it. This is because of the same reason you can't kill the systemd process.

initramfs uses ramfs as a filesystem, and the space occupied by initramfs in memory will be released once the user's root filesystem has been mounted.

 # dmesg | grep Free

```
[    0.813330] Freeing SMP alternatives memory: 36K
[    3.675187] Freeing initrd memory: 32548K     <<<=======<<<<<<===== NOTE
[    5.762702] Freeing unused decrypted memory: 2040K
[    5.767001] Freeing unused kernel image memory: 2272K
[    5.776841] Freeing unused kernel image memory: 2016K
[    5.783116] Freeing unused kernel image memory: 1580K
```

Earlier, instead of initramfs, Linux used to use `initrd` (initial RAM disk), but `initrd` is deprecated now, and hence we will list only a few important points for comparison with initramfs.

initrd

- Being formatted/treated as a block device means `initrd` cannot scale. That means once you bring `initrd` in memory and consider it as a block device, you cannot increase or decrease its size.

- We will waste some of the memory in cache as `initrd` is considered as a block device, because the Linux kernel is designed to keep the block device contents in cache to reduce I/O transactions. In short, unnecessarily the kernel will cache the `initrd` contents, which are already in memory.

Initramfs

- In `initrd`, there will always be the overhead of the filesystem driver and its binaries like `mke2fs`. The `mke2fs` command is used to create ext2/3/4 filesystems. This means some of the RAM area will first be formatted, with the ext2/3/4 filesystem by `mke2fs`, and then `initrd` will be extracted on it, whereas initramfs is just like tmpfs, which you can grow or shrink any time on the fly.

- There is no duplication of data between block devices and cache.

- To use initramfs as the root filesystem, the kernel does not need any driver or binary like `mke2fs` as the initramfs archive will be extracted in main memory as it is.

```
# ls -lh /boot/initramfs-5.3.7-301.fc31.x86_64.img
```

```
-rw--------. 1 root root 32M Dec  9 10:19 /boot/initramfs-5.3.7-301.fc31.
x86_64.img
```

We can use the `lsinitrd` tool to see the contents of initramfs, or we can extract initramfs with the help of the `skipcpio` tool.

#lsinitrd
```
<snip>
Image: /boot/initramfs-5.3.7-301.fc31.x86_64.img: 32M
========================================================================
Early CPIO image
========================================================================
drwxr-xr-x    3 root       root              0 Jul 25  2019 .
-rw-r--r--    1 root       root              2 Jul 25  2019 early_cpio
drwxr-xr-x    3 root       root              0 Jul 25  2019 kernel
drwxr-xr-x    3 root       root              0 Jul 25  2019 kernel/x86
drwxr-xr-x    2 root       root              0 Jul 25  2019 kernel/x86/microcode
-rw-r--r--    1 root       root         100352 Jul 25  2019 kernel/x86/
microcode/GenuineIntel.bin

========================================================================
Version: dracut-049-27.git20181204.fc31.1

Arguments: -f

dracut modules:
bash
systemd
systemd-initrd
nss-softokn
i18n
network-manager
network
ifcfg
drm
plymouth
dm
kernel-modules
kernel-modules-extra
kernel-network-modules
lvm
```

```
qemu
qemu-net
resume
rootfs-block
terminfo
udev-rules
dracut-systemd
usrmount
base
fs-lib
shutdown
================================================================
drwxr-xr-x  12 root       root              0 Jul 25  2019 .
crw-r--r--   1 root       root           5,  1 Jul 25  2019 dev/console
crw-r--r--   1 root       root           1, 11 Jul 25  2019 dev/kmsg
crw-r--r--   1 root       root           1,  3 Jul 25  2019 dev/null
crw-r--r--   1 root       root           1,  8 Jul 25  2019 dev/random
crw-r--r--   1 root       root           1,  9 Jul 25  2019 dev/urandom
lrwxrwxrwx   1 root       root              7 Jul 25  2019 bin -> usr/bin
drwxr-xr-x   2 root       root              0 Jul 25  2019 dev
drwxr-xr-x  11 root       root              0 Jul 25  2019 etc
drwxr-xr-x   2 root       root              0 Jul 25  2019 etc/cmdline.d
drwxr-xr-x   2 root       root              0 Jul 25  2019 etc/conf.d
-rw-r--r--   1 root       root            124 Jul 25  2019 etc/conf.d/systemd.
                                                            conf
-rw-r--r--   1 root       root              0 Jul 25  2019 etc/fstab.empty
-rw-r--r--   1 root       root            240 Jul 25  2019 etc/group
-rw-r--r--   1 root       root             22 Jul 25  2019 etc/hostname
lrwxrwxrwx   1 root       root             25 Jul 25  2019 etc/initrd-release
                                                            -> ../usr/lib/initrd-release
-rw-r--r--   1 root       root           8581 Jul 25  2019 etc/ld.so.cache
-rw-r--r--   1 root       root             28 Jul 25  2019 etc/ld.so.conf
drwxr-xr-x   2 root       root              0 Jul 25  2019 etc/ld.so.conf.d
-rw-r--r--   1 root       root             17 Jul 25  2019 etc/ld.so.conf.d/
                                                            libiscsi-x86_64.conf
```

```
-rw-rw-r--   1 root      root              19 Jul 25   2019 etc/locale.conf
drwxr-xr-x   2 root      root               0 Jul 25   2019 etc/lvm
-rw-r--r--   1 root      root          102256 Jul 25   2019 etc/lvm/lvm.conf
-rw-r--r--   1 root      root            2301 Jul 25   2019 etc/lvm/lvmlocal.conf
-r--r--r--   1 root      root              33 Jul 25   2019 etc/machine-id
drwxr-xr-x   2 root      root               0 Jul 25   2019 etc/modprobe.d
</snip>
```

To extract the contents of initramfs, use the skipcpio binary from /usr/lib/dracut/skipcpio/. The skipcpio is provided by the dracut tool. We will cover dracut in Chapter 6.

#/usr/lib/dracut/skipcpio initramfs-5.3.7-301.fc31.x86_64.img | gunzip -c | cpio -idv

If you look at the extracted initramfs contents, you will be surprised to know that it looks just like the user's root filesystem. Please note that we have extracted initramfs into the /root/boot directory.

 # ls -lh /root/boot/
```
total 44K
lrwxrwxrwx.  1 root root   7 Mar 26 18:03 bin -> usr/bin
drwxr-xr-x.  2 root root 4.0K Mar 26 18:03 dev
drwxr-xr-x. 11 root root 4.0K Mar 26 18:03 etc
lrwxrwxrwx.  1 root root  23 Mar 26 18:03 init -> usr/lib/systemd/systemd
lrwxrwxrwx.  1 root root   7 Mar 26 18:03 lib -> usr/lib
lrwxrwxrwx.  1 root root   9 Mar 26 18:03 lib64 -> usr/lib64
drwxr-xr-x.  2 root root 4.0K Mar 26 18:03 proc
drwxr-xr-x.  2 root root 4.0K Mar 26 18:03 root
drwxr-xr-x.  2 root root 4.0K Mar 26 18:03 run
lrwxrwxrwx.  1 root root   8 Mar 26 18:03 sbin -> usr/sbin
-rwxr-xr-x.  1 root root 3.1K Mar 26 18:03 shutdown
drwxr-xr-x.  2 root root 4.0K Mar 26 18:03 sys
drwxr-xr-x.  2 root root 4.0K Mar 26 18:03 sysroot
drwxr-xr-x.  2 root root 4.0K Mar 26 18:03 tmp
drwxr-xr-x.  8 root root 4.0K Mar 26 18:03 usr
drwxr-xr-x.  3 root root 4.0K Mar 26 18:03 var
```

You will find bin, sbin, usr, etc, var, lib, and lib64-like directories that we used to see in our user's root filesystem. Along with that, you will notice the virtual filesystem directories such as dev, run, proc, sys, etc. So, initramfs is just like the user's root filesystem. Let's explore each directory for the better understanding of the initramfs implementation.

initramfs Implementation

Now we will look as the contents of initramfs and how exactly initramfs is organized. Through this section, you will realize that initramfs is nothing but a small root filesystem.

bin

Normal Binaries

We can use all the following binaries on a system that has finished its booting procedure. Since all these binaries are available inside initramfs, when the system is still booting, we will be able to use all these commands at the time of the boot.

cat, chown, cp, dmesg, echo, grep, gzip, less, ln, mkdir, mv, ps, rm, sed, sleep, umount, uname, vi, loadkeys, kbd_mode, flock, tr, true, stty, mount, sort etc.

```
[root@fedorab boot]# ls -la bin/

total 7208
drwxr-xr-x. 2 root root    4096 Jan 10 12:01 .
drwxr-xr-x. 8 root root    4096 Dec 19 14:30 ..
-rwxr-xr-x. 1 root root 1237376 Dec 19 14:30 bash
-rwxr-xr-x. 1 root root   50160 Dec 19 14:30 cat
-rwxr-xr-x. 1 root root   82688 Dec 19 14:30 chown
-rwxr-xr-x. 1 root root  177144 Dec 19 14:30 cp
-rwxr-xr-x. 1 root root   89344 Dec 19 14:30 dmesg
-rwxr-xr-x. 1 root root    2666 Dec 19 14:30 dracut-cmdline
-rwxr-xr-x. 1 root root     422 Dec 19 14:30 dracut-cmdline-ask
-rwxr-xr-x. 1 root root    1386 Dec 19 14:30 dracut-emergency
-rwxr-xr-x. 1 root root    2151 Dec 19 14:30 dracut-initqueue
```

```
-rwxr-xr-x. 1 root root      1056 Jan 10 12:01 dracut-mount
-rwxr-xr-x. 1 root root       517 Dec 19 14:30 dracut-pre-mount
-rwxr-xr-x. 1 root root       928 Dec 19 14:30 dracut-pre-pivot
-rwxr-xr-x. 1 root root       482 Dec 19 14:30 dracut-pre-trigger
-rwxr-xr-x. 1 root root      1417 Dec 19 14:30 dracut-pre-udev
-rwxr-xr-x. 1 root root     45112 Dec 19 14:30 echo
-rwxr-xr-x. 1 root root     76768 Dec 19 14:30 findmnt
-rwxr-xr-x. 1 root root     38472 Dec 19 14:30 flock
-rwxr-xr-x. 1 root root    173656 Dec 19 14:30 grep
-rwxr-xr-x. 1 root root    107768 Dec 19 14:30 gzip
-rwxr-xr-x. 1 root root     78112 Dec 19 14:30 journalctl
-rwxr-xr-x. 1 root root     17248 Dec 19 14:30 kbd_mode
-rwxr-xr-x. 1 root root    387504 Dec 19 14:30 kmod
-rwxr-xr-x. 1 root root    192512 Dec 19 14:30 less
-rwxr-xr-x. 1 root root     85992 Dec 19 14:30 ln
-rwxr-xr-x. 1 root root    222616 Dec 19 14:30 loadkeys
lrwxrwxrwx. 1 root root         4 Dec 19 14:30 loginctl -> true
-rwxr-xr-x. 1 root root    158056 Dec 19 14:30 ls
-rwxr-xr-x. 1 root root     99080 Dec 19 14:30 mkdir
-rwxr-xr-x. 1 root root     80264 Dec 19 14:30 mkfifo
-rwxr-xr-x. 1 root root     84560 Dec 19 14:30 mknod
-rwsr-xr-x. 1 root root     58984 Dec 19 14:30 mount
-rwxr-xr-x. 1 root root    169400 Dec 19 14:30 mv
-rwxr-xr-x. 1 root root     50416 Dec 19 14:30 plymouth
-rwxr-xr-x. 1 root root    143408 Dec 19 14:30 ps
-rwxr-xr-x. 1 root root     60376 Dec 19 14:30 readlink
-rwxr-xr-x. 1 root root     83856 Dec 19 14:30 rm
-rwxr-xr-x. 1 root root    127192 Dec 19 14:30 sed
-rwxr-xr-x. 1 root root     52272 Dec 19 14:30 setfont
-rwxr-xr-x. 1 root root     16568 Dec 19 14:30 setsid
lrwxrwxrwx. 1 root root         4 Dec 19 14:30 sh -> bash
-rwxr-xr-x. 1 root root     46608 Dec 19 14:30 sleep
-rwxr-xr-x. 1 root root    140672 Dec 19 14:30 sort
-rwxr-xr-x. 1 root root     96312 Dec 19 14:30 stat
```

```
-rwxr-xr-x. 1 root root    92576 Dec 19 14:30 stty
-rwxr-xr-x. 1 root root   240384 Dec 19 14:30 systemctl
-rwxr-xr-x. 1 root root    20792 Dec 19 14:30 systemd-cgls
-rwxr-xr-x. 1 root root    19704 Dec 19 14:30 systemd-escape
-rwxr-xr-x. 1 root root    62008 Dec 19 14:30 systemd-run
-rwxr-xr-x. 1 root root    95168 Dec 19 14:30 systemd-tmpfiles
-rwxr-xr-x. 1 root root   173752 Dec 19 14:30 teamd
-rwxr-xr-x. 1 root root    58400 Dec 19 14:30 tr
-rwxr-xr-x. 1 root root    45112 Dec 19 14:30 true
-rwxr-xr-x. 1 root root   442552 Dec 19 14:30 udevadm
-rwsr-xr-x. 1 root root    41912 Dec 19 14:30 umount
-rwxr-xr-x. 1 root root    45120 Dec 19 14:30 uname
-rwxr-xr-x. 1 root root  1353704 Dec 19 14:30 vi
```

Special Binaries

Special Binary	Purpose
bash	initramfs will provide us with a shell at the time of boot.
mknod	We will be able to create devices.
udevadm	We will be able to manage devices. dracut uses udev, an event-driven tool, which will launch certain programs such as lvm, mdadm, etc., when certain udev rules are matched. For example, whenever certain udev rules are matched, storage volumes and network card device files will appear under /dev.
kmod	A tool to manage the kernel modules.

Networking Binaries

There is only one network related binary available under bin and that is teamd (initramfs can handle the teaming network devices).

Hooks

We will discuss hooks in Chapters 7 and 9.

```
dracut-cmdline          dracut-cmdline-ask
dracut-emergency        dracut -initqueue
dracut-mount            dracut -pre-pivot
dracut - pre-trigger    dracut -pre-udev
```

Systemd Binaries

Binary	Purpose
systemd	This is the parent of every process that is a replacement of init. This is the first process, which runs the moment we enter initramfs.
systemctl	Systemd's service manager.
systemd-cgls	This will list the existing control groups (cgroups).
systemd-escape	This will convert the string in systemd unit format, also called escaping.
systemd-run	This can run the programs as a service but in transient scope.
systemd-tmpfiles	This creates, deletes, and cleans up volatile and temporary files and directories.
journalctl	A tool to deal with systemd journal.

Sbin

Filesystem and Storage-Related Binaries

Binary	Purpose
blkid	To read device attributes
chroot	To change the root filesystem device
e2fsck	To check ext2/3/4 filesystems
fsck, fsck.ext4	To check and repair the filesystem
swapoff	In case you want to stop the swap device

(continued)

Binary	Purpose
dmsetup	A device mapper tool for LVM management
dmeventd	A device mapper event daemon
lvm	An LVM management tool that will provide lvscan, vgscan, vgchange, pvs, etc., commands
lvm_scan	A script to find the LVM devices

Networking Binaries

Binaries	Purpose
dhclient	To get the IP from the DHCP server
losetup	To set the loop device
Netroot	A support for a root over the network
NetworkManager	A tool to manage the network devices

Special Binaries

Binaries	Purpose
depmod	To generate modules.dep (symlink of kmod)
lsmod	To list the loaded modules (symlink of kmod)
modinfo	To print the module's information (symlink of kmod)
modprobe	To load or insert the modules (symlink of kmod)
rmmod	To remove the loaded module (symlink of kmod)
init / systemd	A first process
kexec	A kexec kernel that is used by the Kdump
udevadm	Udev manager

Basic Binaries

Finally, here are the basic binaries:

Halt, poweroff, reboot

```
 [root@fedorab boot]# ls -lah sbin/
total 13M
drwxr-xr-x. 2 root root 4.0K Dec 19 14:30 .
drwxr-xr-x. 8 root root 4.0K Dec 19 14:30 ..
-rwxr-xr-x. 1 root root 126K Dec 19 14:30 blkid
-rwxr-xr-x. 1 root root  50K Dec 19 14:30 chroot
lrwxrwxrwx. 1 root root   11 Dec 19 14:30 depmod -> ../bin/kmod
-rwxr-xr-x. 1 root root 2.9M Dec 19 14:30 dhclient
-r-xr-xr-x. 1 root root  45K Dec 19 14:30 dmeventd
-r-xr-xr-x. 1 root root 159K Dec 19 14:30 dmsetup
-rwxr-xr-x. 2 root root 340K Dec 19 14:30 e2fsck
-rwxr-xr-x. 1 root root  58K Dec 19 14:30 fsck
-rwxr-xr-x. 2 root root 340K Dec 19 14:30 fsck.ext4
lrwxrwxrwx. 1 root root   16 Dec 19 14:30 halt -> ../bin/systemctl
lrwxrwxrwx. 1 root root   22 Dec 19 14:30 init -> ../lib/systemd/systemd
-rwxr-xr-x. 1 root root 1.2K Dec 19 14:30 initqueue
lrwxrwxrwx. 1 root root   11 Dec 19 14:30 insmod -> ../bin/kmod
-rwxr-xr-x. 1 root root  197 Dec 19 14:30 insmodpost.sh
-rwxr-xr-x. 1 root root 203K Dec 19 14:30 kexec
-rwxr-xr-x. 1 root root  496 Dec 19 14:30 loginit
-rwxr-xr-x. 1 root root 117K Dec 19 14:30 losetup
lrwxrwxrwx. 1 root root   11 Dec 19 14:30 lsmod -> ../bin/kmod
-r-xr-xr-x. 1 root root 2.4M Dec 19 14:30 lvm
-rwxr-xr-x. 1 root root 3.5K Dec 19 14:30 lvm_scan
lrwxrwxrwx. 1 root root   11 Dec 19 14:30 modinfo -> ../bin/kmod
lrwxrwxrwx. 1 root root   11 Dec 19 14:30 modprobe -> ../bin/kmod
-rwxr-xr-x. 1 root root 2.7K Dec 19 14:30 netroot
-rwxr-xr-x. 1 root root 5.3M Dec 19 14:30 NetworkManager
-rwxr-xr-x. 1 root root  16K Dec 19 14:30 nologin
-rwxr-xr-x. 1 root root 150K Dec 19 14:30 plymouthd
lrwxrwxrwx. 1 root root   16 Dec 19 14:30 poweroff -> ../bin/systemctl
```

```
-rwxr-xr-x. 1 root root 1.4K Dec 19 14:30 rdsosreport
lrwxrwxrwx. 1 root root   16 Dec 19 14:30 reboot -> ../bin/systemctl
lrwxrwxrwx. 1 root root   11 Dec 19 14:30 rmmod -> ../bin/kmod
-rwxr-xr-x. 1 root root  25K Dec 19 14:30 swapoff
-rwxr-xr-x. 1 root root 6.0K Dec 19 14:30 tracekomem
lrwxrwxrwx. 1 root root   14 Dec 19 14:30 udevadm -> ../bin/udevadm
```

Isn't it amazing to see that without having an actual user's root filesystem we will be able to use and manage the shell, network, modules, devices, etc.? In other words, you do not really need a user's root filesystem, unless a user wants to access their private files, that is. Just kidding.

Now a question comes to mind: where and how can we use all of these commands? These binaries or commands will be automatically used by initramfs. Or, to say it correctly, these binaries or commands will be used by the systemd of initramfs to mount the user's actual root filesystem, but if systemd fails to do so, it will provide us with a shell, and we will be able to use these commands and troubleshoot further. We will discuss this in Chapters 7, 8, and 9.

etc

The binaries from the bin and sbin directories will have their own configuration files, and they will be stored in the etc directory of initramfs.

```
[root@fedorab boot]# tree etc/
etc/
├── cmdline.d
├── conf.d
│   └── systemd.conf
├── fstab.empty
├── group
├── hostname
├── initrd-release -> ../usr/lib/initrd-release
├── ld.so.cache
├── ld.so.conf
├── ld.so.conf.d
│   └── libiscsi-x86_64.conf
```

```
├── locale.conf
├── lvm
│   ├── lvm.conf
│   └── lvmlocal.conf
├── machine-id
├── modprobe.d
│   ├── firewalld-sysctls.conf
│   ├── kvm.conf
│   ├── lockd.conf
│   ├── mlx4.conf
│   ├── nvdimm-security.conf
│   └── truescale.conf
├── mtab -> /proc/self/mounts
├── os-release -> initrd-release
├── passwd
├── plymouth
│   └── plymouthd.conf
├── sysctl.conf
├── sysctl.d
│   └── 99-sysctl.conf -> ../sysctl.conf
├── systemd
│   ├── journald.conf
│   └── system.conf
├── system-release -> ../usr/lib/fedora-release
├── udev
│   ├── rules.d
│   │   ├── 11-dm.rules
│   │   ├── 59-persistent-storage-dm.rules
│   │   ├── 59-persistent-storage.rules
│   │   ├── 61-persistent-storage.rules
│   │   └── 64-lvm.rules
│   └── udev.conf
├── vconsole.conf
└── virc

10 directories, 35 files
```

Virtual Filesystems

Virtual filesystems are the kind of filesystems whose files are not really present on disk; rather, the entire filesystem is available in memory. This has its own advantages and disadvantages; for example, you get a very high throughput, but the filesystem cannot store the data permanently. There are three virtual filesystems available inside initramfs, which are dev, proc, and sys. Here I have given a brief introduction to the filesystems, but we will talk about them in detail in the next chapters:

```
[root@fedorab boot]# ls -lah dev
total 8.0K
drwxr-xr-x.  2 root root  4.0K Dec 19 14:30 .
drwxr-xr-x. 12 root root  4.0K Dec 19 14:33 ..
crw-r--r--.  1 root root 5,  1 Dec 19 14:30 console
crw-r--r--.  1 root root 1, 11 Dec 19 14:30 kmsg
crw-r--r--.  1 root root 1,  3 Dec 19 14:30 null
crw-r--r--.  1 root root 1,  8 Dec 19 14:30 random
crw-r--r--.  1 root root 1,  9 Dec 19 14:30 urandom

[root@fedorab boot]# ls -lah proc/
total 8.0K
drwxr-xr-x.  2 root root 4.0K Dec 19 14:30 .
drwxr-xr-x. 12 root root 4.0K Dec 19 14:33 ..

[root@fedorab boot]# ls -lah sys/
total 8.0K
drwxr-xr-x.  2 root root 4.0K Dec 19 14:30 .
drwxr-xr-x. 12 root root 4.0K Dec 19 14:33 ..
```

dev

As of now, there are only five default device files, but as the system boots up, udev will fully populate this directory. The console, kmsg, null, random, and urandom devices files will be created by the kernel itself, or in other words, these device files are handcrafted by using the mknod command, but the rest of the device files will be populated by udev.

proc and sys

As soon as the kernel takes control of the booting procedure, the kernel will create and populate these directories. The `proc` filesystem will hold all the processes' related information such as `/proc/1/status`, whereas `sys` will hold the device and its driver-related information such as `/sys/fs/ext4/sda5/errors_count`.

usr, var

As we all know, these days `usr` is a separate filesystem hierarchy in the root filesystem. Our `/bin`, `/sbin`, `/lib`, and `/lib64` are nothing but symlinks to `usr/bin`, `usr/sbin`, `usr/lib`, and `usr/lib64`.

 # ls -l bin
```
lrwxrwxrwx. 1 root root 7 Dec 21 12:19 bin -> usr/bin
```

 # ls -l sbin
```
lrwxrwxrwx. 1 root root 8 Dec 21 12:19 sbin -> usr/sbin
```

 # ls -la usr
```
total 40
drwxr-xr-x.  8 root root  4096 Dec 21 12:19 .
drwxr-xr-x. 12 root root  4096 Dec 21 12:19 ..
drwxr-xr-x.  2 root root  4096 Dec 21 12:19 bin
drwxr-xr-x. 12 root root  4096 Dec 21 12:19 lib
drwxr-xr-x.  4 root root 12288 Dec 21 12:19 lib64
drwxr-xr-x.  2 root root  4096 Dec 21 12:19 libexec
drwxr-xr-x.  2 root root  4096 Dec 21 12:19 sbin
drwxr-xr-x.  5 root root  4096 Dec 21 12:19 share
```

 # ls -la var
```
total 12
drwxr-xr-x.  3 root root 4096 Dec 21 12:19 .
drwxr-xr-x. 12 root root 4096 Dec 21 12:19 ..
lrwxrwxrwx.  1 root root   11 Dec 21 12:19 lock -> ../run/lock
lrwxrwxrwx.  1 root root    6 Dec 21 12:19 run -> ../run
drwxr-xr-x.  2 root root 4096 Dec 21 12:19 tmp
```

lib, lib64

There are almost 200 libraries, and almost all of them are provided by glibc, such as libc.so.6.

The lib and lib64 directories are the symlinks of usr/lib and usr/lib64.

```
# ls -l lib
lrwxrwxrwx. 1 root root 7 Dec 21 12:19 lib -> usr/lib
```

```
# ls -l lib64
lrwxrwxrwx. 1 root root 9 Dec 21 12:19 lib64 -> usr/lib64
```

```
# ls -la lib/
total 128
drwxr-xr-x. 12 root root  4096 Dec 21 12:19 .
drwxr-xr-x.  8 root root  4096 Dec 21 12:19 ..
drwxr-xr-x.  3 root root  4096 Dec 21 12:19 dracut
-rwxr-xr-x.  1 root root 34169 Dec 21 12:19 dracut-lib.sh
-rw-r--r--.  1 root root    31 Dec 21 12:19 fedora-release
drwxr-xr-x.  6 root root  4096 Dec 21 12:19 firmware
-rwxr-xr-x.  1 root root  6400 Dec 21 12:19 fs-lib.sh
-rw-r--r--.  1 root root   238 Dec 21 12:19 initrd-release
drwxr-xr-x.  6 root root  4096 Dec 21 12:19 kbd
drwxr-xr-x.  2 root root  4096 Dec 21 12:19 modprobe.d
drwxr-xr-x.  3 root root  4096 Dec 21 12:19 modules
drwxr-xr-x.  2 root root  4096 Dec 21 12:19 modules-load.d
-rwxr-xr-x.  1 root root 25295 Dec 21 12:19 net-lib.sh
lrwxrwxrwx.  1 root root    14 Dec 21 12:19 os-release -> initrd-release
drwxr-xr-x.  2 root root  4096 Dec 21 12:19 sysctl.d
drwxr-xr-x.  5 root root  4096 Dec 21 12:19 systemd
drwxr-xr-x.  2 root root  4096 Dec 21 12:19 tmpfiles.d
drwxr-xr-x.  3 root root  4096 Dec 21 12:19 udev
```

```
# ls -la lib64/libc.so.6
lrwxrwxrwx. 1 root root 12 Dec 21 12:19 lib64/libc.so.6 -> libc-2.30.so
```

```
# dnf whatprovides lib64/libc.so.6
glibc-2.30-5.fc31.x86_64 : The GNU libc libraries
Repo        : @System
Matched from:
Filename    : /lib64/libc.so.6
```

initramfs Booting

The basic flow of booting sequence inside initramfs is easy to understand:

1) Since initramfs is a root filesystem (temporary), it will create the environment that is necessary to run the processes. initramfs will be mounted as a root filesystem (temporary /), and programs like systemd will be started from it.

2) Afterward, a new user's root filesystem from your HDD or network will be mounted on a temporary directory inside initramfs.

3) Once the user's root filesystem is mounted inside initramfs, the kernel will start the init binary, which is a symlink to systemd, the first process of the operating system.

   ```
   # ls init -l
   lrwxrwxrwx. 1 root root 23 Dec 21 12:19 init -> usr/lib/systemd/systemd
   ```

4) Once everything is good, the temporary root filesystem (initramfs root filesystem) will be unmounted, and systemd will take care of the rest of the booting sequence. Chapter 7 will cover systemd booting.

We can cross-verify whether the kernel really launches the init/systemd process as soon as it extracts initramfs. We can modify the init script for this, but the hurdle is that systemd is a binary, whereas init used to be a script. We can edit init easily since it is a script file, but we cannot edit the systemd binary. However, to have good understanding and to verify our booting sequence to see whether systemd is getting called as soon as the kernel extracts initramfs, we will use an init-based system. This would be a fair example since systemd is here to replace the init system. Also, init is still a symlink to systemd. We will use a Centos 6 system, which is an init-based Linux distribution.

First extract initramfs.

```
# zcat  initramfs-2.6.32-573.el6.x86_64.img  |  cpio -idv

[root@localhost initramfs]# ls -lah
total 120K
drwxr-xr-x. 26 root root 4.0K Mar 27 12:56 .
drwxr-xr-x.  3 root root 4.0K Mar 27 12:56 ..
drwxr-xr-x.  2 root root 4.0K Mar 27 12:56 bin
drwxr-xr-x.  2 root root 4.0K Mar 27 12:56 cmdline
drwxr-xr-x.  3 root root 4.0K Mar 27 12:56 dev
-rw-r--r--.  1 root root   19 Mar 27 12:56 dracut-004-388.el6
drwxr-xr-x.  2 root root 4.0K Mar 27 12:56 emergency
drwxr-xr-x.  8 root root 4.0K Mar 27 12:56 etc
-rwxr-xr-x.  1 root root 8.8K Mar 27 12:56 init
drwxr-xr-x.  2 root root 4.0K Mar 27 12:56 initqueue
drwxr-xr-x.  2 root root 4.0K Mar 27 12:56 initqueue-finished
drwxr-xr-x.  2 root root 4.0K Mar 27 12:56 initqueue-settled
drwxr-xr-x.  2 root root 4.0K Mar 27 12:56 initqueue-timeout
drwxr-xr-x.  7 root root 4.0K Mar 27 12:56 lib
drwxr-xr-x.  3 root root 4.0K Mar 27 12:56 lib64
drwxr-xr-x.  2 root root 4.0K Mar 27 12:56 mount
drwxr-xr-x.  2 root root 4.0K Mar 27 12:56 netroot
drwxr-xr-x.  2 root root 4.0K Mar 27 12:56 pre-mount
drwxr-xr-x.  2 root root 4.0K Mar 27 12:56 pre-pivot
drwxr-xr-x.  2 root root 4.0K Mar 27 12:56 pre-trigger
drwxr-xr-x.  2 root root 4.0K Mar 27 12:56 pre-udev
drwxr-xr-x.  2 root root 4.0K Mar 27 12:56 proc
drwxr-xr-x.  2 root root 4.0K Mar 27 12:56 sbin
drwxr-xr-x.  2 root root 4.0K Mar 27 12:56 sys
drwxr-xr-x.  2 root root 4.0K Mar 27 12:56 sysroot
drwxrwxrwt.  2 root root 4.0K Mar 27 12:56 tmp
drwxr-xr-x.  8 root root 4.0K Mar 27 12:56 usr
drwxr-xr-x.  4 root root 4.0K Mar 27 12:56 var
```

Open an init file and add the following banner in it:

#vim init
```
  "We are inside the init process. Init is replaced by Systemd"
<snip>
#!/bin/sh
#
# Licensed under the GPLv2
#
# Copyright 2008-2009, Red Hat, Inc.
# Harald Hoyer <harald@redhat.com>
# Jeremy Katz <katzj@redhat.com>
```
echo "we are inside the init process. Init is replaced by Systemd"
```
wait_for_loginit()
{
    if getarg rdinitdebug; then
        set +x
        exec 0<>/dev/console 1<>/dev/console 2<>/dev/console
        # wait for loginit
        i=0
        while [ $i -lt 10 ]; do
.
.
.

</snip>
```

Repack initramfs with the test.img name.

[root@localhost initramfs]# find . | cpio -o -c | gzip -9 > /boot/test.img
163584 blocks

 # ls -lh /boot/
```
total 66M
-rw-r--r--. 1 root root 105K Jul 23  2015 config-2.6.32-573.el6.x86_64
drwxr-xr-x. 3 root root 1.0K Aug  7  2015 efi
-rw-r--r--. 1 root root 163K Jul 20  2011 elf-memtest86+-4.10
drwxr-xr-x. 2 root root 1.0K Dec 21 16:12 grub
```

```
-rw-------. 1 root root   27M Dec 21 15:55 initramfs-2.6.32-573.el6.
x86_64.img
-rw-------. 1 root root  5.3M Dec 21 16:03 initrd-2.6.32-573.el6.
x86_64kdump.img
drwx------. 2 root root   12K Dec 21 15:54 lost+found
-rw-r--r--. 1 root root  162K Jul 20  2011 memtest86+-4.10
-rw-r--r--. 1 root root  202K Jul 23  2015 symvers-2.6.32-573.el6.x86_64.gz
-rw-r--r--. 1 root root  2.5M Jul 23  2015 System.map-2.6.32-573.el6.x86_64
-rw-r--r--. 1 root root   27M Mar 27 13:16 test.img
-rwxr-xr-x. 1 root root  4.1M Jul 23  2015 vmlinuz-2.6.32-573.el6.x86_64
```

Boot with the new `test.img` initramfs, and you will notice right after unpacking initramfs that our banner is getting printed.

```
<snip>
.
.
.
cpuidle: using governor ladder
cpuidle: using governor menu
EFI Variables Facility v0.08 2004-May-17
usbcore: registered new interface driver hiddev
usbcore: registered new interface driver usbhid
usbhid: v2.6:USB HID core driver
GRE over IPv4 demultiplexor driver
TCP cubic registered
Initializing XFRM netlink socket
NET: Registered protocol family 17
registered taskstats version 1
rtc_cmos 00:01: setting system clock to 2020-03-27 07:53:44 UTC (1585295624)
Initalizing network drop monitor service
Freeing unused kernel memory: 1296k freed
Write protecting the kernel read-only data: 10240k
Freeing unused kernel memory: 732k freed
Freeing unused kernel memory: 1576k freed
we are inside the init process. Init is replaced by Systemd
dracut: dracut-004-388.el6
```

```
dracut: rd_NO_LUKS: removing cryptoluks activation
device-mapper: uevent: version 1.0.3
device-mapper: ioctl: 4.29.0-ioctl (2014-10-28) initialised:
dm-devel@redhat.com
udev: starting version 147
dracut: Starting plymouth daemon
.
.
</snip>
```

How Does the Kernel Extract initramfs from Memory?

Let's take a minute and try to recall whatever we have learned so far.

1) The bootloader runs first.

2) The bootloader copies the kernel and initramfs in memory.

3) The kernel extracts itself.

4) The bootloader passes on the location of initramfs to the kernel.

5) The kernel extracts initramfs in memory.

6) The kernel runs systemd from the extracted initramfs.

The extraction takes place in the kernel's init/initramfs.c file. The populate_rootfs function is responsible for the extraction.

populate_rootfs function:

```
<snip>
.
.
646 static int __init populate_rootfs(void)
647 {
648         /* Load the built in initramfs */
649         char *err = unpack_to_rootfs(__initramfs_start, __initramfs_
            size);
650         if (err)
```

```
651                    panic("%s", err); /* Failed to decompress INTERNAL
                       initramfs */
652
653            if (!initrd_start || IS_ENABLED(CONFIG_INITRAMFS_FORCE))
654                    goto done;
655
656            if (IS_ENABLED(CONFIG_BLK_DEV_RAM))
657                    printk(KERN_INFO "Trying to unpack rootfs image as
                       initramfs...\n");
658            else
659                    printk(KERN_INFO "Unpacking initramfs...\n");
660
661            err = unpack_to_rootfs((char *)initrd_start, initrd_end -
               initrd_start);
662            if (err) {
663                    clean_rootfs();
664                    populate_initrd_image(err);
665            }
666
667 done:
668            /*
669             * If the initrd region is overlapped with crashkernel reserved
                region,
670             * free only memory that is not part of crashkernel region.
671             */
672            if (!do_retain_initrd && initrd_start && !kexec_free_initrd())
673                    free_initrd_mem(initrd_start, initrd_end);
674            initrd_start = 0;
675            initrd_end = 0;
676
677            flush_delayed_fput();
678            return 0;
679 }
.
.
.
</snip>
```

unpack_to_rootfs function:

<snip>

.

.

.

```
443  static char * __init unpack_to_rootfs(char *buf, unsigned long len)
444  {
445          long written;
446          decompress_fn decompress;
447          const char *compress_name;
448          static __initdata char msg_buf[64];
449
450          header_buf = kmalloc(110, GFP_KERNEL);
451          symlink_buf = kmalloc(PATH_MAX + N_ALIGN(PATH_MAX) + 1,
                 GFP_KERNEL);
452          name_buf = kmalloc(N_ALIGN(PATH_MAX), GFP_KERNEL);
453
454          if (!header_buf || !symlink_buf || !name_buf)
455                  panic("can't allocate buffers");
456
457          state = Start;
458          this_header = 0;
459          message = NULL;
460          while (!message && len) {
461                  loff_t saved_offset = this_header;
462                  if (*buf == '0' && !(this_header & 3)) {
463                          state = Start;
464                          written = write_buffer(buf, len);
465                          buf += written;
466                          len -= written;
467                          continue;
468                  }
```

```
469            if (!*buf) {
470                    buf++;
471                    len--;
472                    this_header++;
473                    continue;
474            }
475            this_header = 0;
476            decompress = decompress_method(buf, len, &compress_
               name);
477            pr_debug("Detected %s compressed data\n", compress_
               name);
478            if (decompress) {
479                    int res = decompress(buf, len, NULL, flush_
                       buffer, NULL,
480                            &my_inptr, error);
481                    if (res)
482                            error("decompressor failed");
483            } else if (compress_name) {
484                    if (!message) {
485                            snprintf(msg_buf, sizeof msg_buf,
486                                    "compression method %s not
                                    configured",
487                                    compress_name);
488                            message = msg_buf;
489                    }
490            } else
491                    error("invalid magic at start of compressed
                       archive");
492            if (state != Reset)
493                    error("junk at the end of compressed archive");
494            this_header = saved_offset + my_inptr;
495            buf += my_inptr;
496            len -= my_inptr;
497    }
```

```
498          dir_utime();
499          kfree(name_buf);
500          kfree(symlink_buf);
501          kfree(header_buf);
502          return message;
503 }
.

.

</snip>
```

Inside the populate_rootfs function there is a unpack_to_rootfs function. This is the worker function that unpacks initramfs and returns 0 for failure and 1 for success. Also note the interesting function parameters.

- **__initramfs_start:** This is the exact location/address of a loaded initramfs (initramfs will be loaded by the bootloader, so obviously the address location is also provided by the bootloader through boot_protocol).

- **__initramfs_size:** This is the size of the initramfs image.

How Does the Kernel Mount initramfs as Root?

The initramfs blob is just an (optionally compressed) cpio file. The kernel extracts it by creating a tmpfs/ramfs filesystem in memory as the root filesystem. So, there's not really a fixed location; the kernel just allocates memory for the extracted files as it goes along. We have already seen that GRUB 2/the bootloader places the kernel at a specific location that will be architecture dependent, but initramfs image extraction does not take place at any specific location.

Now before we proceed further with our booting sequence, we need to understand the dracut tool, which generates initramfs. This tool will provide us with a better understanding of initramfs and systemd.

CHAPTER 6

dracut

Put simply, dracut is a tool that creates the initramfs filesystem on Fedora-based systems. Debian- and Ubuntu-based systems use a similar tool called *update-initramfs*. If you want to generate, regenerate, or customize the existing initramfs, then you should know how to use the dracut tool. This chapter will explain how dracut works along with how to generate and customize initramfs. Also, you will learn some of the most common "can't boot" issues related to initramfs.

Getting Started

Every kernel has its own initramfs file, but you might be wondering why you never had to use the dracut command to create initramfs while installing a new kernel. Instead, you just found the respective initramfs in the /boot location. Well, when you install a new kernel, the post-scripts command of the kernel's rpm package calls dracut and makes initramfs for you. Let's see how it works on a Fedora-based system:

```
# rpm -q --scripts kernel-core-5.3.7-301.fc31.x86_64
postinstall scriptlet (using /bin/sh):

if [ `uname -i` == "x86_64" -o `uname -i` == "i386" ] &&
   [ -f /etc/sysconfig/kernel ]; then
  /bin/sed -r -i -e 's/^DEFAULTKERNEL=kernel-smp$/DEFAULTKERNEL=kernel/' /
  etc/sysconfig/kernel || exit $?
fi
preuninstall scriptlet (using /bin/sh):
/bin/kernel-install remove 5.3.7-301.fc31.x86_64 /lib/modules/5.3.7-301.
fc31.x86_64/vmlinuz || exit $?
posttrans scriptlet (using /bin/sh):
/bin/kernel-install add 5.3.7-301.fc31.x86_64 /lib/modules/5.3.7-301.fc31.
x86_64/vmlinuz || exit $?
```

© Yogesh Babar 2020
Y. Babar, *Hands-on Booting*, https://doi.org/10.1007/978-1-4842-5890-3_6

As you can see, the post-scripts command of the kernel package calls the kernel-install script. The kernel-install script executes all the scripts that are available at /usr/lib/kernel/install.d.

 # vim /bin/kernel-install

```
 94 if ! [[ $MACHINE_ID ]]; then
 95     ENTRY_DIR_ABS=$(mktemp -d /tmp/kernel-install.XXXXX) || exit 1
 96     trap "rm -rf '$ENTRY_DIR_ABS'" EXIT INT QUIT PIPE
 97 elif [[ -d /efi/loader/entries ]] || [[ -d /efi/$MACHINE_ID ]]; then
 98     ENTRY_DIR_ABS="/efi/$MACHINE_ID/$KERNEL_VERSION"
 99 elif [[ -d /boot/loader/entries ]] || [[ -d /boot/$MACHINE_ID ]]; then
100     ENTRY_DIR_ABS="/boot/$MACHINE_ID/$KERNEL_VERSION"
101 elif [[ -d /boot/efi/loader/entries ]] || [[ -d /boot/efi/$MACHINE_ID ]];
    then
102     ENTRY_DIR_ABS="/boot/efi/$MACHINE_ID/$KERNEL_VERSION"
103 elif mountpoint -q /efi; then
104     ENTRY_DIR_ABS="/efi/$MACHINE_ID/$KERNEL_VERSION"
105 elif mountpoint -q /boot/efi; then
106     ENTRY_DIR_ABS="/boot/efi/$MACHINE_ID/$KERNEL_VERSION"
107 else
108     ENTRY_DIR_ABS="/boot/$MACHINE_ID/$KERNEL_VERSION"
109 fi
110
111 export KERNEL_INSTALL_MACHINE_ID=$MACHINE_ID
112
113 ret=0
114
115 readarray -t PLUGINS <<<"$(
116     dropindirs_sort ".install" \
117         "/etc/kernel/install.d" \
118         "/usr/lib/kernel/install.d"
119 )"
```

Here you can see the scripts executed by kernel-install:

```
# ls /usr/lib/kernel/install.d/ -lh
total 36K
-rwxr-xr-x. 1 root root  744 Oct 10 18:26 00-entry-directory.install
-rwxr-xr-x. 1 root root 1.9K Oct 19 07:46 20-grubby.install
-rwxr-xr-x. 1 root root 6.6K Oct 10 13:05 20-grub.install
-rwxr-xr-x. 1 root root  829 Oct 10 18:26 50-depmod.install
-rwxr-xr-x. 1 root root 1.7K Jul 25  2019 50-dracut.install
-rwxr-xr-x. 1 root root 3.4K Jul 25  2019 51-dracut-rescue.install
-rwxr-xr-x. 1 root root 3.4K Oct 10 18:26 90-loaderentry.install
-rwxr-xr-x. 1 root root 1.1K Oct 10 13:05 99-grub-mkconfig.install
```

As you can see, this executes the 50-dracut.install script. This particular script executes the dracut command and makes initramfs for a particular kernel.

```
46          for ((i=0; i < "${#BOOT_OPTIONS[@]}"; i++)); do
47              if [[ ${BOOT_OPTIONS[$i]} == root\=PARTUUID\=* ]]; then
48                  noimageifnotneeded="yes"
49                  break
50              fi
51          done
52          dracut -f ${noimageifnotneeded:+--noimageifnotneeded}
            "$BOOT_DIR_ABS/$INITRD" "$KERNEL_VERSION"
53          ret=$?
54          ;;
55      remove)
56          rm -f -- "$BOOT_DIR_ABS/$INITRD"
57          ret=$?
58          ;;
59 esac
60 exit $ret
```

Similarly, there is the script 51-dracut-rescue.install, which will make initramfs for the rescue kernel.

```
100            if [[ ! -f "$BOOT_DIR_ABS/$INITRD" ]]; then
101                dracut -f --no-hostonly -a "rescue" "$BOOT_DIR_ABS/$INITRD"
                   "$KERNEL_VERSION"
102                ((ret+=$?))
103            fi
104
105            if [[ "${BOOT_DIR_ABS}" != "/boot" ]]; then
106                {
107                    echo "title      $PRETTY_NAME - Rescue Image"
108                    echo "version    $KERNEL_VERSION"
109                    echo "machine-id $MACHINE_ID"
110                    echo "options    ${BOOT_OPTIONS[@]} rd.auto=1"
111                    echo "linux      $BOOT_DIR/linux"
112                    echo "initrd     $BOOT_DIR/initrd"
113                } > $LOADER_ENTRY
114            else
115                cp -aT "${KERNEL_IMAGE%/*}/bls.conf" $LOADER_ENTRY
116                sed -i 's/'$KERNEL_VERSION'/0-rescue-'${MACHINE_ID}'/'
                   $LOADER_ENTRY
117            fi
```

Hence, every kernel will have its own initramfs file.

 # ls -lh /boot | grep -e vmlinuz -e initramfs

```
-rw-------. 1 root root  80M Dec  2 18:32 initramfs-0-rescue-280526b3bc5e4c49a
c83c8e5fbdfdb2e.img
-rw-------. 1 root root  28M Dec 23 06:37 initramfs-5.3.16-300.fc31.x86_64.img
-rw-------. 1 root root  30M Dec  2 18:33 initramfs-5.3.7-301.fc31.x86_64.img
-rwxr-xr-x. 1 root root 8.9M Dec  2 18:32 vmlinuz-0-rescue-280526b3bc5e4c49ac8
3c8e5fbdfdb2e
-rwxr-xr-x. 1 root root 8.9M Dec 13 23:51 vmlinuz-5.3.16-300.fc31.x86_64
-rwxr-xr-x. 1 root root 8.9M Oct 22 01:04 vmlinuz-5.3.7-301.fc31.x86_64
```

Note the size of the kernel (vmlinuz) file and its associated initramfs file size. The initramfs file is much bigger than the kernel.

Making an initramfs Image

First check which kernel has been installed on your system with this command:

 # rpm -qa | grep -i kernel-5

kernel-5.3.16-300.fc31.x86_64
kernel-5.3.7-301.fc31.x86_64

Choose the kernel version for which you want to generate a new initramfs image and pass it to dracut.

 # dracut /boot/new.img 5.3.7-301.fc31.x86_64 -v
```
<snip>
dracut: Executing: /usr/bin/dracut /boot/new.img 5.3.7-301.fc31.x86_64 -v
dracut: dracut module 'busybox' will not be installed, because command
'busybox' could not be found!
dracut: dracut module 'stratis' will not be installed, because command
'stratisd-init' could not be found!
dracut: dracut module 'biosdevname' will not be installed, because command
'biosdevname' could not be found!
dracut: dracut module 'busybox' will not be installed, because command
'busybox' could not be found!
dracut: dracut module 'stratis' will not be installed, because command
'stratisd-init' could not be found!
dracut: *** Including module: bash ***
dracut: *** Including module: systemd ***
dracut: *** Including module: systemd-initrd ***
dracut: *** Including module: nss-softokn ***
dracut: *** Including module: i18n ***
dracut: *** Including module: network-manager ***
dracut: *** Including module: network ***
dracut: *** Including module: ifcfg ***
dracut: *** Including module: drm ***
dracut: *** Including module: plymouth ***
.
.
</snip>
```

In the previous code, dracut will create an initramfs file called new.img in the current directory for the 64-bit Fedora kernel, Kernel-5.3.7-301.fc31.x86_64.

ls -lh new.img
```
-rw-------. 1 root root 28M Dec 23 08:16 new.img
```

If the kernel version is not provided, then dracut will make initramfs for the kernel through which the system has been booted. The kernel version that has been passed to dracut must match the kernel directory present in the /lib/modules/ location.

ls /lib/modules/ -l
```
total 4
drwxr-xr-x. 6 root root 4096 Dec  9 10:18 5.3.7-301.fc31.x86_64
```

ls /lib/modules/5.3.7-301.fc31.x86_64/ -l
```
total 18084
-rw-r--r--.  1 root root     249 Oct 22 01:04 bls.conf
lrwxrwxrwx.  1 root root      38 Oct 22 01:04 build -> /usr/src/
kernels/5.3.7-301.fc31.x86_64
-rw-r--r--.  1 root root  213315 Oct 22 01:03 config
drwxr-xr-x.  5 root root    4096 Oct 24 04:44 extra
drwxr-xr-x. 13 root root    4096 Oct 24 04:43 kernel
-rw-r--r--.  1 root root 1127438 Dec  9 10:18 modules.alias
-rw-r--r--.  1 root root 1101059 Dec  9 10:18 modules.alias.bin
-rw-r--r--.  1 root root    1688 Oct 22 01:04 modules.block
-rw-r--r--.  1 root root    8324 Oct 22 01:04 modules.builtin
-rw-r--r--.  1 root root   10669 Dec  9 10:18 modules.builtin.bin
-rw-r--r--.  1 root root   60853 Oct 22 01:04 modules.builtin.modinfo
-rw-r--r--.  1 root root  415475 Dec  9 10:18 modules.dep
-rw-r--r--.  1 root root  574502 Dec  9 10:18 modules.dep.bin
-rw-r--r--.  1 root root     381 Dec  9 10:18 modules.devname
-rw-r--r--.  1 root root     153 Oct 22 01:04 modules.drm
-rw-r--r--.  1 root root      59 Oct 22 01:04 modules.modesetting
-rw-r--r--.  1 root root    2697 Oct 22 01:04 modules.networking
-rw-r--r--.  1 root root  139947 Oct 22 01:04 modules.order
```

```
-rw-r--r--.  1 root root     700 Dec  9 10:18 modules.softdep
-rw-r--r--.  1 root root  468520 Dec  9 10:18 modules.symbols
-rw-r--r--.  1 root root  572778 Dec  9 10:18 modules.symbols.bin
lrwxrwxrwx.  1 root root       5 Oct 22 01:04 source -> build
-rw-------.  1 root root 4426726 Oct 22 01:03 System.map
drwxr-xr-x.  2 root root    4096 Oct 22 01:02 updates
drwxr-xr-x.  2 root root    4096 Oct 24 04:43 vdso
-rwxr-xr-x.  1 root root 9323208 Oct 22 01:04 vmlinuz
```

As we know, initramfs is a temporary root filesystem, and its main purpose is to provide an environment that will help mount the user's root filesystem. The user's root filesystem could be a local to a system, or it could be a network device, and to use that device, the kernel should have drivers (modules) for that hardware and, while booting, get these modules from initramfs.

For example, say the user's root filesystem is a locally connected hard disk, and the HDD is a SCSI device. So, initramfs has to have the SCSI drivers added in its archive.

```
# lsinitrd | grep -i scsi | awk '{ print $9 }'
etc/ld.so.conf.d/libiscsi-x86_64.conf
usr/lib/modules/5.3.7-301.fc31.x86_64/kernel/drivers/firmware/iscsi_ibft.
ko.xz
usr/lib/modules/5.3.7-301.fc31.x86_64/kernel/drivers/scsi
usr/lib/modules/5.3.7-301.fc31.x86_64/kernel/drivers/scsi/iscsi_boot_sysfs.
ko.xz
usr/lib/modules/5.3.7-301.fc31.x86_64/kernel/drivers/scsi/libiscsi.ko.xz
usr/lib/modules/5.3.7-301.fc31.x86_64/kernel/drivers/scsi/qla4xxx
usr/lib/modules/5.3.7-301.fc31.x86_64/kernel/drivers/scsi/qla4xxx/qla4xxx.
ko.xz
usr/lib/modules/5.3.7-301.fc31.x86_64/kernel/drivers/scsi/scsi_transport_
iscsi.ko.xz
usr/lib/modules/5.3.7-301.fc31.x86_64/kernel/drivers/scsi/scsi_transport_
srp.ko.xz
usr/lib/modules/5.3.7-301.fc31.x86_64/kernel/drivers/scsi/virtio_scsi.ko.xz
usr/lib/udev/scsi_id
```

On top of the SCSI device, users might have configured a RAID device. If they have, then the kernel needs to have RAID device drivers to identify and assemble the RAID device. Similarly, some of the users' HDDs could be connected through an HBA card. In such situations, the kernel needs a qlaXxxx-like modules.

```
# lsinitrd | grep -i qla
        usr/lib/modules/5.3.7-301.fc31.x86_64/kernel/drivers/scsi/qla4xxx
        usr/lib/modules/5.3.7-301.fc31.x86_64/kernel/drivers/scsi/qla4xxx/
        qla4xxx.ko.xz
```

Please note that these days '/lib' is a symlink to '/usr/lib/'.

In the case of some users, the HDD could be coming from Fiber Channel over Ethernet. Then the kernel needs FCOE modules. In a virtualized environment, the HDD could be a virtual disk exposed by a hypervisor. In that case, to mount the user's root filesystem, the virtIO module is necessary. This way, the list of hardware and their respective modules goes on.

Obviously, the kernel cannot store all of these necessary module files (.ko) in its own binary (vmlinuz). Hence, one of the main jobs of initramfs is to store all the modules that are necessary to mount the user's root filesystem. This is also one of the reasons why the initramfs file size is much bigger compared to the kernel file. But remember, initramfs is not the source of the modules. The modules will always be provided by the kernel and archived in initramfs by dracut. The kernel (vmlinuz) is the source of all the modules, but as you can rightly guess, the kernel size will be huge if the kernel stores all the modules in its vmlinuz binary. Hence, along with a kernel package, a new package named kernel-modules has been introduced, and this package provides all the modules that are present at the /lib/modules/<kernel-version-arch> location; dracut pulls only those modules (.ko files) that are necessary for mounting the user's root filesystem.

```
# rpm -qa | grep -i kernel
        Kernel-headers-5.3.6-300.fc31.x86_64
        kernel-modules-extra-5.3.7-301.fc31.x86_64
        kernel-modules-5.3.7-301.fc31.x86_64
        kernel-core-5.3.16-300.fc31.x86_64
        kernel-core-5.3.7-301.fc31.x86_64
```

kernel-5.3.16-300.fc31.x86_64
abrt-addon-kerneloops-2.12.2-1.fc31.x86_64
kernel-5.3.7-301.fc31.x86_64
libreport-plugin-kerneloops-2.10.1-2.fc31.x86_64
Kernel-modules-5.3.16-300.fc31.x86_64

```
# rpm -ql kernel-modules-5.3.7-301.fc31.x86_64 | wc -l
    1698

    # rpm -ql kernel-modules-5.3.7-301.fc31.x86_64
    <snip>
    /lib/modules/5.3.7-301.fc31.x86_64/kernel/drivers/atm/atmtcp.ko.xz
    /lib/modules/5.3.7-301.fc31.x86_64/kernel/drivers/atm/eni.ko.xz
    /lib/modules/5.3.7-301.fc31.x86_64/kernel/drivers/atm/firestream.ko.xz
    /lib/modules/5.3.7-301.fc31.x86_64/kernel/drivers/atm/he.ko.xz
    /lib/modules/5.3.7-301.fc31.x86_64/kernel/drivers/atm/nicstar.ko.xz
    /lib/modules/5.3.7-301.fc31.x86_64/kernel/drivers/atm/solos-pci.ko.xz
    /lib/modules/5.3.7-301.fc31.x86_64/kernel/drivers/atm/suni.ko.xz
    /lib/modules/5.3.7-301.fc31.x86_64/kernel/drivers/auxdisplay/cfag12864b.
    ko.xz
    /lib/modules/5.3.7-301.fc31.x86_64/kernel/drivers/auxdisplay/cfag12864bfb.
    ko.xz
    /lib/modules/5.3.7-301.fc31.x86_64/kernel/drivers/auxdisplay/charlcd.ko.xz
    /lib/modules/5.3.7-301.fc31.x86_64/kernel/drivers/auxdisplay/hd44780.ko.xz
    /lib/modules/5.3.7-301.fc31.x86_64/kernel/drivers/auxdisplay/ks0108.ko.xz
    /lib/modules/5.3.7-301.fc31.x86_64/kernel/drivers/bcma/bcma.ko.xz
    /lib/modules/5.3.7-301.fc31.x86_64/kernel/drivers/bluetooth/ath3k.ko.xz
    /lib/modules/5.3.7-301.fc31.x86_64/kernel/drivers/bluetooth/bcm203x.ko.xz
    /lib/modules/5.3.7-301.fc31.x86_64/kernel/drivers/bluetooth/bfusb.ko.xz
    /lib/modules/5.3.7-301.fc31.x86_64/kernel/drivers/bluetooth/bluecard_
    cs.ko.xz
    /lib/modules/5.3.7-301.fc31.x86_64/kernel/drivers/bluetooth/bpa10x.ko.xz
    .
    .
    </snip>
```

As you can see, the `kernel-modules` package that came with `kernel-5.3.7-301` provides almost 1,698 modules. Also, the `kernel-module` package will be a dependency of the `kernel` package; hence, whenever `kernel` is installed, `kernel-modules` will be pulled and installed by a Fedora-based operating system.

Dracut and Modules

We'll now review the dracut modules.

How Does dracut Select Modules?

To understand how dracut pulls the modules in initramfs, first we need to understand the `depmod` command. `depmod` analyzes all the kernel modules in the `/lib/modules/<kernel-version-arch>` location and makes a list of all the modules along with their dependency modules. It keeps this list in the `modules.dep` file. (Note that on Fedora-based systems, it is good to refer to the module's location as `/usr/lib/modules/<kernel_version>/*`.) Here's an example:

```
# vim /lib/modules/5.3.7-301.fc31.x86_64/modules.dep
<snip>
.

.

kernel/arch/x86/kernel/cpu/mce/mce-inject.ko.xz:
kernel/arch/x86/crypto/des3_ede-x86_64.ko.xz: kernel/crypto/des_generic.ko.xz
kernel/arch/x86/crypto/camellia-x86_64.ko.xz:
kernel/arch/x86/crypto/blowfish-x86_64.ko.xz: kernel/crypto/blowfish_
common.ko.xz
kernel/arch/x86/crypto/twofish-x86_64.ko.xz: kernel/crypto/twofish_common.
ko.xz
.

.

</snip>
```

In this code, you can see that the module named des3_ede needs the module des_generic to work properly. In another example, you can see that the blowfish modules have a blowfish_comman module as a dependency. So, dracut reads the modules. dep file and starts pulling the kernel modules in the initramfs image from the /lib/ modules/5.3.7-301.fc31.x86_64/kernel/ location.

```
# ls /lib/modules/5.3.7-301.fc31.x86_64/kernel/ -l
total 44
drwxr-xr-x.  3 root root 4096 Oct 24 04:43 arch
drwxr-xr-x.  4 root root 4096 Oct 24 04:43 crypto
drwxr-xr-x. 80 root root 4096 Oct 24 04:43 drivers
drwxr-xr-x. 43 root root 4096 Oct 24 04:43 fs
drwxr-xr-x.  4 root root 4096 Oct 24 04:43 kernel
drwxr-xr-x.  8 root root 4096 Oct 24 04:43 lib
drwxr-xr-x.  2 root root 4096 Oct 24 04:43 mm
drwxr-xr-x. 51 root root 4096 Oct 24 04:43 net
drwxr-xr-x.  3 root root 4096 Oct 24 04:43 security
drwxr-xr-x. 13 root root 4096 Oct 24 04:43 sound
drwxr-xr-x.  3 root root 4096 Oct 24 04:43 virt
```

The kernel provides thousands of modules, but every module does not need to be added in initramfs. Hence, while collecting the modules, dracut pulls very specific modules.

```
# find /lib/modules/5.3.7-301.fc31.x86_64/ -name '*.ko.xz' | wc -l
3539
```

If dracut pulled every module, then the size of initramfs would be large. Also, why pull every module when it is not necessary? So, dracut pulls only those modules that are necessary to mount the user's root filesystem on that system.

```
# lsinitrd | grep -i '.ko.xz'  | wc -l
221
```

As you can see, initramfs has only 221 modules, whereas the kernel has almost 3,539 modules in it.

If we include 3,539 modules in initramfs, it would make initramfs huge, which will eventually slow down the booting performance because the initramfs archive loading and decompression time will be high. Also, we need to understand that initramfs' main task is to mount the user's root filesystem. Therefore, it makes sense to include only those modules that are necessary to mount the root filesystem. For example, the Bluetooth-related modules are not necessary to add in initramfs since the root filesystem will never be coming from a Bluetooth-connected device. So, you will not find any Bluetooth-related modules in initramfs, even though there are a couple of `bluetooth` modules provided by the kernel (`kernel-modules`).

```
# find /lib/modules/5.3.7-301.fc31.x86_64/ -name 'bluetooth'
    /lib/modules/5.3.7-301.fc31.x86_64/kernel/net/bluetooth
    /lib/modules/5.3.7-301.fc31.x86_64/kernel/drivers/bluetooth
```

```
# lsinitrd | grep -i blue
    <no_output>
```

By default, dracut will add only host-specific modules in initramfs. It does this by inspecting the current system state and the modules that are currently used by the system. Being host-specific is the default approach of every leading Linux distribution. Fedora and Ubuntu-like systems also create a generic initramfs image, called a *rescue initramfs image*. The rescue initramfs includes all possible modules for devices on which users can possibly make a root filesystem. The idea is that the generic initramfs should be applicable to all the systems. Therefore, the rescue initramfs will always be bigger in size compared to the host-specific initramfs. dracut has a bunch of logic to decide which modules are needed to mount the root filesystem. This is what man page of dracut says, but remember in Fedora-based Linux, `--hostonly` is the default.

> *"If you want to create lighter, smaller initramfs images, you may want to specify the --hostonly or -H option. Using this option, the resulting image will contain only those dracut modules, kernel modules and filesystems, which are needed to boot this specific machine. This has the drawback, that you can't put the disk on another controller or machine, and that you can't switch to another root filesystem, without recreating the initramfs image. The usage of the --hostonly option is only for experts and you will have to keep the broken pieces. At least keep a copy of a general purpose image (and corresponding kernel) as a fallback to rescue your system."*

In the Chapter 5 we saw that there are a number of binaries, modules, and configuration files that were chosen by dracut and added in initramfs, but how does dracut choose files from the user's large root filesystem?

The files are chosen by running the scripts in the location /usr/lib/dracut/ modules.d. This is the place where all the scripts of dracut are stored. dracut runs these scripts while generating initramfs, as shown here:

```
# ls /usr/lib/dracut/modules.d/ -l
total 288
drwxr-xr-x. 2 root root 4096 Oct 24 04:43 00bash
drwxr-xr-x. 2 root root 4096 Oct 24 04:43 00systemd
drwxr-xr-x. 2 root root 4096 Oct 24 04:43 00warpclock
drwxr-xr-x. 2 root root 4096 Oct 24 04:43 01fips
drwxr-xr-x. 2 root root 4096 Oct 24 04:43 01systemd-initrd
drwxr-xr-x. 2 root root 4096 Oct 24 04:43 02systemd-networkd
drwxr-xr-x. 2 root root 4096 Oct 24 04:43 03modsign
drwxr-xr-x. 2 root root 4096 Oct 24 04:43 03rescue
drwxr-xr-x. 2 root root 4096 Oct 24 04:43 04watchdog
drwxr-xr-x. 2 root root 4096 Oct 24 04:43 05busybox
drwxr-xr-x. 2 root root 4096 Oct 24 04:42 05nss-softokn
drwxr-xr-x. 2 root root 4096 Oct 24 04:43 05rdma
drwxr-xr-x. 2 root root 4096 Oct 24 04:43 10i18n
drwxr-xr-x. 2 root root 4096 Oct 24 04:43 30convertfs
drwxr-xr-x. 2 root root 4096 Oct 24 04:43 35network-legacy
drwxr-xr-x. 2 root root 4096 Oct 24 04:43 35network-manager
drwxr-xr-x. 2 root root 4096 Oct 24 04:43 40network
drwxr-xr-x. 2 root root 4096 Oct 24 04:43 45ifcfg
drwxr-xr-x. 2 root root 4096 Oct 24 04:43 45url-lib
drwxr-xr-x. 2 root root 4096 Oct 24 04:43 50drm
drwxr-xr-x. 2 root root 4096 Oct 24 04:43 50plymouth
drwxr-xr-x. 2 root root 4096 Oct 24 04:43 80lvmmerge
drwxr-xr-x. 2 root root 4096 Oct 24 04:42 90bcache
drwxr-xr-x. 2 root root 4096 Oct 24 04:43 90btrfs
drwxr-xr-x. 2 root root 4096 Oct 24 04:43 90crypt
drwxr-xr-x. 2 root root 4096 Oct 24 04:43 90dm
drwxr-xr-x. 2 root root 4096 Oct 24 04:43 90dmraid
drwxr-xr-x. 2 root root 4096 Oct 24 04:44 90dmsquash-live
drwxr-xr-x. 2 root root 4096 Oct 24 04:44 90dmsquash-live-ntfs
drwxr-xr-x. 2 root root 4096 Oct 24 04:43 90kernel-modules
```

```
drwxr-xr-x. 2 root root 4096 Oct 24 04:43 90kernel-modules-extra
drwxr-xr-x. 2 root root 4096 Oct 24 04:43 90kernel-network-modules
drwxr-xr-x. 2 root root 4096 Oct 24 04:44 90livenet
drwxr-xr-x. 2 root root 4096 Oct 24 04:43 90lvm
drwxr-xr-x. 2 root root 4096 Oct 24 04:43 90mdraid
drwxr-xr-x. 2 root root 4096 Oct 24 04:43 90multipath
drwxr-xr-x. 2 root root 4096 Oct 24 04:43 90qemu
drwxr-xr-x. 2 root root 4096 Oct 24 04:43 90qemu-net
drwxr-xr-x. 2 root root 4096 Oct 24 04:43 90stratis
drwxr-xr-x. 2 root root 4096 Oct 24 04:43 91crypt-gpg
drwxr-xr-x. 2 root root 4096 Oct 24 04:43 91crypt-loop
drwxr-xr-x. 2 root root 4096 Oct 24 04:43 95cifs
drwxr-xr-x. 2 root root 4096 Oct 24 04:43 95debug
drwxr-xr-x. 2 root root 4096 Oct 24 04:43 95fcoe
drwxr-xr-x. 2 root root 4096 Oct 24 04:43 95fcoe-uefi
drwxr-xr-x. 2 root root 4096 Oct 24 04:43 95fstab-sys
drwxr-xr-x. 2 root root 4096 Oct 24 04:43 95iscsi
drwxr-xr-x. 2 root root 4096 Oct 24 04:43 95lunmask
drwxr-xr-x. 2 root root 4096 Oct 24 04:43 95nbd
drwxr-xr-x. 2 root root 4096 Oct 24 04:43 95nfs
drwxr-xr-x. 2 root root 4096 Oct 24 04:43 95resume
drwxr-xr-x. 2 root root 4096 Oct 24 04:43 95rootfs-block
drwxr-xr-x. 2 root root 4096 Oct 24 04:43 95ssh-client
drwxr-xr-x. 2 root root 4096 Oct 24 04:43 95terminfo
drwxr-xr-x. 2 root root 4096 Oct 24 04:43 95udev-rules
drwxr-xr-x. 2 root root 4096 Oct 24 04:43 95virtfs
drwxr-xr-x. 2 root root 4096 Oct 24 04:43 97biosdevname
drwxr-xr-x. 2 root root 4096 Jan  6 12:42 98dracut-systemd
drwxr-xr-x. 2 root root 4096 Oct 24 04:43 98ecryptfs
drwxr-xr-x. 2 root root 4096 Oct 24 04:44 98ostree
drwxr-xr-x. 2 root root 4096 Oct 24 04:43 98pollcdrom
drwxr-xr-x. 2 root root 4096 Oct 24 04:43 98selinux
drwxr-xr-x. 2 root root 4096 Oct 24 04:43 98syslog
drwxr-xr-x. 2 root root 4096 Oct 24 04:43 98usrmount
drwxr-xr-x. 2 root root 4096 Oct 24 04:43 99base
```

```
drwxr-xr-x. 2 root root 4096 Oct 24 04:43 99earlykdump
drwxr-xr-x. 2 root root 4096 Oct 24 04:43 99fs-lib
drwxr-xr-x. 2 root root 4096 Oct 24 04:44 99img-lib
drwxr-xr-x. 2 root root 4096 Oct 24 04:43 99kdumpbase
drwxr-xr-x. 2 root root 4096 Oct 24 04:43 99shutdown
drwxr-xr-x. 2 root root 4096 Oct 24 04:43 99squash
drwxr-xr-x. 2 root root 4096 Oct 24 04:43 99uefi-lib
```

The same output can be viewed by using #dracut --list-modules.

Whenever we try to make an initramfs filesystem, dracut starts executing the module-setup.sh script files in each directory in /usr/lib/dracut/modules.d/.

find /usr/lib/dracut/modules.d/ -name 'module-setup.sh'

```
/usr/lib/dracut/modules.d/95iscsi/module-setup.sh
/usr/lib/dracut/modules.d/98ecryptfs/module-setup.sh
/usr/lib/dracut/modules.d/30convertfs/module-setup.sh
/usr/lib/dracut/modules.d/90crypt/module-setup.sh
/usr/lib/dracut/modules.d/10i18n/module-setup.sh
/usr/lib/dracut/modules.d/99earlykdump/module-setup.sh
/usr/lib/dracut/modules.d/95nbd/module-setup.sh
.
.
.
/usr/lib/dracut/modules.d/04watchdog/module-setup.sh
/usr/lib/dracut/modules.d/90lvm/module-setup.sh
/usr/lib/dracut/modules.d/35network-legacy/module-setup.sh
/usr/lib/dracut/modules.d/01systemd-initrd/module-setup.sh
/usr/lib/dracut/modules.d/99squash/module-setup.sh
/usr/lib/dracut/modules.d/05busybox/module-setup.sh
/usr/lib/dracut/modules.d/50drm/module-setup.sh
```

This module-setup.sh script will pick the module, binary, and configuration files that are specific to that host. For example, the first module-setup.sh script, which will run from the 00bash directory, will include the bash binary in initramfs.

vim /usr/lib/dracut/modules.d/00bash/module-setup.sh

```
 1 #!/usr/bin/bash
 2
 3 # called by dracut
 4 check() {
 5     require_binaries /bin/bash
 6 }
 7
 8 # called by dracut
 9 depends() {
10     return 0
11 }
12
13 # called by dracut
14 install() {
15     # If another shell is already installed, do not use bash
16     [[ -x $initdir/bin/sh ]] && return
17
18     # Prefer bash as /bin/sh if it is available.
19     inst /bin/bash && ln -sf bash "${initdir}/bin/sh"
20 }
21
```

As you can see, the script file is adding the /bin/bash binary in initramfs. Let's look at another example, this one of plymouth.

vim /usr/lib/dracut/modules.d/50plymouth/module-setup.sh

```
 1 #!/usr/bin/bash
 2
 3 pkglib_dir() {
 4     local _dirs="/usr/lib/plymouth /usr/libexec/plymouth/"
 5     if type -P dpkg-architecture &>/dev/null; then
 6         _dirs+=" /usr/lib/$(dpkg-architecture -qDEB_HOST_MULTIARCH)/
         plymouth"
 7     fi
 8     for _dir in $_dirs; do
```

```
9          if [ -x $_dir/plymouth-populate-initrd ]; then
10             echo $_dir
11             return
12         fi
13     done
14 }
15
16 # called by dracut
17 check() {
18     [[ "$mount_needs" ]] && return 1
19     [ -z $(pkglib_dir) ] && return 1
20
21     require_binaries plymouthd plymouth plymouth-set-default-theme
22 }
23
24 # called by dracut
25 depends() {
26     echo drm
27 }
28
29 # called by dracut
30 install() {
31     PKGLIBDIR=$(pkglib_dir)
32     if grep -q nash ${PKGLIBDIR}/plymouth-populate-initrd \
33         || [ ! -x ${PKGLIBDIR}/plymouth-populate-initrd ]; then
34         . "$moddir"/plymouth-populate-initrd.sh
35     else
36         PLYMOUTH_POPULATE_SOURCE_FUNCTIONS="$dracutfunctions" \
37             ${PKGLIBDIR}/plymouth-populate-initrd -t "$initdir"
38     fi
39
40     inst_hook emergency 50 "$moddir"/plymouth-emergency.sh
41
42     inst_multiple readlink
43
```

```
44      if ! dracut_module_included "systemd"; then
45          inst_hook pre-trigger 10 "$moddir"/plymouth-pretrigger.sh
46          inst_hook pre-pivot 90 "$moddir"/plymouth-newroot.sh
47      fi
48  }
```

Simply grepping require_binaries will show all the binaries that dracut will add in the generic initramfs.

grep -ir "require_binaries" /usr/lib/dracut/modules.d/

/usr/lib/dracut/modules.d/90mdraid/module-setup.sh: require_binaries mdadm expr || return 1

/usr/lib/dracut/modules.d/80lvmmerge/module-setup.sh: require_binaries lvm dd swapoff || return 1

/usr/lib/dracut/modules.d/95cifs/module-setup.sh: require_binaries mount.cifs || return 1

/usr/lib/dracut/modules.d/91crypt-gpg/module-setup.sh: require_binaries gpg || return 1

/usr/lib/dracut/modules.d/91crypt-gpg/module-setup.sh: require_ binaries gpg-agent &&

/usr/lib/dracut/modules.d/91crypt-gpg/module-setup.sh: require_ binaries gpg-connect-agent &&

/usr/lib/dracut/modules.d/91crypt-gpg/module-setup.sh: require_ binaries /usr/libexec/scdaemon &&

/usr/lib/dracut/modules.d/45url-lib/module-setup.sh: require_binaries curl || return 1

/usr/lib/dracut/modules.d/90stratis/module-setup.sh: require_binaries stratisd-init thin_check thin_repair mkfs.xfs xfs_admin xfs_growfs || return 1

/usr/lib/dracut/modules.d/90multipath/module-setup.sh: require_binaries multipath || return 1

/usr/lib/dracut/modules.d/95iscsi/module-setup.sh: require_binaries iscsi-iname iscsiadm iscsid || return 1

/usr/lib/dracut/modules.d/95ssh-client/module-setup.sh: require_binaries ssh scp || return 1

/usr/lib/dracut/modules.d/35network-manager/module-setup.sh: require_
binaries sed grep || return 1
/usr/lib/dracut/modules.d/90dmsquash-live-ntfs/module-setup.sh: require_
binaries ntfs-3g || return 1
/usr/lib/dracut/modules.d/91crypt-loop/module-setup.sh: require_binaries
losetup || return 1
/usr/lib/dracut/modules.d/05busybox/module-setup.sh: require_binaries
busybox || return 1
/usr/lib/dracut/modules.d/99img-lib/module-setup.sh: require_binaries
tar gzip dd bash || return 1
/usr/lib/dracut/modules.d/90dm/module-setup.sh: require_binaries dmsetup
|| return 1
/usr/lib/dracut/modules.d/03modsign/module-setup.sh: require_binaries
keyctl || return 1
/usr/lib/dracut/modules.d/97biosdevname/module-setup.sh: require_
binaries biosdevname || return 1
/usr/lib/dracut/modules.d/95nfs/module-setup.sh: require_binaries rpc.
statd mount.nfs mount.nfs4 umount || return 1
/usr/lib/dracut/modules.d/90dmraid/module-setup.sh: require_binaries
dmraid || return 1
/usr/lib/dracut/modules.d/95fcoe/module-setup.sh: require_binaries
dcbtool fipvlan lldpad ip readlink fcoemon fcoeadm || return 1
/usr/lib/dracut/modules.d/00warpclock/module-setup.sh: require_binaries
/sbin/hwclock || return 1
/usr/lib/dracut/modules.d/35network-legacy/module-setup.sh: require_
binaries ip dhclient sed awk grep || return 1
/usr/lib/dracut/modules.d/00bash/module-setup.sh: require_binaries /bin/
bash
/usr/lib/dracut/modules.d/95nbd/module-setup.sh: require_binaries nbd-
client || return 1
/usr/lib/dracut/modules.d/90btrfs/module-setup.sh: require_binaries
btrfs || return 1
/usr/lib/dracut/modules.d/00systemd/module-setup.sh: if require_binaries
$systemdutildir/systemd; then

/usr/lib/dracut/modules.d/10i18n/module-setup.sh: require_binaries
setfont loadkeys kbd_mode || return 1
/usr/lib/dracut/modules.d/90lvm/module-setup.sh: require_binaries lvm ||
return 1
/usr/lib/dracut/modules.d/50plymouth/module-setup.sh: require_binaries
plymouthd plymouth plymouth-set-default-theme
/usr/lib/dracut/modules.d/95fcoe-uefi/module-setup.sh: require_binaries
dcbtool fipvlan lldpad ip readlink || return 1

Once again, dracut does not include every module from /usr/lib/dracut/
modules.d. It includes only host-specific modules. In the following section, you will learn
how to add or omit specific modules from initramfs.

Customizing initramfs

Dracut also has its own modules. The kernel modules and dracut modules are different.
Dracut collects the host-specific binaries, the associated libraries, the configuration files,
and the hardware device modules and groups them under the name *dracut modules*.
The kernel modules consist of the .ko files of the hardware device. You can see the
dracut modules list either from /usr/lib/dracut/modules.d/ or from the dracut
--list-modules command.

dracut --list-modules | xargs -n6
bash systemd warpclock fips systemd-initrd systemd-networkd
modsign rescue watchdog busybox nss-softokn rdma
i18n convertfs network-legacy network-manager network ifcfg
url-lib drm plymouth lvmmerge bcache btrfs
crypt dm dmraid dmsquash-live dmsquash-live-ntfs kernel-modules
kernel-modules-extra kernel-network-modules livenet lvm mdraid multipath
qemu qemu-net stratis crypt-gpg crypt-loop cifs
debug fcoe fcoe-uefi fstab-sys iscsi lunmask
nbd nfs resume rootfs-block ssh-client terminfo
udev-rules virtfs biosdevname dracut-systemd ecryptfs ostree
pollcdrom selinux syslog usrmount base earlykdump
fs-lib img-lib kdumpbase shutdown squash uefi-lib

If you want to add or omit specific dracut modules (not the hardware device module) from initramfs, then `dracut.conf` plays a vital role here. Note that `dracut.conf` is a configuration file of dracut, not of initramfs; hence, it will not be available inside initramfs.

```
# lsinitrd | grep -i 'dracut.conf'
   <no output>
```

dracut will refer to the `dracut.conf file` while generating initramfs. By default it will be an empty file.

```
# cat /etc/dracut.conf
   # PUT YOUR CONFIG IN separate files
   # in /etc/dracut.conf.d named "<name>.conf"
   # SEE man dracut.conf(5) for options
```

There are various options provided by `dracut.conf` that you can use to add or omit the module.

Suppose you want to omit the `plymouth`-related files (binaries, configuration files, modules, etc.) from initramfs; then you can either add a `omit_dracutmodules+=plymouth` in `dracut.conf` or use the `omit (-o)` switch of the `dracut` binary. Here's an example:

```
# lsinitrd | grep -i plymouth | wc -l
   118
```

There are almost 118 `plymouth`-related files present in the currently booted kernel. Let's try to omit `plymouth`-related files now.

```
# dracut -o plymouth /root/new.img
```

```
# lsinitrd /root/new.img | grep -i plymouth | wc -l
   4
```

As you can clearly see, all `plymouth`-related dracut modules have been eliminated from our newly built initramfs. Therefore, the `plymouth`-related binaries, configuration files, libraries, and hardware device modules (if available) will not be captured by dracut in initramfs. The same result can be achieved by adding `omit_dracutmodules+=` `plymouth` in `dracut.conf`.

```
# cat /etc/dracut.conf | grep -v '#'
    omit_dracutmodules+=plymouth
```

```
# dracut /root/new.img --force
```

```
# lsinitrd /root/new.img | grep -i plymouth
```

```
-rw-r--r--    1 root      root             454 Jul 25   2019 usr/lib/systemd/
system/systemd-ask-password-plymouth.path
-rw-r--r--    1 root      root             435 Jul 25   2019 usr/lib/systemd/
system/systemd-ask-password-plymouth.service
drwxr-xr-x    2 root      root               0 Jul 25   2019 usr/lib/systemd/
system/systemd-ask-password-plymouth.service.wants
lrwxrwxrwx    1 root      root              33 Jul 25   2019 usr/lib/systemd/
system/systemd-ask-password-plymouth.service.wants/systemd-vconsole-setup.
service -> ../systemd-vconsole-setup.service
```

The following comes from the man page:

Omitting dracut Modules

Sometimes you don't want a dracut module to be included for reasons of speed, size or functionality. To do this, either specify the omit_dracutmodules variable in the dracut.conf or /etc/dracut.conf.d/myconf.conf configuration file (see dracut.conf(5)), or use the -o or --omit option on the command line: # dracut -o "multipath lvm" no-multipath-lvm.img

Like when we omitted the dracut module, we can add any module that is available in /usr/lib/dracut/modules.d. We can use the --add switch of dracut or can use add_dracutmodules+= in dracut.conf. For example, you can see that we do not have NFS modules/files/binaries added in our new.img initramfs because my test system is not booting from NFS and not using any NFS mount point in it. Obviously, dracut will skip the nfs module from /usr/lib/dracut/modules.d. So, let's add it in our initramfs.

```
#lsinitrd | grep -i nfs
<no_output>
```

```
# cat /etc/dracut.conf
    # PUT YOUR CONFIG IN separate files
    # in /etc/dracut.conf.d named "<name>.conf"
    # SEE man dracut.conf(5) for options
```

```
    #omit_dracutmodules+=plymouth
    add_dracutmodules+=nfs
# dracut /root/new.img --force
# lsinitrd /root/new.img | grep -i nfs | wc -l
    33
```

We can also achieve this by using the dracut command with the --add switch.

```
# lsinitrd /root/new.img | grep -i nfs
# dracut --add nfs /root/new.img --force
# lsinitrd /root/new.img | grep -i nfs
Arguments: --add 'nfs' --force
nfs
-rw-r--r--    1 root      root              15 Jul 25  2019 etc/modprobe.d/nfs.conf
drwxr-xr-x    2 root      root               0 Jul 25  2019 usr/lib64/libnfsidmap
-rwxr-xr-x    1 root      root           50416 Jul 25  2019 usr/lib64/
libnfsidmap/nsswitch.so
-rwxr-xr-x    1 root      root           54584 Jul 25  2019 usr/lib64/
libnfsidmap.so.1.0.0
lrwxrwxrwx    1 root      root              20 Jul 25  2019 usr/lib64/
libnfsidmap.so.1 -> libnfsidmap.so.1.0.0
-rwxr-xr-x    1 root      root           42744 Jul 25  2019 usr/lib64/
libnfsidmap/sss.so
-rwxr-xr-x    1 root      root           46088 Jul 25  2019 usr/lib64/
libnfsidmap/static.so
-rwxr-xr-x    1 root      root           62600 Jul 25  2019 usr/lib64/
libnfsidmap/umich_ldap.so
-rwxr-xr-x    1 root      root             849 Oct  8  2018 usr/lib/dracut/hooks/
cleanup/99-nfsroot-cleanup.sh
-rwxr-xr-x    1 root      root            3337 Oct  8  2018 usr/lib/dracut/hooks/
cmdline/90-parse-nfsroot.sh
-rwxr-xr-x    1 root      root             874 Oct  8  2018 usr/lib/dracut/hooks/
pre-udev/99-nfs-start-rpc.sh
drwxr-xr-x    5 root      root               0 Jul 25  2019 usr/lib/
modules/5.3.7-301.fc31.x86_64/kernel/fs/nfs
```

```
drwxr-xr-x   2 root     root            0 Jul 25  2019 usr/lib/
modules/5.3.7-301.fc31.x86_64/kernel/fs/nfs/blocklayout
-rw-r--r--   1 root     root        16488 Jul 25  2019 usr/lib/modules/
5.3.7-301.fc31.x86_64/kernel/fs/nfs/blocklayout/blocklayoutdriver.ko.xz
drwxr-xr-x   2 root     root            0 Jul 25  2019 usr/lib/
modules/5.3.7-301.fc31.x86_64/kernel/fs/nfs_common
-rw-r--r--   1 root     root         2584 Jul 25  2019 usr/lib/
modules/5.3.7-301.fc31.x86_64/kernel/fs/nfs_common/grace.ko.xz
-rw-r--r--   1 root     root         3160 Jul 25  2019 usr/lib/
modules/5.3.7-301.fc31.x86_64/kernel/fs/nfs_common/nfs_acl.ko.xz
drwxr-xr-x   2 root     root            0 Jul 25  2019 usr/lib/
modules/5.3.7-301.fc31.x86_64/kernel/fs/nfs/filelayout
-rw-r--r--   1 root     root        11220 Jul 25  2019 usr/lib/modules/
5.3.7-301.fc31.x86_64/kernel/fs/nfs/filelayout/nfs_layout_nfsv41_files.ko.xz
drwxr-xr-x   2 root     root            0 Jul 25  2019 usr/lib/
modules/5.3.7-301.fc31.x86_64/kernel/fs/nfs/flexfilelayout
-rw-r--r--   1 root     root        20872 Jul 25  2019 usr/lib/
modules/5.3.7-301.fc31.x86_64/kernel/fs/nfs/flexfilelayout/nfs_layout_
flexfiles.ko.xz
-rw-r--r--   1 root     root       109684 Jul 25  2019 usr/lib/
modules/5.3.7-301.fc31.x86_64/kernel/fs/nfs/nfs.ko.xz
-rw-r--r--   1 root     root        18028 Jul 25  2019 usr/lib/
modules/5.3.7-301.fc31.x86_64/kernel/fs/nfs/nfsv3.ko.xz
-rw-r--r--   1 root     root       182756 Jul 25  2019 usr/lib/
modules/5.3.7-301.fc31.x86_64/kernel/fs/nfs/nfsv4.ko.xz
-rwxr-xr-x   1 root     root         4648 Oct  8  2018 usr/lib/nfs-lib.sh
-rwsr-xr-x   1 root     root       187680 Jul 25  2019 usr/sbin/mount.nfs
lrwxrwxrwx   1 root     root            9 Jul 25  2019 usr/sbin/mount.nfs4
-> mount.nfs
-rwxr-xr-x   1 root     root          719 Oct  8  2018 usr/sbin/nfsroot
drwxr-xr-x   4 root     root            0 Jul 25  2019 var/lib/nfs
drwxr-xr-x   2 root     root            0 Jul 25  2019 var/lib/nfs/rpc_pipefs
drwxr-xr-x   3 root     root            0 Jul 25  2019 var/lib/nfs/statd
drwxr-xr-x   2 root     root            0 Jul 25  2019 var/lib/nfs/statd/sm
```

Like we added the extra nfs dracut module in our initramfs, the same way we can have only the nfs module in our initramfs with the help of adding dracutmodules+= in dracut.conf. This means the resultant initramfs will have only the nfs module in it. The rest of the modules from /usr/lib/dracut/modules.d/ will be discarded.

cat /etc/dracut.conf

```
#omit_dracutmodules+=plymouth
#add_dracutmodules+=nfs
dracutmodules+=nfs
```

dracut /root/new.img —force

lsinitrd /root/new.img

```
Image: /root/new.img: 20M
=========================================================================
Early CPIO image
=========================================================================
drwxr-xr-x  3 root      root           0 Jul 25  2019 .
-rw-r—r--  1 root      root           2 Jul 25  2019 early_cpio
drwxr-xr-x  3 root      root           0 Jul 25  2019 kernel
drwxr-xr-x  3 root      root           0 Jul 25  2019 kernel/x86
drwxr-xr-x  2 root      root           0 Jul 25  2019 kernel/x86/microcode
-rw-r—r--  1 root      root      100352 Jul 25  2019 kernel/x86/microcode/
GenuineIntel.bin
=========================================================================
Version:
Arguments: --force
dracut modules:
nss-softokn
network-manager
network
kernel-network-modules
nfs
=========================================================================
```

As you can see, only the nfs module has been added along with its dependencies like the network dracut module. Also, notice the size difference between both versions of initramfs.

```
# ls -lh initramfs-5.3.16-300.fc31.x86_64.img
    -rw-------. 1 root root 28M Dec 23 06:37 initramfs-5.3.16-300.fc31.
    x86_64.img
```

```
# ls -lh /root/new.img
    -rw-------. 1 root root 20M Dec 24 11:05 /root/new.img
```

The same can be achieved by using the -m or --modules switch of dracut.

```
# dracut -m nfs /root/new.img --force
```

If you want to add only the hardware device module, then please note that *hardware device module* means the *.ko files provided by the kernel-modules package at /lib/modules/<kernel-version>/drivers/<module-name>. Then the --add switch of dracut or add_dracutmodules+= will not help because these two switches add the dracut modules and not the kernel module (.ko) file. So, to add the kernel module, we need to use either a --add-drivers switch of dracut or drivers+= or add_drivers+= in dracut.conf. Here's an example:

```
# lsinitrd /root/new.img | grep -i ath3k
```

The Bluetooth-related module named ath3k is not present in our initramfs, but it is one of the modules provided by the kernel.

```
#ls -lh /lib/modules/5.3.16-300.fc31.x86_64/kernel/drivers/bluetooth/ath3k.
ko.xz
```

Let's add it, as shown here:

```
# dracut --add-drivers ath3k /root/new.img --force
```

Now it has been added, as shown here:

```
# lsinitrd /root/new.img | grep -i ath3k
Arguments: --add-drivers 'ath3k' --force
-rw-r--r-- 1 root  root 246804 Jul 25 03:54 usr/lib/firmware/ath3k-1.fw
-rw-r--r-- 1 root  root   5652 Jul 25 03:54 usr/lib/modules/5.3.7-301.fc31.
x86_64/kernel/drivers/bluetooth/ath3k.ko.xz
```

As you can see, the ath3k.ko module has been added in initramfs.

dracut Module or Kernel Module?

Let's examine when to add a dracut module and when to add a kernel module. Here's a scenario: your host root filesystem is on a normal SCSI device. So, obviously, your initramfs has neither a `multipath.ko` kernel module nor a `multipath.conf`-like configuration file for it.

1) All of sudden you decide to shift your root filesystem from the normal local disk to a SAN (I would never recommend such change on a production system), and the SAN is connected through a multipath device.

2) To get the entire environment of the multipath device, you need to add the multipath dracut module here so that the entire environment of multipath will be pulled into initramfs.

3) After a few days, you add a new NIC card on the same system, and the NIC card vendor has provided drivers for it. A driver is nothing but a `.ko` file (kernel object). To add this module in your initramfs, you have to choose to add the `kernel module` option. This will add the driver of only the NIC card, not the entire environment.

But what if you want to add some specific file to the initramfs, which is neither a kernel module nor a dracut module? dracut provides the `install_items+=` and `--include` variables of `dracut.conf` through which we can add specific files. The files could be anything from a normal text to a binary file, etc.

#lsinitrd /root/new.img | grep -i date

    <no_output>

The date binary is not by default present in initramfs. But to add a binary, we can use an `install_itsems+` switch.

 # cat /etc/dracut.conf

    # PUT YOUR CONFIG IN separate files
    # in /etc/dracut.conf.d named "<name>.conf"
    # SEE man dracut.conf(5) for options

```
    #omit_dracutmodules+=plymouth
    #add_dracutmodules+=nfs
    #dracutmodules+=nfs
    install_items+=date
```

dracut /root/new.img --force

lsinitrd /root/new.img | grep -i date
```
-rwxr-xr-x   1 root      root        122456 Jul 25 02:36 usr/bin/date
```

As you can see, the date binary has been added, but the most important thing is it does not only add the binary; rather, it also adds the library that is necessary to run the date command. The same can be achieved with the --install switch of the dracut command. But this has a limitation; it cannot add the user-made custom binaries. To do that, we need to use the --include switch of dracut. With --include, you can include the normal files, directories, or even a binary in initramfs. In the case of the binary, if your binary needs a supporting library, then you have to specify that library name with its absolute path.

"Can't Boot" Issue 4 (initramfs)

Issue: A Linux production system has been rebooted after four months for regular maintenance, and it has stopped booting. It keeps throwing this error message on the screen:

```
<snip>
.
dracut-initqueue[444]: warning: dracut-initqueue timeout - starting timeout
scripts
dracut-initqueue[444]: warning: dracut-initqueue timeout - starting timeout
scripts
dracut-initqueue[444]: warning: dracut-initqueue timeout - starting timeout
scripts
dracut-initqueue[444]: warning: dracut-initqueue timeout - starting timeout
scripts
.
</snip>
```

Resolution: Here are the steps to resolve the issue:

1. The error message starts by saying it is not able to reach the swap device, and then the process times out.

   ```
   [TIME] Timed out waiting for device /dev/mapper/fedora_localhost--live-swap
   ```

   This is a crucial piece of information since this tells you that something is wrong with this system's filesystems.

2. The swap device is based on an HDD, and the swap filesystem has been created on it. Now the swap device itself is missing. So, either the underlying disk itself is not accessible or the swap filesystem is corrupted. With this understanding, we can now concentrate on the storage side only. The isolation of the issue is important since the "can't boot" issue has thousands of situations that could cause the system to stop booting.

3. Either we will boot with rescue mode or we can use a live image of the same distribution and version. This is a Fedora 31 system, and as shown in Figure 6-1, I will use the rescue option from GRUB.

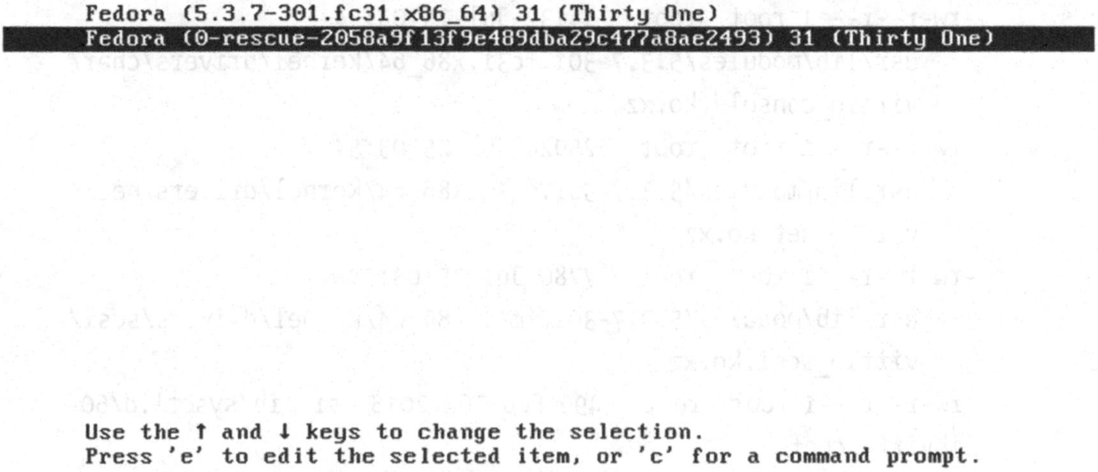

```
Fedora (5.3.7-301.fc31.x86_64) 31 (Thirty One)
Fedora (0-rescue-2058a9f13f9e489dba29c477a8ae2493) 31 (Thirty One)




Use the ↑ and ↓ keys to change the selection.
Press 'e' to edit the selected item, or 'c' for a command prompt.
```

Figure 6-1. *The GRUB splash screen*

4. Once we boot into rescue mode, we will mount the user's root filesystem and chroot into it. Now why is rescue mode able to boot when the normal kernel is not able to boot on the same system? This is a valid question, and the answer will be covered in Chapter 10.

5. Since we are able to mount the root filesystem in a rescue kernel but not able to mount the root filesystem with the normal kernel, that means something is wrong with the initramfs image. Maybe some module that is necessary to handle the HDD is missing. Let's verify this theory.

6. This is a virtualized system, which means it has a virtual disk. This can be seen from the /dev directory.

#ls /dev/vd*
vda vda1 vda2

7. To handle the virtualized disks, we need to have a virtio_blk module present in initramfs.

#lsinitrd /boot/new.img | grep -i virt
Arguments: --omit-drivers virtio_blk
-rw-r--r-- 1 root   root   14132 Jul 25 03:54
    usr/lib/modules/5.3.7-301.fc31.x86_64/kernel/drivers/char/
    virtio_console.ko.xz
-rw-r--r-- 1 root   root   25028 Jul 25 03:54
    usr/lib/modules/5.3.7-301.fc31.x86_64/kernel/drivers/net/
    virtio_net.ko.xz
-rw-r--r-- 1 root   root   7780 Jul 25 03:54
    usr/lib/modules/5.3.7-301.fc31.x86_64/kernel/drivers/scsi/
    virtio_scsi.ko.xz
-rw-r--r-- 1 root   root   499 Feb 26 2018 usr/lib/sysctl.d/60-
libvirtd.conf

As you can see, the virtio_blk module is missing.

8. Since virtio_blk is missing, obviously the kernel cannot detect and access the vda disk, which is where the user has the root filesystem as well as the swap filesystem.

9. To fix this issue, we need to add the missing `virtio_blk` module in initramfs.

```
#dracut --add-drivers=virtio_blk /boot/new.img --force
```

```
# lsinitrd | grep -i virtio_blk
    -rw-r--r--   1 root      root          8356 Jul 25 03:54 usr/
    lib/modules/5.3.7-301.fc31.x86_64/kernel/drivers/block/virtio_
    blk.ko.xz
```

10. We will boot by using our `new.img` initramfs. How to boot the system manually with the help of the GRUB command prompt was already discussed in "can't boot" issue 1.

11. After adding the missing `virtio_blk` module, the "can't boot" issue has been fixed. You can see the successfully booted system in Figure 6-2.

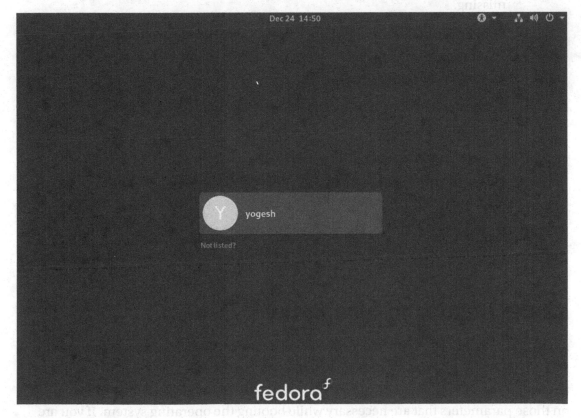

Figure 6-2. *The login screen of Fedora*

"Can't Boot" Issue 5 (initramfs)

Issue: Figure 6-3 shows what is visible on-screen.

```
error: ../../grub-core/fs/fshelp.c:257:file
`/boot/initramfs-5.3.16-300.fc31.img' not found.

Press any key to continue..._
```

Figure 6-3. *The console messages*

Resolution: Here are the steps to resolve the issue:

1) Now this is easy to understand and to resolve.

2) The error message is self-explanatory; the initramfs file itself is missing.

3) Either the initramfs itself is missing or it's just that the `/boot/loader/entries/*` file has a wrong entry in it. In this case, initramfs itself is missing.

4) So, we need to boot in rescue mode and mount the user's root filesystem.

5) Either reinstall the kernel's `rpm` package so that the `postscripts` part of the package will regenerate the missing initramfs and will also update the BLS entries accordingly.

6) Or you can regenerate initramfs with the help of the `dracut` command.

Kernel Command-Line Options

As we have already seen, GRUB accepts kernel command-line parameters and passes them to the kernel. The kernel has hundreds of command-line parameters, and it is almost impossible for anyone to cover each and every parameter. So, we will focus only on those parameters that are necessary while booting the operating system. If you are interested in all of the kernel command-line parameters, then visit the following page: https://www.kernel.org/doc/html/v4.14/admin-guide/kernel-parameters.html.

The list of parameters on that page are of the series 4 of kernels, but most of the parameter explanations are applicable to series 5 kernels as well. The best option is to always look at the kernel documentation at /usr/share/doc/.

root

- This is one of the main kernel's command-line parameters. The ultimate aim of booting is to mount the user's root filesystem. The root kernel command-line parameter provides the name of the user's root filesystem, which the kernel is supposed to mount.

- On behalf of the kernel, systemd, which ran from initramfs, mounts the user's root filesystem.

- If the user's root filesystem is not available or if the kernel is not able to mount it, then it will be considered a panic situation for the kernel.

init

- The kernel runs systemd from initramfs, and that becomes the first process. It's also called PID-1 and is the parent of every process.

- But if you are a developer and you want to run your own binary instead of systemd, then you can use the init kernel command-line parameter. Here's an example:

    init=/sbin/yogesh

As you can see in Figure 6-4, this will run the yogesh binary instead of systemd.

```
load_video
set gfx_payload=keep
insmod gzio
linux ($root)/boot/vmlinuz-5.3.16-300.fc31.x86_64 root=UUID=6588b8f1-7f37-4162\
-968c-8f99eacdf32e ro init=/sbin/yogesh_
initrd ($root)/boot/initramfs-5.3.16-300.fc31.x86_64.img
```

Figure 6-4. *The kernel command-line parameters*

But yogesh is not available on the actual root filesystem; hence, as shown in Figure 6-5, it will fail to boot.

```
         Starting File System Check on /dev/disk/by-uuid/6588b8f1-7f37-4162-968c-8f99eacdf32e...
[  OK  ] Started File System Check on /dev/disk/by-uuid/6588b8f1-7f37-4162-968c-8f99eacdf32e.
[    4.918340] audit: type=1130 audit(1577216447.044:10): pid=1 uid=0 auid=4294967295 ses=4294967295 subj=kernel msg='unit=syste
md-fsck-root comm="systemd" exe="/usr/lib/systemd/systemd" hostname=? addr=? terminal=? res=success'
         Mounting /sysroot...
[    4.929126] EXT4-fs (sda5): mounted filesystem with ordered data mode. Opts: (null)
[  OK  ] Mounted /sysroot.
[  OK  ] Reached target Initrd Root File System.
         Starting Reload Configuration from the Real Root...
[  OK  ] Started Reload Configuration from the Real Root.
[  OK  ] Reached target Initrd File Systems.
[  OK  ] Reached target Initrd Default Target.
         Starting dracut pre-pivot and cleanup hook...
[  OK  ] Started dracut pre-pivot and cleanup hook.
         Starting Cleaning Up and Shutting Down Daemons...
[  OK  ] Stopped target Timers.
[  OK  ] Stopped dracut pre-pivot and cleanup hook.
[  OK  ] Stopped target Initrd Default Target.
[  OK  ] Stopped target Basic System.
[  OK  ] Stopped target Initrd Root Device.
[  OK  ] Stopped target Paths.
[  OK  ] Stopped target Remote File Systems.
[  OK  ] Stopped target Remote File Systems (Pre).
[  OK  ] Stopped target Slices.
[  OK  ] Stopped target Sockets.
[  OK  ] Stopped target System Initialization.
[  OK  ] Stopped target Swap.
[  OK  ] Stopped dracut initqueue hook.
         Starting Plymouth switch root service...
[  OK  ] Stopped Apply Kernel Variables.
[  OK  ] Stopped Load Kernel Modules.
[  OK  ] Stopped Create Volatile Files and Directories.
[  OK  ] Stopped target Local File Systems.
[  OK  ] Stopped udev Coldplug all Devices.
         Stopping udev Kernel Device Manager...
         Starting Setup Virtual Console...
[  OK  ] Started Cleaning Up and Shutting Down Daemons.

Generating "/run/initramfs/rdsosreport.txt"


Entering emergency mode. Exit the shell to continue.
Type "journalctl" to view system logs.
You might want to save "/run/initramfs/rdsosreport.txt" to a USB stick or /boot
after mounting them and attach it to a bug report.


:/#
```

Figure 6-5. *The emergency shell*

- The system has dropped us in the emergency shell. Refer to Chapter 8 for a detailed discussion about debugging shells.

- The reason for dropping us in the emergency shell and the reason for the "can't boot" issue is mentioned in /run/initramfs/ rdsosreport.txt. Figure 6-6 shows a snippet of the rdsosreport. txt file.

```
[    5.639115] localhost.localdomain systemd[1]: Reached target Switch Root.
[    5.639700] localhost.localdomain systemd[1]: Starting Switch Root...
[    5.653897] localhost.localdomain systemctl[726]: Failed to switch root: Could not resolve init executable /sbin/yogesh: No s
uch file or directory
[    5.654883] localhost.localdomain systemd[1]: initrd-switch-root.service: Main process exited, code=exited, status=1/FAILURE
[    5.655047] localhost.localdomain systemd[1]: initrd-switch-root.service: Failed with result 'exit-code'.
[    5.655396] localhost.localdomain systemd[1]: Failed to start Switch Root.
[    5.655589] localhost.localdomain systemd[1]: Startup finished in 3.460s (kernel) + 0 (initrd) + 2.195s (userspace) = 5.655s.
[    5.655664] localhost.localdomain systemd[1]: initrd-switch-root.service: Triggering OnFailure= dependencies.
[    5.655952] localhost.localdomain audit[1]: SERVICE_START pid=1 uid=0 auid=4294967295 ses=4294967295 subj=kernel msg='unit=in
itrd-switch-root comm="systemd" exe="/usr/lib/systemd/systemd" hostname=? addr=? terminal=? res=failed'
[    5.656754] localhost.localdomain systemd[1]: Starting Setup Virtual Console...
[    5.739335] localhost.localdomain systemd[1]: systemd-vconsole-setup.service: Succeeded.
[    5.739735] localhost.localdomain systemd[1]: Started Setup Virtual Console.
[    5.740002] localhost.localdomain audit[1]: SERVICE_START pid=1 uid=0 auid=4294967295 ses=4294967295 subj=kernel msg='unit=sy
stemd-vconsole-setup comm="systemd" exe="/usr/lib/systemd/systemd" hostname=? addr=? terminal=? res=success'
[    5.740006] localhost.localdomain audit[1]: SERVICE_STOP pid=1 uid=0 auid=4294967295 ses=4294967295 subj=kernel msg='unit=sys
temd-vconsole-setup comm="systemd" exe="/usr/lib/systemd/systemd" hostname=? addr=? terminal=? res=success'
[    5.741630] localhost.localdomain systemd[1]: Started Emergency Shell.
[    5.741933] localhost.localdomain audit[1]: SERVICE_START pid=1 uid=0 auid=4294967295 ses=4294967295 subj=kernel msg='unit=em
```

Figure 6-6. *The rdsosreport.txt file*

- The interesting part to note here is that our /sbin/yogesh binary will be called at the time of the chroot'ing to the actual root filesystem. We have not discussed chroot yet; you can find a detailed discussion in Chapter 10.

ro

- This is a supporting parameter to the root kernel command-line parameter. ro stands for "read-only" file system. The user's root filesystem will be mounted inside initramfs, and it will be mounted in read-only mode if the ro kernel command-line parameter has been passed. The ro is the default choice of every major Linunx distribution.

rhgb and quite

- Almost every Linux distribution shows the animation at the time of booting to make the booting procedure more exciting, but the important console messages that are required to analyze the booting sequence will be hidden behind the animation. To stop the animation and to see the verbose console messages on-screen, remove the rhgb and quite parameters.

- When rhgb and quite are passed, as you can see in Figure 6-7, the plymouth animation will be shown.

Figure 6-7. *The plymouth screen*

- When rhgb and quite are removed, as you can see in Figure 6-8, the
  console messages will be exposed to the user.

```
[  OK  ] Mounted Huge Pages File System.
[  OK  ] Mounted POSIX Message Queue File System.
[  OK  ] Mounted Kernel Debug File System.
[  OK  ] Mounted Temporary Directory (/tmp).
[  OK  ] Started Create list of static device nodes for the current kernel.
[  OK  ] Started Preprocess NFS configuration convertion.
[  OK  ] Started Load Kernel Modules.
[  OK  ] Started Remount Root and Kernel File Systems.
         Mounting FUSE Control File System...
         Starting Load/Save Random Seed...
         Starting Apply Kernel Variables...
         Starting Create Static Device Nodes in /dev...
[  OK  ] Mounted FUSE Control File System.
[  OK  ] Started Apply Kernel Variables.
[  OK  ] Started Load/Save Random Seed.
[  OK  ] Started Create Static Device Nodes in /dev.
         Starting udev Kernel Device Manager...
[  OK  ] Started Setup Virtual Console.
[  OK  ] Started udev Coldplug all Devices.
         Starting udev Wait for Complete Device Initialization...
[  OK  ] Started Journal Service.
         Starting Flush Journal to Persistent Storage...
[  OK  ] Started Flush Journal to Persistent Storage.
[  OK  ] Started udev Kernel Device Manager.
[  OK  ] Listening on Load/Save RF Kill Switch Status /dev/rfkill Watch.
[  OK  ] Started Monitoring of LVM2 mirrors, snapshots etc. using dmeventd or progress polling.
         Starting Load/Save RF Kill Switch Status...
[  OK  ] Started Load/Save RF Kill Switch Status.
```

Figure 6-8. *The console messages*

- You can also press Escape at the animation (plymouth) screen and
  can see the console messages, but for that, you have to be physically
  present in front of the production system, which is unlikely.

selinux

- Sometimes to resolve the "can't boot" issues, you want to completely get rid of SELinux. You can pass `selinux=0` kernel command line parameter at that time. This will disable SELinux altogether.

These were some of the kernel command-line parameters that directly affect the booting sequence. Like with the kernel command-line parameters, GRUB can accept dracut command-line parameters too, which will be accepted by initramfs or more precisely by systemd of initramfs.

dracut Command-Line Options

In layperson's terms, you can consider command-line parameters starting with `rd.` to be dracut command-line parameters that will be understood by initramfs.

rd.auto (rd.auto=1)

- According to the man page, this enables auto assembly of special devices such as cryptoLUKS, dmraid, mdraid, or lvm. The default is off.

- Consider a scenario like earlier where your system did not have `mdraid (s/w raid)` configured, but now you have recently implemented it, and you want that device to be activated at the time of the boot. In other words, the storage state of the machine is changed at the time of the initramfs creation. Now, without regenerating the new initramfs, you want the new configuration (LVM or LUKS) to be activated at the time of the boot.

rd.hostonly=0

- According to the man page, this removes all compiled in the configuration of the host system that the initramfs image was built on. This helps booting, if any disk layout has changed, especially in combination with `rd.auto` or other parameters specifying the layout.

- Say that your graphics card provider (such as Nvidia) has given you special drivers/modules that are present in your initramfs, but the modules have started creating a problem. Since the graphics driver will be loaded at an early stage of booting, you want to avoid the use of that module; instead, you want to use a generic driver (vesa). In that scenario, you can use rd.hostonly=0. With this parameter, initramfs will load the generic driver and will avoid the host-specific Nvidia driver.

rd.fstab = 0

- According to the man page, use this parameter if you do not want to honor special mount options for the root filesystem found in /etc/fstab of the real root.

rd.skipfsck

- According to the man page, this skips fsck for rootfs and /usr. If you're mounting /usr to be read-only and the init system performs fsck before the remount, you might want to use this option to avoid duplication.

- Most Linux administrators have a misconception about fsck and how it is combined with the ro kernel command-line parameter. Most of us think that the kernel first mounts the actual root filesystem in ro mode and then performs an fsck on it so that the fsck operation will not corrupt the root filesystem data. Once the fsck is successful, it will remount the root filesystem in read-write mode by referring to /etc/fstab.

- But this understanding has a basic flaw, which is that fsck cannot be performed on a mounted filesystem irrespective of ro or rw mode.

The following Fedora system's user root filesystem is on the sda5 device, and it is currently mounted in read-only mode, so fsck would fail since the filesystem is mounted:

```
# fsck.ext4 /dev/sda5
    e2fsck 1.45.3 (14-Jul-2019)
    /dev/sda5 is mounted.
    e2fsck: Cannot continue, aborting.
```

Hence, it is proved that the purpose of the user's root filesystem getting mounted in ro mode is not to perform a fsck. Then what is the reason to pass the ro command-line parameter to the kernel? Let's discuss it through the booting sequence.

- The kernel extracts initramfs and passes command-line parameters like root and ro to systemd, which will start from initramfs.

- systemd will find the actual root filesystem.

- Once the root filesystem (device) is identified, systemd will perform the fsck on it.

- If the fsck is successful, then systemd will mount the root filesystem as ro (as per the passed kernel command-line parameter) inside initramfs itself. It will be mounted as read-only in the /sysroot directory of initramfs.

- As you can see in Figure 6-9, the kernel has extracted initramfs and started systemd from it (I have removed the rhgb and quite parameters).

```
[    3.438934] [drm] Initialized qxl 0.1.0 20120117 for 0000:00:01.0 on minor 0
[    3.440303] fbcon: qxldrmfb (fb0) is primary device
[    3.442409] Console: switching to colour frame buffer device 128x48
[    3.449070] qxl 0000:00:01.0: fb0: qxldrmfb frame buffer device
[  OK  ] Found device /dev/mapper/fedora_localhost--live-root.
[  OK  ] Reached target Initrd Root Device.
[  OK  ] Found device /dev/mapper/fedora_localhost--live-swap.
        Starting Resume from hibernation using device /dev/mapper/fedora_localhost--live-swap
...
[  OK       3.751667] audit: type=1130 audit(1577266230.433:10): pid=1 uid=0 auid=4294967295 se
s=4294967295 subj=kernel msg='unit=systemd-hibernate-resume@dev-mapper-fedora_localhost\x2d\x2
dlive\x2dswap comm="systemd" exe="/usr/lib/systemd/systemd" hostname=? addr=? terminal=? res=s
uccess'
0m] Started Resume from hibernation using device /dev/mapper/fedora_localhost--live-swap.
[  OK  ] Reached target Local File Systems (Pre).
[  OK  ] Reached target Local File Systems.
        Starting Create Volatile Files and Directories...
[  OK  ] Started Create Volatile Files and Directories.
[  OK  ] Reached target System Initialization.
[  OK  ] Reached target Basic System.
[  OK  ] Started dracut initqueue hook.
[  OK  ] Reached target Remote File Systems (Pre).
[  OK  ] Reached target Remote File Systems.
        Starting File System Check on /dev/mapper/fedora_localhost--live-root...
[    3.799893] pcieport 0000:00:02.6: pciehp: Failed to check link status
[  OK  ] Started File System Check on /dev/mapper/fedora_localhost--live-root.
        Mounting /sysroot...
[    3.811283] EXT4-fs (dm-0): mounted filesystem with ordered data mode. Opts: (null)
[  OK  ] Mounted /sysroot.
[  OK  ] Reached target Initrd Root File System.
```

Figure 6-9. *The console messages*

Systemd then scanned the connected storage devices for the root filesystem and found one. Before mounting the user's root filesystem, it first performed the fsck on it and later mounted it inside initramfs on the directory sysroot. The user's root filesystem will be mounted in read-only mode.

- The reason for mounting it in read-only mode is simple to understand. Suppose the system fails to boot, but it has managed to mount the user's root filesystem on sysroot and has provided us with a shell to fix the "can't boot" issue. Users might accidentally corrupt or even delete the user's root filesystem that is mounted under sysroot. So, to prevent the user's root filesystem from such accidents, it is preferred to mount it in read-only mode.

#switch_root:/# ls -ld /sysroot/
```
dr-xr-xr-x 19 root 0 4096 Sep 10  2017 /sysroot/
```

- How to use the debugging shells and how initramfs provides them will be discussed in Chapter 8.

- Figure 6-10 shows systemd continuing its booting sequence and leaving the initramfs environment.

```
[  OK  ] Stopped Create list of static device nodes for the current kernel.
[  OK  ] Started Cleanup udevd DB.
[  OK  ] Started Setup Virtual Console.
[  OK  ] Reached target Switch Root.
         Starting Switch Root...
[    4.113676] systemd-journald[317]: Received SIGTERM from PID 1 (systemd).
[    4.131928] printk: systemd: 20 output lines suppressed due to ratelimiting
[    4.345867] IPv6: ADDRCONF(NETDEV_CHANGE): enp1s0: link becomes ready
[    4.553209] SELinux:  policy capability network_peer_controls=1
[    4.554336] SELinux:  policy capability open_perms=1
[    4.555321] SELinux:  policy capability extended_socket_class=1
[    4.556442] SELinux:  policy capability always_check_network=0
[    4.557533] SELinux:  policy capability cgroup_seclabel=1
[    4.558563] SELinux:  policy capability nnp_nosuid_transition=1
[    4.577426] systemd[1]: Successfully loaded SELinux policy in 419.553ms.
[    4.619094] systemd[1]: Relabelled /dev, /dev/shm, /run, /sys/fs/cgroup in 23.614ms.
[    4.623723] systemd[1]: systemd v243-4.gitef67743.fc31 running in system mode. (+PAM +AUDIT
 +SELINUX +IMA -APPARMOR +SMACK +SYSVINIT +UTMP +LIBCRYPTSETUP +GCRYPT +GNUTLS +ACL +XZ +LZ4 +
SECCOMP +BLKID +ELFUTILS +KMOD +IDN2 -IDN +PCRE2 default-hierarchy=unified)
[    4.628180] systemd[1]: Detected virtualization kvm.
[    4.629988] systemd[1]: Detected architecture x86-64.
[    4.633597] systemd[1]: Set hostname to <localhost.localdomain>.

Welcome to Fedora 31 (Workstation Edition)!

[    4.740509] systemd[1]: /usr/lib/systemd/system/sssd.service:12: PIDFile= references a path
 below legacy directory /var/run/, updating /var/run/sssd.pid → /run/sssd.pid; please update t
he unit file accordingly.
```

Figure 6-10. *The console messages*

- As you can see Figure 6-10, the switch root leaves the current initramfs environment and changes the root from initramfs' temporary root filesystem to /sysroot, which has the user's root filesystem mounted. (The switch root process will be discussed in Chapter 9.)

- Right after entering into the user's root filesystem, systemd of the user's root filesystem reads /etc/fstab and takes the appropriate action on mount points. For example, on this Fedora system, there is the user's root filesystem entry as well as the /boot entry (boot is on separate partition):

#**cat /etc/fstab**

```
/dev/mapper/fedora_localhost--live-root  /     ext4      defaults      1 1
UUID=eea3d947-0618-4d8c-b083-87daf15b2679 /boot ext4      defaults      1 2
/dev/mapper/fedora_localhost--live-swap none   swap      defaults      0 0
```

- As you can see in Figure 6-11, at this stage, systemd will perform fsck only on the boot device before mounting it. Please note that it is not performing fsck on the user's root filesystem since it has already been performed inside an initramfs environment. Also the user's root filesystem is currently mounted, and we all know that it does not make sense to do an fsck on the swap device.

```
[  OK  ] Started Activation of DM RAID sets.
[    5.939178] audit: type=1131 audit(1577266232.607:63): pid=1 uid=0 auid=4294967295 ses=4294
967295 subj=system_u:system_r:init_t:s0 msg='unit=dmraid-activation comm="systemd" exe="/usr/l
ib/systemd/systemd" hostname=? addr=? terminal=? res=success'
[  OK  ] Reached target Local Encrypted Volumes.
[  OK  ] Reached target Local File Systems (Pre).
         Starting File System Check on /dev/disk/by-uuid/eea3d947-0618-4d8c-b083-87daf15b2679.
..
[  OK  ] Started File System Check on /dev/disk/by-uuid/eea3d947-0618-4d8c-b083-87daf15b2679.
[    6.036310] audit: type=1130 audit(1577266232.718:64): pid=1 uid=0 auid=4294967295 ses=4294
967295 subj=system_u:system_r:init_t:s0 msg='unit=systemd-fsck@dev-disk-by\x2duuid-eea3d947\x2
d0618\x2d4d8c\x2db083\x2d87daf15b2679 comm="systemd" exe="/usr/lib/systemd/systemd" hostname=?
 addr=? terminal=? res=success'
[    6.066303] EXT4-fs (vda1): mounted filesystem with ordered data mode. Opts: (null)
         Mounting /boot...
[  OK  ] Mounted /boot.
[  OK  ] Reached target Local File Systems.
```

Figure 6-11. *The fsck console messages*

- If there had been any other extra mount points like /usr, it would have performed fsck on that device too.

- fsck depends on the fifth parameter of /etc/fstab. If it is 1, then fsck will be performed at the time of boot. This fstab setting is not applicable to the user's root filesystem since fsck will be compulsory performed on user's root filesystem inside initramfs, which is before reading the /etc/fstab file.

- rd.skipfsck is applicable only to root and the user's root filesystem. It is not applicable to any other filesystem like /boot.

rd.driver.blacklist, rd.driver.pre, and rd.driver.post

This is from the man page of rd.driver.blacklist:

rd.driver.blacklist=<drivername>[,<drivername>,...]

do not load kernel module <drivername>. This parameter can be specified multiple times.

rd.driver.blacklist is one of the most important dracut command-line parameters. As the name suggests, it will blacklist the specified modules. Let's try to blacklist the virtio-related drivers that are quite important for virtual guest systems.

lsmod | grep -i virt
```
virtio_balloon          24576 0
virtio_net              57344 0
virtio_console          40960 2
virtio_blk              20480 3
net_failover            20480 1 virtio_net
```

It is available in initramfs as well.

lsinitrd | grep -i virtio
```
-rw-r--r-- 1 root  root  8356 Jul 25 03:54 usr/lib/modules/5.3.7-301.fc31.
x86_64/kernel/drivers/block/virtio_blk.ko.xz
-rw-r--r--   1 root     root       14132 Jul 25 03:54 usr/lib/
modules/5.3.7-301.fc31.x86_64/kernel/drivers/char/virtio_console.ko.xz
-rw-r--r--   1 root     root       25028 Jul 25 03:54 usr/lib/
modules/5.3.7-301.fc31.x86_64/kernel/drivers/net/virtio_net.ko.xz
-rw-r--r--   1 root     root        7780 Jul 25 03:54 usr/lib/
modules/5.3.7-301.fc31.x86_64/kernel/drivers/scsi/virtio_scsi.ko.xz
```

Remember, to blacklist the module, as you can see in Figure 6-12, you need to make sure that every other dependent module also has to be blacklisted; otherwise, the dependent modules would pull the blacklisted module. For example, in this case, the virtio_balloon, virtio_net, virtio_console, virtio_blk, and virtio_pci modules are dependent on each other. That means if we blacklist only virtio_blk, the other dependent modules will still load the virtio_blk module.

```
load_video
set gfx_payload=keep
insmod gzio
linux ($root)/vmlinuz-5.3.7-301.fc31.x86_64 root=/dev/mapper/fedora_localhost-\
-live-root ro resume=/dev/mapper/fedora_localhost--live-swap rd.lvm.lv=fedora_\
localhost-live/root rd.lvm.lv=fedora_localhost-live/swap rd.driver.blacklist=v\
irtio_balloon,virtio_net,virtio_console,virtio_blk,net_failover_
initrd ($root)/initramfs-5.3.7-301.fc31.x86_64.img
```

Figure 6-12. *The kernel command-line parameter*

The `virtio`-related drivers are important. This is the same driver through which virtual disks and networks of hypervisors get exposed to the guest operating system. Since we blacklisted them, the guest OS will stop booting. You can see the "can't boot" console messages in Figure 6-13.

```
[    2.270151] [drm] qxl: 64M of Surface memory size
[    2.294709] [drm] slot 0 (main): base 0xc4000000, size 0x03ffe000, gpu_offset
0x2000000000
[    2.294806] [drm] slot 1 (surfaces): base 0xc0000000, size 0x04000000, gpu_of
fset 0x3000000000
[    2.295342] [drm] Initialized qxl 0.1.0 20120117 for 0000:00:01.0 on minor 0
[    2.296038] fbcon: qxldrmfb (fb0) is primary device
[    2.297400] Console: switching to colour frame buffer device 128x48
[    2.304178] qxl 0000:00:01.0: fb0: qxldrmfb frame buffer device
[    3.000212] pcieport 0000:00:02.6: pciehp: Failed to check link status
[ TIME ] Timed out waiting for device /dev/mapper/fedora_localhost--live-swap.
[DEPEND] Dependency failed for Resume from hibernation using device /dev/mapper/fedora_localhost--live-swap.
[  OK  ] Reached target Local File Systems (Pre).
[  OK  ] Reached target Local File Systems.
         Starting Create Volatile Files and Directories...
[   92.073420] audit: type=1130 audit(1577343768.641:6): pid=1 uid=0 auid=4294967295 ses=4294967295 subj=kernel msg='unit=system
d-tmpfiles-setup comm="systemd" exe="/usr/lib/systemd/systemd" hostname=? addr=? terminal=? res=success'

[  OK  ] Reached target System Initialization.
[  OK  ] Reached target Basic System.
[  146.178823] dracut-initqueue[449]: Warning: dracut-initqueue timeout - starting timeout scripts
[  146.869519] dracut-initqueue[449]: Warning: dracut-initqueue timeout - starting timeout scripts
[  147.532546] dracut-initqueue[449]: Warning: dracut-initqueue timeout - starting timeout scripts
```

Figure 6-13. *The console messages*

So, the blacklisting of the `virtio` modules is successful, but there are two issues in this approach.

- `rd.driver.blacklist` will only block the modules that are loading from initramfs.

- We need to manually provide the list of modules to `rd.driver.blacklist` every time.

If the module is not in initramfs, then you cannot really block it from loading. For example, the bluetooth module is not loaded from initramfs, but the kernel loads it after the initramfs environment.

lsmod | grep -i bluetooth

```
bluetooth            626688  37 btrtl,btintel,btbcm,bnep,btusb,rfcomm
ecdh_generic          16384   1 bluetooth
rfkill                28672   5 bluetooth
```

lsinitrd | grep -i bluetooth

```
<no_output>
```

To block the kernel from loading the bluetooth module, we need to tell the modprobe command to block the module from loading. modprobe is a binary that loads or removes modules on behalf of the kernel.

Make a new blacklist.conf file. (You can choose any name, but it has to have a .conf suffix) and blacklist the module.

#**cat /etc/modprobe.d/blacklist.conf**

```
blacklist bluetooth
```

But after reboot, you will find that bluetooth is again loaded by kernel.

#**lsmod | grep -i bluetooth**

```
bluetooth            626688  37 btrtl,btintel,btbcm,bnep,btusb,rfcomm
ecdh_generic          16384   1 bluetooth
rfkill                28672   5 bluetooth
```

This is because the bluetooth module is a dependency of multiple other modules such as btrtl, btintel, btbcm, bnep, btusb, rfcomm, and rfkill. Hence, modprobe has loaded bluetooth as a dependency of other modules. In such situations, we need to fool the modprobe command by adding the install bluetooth /bin/true line in the blacklist.conf file, as shown here:

cat /etc/modprobe.d/blacklist.conf

```
install bluetooth /bin/true
```

After rebooting, you will find the `bluetooth` module has been blocked.

```
# lsmod | grep -i bluetooth
    <no_output>
```

You can also use `/bin/false` instead of `/bin/true`.

After the explanation of `rd.driver.blacklist`, the `rd.driver.pre` and `rd.driver.post` dracut command-line parameters are easier to understand, and the man pages are self-explanatory, shown here:

rd.driver.pre=<drivername>[,<drivername>,...]

> *force loading kernel module <drivername>. This parameter can be specified multiple times.*

rd.driver.post=<drivername>[,<drivername>,...]

> *force loading kernel module <drivername> after all automatic loading modules have been loaded. This parameter can be specified multiple times.*

rd.debug

This comes from the man page:

> *set -x for the dracut shell. If systemd is active in the initramfs, all output is logged to the systemd journal, which you can inspect with "journalctl -ab". If systemd is not active, the logs are written to dmesg and /run/initramfs/init.log. If "quiet" is set, it also logs to the console.*

`rd.debug` will enable the debug logging of systemd, which will log huge messages on the console as well as in the systemd journals. The detailed messages provided by `rd.debug` will be helpful in identifying systemd-related "can't boot" issues.

rd.memdebug= [0-4]

This comes from the man page:

> *Print memory usage info at various points, set the verbose level from 0 to 4. Higher level means more debugging output:*

```
0 - no output
1 - partial /proc/meminfo
```

```
2 - /proc/meminfo
3 - /proc/meminfo + /proc/slabinfo
4 - /proc/meminfo + /proc/slabinfo + tracekomem
```

- This will print all the memory subsystem–related information on-screen, such as the meminfo and slabinfo file contents.

lvm, raid, and Multipath-Related dracut Command-Line Parameters

This comes from the man pages:

rd.lvm=0

disable LVM detection

rd.lvm.vg=<volume group name>

only activate the volume groups with the given name. rd.lvm.vg can be specified multiple times on the kernel command line.

rd.lvm.lv=<logical volume name>

only activate the logical volumes with the given name. rd.lvm.lv can be specified multiple times on the kernel command line.

rd.lvm.conf=0

remove any /etc/lvm/lvm.conf, which may exist in the initramfs

- Out of these parameters, you must have at least observed the rd.lvm.lv option passed by GRUB. The purpose of rd.lvm.lv is to activate the given LVM device at an early stage of booting. By default, the major Linux distributors activate only root and swap (if configured) LV devices. Activating only the root filesystem at the time of the boot speeds up the booting procedure. After switching the root from initramfs to the actual root filesystem, systemd can activate the remaining volume groups as per the list at /etc/fstab.

- Similarly, dracut provides multipath and RAID-related command-line parameters, which are again self-explanatory.

MD RAID

    `rd.md=0`

disable MD RAID detection

    `rd.md.imsm=0`

disable MD RAID for imsm/isw raids, use DM RAID instead

    `rd.md.ddf=0`

disable MD RAID for SNIA ddf raids, use DM RAID instead

    `rd.md.conf=0`

ignore mdadm.conf included in initramfs

    `rd.md.waitclean=1`

wait for any resync, recovery, or reshape activity to finish before continuing

    `rd.md.uuid=<md raid uuid>`

only activate the raid sets with the given UUID. This parameter can be specified multiple times.

DM RAID

    `rd.dm=0`

disable DM RAID detection

    `rd.dm.uuid=<dm raid uuid>`

only activate the raid sets with the given UUID. This parameter can be specified multiple times.

MULTIPATH

    `rd.multipath=0`

disable multipath detection

- dracut provides *n* number of command-line parameters for networks, NFS, CIFS, iSCSI, FCoE, etc. It also means these are the various options on which you can put your root filesystem, but it is almost impossible to cover each and every dracut command-line parameter. Also, I am not in favor of booting the system from all these complex structures. I believe in keeping the user's root filesystem always on the local disk so that the booting procedure will be easy and mainly because the simpler booting sequence is quicker to fix in the case of a "can't boot" situation.

rd.break and rd.shell

rd.shell will provide us with the shell at the end of the booting sequence, and with rd.break, we can break the booting sequence. But to understand these parameters, we need to have a good understanding of systemd. Hence, before discussing rd.break and the dracut hooks, we will discuss systemd first in our next chapter. The following are the parameters accepted by rd.break:

Parameters	Purpose
cmdline	This hook collects the kernel command-line parameters.
pre-udev	This hook starts before starting the udev handler.
pre-trigger	In this hook, you can set udev environment variables with 'udevadm' control --property=KEY=value or control the further execution of udev.
pre-mount	This hook starts before mounting the user's root filesystem at /sysroot.
mount	The hook will be started after mounting the root filesystem at /sysroot.
pre-pivot	The hook will be executed just before switching to actual root filesystem.

CHAPTER 7

systemd (Part I)

Here is what we know about the booting sequence so far:

1) The bootloader loads the kernel and initramfs in memory.

2) The kernel will be loaded at a specific location (an architecture-specific location), whereas initramfs will be loaded at any available location.

3) The kernel extracts itself with the help of the header of the `vmlinuz` file.

4) The kernel extracts initramfs in main memory (`init/initramfs.c`) and mounts it as a temporary root filesystem (`/`) in main memory.

5) The kernel launches (`init/main.c`) the systemd as a first process with PID-1 from a temporary root filesystem.

6) systemd will find the user's root filesystem and will `chroot` into it.

This chapter will address how systemd, which is forked from initramfs, manages to mount the user's root filesystem, and we will also see the detailed booting sequence of systemd inside initramfs. But before that, we need to understand systemd as a process.

I will let systemd's man page do the talking here:

> *"After the root file system is found and mounted, the `initrd` hands over control to the host's system manager (such as systemd(1)) stored in the root file system, which is then responsible for probing all remaining hardware, mounting all necessary file systems and spawning all configured services."*

© Yogesh Babar 2020
Y. Babar, *Hands-on Booting*, https://doi.org/10.1007/978-1-4842-5890-3_7

Structure

systemd was first introduced in Fedora 15. We all know that systemd is a replacement for init scripts (quite literally, /sbin/init is now a symlink to /usr/lib/systemd/systemd), and it amazingly reduces the boot time. However, in reality, systemd is much bigger than just a replacement for init. This is what systemd does:

1) It maintains logs with journalctl.

2) It extensively uses cgroups version 1 and 2.

3) It reduces boot time.

4) It manages units. service is just one type of unit that systemd handles. The following are the units that systemd provides and manages:

Unit	Purpose
systemd.service	To manage the services
systemd.socket	To create and manage the sockets
systemd.device	To create and use devices based on udev's inputs
systemd.mount	To mount the filesystem
systemd.automount	To automount the filesystem
systemd.swap	To make and manage swap devices
systemd.target	Group of services instead of runlevels
systemd.path	Information about a path monitored by systemd, for path-based activation
systemd.timer	For time-based activation
systemd.slice	Resource management such as CPU, memory, I/O for service units

Unit files will be stored and loaded from these three locations:

Path	Description
/etc/systemd/system	Local configuration
/run/systemd/system	Runtime units
/usr/lib/systemd/system	Units of installed packages

/etc/systemd/system is an admin location, whereas /usr/lib/systemd/system is an application vendor location. This means the admin's location will get precedence over the application vendor's location if the same unit file is present at both locations. Please note that in this chapter all the commands are executed from the directory in which initramfs has been extracted.

```
# tree etc/systemd/
      etc/systemd/
      ├── journald.conf
      └── system.conf
0 directories, 2 files
```

```
#ls usr/lib/systemd/system | column
```

basic.target	plymouth-switch-root.service
cryptsetup.target	poweroff.target
ctrl-alt-del.target	poweroff.target.wants
default.target	reboot.target
dracut-cmdline-ask.service	reboot.target.wants
dracut-cmdline.service	remote-fs-pre.target
dracut-emergency.service	remote-fs.target
dracut-initqueue.service	rescue.service
dracut-mount.service	rescue.target
dracut-pre-mount.service	rescue.target.wants
dracut-pre-pivot.service	rpcbind.target
dracut-pre-trigger.service	shutdown.target
dracut-pre-udev.service	sigpwr.target
emergency.service	slices.target
emergency.target	sockets.target
emergency.target.wants	sockets.target.wants
final.target	swap.target
halt.target	sysinit.target
halt.target.wants	sysinit.target.wants
initrd-cleanup.service	sys-kernel-config.mount
initrd-fs.target	syslog.socket
initrd-parse-etc.service	systemd-ask-password-console.path
initrd-root-device.target	systemd-ask-password-console.service

initrd-root-fs.target	systemd-ask-password-console.service.wants
initrd-switch-root.service	systemd-ask-password-plymouth.path
initrd-switch-root.target	systemd-ask-password-plymouth.service
initrd-switch-root.target.wants	systemd-ask-password-plymouth.service.wants
initrd.target	systemd-fsck@.service
initrd.target.wants	systemd-halt.service
initrd-udevadm-cleanup-db.service	systemd-journald-audit.socket
kexec.target	systemd-journald-dev-log.socket
kexec.target.wants	systemd-journald.service
kmod-static-nodes.service	systemd-journald.socket
local-fs-pre.target	systemd-kexec.service
local-fs.target	systemd-modules-load.service
multi-user.target	systemd-poweroff.service
multi-user.target.wants	systemd-random-seed.service
network-online.target	systemd-reboot.service
network-pre.target	systemd-sysctl.service
network.target	systemd-tmpfiles-setup-dev.service
nss-lookup.target	systemd-tmpfiles-setup.service
nss-user-lookup.target	systemd-udevd-control.socket
paths.target	systemd-udevd-kernel.socket
plymouth-halt.service	systemd-udevd.service
plymouth-kexec.service	systemd-udev-settle.service
plymouth-poweroff.service	systemd-udev-trigger.service
plymouth-quit.service	systemd-vconsole-setup.service
plymouth-quit-wait.service	timers.target
plymouth-reboot.service	umount.target
plymouth-start.service	

The third location, /run/systemd/system, is a temporary location and will be used internally by systemd to manage units. For example, it will be used extensively while creating the sockets. In fact, /run is a separate filesystem introduced with systemd to store runtime data. As of now, the /run directory of initramfs is empty, which is obvious because initramfs is not in use.

#ls run/

    <no_output>

Also, it is expected that there are fewer unit files that are present in initramfs than the ones that are available on the user's root filesystem. dracut will collect only those systemd unit files that are necessary to mount the user's root filesystem. For example, it does not make sense to add the httpd or mysql related systemd unit files in initramfs. Let's try to understand one of the service unit files of systemd, as shown here:

```
# cat /usr/lib/systemd/system/sshd.service
[Unit]
Description=OpenSSH server daemon
Documentation=man:sshd(8) man:sshd_config(5)
After=network.target sshd-keygen.target
Wants=sshd-keygen.target

[Service]
Type=notify
EnvironmentFile=-/etc/crypto-policies/back-ends/opensshserver.config
EnvironmentFile=-/etc/sysconfig/sshd-permitrootlogin
EnvironmentFile=-/etc/sysconfig/sshd
ExecStart=/usr/sbin/sshd -D $OPTIONS $CRYPTO_POLICY $PERMITROOTLOGIN
ExecReload=/bin/kill -HUP $MAINPID
KillMode=process
Restart=on-failure
RestartSec=42s

[Install]
WantedBy=multi-user.target
```

This sshd service unit file will not be part of initramfs since you do not need an ssh service to mount the user's root filesystem. The service unit file is divided into three parts: [unit], [service], [install].

- **[unit]**:

  After=network.target sshd-keygen.target
  The sshd service will start only if network.target (listed units) and sshd-keygen (listed units) have successfully started. If either of them fails, then the sshd service will also fail.

Wants=sshd-keygen.target

This is a less severe version of Requires. If any of the units that are mentioned in wants fails, then also the sshd service (or that particular service) will start, whereas in Requires the sshd service will start only if the units mentioned under Requires have been successfully started. Before is the opposite of After The Wants, After, Before, and Requires all work independently of each other. It is a common practice to use Wants and After together.

Conflicts=

This can be used to list the units that are conflicting with the current unit. Starting this unit might stop the listed conflicting units.

OnFailure=

OnFailure units will start when any given unit reaches the failed state.

- **[Service]:**

ExecStart=/usr/sbin/sshd

Starting an sshd service unit just starts the binary mentioned after ExecStart.

- **[Install]:**

The Install section of a unit file is not used by systemd. Rather, it is used by the systemctl enable, or disable command. It will be used by systemctl to create or destroy the symlinks.

How Does systemd Reduce Boot Time?

Lennart Poettering, the creator of systemd, gives a classic example of how systemd reduces the boot time in his blog at http://0pointer.de/blog/projects/systemd.html. This blog is one of the best resources if you really want to deep dive into the systemd world.

There are four daemons: syslog, dbus, avahi, and bluetooth.

syslog is necessary for every daemon to log the messages. So, syslog is a requirement for every other daemon. avahi needs syslog and dbus to run. bluetooth needs dbus and syslog but does not need avahi to be running. With the Sysv/init script model, this happens:

1) syslog will start first.

2) When it is completely ready, the dbus service will be started.

3) After dbus, avahi will be started.

4) Finally, the bluetooth service will be started. See Figure 7-1.

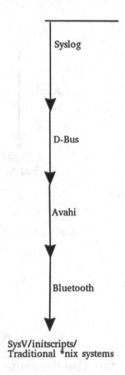

Figure 7-1. *The init model*

bluetooth and avahi are not dependent on each other, but bluetooth has to wait until avahi starts. Ubuntu-like distributions use upstart instead of init, which improves the boot time to some extent. In upstart, the services that are not dependent on each other will start in parallel, meaning avahi and bluetooth will start together. Please see Figure 7-2 for reference.

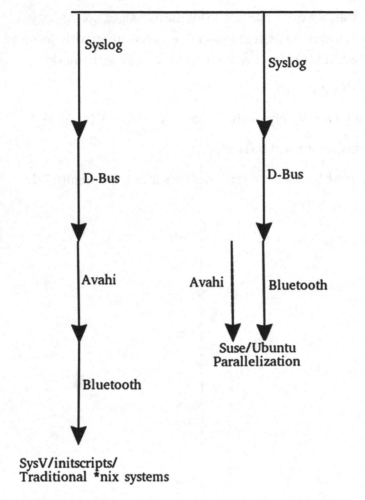

Figure 7-2. *The upstart model*

In systemd, all the services are started at the same time with the help of sockets. Here's an example:

1) systemd will create a socket for syslog (which has been replaced with journald).

2) A socket /dev/log is a symlink to /run/systemd/journal/dev-log.

 # file /dev/log
```
/dev/log: symbolic link to /run/systemd/journal/dev-log
```

 # file /run/systemd/journal/dev-log
```
/run/systemd/journal/dev-log: socket
```

As mentioned earlier, the run filesystem will be used by systemd for socket file creation.

3) For dbus, the socket is created at /run/dbus/system_bus_socket. To run, dbus needs journald to be running, but since the system is still booting and journald/syslog is not fully started yet, dbus will log its messages to journald's socket /dev/log, and whenever the journald service is fully ready, it will fetch the messages from the socket.

4) It's the same for the bluetooth service; it needs the dbus service to be running to start. So, systemd will create a /run/dbus/system_bus_socket socket before the dbus service starts. The bluetooth service will not wait for dbus to start. You can refer to Figure 7-3 for a better understanding.

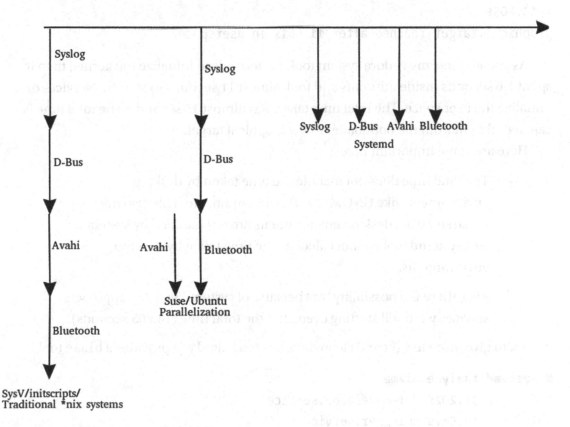

Figure 7-3. *The systemd model*

5) If the systemd created socket runs out of buffer, then the
    bluetooth service will be blocked until the socket is available.
    This socket approach will drastically reduce the boot time.

This socket-based approach was originally tried in macOS. It was called launchd at
that time. Lennart Poettering took inspiration from it.

systemd-analyze

systemd provides the systemd-analyze tool to check the time taken by the system to boot.

```
# systemd-analyze
Startup finished in 1.576s (kernel) + 1.653s (initrd) + 11.574s (userspace)
= 14.805s
graphical.target reached after 11.561s in userspace
```

As you can see, my Fedora system took 1.5 seconds to initialize the kernel; then it
spent 1.6 seconds inside initramfs and took almost 11 seconds to start the services or
initialize the user space. The total time taken was almost 15 seconds. The total time is
calculated right from the bootloader to the graphical target.

Here are some important notes:

- The total time does not include the time taken by desktop
  environments like GNOME, KDE, Cinnamon, etc. This also makes
  sense since the desktop environments are not handled by systemd,
  so a systemd tool cannot calculate the time taken by desktop
  environments.

- Also, there is a possibility that because of systemd's socket approach,
  services were still starting even after the total time (14.805 seconds).

So, to give more insight and clean data, systemd-analyse provides a blame tool.

```
# systemd-analyze blame
        31.202s dnf-makecache.service
        10.517s pmlogger.service
        9.264s NetworkManager-wait-online.service
        4.977s plymouth-switch-root.service
        2.994s plymouth-quit-wait.service
        1.674s systemd-udev-settle.service
```

```
1.606s lightdm.service
1.297s pmlogger_check.service
 938ms docker.service
 894ms dracut-initqueue.service
 599ms pmcd.service
 590ms lvm2-monitor.service
 568ms abrtd.service
 482ms firewalld.service
 461ms systemd-logind.service
 430ms lvm2-pvscan@259:3.service
 352ms initrd-switch-root.service
 307ms bolt.service
 290ms systemd-machined.service
 288ms registries.service
 282ms udisks2.service
 269ms libvirtd.service
 255ms sssd.service
 209ms systemd-udevd.service
 183ms systemd-journal-flush.service
 180ms docker-storage-setup.service
 169ms systemd-journald.service
 156ms polkit.service
 .
 .
 .
</snip>
```

The blame output could easily be misunderstood; i.e., two services might be initializing at the same time, and thus the time spent to initialize both services is much less than the sum of both individual times combined. For more precise data, you can use the plot tool of systemd-analyse, which will generate the graph and provide many more details about the boot time. You can see the generated plot image in Figure 7-4.

```
# systemd-analyze plot > plot.svg

# eog plot.svg
```

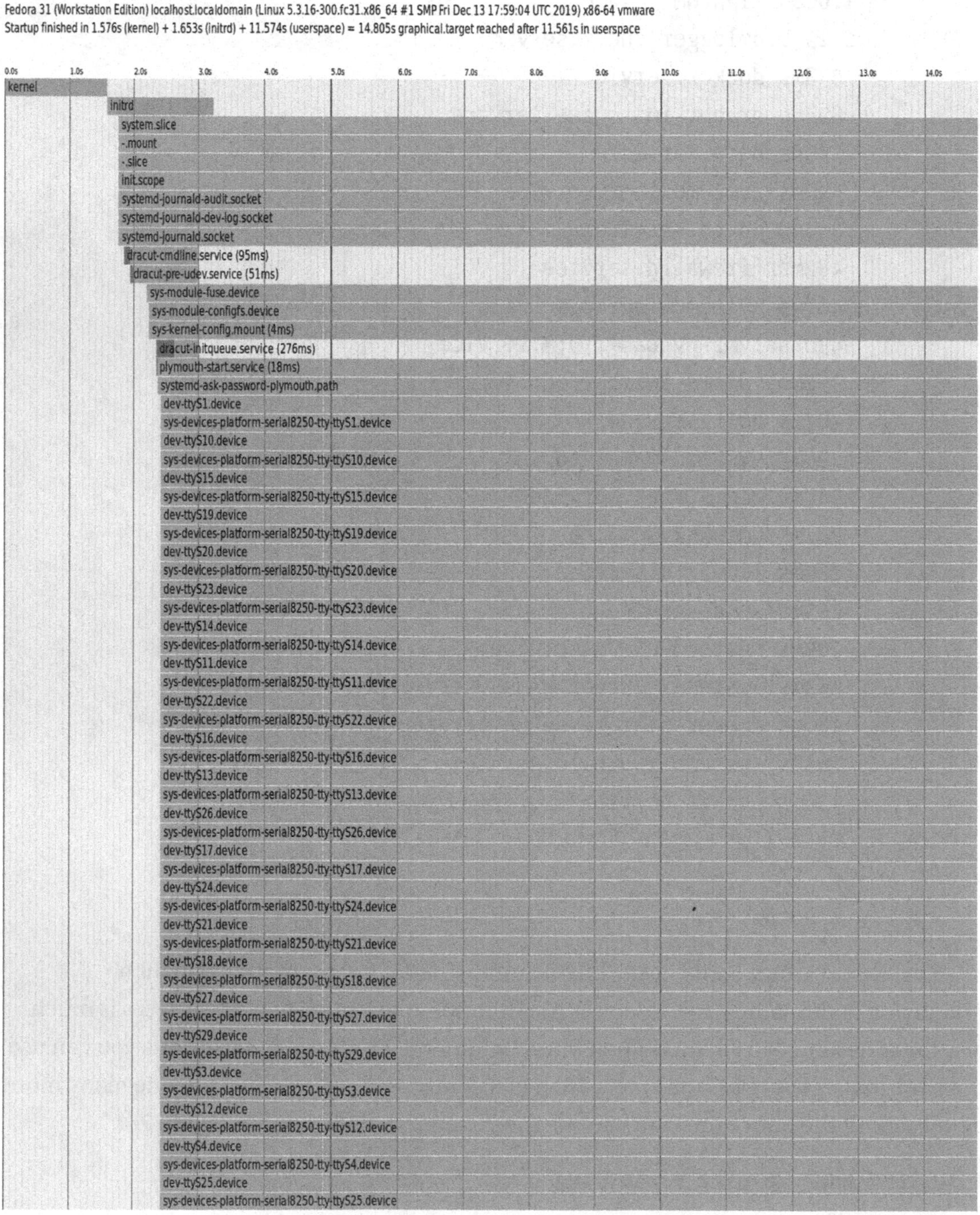

Fedora 31 (Workstation Edition) localhost.localdomain (Linux 5.3.16-300.fc31.x86_64 #1 SMP Fri Dec 13 17:59:04 UTC 2019) x86-64 vmware
Startup finished in 1.576s (kernel) + 1.653s (initrd) + 11.574s (userspace) = 14.805s graphical.target reached after 11.561s in userspace

Figure 7-4. *The generated plot image*

The following are some of the other tools that systemd-analyse provides that can be used to identify the boot time.

systemd-analyze <tool>	Description
time	Prints time spent in the kernel
blame	Prints list of running units ordered by time to init
critical-chain [UNIT...]	Prints a tree of the time-critical chain of units
plot	Outputs SVG graphic showing service initialization
dot [UNIT...]	Outputs dependency graph in dot(1) format
log-level [LEVEL]	Gets/sets logging threshold for manager
log-target [TARGET]	Gets/sets logging target for manager
dump	Output state serialization of service manager
cat-config	Shows configuration file and drop-ins
unit-files	Lists files and symlinks for units
units-paths	Lists load directories for units
exit-status [STATUS...]	Lists exit status definitions
syscall-filter [NAME...]	Prints list of syscalls in seccomp filter
condition...	Evaluates conditions and asserts
verify FILE...	Checks unit files for correctness

(*continued*)

systemd-analyze <tool>	Description
service-watchdogs [BOOL]	Gets/sets service watchdog state
calendar SPEC...	Validates repetitive calendar time events
timestamp...	Validates a timestamp
timespan SPAN...	Validates a time span
security [UNIT...]	Analyzes security of unit

"Can't Boot" Issue 6 (systemd)

Issue: The system successfully boots, but the nagios service fails to start at the time of the boot.

Here are the steps to resolve this issue:

1) We need to isolate the issue first. Remove the rhgb quiet kernel command-line parameters when GRUB appears on the screen.

2) The verbose logs show that the system is able to boot, but the nagios service fails to start while booting. As you can see, the NetworkManager service of systemd which is responsible for the network has successfully started. This means it is not a network communication issue.

```
13:23:52    systemd: Starting Network Manager...
13:23:52    systemd: Started Kernel Samepage Merging (KSM)
            Tuning Daemon.
13:23:52    systemd: Started Install ABRT coredump hook.
13:23:52    abrtd: Init complete, entering main loop
13:23:52    systemd: Started Load CPU microcode update.
13:23:52    systemd: Started Authorization Manager.
13:23:53    NetworkManager[1356]: <info>  [1534389833.1078]
            NetworkManager is starting... (for the first time)
```

```
13:23:53   NetworkManager[1356]: <info>  [1534389833.1079] Read
           config: /etc/NetworkManager/NetworkManager.conf (lib:
           00-server.conf, 10-slaves-order.conf)
13:23:53   NetworkManager[1356]: <info>  [1534389833.1924]
           manager[0x558b0496a0c0]: monitoring kernel firmware
           directory '/lib/firmware'.
13:23:53   NetworkManager[1356]: <info>  [1534389833.2051] dns-
           mgr[0x558b04971150]: init: dns=default, rc-manager=file
13:23:53   systemd: Started Network Manager.
```

3) The nagios service tries to execute right after the NetworkManager
   service. This means nagios must have mentioned after=Network.
   target in its service unit file. But the nagios service fails to start.

```
13:24:03   nagios: Nagios 4.2.4 starting... (PID=5006)
13:24:03   nagios: Local time is Thu  13:24:03 AEST 2018
13:24:03   nagios: LOG VERSION: 2.0
13:24:03   nagios: qh: Socket '/usr/local/nagios/var/rw/nagios.qh'
           successfully initialized
13:24:03   nagios: qh: core query handler registered
13:24:03   nagios: nerd: Channel hostchecks registered
           successfully
13:24:03   nagios: nerd: Channel servicechecks registered
           successfully
13:24:03   nagios: nerd: Channel opathchecks registered
           successfully
13:24:03   nagios: nerd: Fully initialized and ready to
           rock!  Nagios Can't ping devices (not 100% packet loss
           at the end of each line)
13:24:04   nagios: HOST ALERT:  X ;DOWN;SOFT;1;CRITICAL -  X: Host
           unreachable @  X. rta nan, lost 100%
```

Resolution: The strange thing is that the nagios error message says it failed to
start because it is not able to connect to the network, but as per NetworkManager, it has
successfully started, and the system has already been placed in network.

The issue is clearly created by systemd's "speeding up the booting procedure" approach. To place the system in the network, systemd has to do a lot of work: initialize the network cards, activate the link, put the IP on the NIC card, check if any duplicate IPs are already available, start communicating on the network, etc. Obviously, to finish every bit of this, systemd will take some time. On my test system, it took almost 20 seconds to fully populate the network. Of course, systemd cannot pause the booting sequence for that whole time. If systemd waits until the network fully populates, then one of the main aspects of systemd's innovation to speed up the booting process will be ruined.

systemd with the help of NetworkManager will give its best shot to make sure we are on the network, but it will not wait for the user-specified network spawning and will not wait until every rule of topology is achieved.

In some situations like this "can't boot" issue, it is possible that NetworkManager has told systemd to initialize nagios, which was dependent on network.target, but the network is not yet fully up, so nagios might not be able to contact its servers.

1) To solve such issues, systemd suggests enabling NetworkManager-wait-online.service. This service will make NetworkManager wait until the network fully comes up. Once the network is fully populated, NetworkManager will signal to systemd to start the services that are dependent on network.target.

```
# cat /usr/lib/systemd/system/NetworkManager-wait-online.service
[Unit]
Description=Network Manager Wait Online
Documentation=man:nm-online(1)
Requires=NetworkManager.service
After=NetworkManager.service
Before=network-online.target

[Service]
Type=oneshot
ExecStart=/usr/bin/nm-online -s -q --timeout=30
RemainAfterExit=yes

[Install]
WantedBy=network-online.target
```

This simply calls the nm-online binary and passes the -s switch to it. The service will hold NetworkManager for a maximum of 30 seconds.

This is what the man page has to say about the nm-online:

"Wait for NetworkManager startup to complete, rather than waiting for network connectivity specifically. Startup is considered complete once NetworkManager has activated (or attempted to activate) every auto-activate connection which is available given the current network state. (This is generally only useful at boot time; after startup has completed, nm-online -s will just return immediately, regardless of the current network state.) "

   2)   After enabling `NetworkManager-wait-online-service`, the issue has been resolved, but the boot time has been reduced slightly. As you can see in Figure 7-5, most of the boot time has been eaten up by `NetworkManager-wait-online-service`, which is expected.

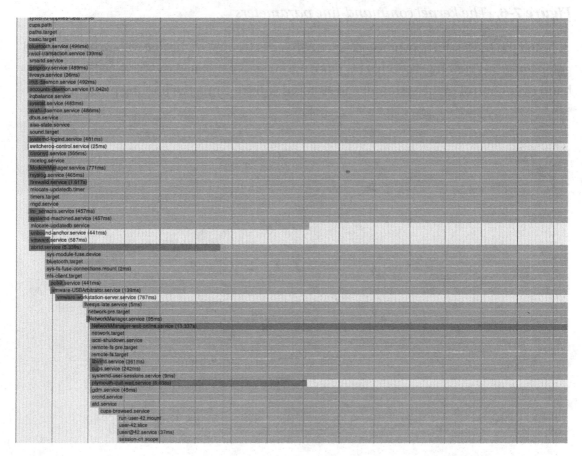

Figure 7-5. *The plot after enabling NetworkManager-wait-online-service*

systemd provides one more tool, bootchart, which is basically a daemon through which you can conduct a performance analysis of the Linux boot process. It will collect the data at boot time and make a graph out of it. You can consider bootchart to be an advanced version of a systemd-analyze plot. To use this tool, as shown in Figure 7-6, you need to pass the full path of the systemd-bootchart binary to the init kernel command-line parameter.

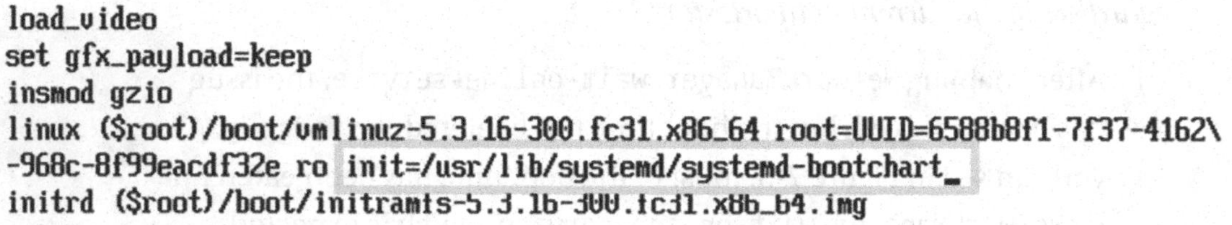

```
load_video
set gfx_payload=keep
insmod gzio
linux ($root)/boot/vmlinuz-5.3.16-300.fc31.x86_64 root=UUID=6588b8f1-7f37-4162\
-968c-8f99eacdf32e ro init=/usr/lib/systemd/systemd-bootchart_
initrd ($root)/boot/initramfs-5.3.16-300.fc31.x86_64.img
```

Figure 7-6. *The kernel command-line parameters*

After the successful boot process, as you can see in Figure 7-7, the tool will create a detailed graph image at /run/log/bootchart*. Once the image is generated, systemd-bootchart will hand over control to the systemd, and systemd will continue the booting procedure.

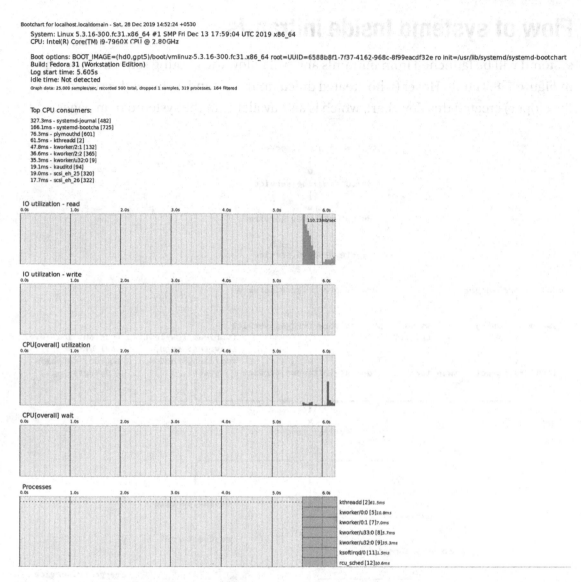

Figure 7-7. *The bootchart graph*

Since we now understand the basics of systemd, we can continue our paused booting sequence. So far, we have reached the stage where the kernel has extracted initramfs in RAM and started the systemd binary from it. Once the systemd process starts, it will follow the regular booting sequence.

Flow of systemd Inside initramfs

systemd will be launched from initramfs and will follow the booting sequence shown in Figure 7-8. Harald Hoyer (who created dracut initramfs and is the lead systemd developer) created this flowchart, which is also available in the systemd man pages.

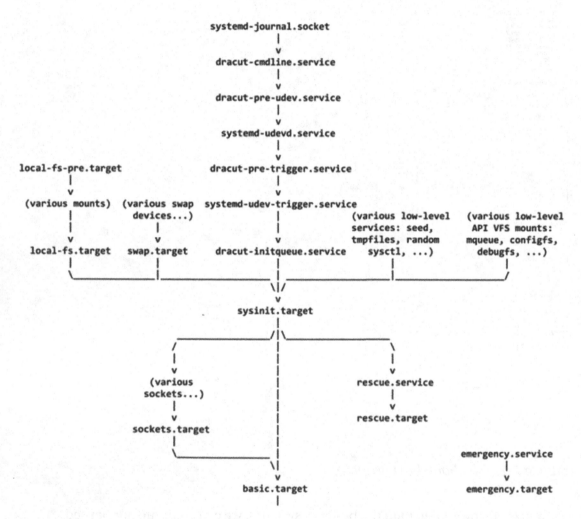

Figure 7-8. *The booting flowchart*

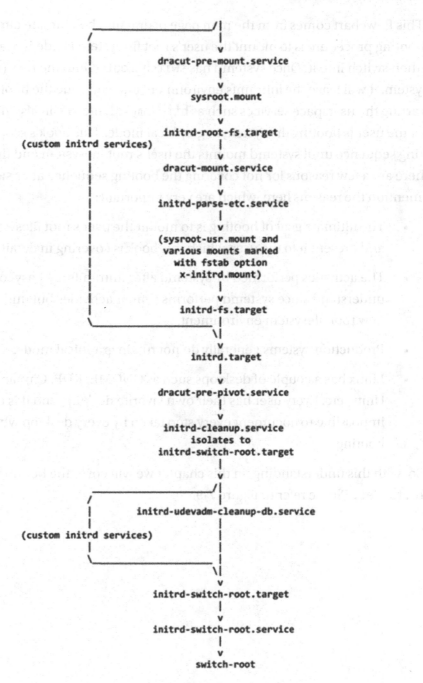

Figure 7-8. *(continued)*

This flowchart comes from the man page of dracut. The ultimate aim of systemd in the booting procedure is to mount the user's root filesystem inside initramfs (`sysroot`) and then switch into it. Once systemd has `switch_rooted` into the new (user's) root filesystem, it will leave the initramfs environment and continue the booting procedure by starting the userspace services such as `httpd`, `mysql`, etc. It will also draw a desktop/ GUI if the user is booting the system in graphical mode. This book's scope is to cover the booting sequence until systemd mounts the user's root filesystem and then switches into it. There are a few reasons for not covering the booting sequence after `switch_root`. I will mention the reasons here, which are very important:

- The ultimate goal of booting is to mount the user's root filesystem and present it to the user, which this book is covering in detail.

- The activities performed by systemd after initramfs are easy to understand since systemd performs similar activities but under the new root filesystem environment.

- Production systems generally do not run in graphical mode.

- Linux has a couple of desktops such as GNOME, KDE, Cinnamon, Unity, etc. Every user has their own favorite desktop, and it is almost impossible to document every step taken by every desktop while booting.

So, with this understanding, in this chapter we will cover the booting sequence up to `basic.target`. Please refer to Figure 7-9.

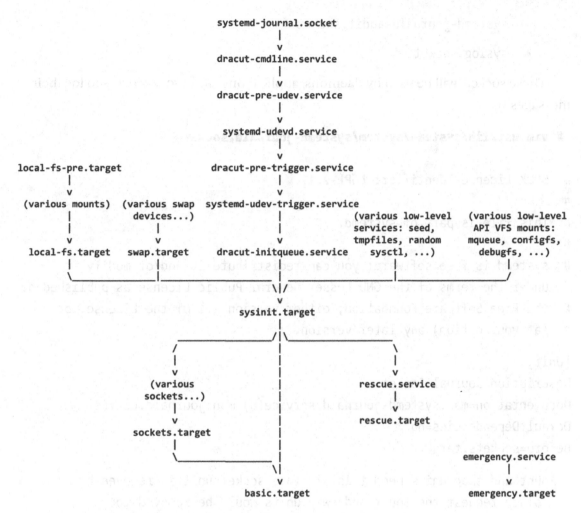

Figure 7-9. *The boot sequence up to basic.target*

systemd-journal.socket

Every process has to log its messages. In fact, a process, service, or daemon will start only if it is able to log its messages in the OS logging mechanism. These days, the OS logging mechanism is journald. So, it is obvious that the journald service has to be started first, but as we know, systemd won't wait until the services fully start. To speed up the procedure, it uses the socket approach. Hence, systemd has to start the journald sockets first. The journald service creates the following four sockets and listens for messages:

- systemd-journald.socket

- systemd-journald-dev-log.socket

- systemd-journald-audit.socket

- syslog.socket

These sockets will be used by daemons, applications, and every process to log their messages.

 # vim usr/lib/systemd/system/systemd-journald.socket

```
# SPDX-License-Identifier: LGPL-2.1+
#
# This file is part of systemd.
#
# systemd is free software; you can redistribute it and/or modify it
# under the terms of the GNU Lesser General Public License as published by
# the Free Software Foundation; either version 2.1 of the License, or
# (at your option) any later version.

[Unit]
Description=Journal Socket
Documentation=man:systemd-journald.service(8) man:journald.conf(5)
DefaultDependencies=no
Before=sockets.target

# Mount and swap units need this. If this socket unit is removed by an
# isolate request the mount and swap units would be removed too,
# hence let's exclude this from isolate requests.
IgnoreOnIsolate=yes

[Socket]
ListenStream=/run/systemd/journal/stdout
ListenDatagram=/run/systemd/journal/socket
SocketMode=0666
PassCredentials=yes
PassSecurity=yes
ReceiveBuffer=8M
Service=systemd-journald.service
```

 # cat usr/lib/systemd/system/systemd-journald-dev-log.socket | grep -v '#'

```
[Unit]
Description=Journal Socket (/dev/log)
Documentation=man:systemd-journald.service(8) man:journald.conf(5)
DefaultDependencies=no
Before=sockets.target

IgnoreOnIsolate=yes

[Socket]
Service=systemd-journald.service
ListenDatagram=/run/systemd/journal/dev-log
Symlinks=/dev/log
SocketMode=0666
PassCredentials=yes
PassSecurity=yes

ReceiveBuffer=8M
SendBuffer=8M
```

We have already discussed the way sockets work, especially the /dev/log socket. The next step in the booting sequence is dracut-cmdline.service.

dracut-cmdline.service

After initializing journald sockets, systemd collects the kernel command-line parameters such as the root, rflags, and fstype variables through usr/lib/systemd/system/dracut-cmdline.service. This is also called a *cmdline hook* of initramfs, which we mentioned at the end of Chapter 6. The hook can be called by passing the cmdline value to rd.break (a dracut command-line parameter). We will explore this stage of the booting process by using the cmdline hook. We need to pass the rd.break=cmdline dracut command-line parameter to the kernel at the time of the boot.

Inside initramfs, systemd calls this hook from usr/lib/systemd/system/dracut-cmdline.service.

 # cat usr/lib/systemd/system/dracut-cmdline.service

```
#  This file is part of dracut.
#
# See dracut.bootup(7) for details

[Unit]
Description=dracut cmdline hook
Documentation=man:dracut-cmdline.service(8)
DefaultDependencies=no
Before=dracut-pre-udev.service
After=systemd-journald.socket
Wants=systemd-journald.socket
ConditionPathExists=/usr/lib/initrd-release
ConditionPathExistsGlob=|/etc/cmdline.d/*.conf
ConditionDirectoryNotEmpty=|/lib/dracut/hooks/cmdline
ConditionKernelCommandLine=|rd.break=cmdline
ConditionKernelCommandLine=|resume
ConditionKernelCommandLine=|noresume
Conflicts=shutdown.target emergency.target
[Service]
Environment=DRACUT_SYSTEMD=1
Environment=NEWROOT=/sysroot
Type=oneshot
ExecStart=-/bin/dracut-cmdline
StandardInput=null
StandardOutput=syslog
StandardError=syslog+console
KillMode=process
RemainAfterExit=yes

# Bash ignores SIGTERM, so we send SIGHUP instead, to ensure that bash
# terminates cleanly.
KillSignal=SIGHUP
```

As you can see, systemd has called a dracut-cmdline script. The script is available in initramfs itself, which will collect the kernel command-line parameters.

 # vim bin/dracut-cmdline

```
24 # Get the "root=" parameter from the kernel command line, but
      differentiate
25 # between the case where it was set to the empty string and the case
      where it
26 # wasn't specified at all.
27 if ! root="$(getarg root=)"; then
28     root_unset='UNSET'
29 fi
30
31 rflags="$(getarg rootflags=)"
32 getargbool 0 ro && rflags="${rflags},ro"
33 getargbool 0 rw && rflags="${rflags},rw"
34 rflags="${rflags#,}"
35
36 fstype="$(getarg rootfstype=)"
37 if [ -z "$fstype" ]; then
38     fstype="auto"
39 fi
40
41 export root
42 export rflags
43 export fstype
44
45 make_trace_mem "hook cmdline" '1+:mem' '1+:iomem' '3+:slab' '4+:komem'
46 # run scriptlets to parse the command line
47 getarg 'rd.break=cmdline' -d 'rdbreak=cmdline' && emergency_shell -n
   cmdline "Break before cmdline"
48 source_hook cmdline
49
50 [ -f /lib/dracut/parse-resume.sh ] && . /lib/dracut/parse-resume.sh
51
52 case "${root}${root_unset}" in
53     block:LABEL=*|LABEL=*)
54         root="${root#block:}"
```

```
55            root="$(echo $root | sed 's,/,\\x2f,g')"
56            root="block:/dev/disk/by-label/${root#LABEL=}"
57            rootok=1 ;;
58      block:UUID=*|UUID=*)
59            root="${root#block:}"
60            root="block:/dev/disk/by-uuid/${root#UUID=}"
61            rootok=1 ;;
62      block:PARTUUID=*|PARTUUID=*)
63            root="${root#block:}"
64            root="block:/dev/disk/by-partuuid/${root#PARTUUID=}"
65            rootok=1 ;;
66      block:PARTLABEL=*|PARTLABEL=*)
67            root="${root#block:}"
68            root="block:/dev/disk/by-partlabel/${root#PARTLABEL=}"
69            rootok=1 ;;
70      /dev/*)
71            root="block:${root}"
72            rootok=1 ;;
73      UNSET|gpt-auto)
74            # systemd's gpt-auto-generator handles this case.
75            rootok=1 ;;
76 esac
77
78 [ -z "${root}${root_unset}" ] && die "Empty root= argument"
79 [ -z "$rootok" ] && die "Don't know how to handle 'root=$root'"
80
81 export root rflags fstype netroot NEWROOT
82
83 export -p > /dracut-state.sh
84
85 exit 0
```

Basically, there are three parameters (kernel command-line parameters) that will be exported in this hook:

- **root** = User's root file system name

- **rflags** = User's root filesystem flags (ro or rw)

- **fstype** = Auto (auto mounting or not)

Let's see how these parameters are discovered by initramfs (or in the cmdline hook of initramfs). The getarg named function will be used to get these three kernel command-line parameters.

```
root="$(getarg root=)
rflags="$(getarg rootflags=)
fstype="$(getarg rootfstype=)"
.

.

export root
export rflags
export fstype
```

The getarg function is defined in the usr/lib/dracut-lib.sh file of initramfs.

#vim usr/lib/dracut-lib.sh
```
201 getarg() {
202     debug_off
203     local _deprecated _newoption
204     while [ $# -gt 0 ]; do
205         case $1 in
206             -d) _deprecated=1; shift;;
207             -y) if _dogetarg $2 >/dev/null; then
208                     if [ "$_deprecated" = "1" ]; then
209                         [ -n "$_newoption" ] && warn "Kernel command
                            line option '$2' is deprecated, use '$_
                            newoption' instead." || warn "Option '$2' is
                            deprecated."
210                     fi
211                     echo 1
212                     debug_on
213                     return 0
214                 fi
215                 _deprecated=0
```

```
216                     shift 2;;
217            -n) if _dogetarg $2 >/dev/null; then
218                    echo 0;
219                    if [ "$_deprecated" = "1" ]; then
220                        [ -n "$_newoption" ] && warn "Kernel command
                           line option '$2' is deprecated, use '$_
                           newoption=0' instead." || warn "Option '$2'
                           is deprecated."
221                    fi
222                    debug_on
223                    return 1
224                fi
225                _deprecated=0
226                shift 2;;
227            *)  if [ -z "$_newoption" ]; then
228                    _newoption="$1"
229                fi
230                if _dogetarg $1; then
231                    if [ "$_deprecated" = "1" ]; then
232                        [ -n "$_newoption" ] && warn "Kernel command
                           line option '$1' is deprecated, use '$_
                           newoption' instead." || warn "Option '$1' is
                           deprecated."
233                    fi
234                    debug_on
235                    return 0;
236                fi
237                _deprecated=0
238                shift;;
239        esac
240    done
241    debug_on
242    return 1
243 }
```

The getarg function is calling the _dogetarg function from the same file.

```
165 _dogetarg() {
166     local _o _val _doecho
167     unset _val
168     unset _o
169     unset _doecho
170     CMDLINE=$(getcmdline)
171
172     for _o in $CMDLINE; do
173         if [ "${_o%%=*}" = "${1%%=*}" ]; then
174             if [ -n "${1#*=}" -a "${1#*=}" != "${1}" ]; then
175                 # if $1 has a "=<value>", we want the exact match
176                 if [ "$_o" = "$1" ]; then
177                     _val="1";
178                     unset _doecho
179                 fi
180                 continue
181             fi
182
183             if [ "${_o#*=}" = "$_o" ]; then
184                 # if cmdline argument has no "=<value>", we assume "=1"
185                 _val="1";
186                 unset _doecho
187                 continue
188             fi
189
190             _val="${_o#*=}"
191             _doecho=1
192         fi
193     done
194     if [ -n "$_val" ]; then
195         [ "x$_doecho" != "x" ] && echo "$_val";
196         return 0;
197     fi
198     return 1;
199 }
```

Then the _dogetarg() function calls the getcmdline named function, which collects the actual kernel command-line parameters from /proc/cmdline.

```
137 getcmdline() {
138     local _line
139     local _i
140     local CMDLINE_ETC_D
141     local CMDLINE_ETC
142     local CMDLINE_PROC
143     unset _line
144
145     if [ -e /etc/cmdline ]; then
146         while read -r _line || [ -n "$_line" ]; do
147             CMDLINE_ETC="$CMDLINE_ETC $_line";
148         done </etc/cmdline;
149     fi
150     for _i in /etc/cmdline.d/*.conf; do
151         [ -e "$_i" ] || continue
152         while read -r _line || [ -n "$_line" ]; do
153             CMDLINE_ETC_D="$CMDLINE_ETC_D $_line";
154         done <"$_i";
155     done
156     if [ -e /proc/cmdline ]; then
157         while read -r _line || [ -n "$_line" ]; do
158             CMDLINE_PROC="$CMDLINE_PROC $_line"
159         done </proc/cmdline;
160     fi
161     CMDLINE="$CMDLINE_ETC_D $CMDLINE_ETC $CMDLINE_PROC"
162     printf "%s" "$CMDLINE"
163 }
```

Here is the booting sequence so far:

1. The bootloader collects the kernel command-line parameters from the user and stores them in its own configuration file (grub.cfg).

2. It passes those command-line parameters to the kernel by filling the kernel header.

3. The kernel extracts itself and copies the kernel command-line parameters found in the kernel header.

4. The kernel extracts initramfs in memory and uses it as a temporary root filesystem.

5. In the same procedure, the kernel prepares the virtual filesystems such as proc, sys, dev, devpts, shm, etc.

6. The kernel stores the command-line parameters in the /proc/cmdline file.

7. systemd collects the kernel command-line parameters by reading the /proc/cmdline file and stores them in the root, rootfs, and fstype variables.

We can verify this procedure by using the cmdline hook.

Getting back to the /bin/dracut-cmdline script, let's take a look:

```
41 export root
42 export rflags
43 export fstype
44
45 make_trace_mem "hook cmdline" '1+:mem' '1+:iomem' '3+:slab' '4+:komem'
46 # run scriptlets to parse the command line
47 getarg 'rd.break=cmdline' -d 'rdbreak=cmdline' && emergency_shell -n
cmdline "Break before cmdline"
48 source_hook cmdline
49
50 [ -f /lib/dracut/parse-resume.sh ] && . /lib/dracut/parse-resume.sh
```

The condition says if the user has passed the `rd.break=cmdline` parameter on the kernel stanza of GRUB, then execute the `emergency_shell` function. Figure 7-10 shows the condition.

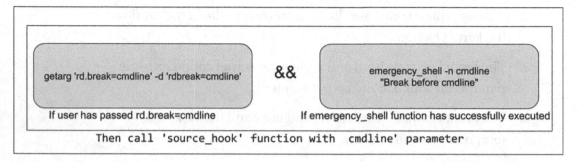

Figure 7-10. *The condition*

If the user has passed `rd.break=cmdline`, then the script calls the function named `emergency_shell`. As the name suggests, it will provide the debugging shell, and if the debugging shell has successfully launched, then it calls another function named `source_ hook` and passes the `cmdline` parameter to it. Whoever wrote this code to provide users with a debugging shell is a genius programmer!

We will not discuss the emergency shell function at this stage since we need to understand systemd more first. Hence, we will discuss it in much more detail in Chapter 8.

Figure 7-11 shows the flowchart of the `dracut-cmdline.service` units working.

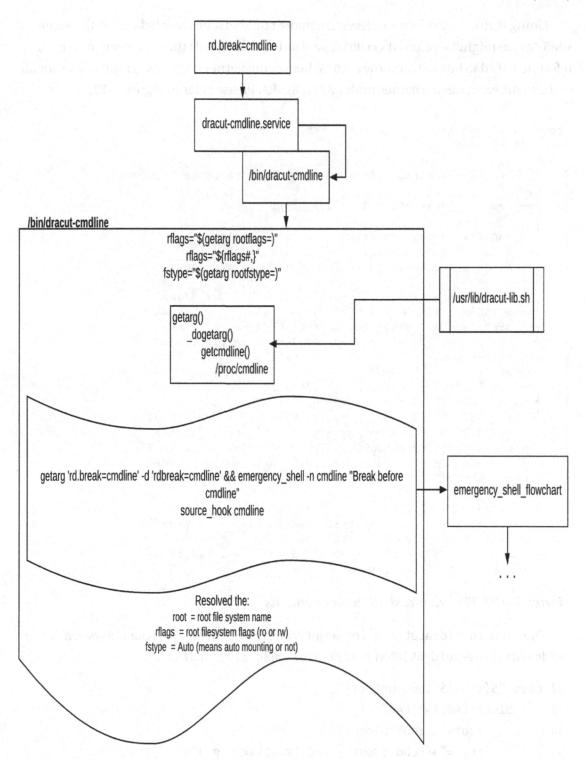

Figure 7-11. *The flowchart of dracut-cmdline.service*

Going further, a user's root filesystem name could just be /dev/sda5, but the same sda5 device might be referred via uuid, partuuid, or label. At the end, every other reference of sda5 has to reach /dev/sda5; hence, the kernel prepares symlinks files for all of these different device names under /dev/disk/. Please refer to Figure 7-12.

```
[root@localhost boot]# tree /dev/disk/
/dev/disk/
├── by-id
│   └── ata-VMware_Virtual_SATA_CDRW_Drive_01000000000000000001 -> ../../sr0
├── by-label
│   └── Fedora-WS-Live-31-1-9 -> ../../sr0
├── by-partlabel
│   ├── Basic\x20data\x20partition -> ../../sda4
│   ├── EFI\x20System\x20Partition -> ../../sda1
│   └── Microsoft\x20reserved\x20partition -> ../../sda3
├── by-partuuid
│   ├── 4fb8ac07-ca42-41c9-910b-e323bcbd82fd -> ../../sda3
│   ├── 557553aa-f11f-4d67-a4c9-68944e3d3c33 -> ../../sda1
│   ├── a500e83e-8702-4cb6-a80b-85ec28f59f47 -> ../../sda5
│   ├── b49bd562-70f9-4477-a0d3-0143f07e89e6 -> ../../sda2
│   └── be7e9e01-b172-42f5-b95d-6e378e6a2c93 -> ../../sda4
├── by-path
│   ├── pci-0000:02:04.0-ata-2 -> ../../sr0
│   ├── pci-0000:03:00.0-sas-phy0-lun-0 -> ../../sda
│   ├── pci-0000:03:00.0-sas-phy0-lun-0-part1 -> ../../sda1
│   ├── pci-0000:03:00.0-sas-phy0-lun-0-part2 -> ../../sda2
│   ├── pci-0000:03:00.0-sas-phy0-lun-0-part3 -> ../../sda3
│   ├── pci-0000:03:00.0-sas-phy0-lun-0-part4 -> ../../sda4
│   └── pci-0000:03:00.0-sas-phy0-lun-0-part5 -> ../../sda5
└── by-uuid
    ├── 2019-10-23-23-21-29-00 -> ../../sr0
    ├── 6588b8f1-7f37-4162-968c-8f99eacdf32e -> ../../sda5
    ├── C27C4E0C7C4DFC23 -> ../../sda4
    ├── cc6a7fe8-d67a-4793-b9b0-21557732cbe8 -> ../../sda2
    └── FBC0-BBD6 -> ../../sda1
```

Figure 7-12. *The /dev/disk directory contents*

The same /bin/dracut-cmdline script converts the mear sda5 root filesystem name to /dev/disk/by-uuid/6588b8f1-7f37-4162-968c-8f99eacdf32e.

```
52 case "${root}${root_unset}" in
53    block:LABEL=*|LABEL=*)
54        root="${root#block:}"
55        root="$(echo $root | sed 's,/,\\x2f,g')"
```

```
56          root="block:/dev/disk/by-label/${root#LABEL=}"
57          rootok=1 ;;
58      block:UUID=*|UUID=*)
59          root="${root#block:}"
60          root="block:/dev/disk/by-uuid/${root#UUID=}"
61          rootok=1 ;;
62      block:PARTUUID=*|PARTUUID=*)
63          root="${root#block:}"
64          root="block:/dev/disk/by-partuuid/${root#PARTUUID=}"
65          rootok=1 ;;
66      block:PARTLABEL=*|PARTLABEL=*)
67          root="${root#block:}"
68          root="block:/dev/disk/by-partlabel/${root#PARTLABEL=}"
69          rootok=1 ;;
70      /dev/*)
71          root="block:${root}"
72          rootok=1 ;;
73      UNSET|gpt-auto)
74          # systemd's gpt-auto-generator handles this case.
75          rootok=1 ;;
76 esac
77
78 [ -z "${root}${root_unset}" ] && die "Empty root= argument"
79 [ -z "$rootok" ] && die "Don't know how to handle 'root=$root'"
80
81 export root rflags fstype netroot NEWROOT
82
83 export -p > /dracut-state.sh
84
85 exit 0
```

Let's see the cmdline hook in action. As shown in Figure 7-13, pass rd.
break=cmdline on the kernel stanza of GRUB.

```
load_video
set gfx_payload=keep
insmod gzio
linux ($root)/boot/vmlinuz-5.3.16-300.fc31.x86_64 root=UUID=6588b8f1-7f37-4162\
-968c-8f99eacdf32e ro rd.break=cmdline_
initrd ($root)/boot/initramfs-5.3.16-300.fc31.x86_64.img
```

Figure 7-13. *The kernel command-line parameter*

The kernel will extract initramfs, the systemd process will launch, systemd will
initialize the journald sockets, and as you can see in Figure 7-14, systemd will drop us
on a cmdline shell since we told systemd to break (hook) the booting sequence before
executing the dracut-cmdline hook.

```
        Starting Create Volatile Files and Directories...
[  OK  ] Started Create Volatile Files and Directories.
[   2.140892] audit: type=1130 audit(1577617801.064:5): pid=1 uid=0 auid=4294967295 ses=4294967295 subj=kernel msg='unit=system
d-tmpfiles-setup comm="systemd" exe="/usr/lib/systemd/systemd" hostname=? addr=? terminal=? res=success'
Warning: /dev/disk/by-uuid/6588b8f1-7f37-4162-968c-8f99eacdf32e does not exist

Generating "/run/initramfs/rdsosreport.txt"


Entering emergency mode. Exit the shell to continue.
Type "journalctl" to view system logs.
You might want to save "/run/initramfs/rdsosreport.txt" to a USB stick or /boot
after mounting them and attach it to a bug report.


cmdline:/# [   2.293496] pcieport 0000:00:15.1: pciehp: Failed to check link status
[   2.306670] pcieport 0000:00:15.3: pciehp: Failed to check link status
[   2.307571] pcieport 0000:00:15.4: pciehp: Failed to check link status
[   2.307640] pcieport 0000:00:15.5: pciehp: Failed to check link status
[   2.307688] pcieport 0000:00:15.2: pciehp: Failed to check link status
[   2.312566] pcieport 0000:00:15.6: pciehp: Failed to check link status
[   2.317572] pcieport 0000:00:15.7: pciehp: Failed to check link status
[   2.319658] pcieport 0000:00:16.2: pciehp: Failed to check link status
[   2.324680] pcieport 0000:00:16.1: pciehp: Failed to check link status
[   2.329580] pcieport 0000:00:16.3: pciehp: Failed to check link status
[   2.330482] pcieport 0000:00:16.5: pciehp: Failed to check link status
[   2.331631] pcieport 0000:00:16.4: pciehp: Failed to check link status
[   2.332500] pcieport 0000:00:17.1: pciehp: Failed to check link status
[   2.334463] pcieport 0000:00:17.2: pciehp: Failed to check link status
[   2.335390] pcieport 0000:00:16.6: pciehp: Failed to check link status
[   2.336806] pcieport 0000:00:17.4: pciehp: Failed to check link status
[   2.336901] pcieport 0000:00:17.3: pciehp: Failed to check link status
[   2.346494] pcieport 0000:00:16.7: pciehp: Failed to check link status
[   2.350520] pcieport 0000:00:18.2: pciehp: Failed to check link status
[   2.351546] pcieport 0000:00:18.3: pciehp: Failed to check link status
[   2.351591] pcieport 0000:00:17.5: pciehp: Failed to check link status
[   2.352406] pcieport 0000:00:18.5: pciehp: Failed to check link status
[   2.352444] pcieport 0000:00:17.7: pciehp: Failed to check link status
[   2.353291] pcieport 0000:00:17.6: pciehp: Failed to check link status
[   2.353373] pcieport 0000:00:18.4: pciehp: Failed to check link status
[   2.355288] pcieport 0000:00:18.1: pciehp: Failed to check link status
[   2.356370] pcieport 0000:00:18.0: pciehp: Failed to check link status
[   2.370067] pcieport 0000:00:18.7: pciehp: Failed to check link status
[   2.375153] pcieport 0000:00:18.6: pciehp: Failed to check link status

cmdline:/# _
```

Figure 7-14. *The command-line hook*

Currently, we are inside initramfs, and we have paused (dracut hooked) systemd's booting sequence after `systemd-journal.socket`. Since `dracut-cmdline.service` has not yet started, systemd has not yet collected the kernel command-line parameters such as `root`, `rsflags`, and `fstype` from `/proc/cmdline`. Please see Figure 7-15 for a better understanding. Also, the symlinks under `/dev/disk` have not yet been created by dracut.

```
cmdline:/# echo $root

cmdline:/#
cmdline:/# echo $rflags

cmdline:/#
cmdline:/# echo $fstype

cmdline:/#
cmdline:/# ls /dev/disk -l
ls: cannot access '/dev/disk': No such file or directory
cmdline:/#
```

Figure 7-15. *The command-line hook*

Since systemd has not yet collected the name of the user's root filesystem, there is no question that you will not find user's root filesystem mounted inside initramfs. `sysroot` is a directory inside initramfs where systemd mounts the user's root filesystem. Refer to Figure 7-16.

```
cmdline:/# ls -l /
total 8
lrwxrwxrwx   1 root root      7 Jul 24 22:24 bin -> usr/bin
drwxr-xr-x  10 root root   3100 Dec 29 11:10 dev
-rw-r--r--   1 root root      2 Jul 24 22:24 early_cpio
drwxr-xr-x  10 root root      0 Dec 29 11:10 etc
lrwxrwxrwx   1 root root     23 Jul 24 22:24 init -> usr/lib/systemd/systemd
drwxr-xr-x   3 root root      0 Jul 24 22:24 kernel
lrwxrwxrwx   1 root root      7 Jul 24 22:24 lib -> usr/lib
lrwxrwxrwx   1 root root      9 Jul 24 22:24 lib64 -> usr/lib64
dr-xr-xr-x 293 root root      0 Dec 29 11:09 proc
drwxr-xr-x   2 root root      0 Jul 24 22:24 root
drwxr-xr-x  10 root root    220 Dec 29 11:10 run
lrwxrwxrwx   1 root root      8 Jul 24 22:24 sbin -> usr/sbin
-rwxr-xr-x   1 root root   3121 Jul 24 22:24 shutdown
dr-xr-xr-x  13 root root      0 Dec 29 11:10 sys
drwxr-xr-x   2 root root      0 Jul 24 22:24 sysroot
drwxr-xr-x   2 root root      0 Jul 24 22:24 tmp
drwxr-xr-x   8 root root      0 Jul 24 22:24 usr
drwxr-xr-x   5 root root      0 Dec 29 11:10 var
cmdline:/#
cmdline:/# ls /sysroot
cmdline:/#
cmdline:/# exit_
```

Figure 7-16. *The sysroot directory*

But if we do not pass any argument to rd.break or simply exit from the current cmdline shell, we will be dropped at the switch_root shell. The switch_root shell is the final stage of systemd's boot sequence inside initramfs. In Figure 7-17, you can see that we are passing rd.break without any arguments.

```
load_video
set gfx_payload=keep
insmod gzio
linux ($root)/boot/vmlinuz-5.3.16-300.fc31.x86_64 root=UUID=6588b8f1-7f37-4162\
-968c-8f99eacdf32e ro rd.break_
initrd ($root)/boot/initramfs-5.3.16-300.fc31.x86_64.img
```

Figure 7-17. *The rd.break kernel command-line parameter*

As you can see in Figure 7-18, in the switch_root shell since the dracut-cmdline. service has been executed, you will find the kernel command-line parameters have been collected by systemd. Also, the user's root filesystem has been mounted inside initramfs under sysroot.

```
[ OK ] Started Setup Virtual Console.
        Starting Dracut Emergency Shell...

Generating "/run/initramfs/rdsosreport.txt"


Entering emergency mode. Exit the shell to continue.
Type "journalctl" to view system logs.
You might want to save "/run/initramfs/rdsosreport.txt" to a USB stick or /boot
after mounting them and attach it to a bug report.


switch_root:/# echo $root
block:/dev/disk/by-uuid/6588b8f1-7f37-4162-968c-8f99eacdf32e
switch_root:/#
switch_root:/# echo $rflags
ro
switch_root:/#
switch_root:/# echo $fstype
auto
switch_root:/#
switch_root:/# ls /sysroot/
bin boot dev etc home lib lib64 lost+found media mnt opt proc root run sbin srv sys tmp usr var
switch_root:/#
switch_root:/# exit_
```

Figure 7-18. *The switch_root hook*

If we exit from this stage, switch_root (pivot_root) will be performed by systemd, and it will leave the initramfs environment. Later systemd will carry the remaining booting procedure, and as shown in Figure 7-19, eventually we will get the desktop.

Figure 7-19. *The login screen of Fedora*

Coming back to our booting sequence so far, we have reached the pre-udev stage. You can refer to Figure 7-20 for this.

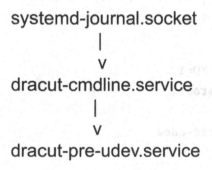

Figure 7-20. *The booting sequence covered so far*

dracut-pre-udev.service

Next systemd will deal with the attached devices. For that, systemd has to start the udev daemon, but before starting the udev service, it checks whether users want to stop the booting procedure before udev kicks in. If a user has passed the rd.break=pre-udev dracut command-line parameter, systemd will stop the booting sequence just before executing the udev daemon.

 # cat usr/lib/systemd/system/dracut-pre-udev.service | grep -v '#'

```
[Unit]
Description=dracut pre-udev hook
Documentation=man:dracut-pre-udev.service(8)
DefaultDependencies=no
Before=systemd-udevd.service dracut-pre-trigger.service
After=dracut-cmdline.service
Wants=dracut-cmdline.service
ConditionPathExists=/usr/lib/initrd-release
ConditionDirectoryNotEmpty=|/lib/dracut/hooks/pre-udev
ConditionKernelCommandLine=|rd.break=pre-udev
ConditionKernelCommandLine=|rd.driver.blacklist
ConditionKernelCommandLine=|rd.driver.pre
ConditionKernelCommandLine=|rd.driver.post
ConditionPathExistsGlob=|/etc/cmdline.d/*.conf
Conflicts=shutdown.target emergency.target

[Service]
Environment=DRACUT_SYSTEMD=1
Environment=NEWROOT=/sysroot
Type=oneshot
ExecStart=-/bin/dracut-pre-udev
StandardInput=null
StandardOutput=syslog
StandardError=syslog+console
KillMode=process
RemainAfterExit=yes

KillSignal=SIGHUP
```

It will drop us on a pre-udev shell. Notice the after, before, and wants variables. Executing dracut-pre-udev.service just starts a /bin/dracut-pre-udev binary from initramfs. In Figure 7-21, we have passed rd.break=pre-udev as a kernel command-line parameter.

```
load_video
set gfx_payload=keep
insmod gzio
linux ($root)/boot/vmlinuz-5.3.16-300.fc31.x86_64 root=UUID=6588b8f1-7f37-4162\
-968c-8f99eacdf32e ro rd.break=pre-udev_
initrd ($root)/boot/initramfs-5.3.16-300.fc31.x86_64.img
```

Figure 7-21. *Passing the pre-udev kernel command-line parameter*

To understand the pre-udev hook, you can simply list the contents of /dev, and in Figure 7-22 you will notice there is no device file named sda. sda is our HDD where we have our root filesystem.

```
Entering emergency mode. Exit the shell to continue.
Type "journalctl" to view system logs.
You might want to save "/run/initramfs/rdsosreport.txt" to a USB stick or /boot
after mounting them and attach it to a bug report.

pre-udev:/#
pre-udev:/# ls /dev
agpgart          hidraw1             nvram     stdout  tty19  tty30  tty42  tty54  tty9    ttyS2   ttyS31  usbmon3
autofs           hpet                port      tty     tty2   tty31  tty43  tty55  ttyS0   ttyS20  ttyS4   usbmon4
bsg              hwrng               ptmx      tty0    tty20  tty32  tty44  tty56  ttyS1   ttyS21  ttyS5   vcs
bus              input               pts       tty1    tty21  tty33  tty45  tty57  ttyS10  ttyS22  ttyS6   vcs1
console          kmsg                random    tty10   tty22  tty34  tty46  tty58  ttyS11  ttyS23  ttyS7   vcsa
core             log                 raw       tty11   tty23  tty35  tty47  tty59  ttyS12  ttyS24  ttyS8   vcsa1
cpu              mapper              rtc0      tty12   tty24  tty36  tty48  tty6   ttyS13  ttyS25  ttyS9   vcsu
cpu_dma_latency  mcelog              sg0       tty13   tty25  tty37  tty49  tty60  ttyS14  ttyS26  udmabuf vcsu1
fb0              mem                 shm       tty14   tty26  tty38  tty5   tty61  ttyS15  ttyS27  uhid    vga_arbiter
fd               memory_bandwidth    snapshot  tty15   tty27  tty39  tty50  tty62  ttyS16  ttyS28  urandom zero
full             network_latency     sr0       tty16   tty28  tty4   tty51  tty63  ttyS17  ttyS29  usbmon0
fuse             network_throughput  stderr    tty17   tty29  tty40  tty52  tty7   ttyS18  ttyS3   usbmon1
hidraw0          null                stdin     tty18   tty3   tty41  tty53  tty8   ttyS19  ttyS30  usbmon2
pre-udev:/# _
```

Figure 7-22. *The pre-udev hook*

The reason for the absence of sda device files is because the udev daemon has not started yet. The daemon will be started by the /usr/lib/systemd/system/systemd-udevd.service unit file, which will start after the pre-udev hook.

```
# cat usr/lib/systemd/system/systemd-udevd.service | grep -v '#'
```

```
[Unit]
Description=udev Kernel Device Manager
Documentation=man:systemd-udevd.service(8) man:udev(7)
DefaultDependencies=no
After=systemd-sysusers.service systemd-hwdb-update.service
Before=sysinit.target
ConditionPathIsReadWrite=/sys

[Service]
Type=notify
OOMScoreAdjust=-1000
Sockets=systemd-udevd-control.socket systemd-udevd-kernel.socket
Restart=always
RestartSec=0
ExecStart=/usr/lib/systemd/systemd-udevd
KillMode=mixed
WatchdogSec=3min
TasksMax=infinity
PrivateMounts=yes
ProtectHostname=yes
MemoryDenyWriteExecute=yes
RestrictAddressFamilies=AF_UNIX AF_NETLINK AF_INET AF_INET6
RestrictRealtime=yes
RestrictSUIDSGID=yes
SystemCallFilter=@system-service @module @raw-io
SystemCallErrorNumber=EPERM
SystemCallArchitectures=native
LockPersonality=yes
IPAddressDeny=any
```

Let's try to understand how udev works and how it creates device files under /dev.

It's the kernel that detects the connected hardware to the system; more precisely, it's the drivers that are compiled inside kernels or the modules inserted later that will detect the hardware and will register their objects with sysfs (/sys mount point). Because of the /sys mount point, this data becomes available to userspace and to tools like udev. So, it's the kernel that detects the hardware through drivers and creates a device file in /dev, which is a devfs filesystem. After this, the kernel sends a uevent to udevd, and udevd changes the device file's name, owner, or group, or it sets the proper permissions according to the rules defined here:

```
/etc/udev/rules.d,
/lib/udev/rules.d, and
/run/udev/rules.d
```

```
# ls etc/udev/rules.d/
    59-persistent-storage.rules  61-persistent-storage.rules
```

```
# ls lib/udev/rules.d/
    50-udev-default.rules         70-uaccess.rules      75-net-description.
    rules  85-nm-unmanaged.rules
    60-block.rules                71-seat.rules         80-drivers.rules
    90-vconsole.rules
    60-persistent-storage.rules  73-seat-late.rules    80-net-setup-link.
    rules    99-systemd.rules
```

initramfs has few udev rules files compared to the available udev rules present on the user's root filesystem. Basically, it has only those rules that are necessary to manage the user's root filesystem devices. Once udevd is in control, it will call the respective systemd units based on lib/udev/rules.d/99-systemd.rules. Here's an example:

 # cat lib/udev/rules.d/99-systemd.rules
```
SUBSYSTEM=="net", KERNEL!="lo", TAG+="systemd", ENV{SYSTEMD_ALIAS}+="/sys/
subsystem/net/devices/$name"
SUBSYSTEM=="bluetooth", TAG+="systemd", ENV{SYSTEMD_ALIAS}+="/sys/
subsystem/bluetooth/devices/%k"
```

**SUBSYSTEM=="bluetooth", TAG+="systemd", ENV{SYSTEMD_WANTS}+="bluetooth.
target", ENV{SYSTEMD_USER_WANTS}+="bluetooth.target"**
```
ENV{ID_SMARTCARD_READER}=="?*", TAG+="systemd", ENV{SYSTEMD_
WANTS}+="smartcard.target", ENV{SYSTEMD_USER_WANTS}+="smartcard.target"
SUBSYSTEM=="sound", KERNEL=="card*", TAG+="systemd", ENV{SYSTEMD_
WANTS}+="sound.target", ENV{SYSTEMD_USER_WANTS}+="sound.target"
```

```
SUBSYSTEM=="printer", TAG+="systemd", ENV{SYSTEMD_WANTS}+="printer.target",
ENV{SYSTEMD_USER_WANTS}+="printer.target"
SUBSYSTEM=="usb", KERNEL=="lp*", TAG+="systemd", ENV{SYSTEMD_
WANTS}+="printer.target", ENV{SYSTEMD_USER_WANTS}+="printer.target"
```

```
SUBSYSTEM=="usb", ENV{DEVTYPE}=="usb_device", ENV{ID_USB_
INTERFACES}=="*:0701??:*", TAG+="systemd", ENV{SYSTEMD_WANTS}+="printer.
target", ENV{SYSTEMD_USER_WANTS}+="printer.target"
```

```
SUBSYSTEM=="udc", ACTION=="add", TAG+="systemd", ENV{SYSTEMD_WANTS}+="usb-
gadget.target"
```

The rule is tagged with the systemd tag. That means whenever a bluetooth device is detected, udevd will call systemd's bluetooth.target. The bluetooth.target will execute the /usr/libexec/bluetooth/bluetoothd binary, which will take care of the rest of the bluetooth device handling. So, the complete sequence of udevd handling the bluetooth device is as follows:

1) If a user has a bluetooth device connected to the system while booting, it's the kernel or drivers compiled in the kernel or modules inserted later that will detect the bluetooth device and register its object with /sys.

2) Later the kernel will create a device file in the /dev mount point. After the device file creation, the kernel will send a uevent to udevd.

3) udevd will refer to lib/udev/rules.d/99-systemd.rules from initramfs and will call systemd. As per the tag, systemd is supposed to handle the rest of it.

4) systemd will execute the bluetooth.target, which will execute the bluetoothd binary, and the bluetooth hardware will be ready to be used.

Of course, bluetooth is not the kind of hardware that is necessary at the time of the boot. I have taken this example just for the ease of understanding.

So, we have reached up to systemd-udev.service. systemd will continue its booting sequence and will execute dracut-pre-trigger.service. You can see the booting sequence in Figure 7-23.

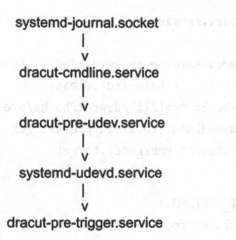

Figure 7-23. *The boot sequence covered so far*

dracut-pre-trigger.service

systemd's initramfs boot sequence will be broken (hooked) if the user has passed the
rd.break=pre-trigger dracut command-line parameter. You can see in Figure 7-24
that we have passed pre-trigger as an argument to the rd.break kernel command-line
parameter.

```
load_video
set gfx_payload=keep
insmod gzio
linux ($root)/boot/vmlinuz-5.3.16-300.fc31.x86_64 root=UUID=6588b8f1-7f37-4162\
-968c-8f99eacdf32e ro rd.break=pre-trigger_
initrd ($root)/boot/initramfs-5.3.16-300.fc31.x86_64.img
```

Figure 7-24. *The rd.break=pre-trigger kernel command-line parameter*

It will drop us on a pre-trigger shell, which is just after starting the udevd service.
First let's see how it drops on a pre-trigger shell.

```
# cat usr/lib/systemd/system/dracut-pre-trigger.service | grep -v '#'
[Unit]
Description=dracut pre-trigger hook
Documentation=man:dracut-pre-trigger.service(8)
DefaultDependencies=no
Before=systemd-udev-trigger.service dracut-initqueue.service
```

```
After=dracut-pre-udev.service systemd-udevd.service systemd-tmpfiles-setup-
dev.service
Wants=dracut-pre-udev.service systemd-udevd.service
ConditionPathExists=/usr/lib/initrd-release
ConditionDirectoryNotEmpty=|/lib/dracut/hooks/pre-trigger
ConditionKernelCommandLine=|rd.break=pre-trigger
Conflicts=shutdown.target emergency.target

[Service]
Environment=DRACUT_SYSTEMD=1
Environment=NEWROOT=/sysroot
Type=oneshot
ExecStart=-/bin/dracut-pre-trigger
StandardInput=null
StandardOutput=syslog
StandardError=syslog+console
KillMode=process
RemainAfterExit=yes

KillSignal=SIGHUP
```

Please note the After, Before, and wants sections of the service unit file.
This service file will execute /bin/dracut-pre-trigger from initramfs if this
ConditionDirectoryNotEmpty=|/lib/dracut/hooks/pre-trigger directory exists and
if the user has passed rd.break=pre-trigger as a command-line parameter.

```
[root@fedorab boot]# cat bin/dracut-pre-trigger
#!/usr/bin/sh

export DRACUT_SYSTEMD=1
if [ -f /dracut-state.sh ]; then
    . /dracut-state.sh 2>/dev/null
fi
type getarg >/dev/null 2>&1 || . /lib/dracut-lib.sh
source_conf /etc/conf.d
make_trace_mem "hook pre-trigger" '1:shortmem' '2+:mem' '3+:slab'
'4+:komem'
source_hook pre-trigger
```

CHAPTER 7   SYSTEMD (PART I)

```
getarg 'rd.break=pre-trigger' 'rdbreak=pre-trigger' && emergency_shell -n
pre-trigger "Break pre-trigger"
udevadm control --reload >/dev/null 2>&1 || :
export -p > /dracut-state.sh
exit 0
```

As you can see, it is checking the passed dracut command-line parameters
(rd.break=pre-trigger) through the getarg function. We saw how getarg works
earlier in this chapter. If the user has passed rd.break=pre-trigger, then it will call
the emergency_shell function with pre-trigger as a parameter passed to it. The
emergency_shell function is written in the dracut-lib.sh file. This function will
provide us with the pre-trigger shell. Chapter 8 covers the procedure behind providing
an emergency shell.

As the pre-trigger name suggests, and as you can see in Figure 7-25, we have
stopped the booting sequence just before the udev triggers. Hence, the sda disk is not yet
available under dev.

```
        Starting Dracut Emergency Shell...
Warning: /dev/disk/by-uuid/6588b8f1-7f37-4162-968c-8f99eacdf32e does not exist

Generating "/run/initramfs/rdsosreport.txt"


Entering emergency mode. Exit the shell to continue.
Type "journalctl" to view system logs.
You might want to save "/run/initramfs/rdsosreport.txt" to a USB stick or /boot
after mounting them and attach it to a bug report.


pre-trigger:/# ls /dev/sda
ls: cannot access '/dev/sda': No such file or directory
```

Figure 7-25. *The pre-trigger hook*

This is because the udevadm trigger has not been executed yet. The service dracut-
pre-trigger.service executes only udevadm control --reload, which reloads the
udev rules. As shown in Figure 7-26, the service systemd-udev.service has been
started, but the systemd-udev-trigger service has not yet started.

333

```
pre-trigger:/# systemctl status systemd-udevd.service
● systemd-udevd.service - udev Kernel Device Manager
   Loaded: loaded (/usr/lib/systemd/system/systemd-udevd.service; static; vendor preset: enabled)
   Active: active (running) since Mon 2019-12-30 04:48:22 UTC; 1min 3s ago
     Docs: man:systemd-udevd.service(8)
           man:udev(7)
 Main PID: 553 (systemd-udevd)
   Status: "Processing with 48 children at max"
    Tasks: 1
   Memory: 3.2M
      CPU: 255ms
   CGroup: /system.slice/systemd-udevd.service
           └─553 /usr/lib/systemd/systemd-udevd

Dec 30 04:48:22 localhost.localdomain systemd[1]: Started udev Kernel Device Manager.
pre-trigger:/#
pre-trigger:/# systemctl status systemd-udev-trigger.service
● systemd-udev-trigger.service - udev Coldplug all Devices
   Loaded: loaded (/usr/lib/systemd/system/systemd-udev-trigger.service; static; vendor preset: enabled)
   Active: inactive (dead)
     Docs: man:udev(7)
           man:systemd-udevd.service(8)
pre-trigger:/#
pre-trigger:/# exit_
```

Figure 7-26. *The pre-trigger hook*

systemd-udev-trigger.service

Figure 7-27 shows the stage of booting we have reached.

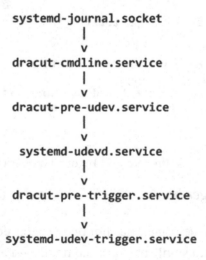

Figure 7-27. *The booting sequence so far*

As we have seen, with pre-udev the /dev was not populated since the systemd-udevd. service itself was not started. With pre-trigger, it's the same: /dev is not populated, but the udevd service has started. The udevd service will create an environment to start/run the various udev tools like udevadm. By using the environment provided by the udevd daemon, as you can see in Figure 7-28, inside pre-trigger we will be able to execute the udevadm, which we were not able to use at the pre-udev shell.

```
        Starting Dracut Emergency Shell...
Warning: /dev/disk/by-uuid/6588b8f1-7f37-4162-968c-8f99eacdf32e does not exist

Generating "/run/initramfs/rdsosreport.txt"


Entering emergency mode. Exit the shell to continue.
Type "journalctl" to view system logs.
You might want to save "/run/initramfs/rdsosreport.txt" to a USB stick or /boot
after mounting them and attach it to a bug report.


pre-trigger:/# ls /dev/sda
ls: cannot access '/dev/sda': No such file or directory
pre-trigger:/#
pre-trigger:/# udevadm trigger --type=subsystems --action=add;
pre-trigger:/#          Mounting Kernel Configuration File System...
[  OK  ] Mounted Kernel Configuration File System.

pre-trigger:/# ls /dev/sda
ls: cannot access '/dev/sda': No such file or directory
pre-trigger:/#
pre-trigger:/# udevadm trigger --type=devices --action=add;
```

Figure 7-28. *The pre-trigger hook*

As you can see inside the pre-trigger switch, the sda device has not been created yet. But since we have a udevadm environment ready, we can discover the devices through it. As shown in Figure 7-29, we will first mount the kernel configuration filesystem.

pre-trigger:/ # **udevadm trigger --type=subsystems --action=add**

Then we will trigger udevadm to add the devices.

pre-trigger:/ # **udevadm trigger --type=devices --action=add**

```
[  175.767498] scsi 32:0:0:0: Direct-Access      VMware,  VMware Virtual S 1.0  P
[  175.769872] sd 32:0:0:0: Attached scsi generic sg1 type 0
[  175.770416] sd 32:0:0:0: [sda] 125829120 512-byte logical blocks: (64.4 GB/60
[  175.771153] e1000e 0000:0b:00.0 ens192: renamed from eth0
[  175.771904] sd 32:0:0:0: [sda] Write Protect is off
[  175.774422] sd 32:0:0:0: [sda] Cache data unavailable
[  175.775519] sd 32:0:0:0: [sda] Assuming drive cache: write through
[  175.777279] fb0: switching to svgadrmfb from EFI VGA
[  175.777911] Console: switching to colour dummy device 80x25
pre-trigger:/# [  175.778142] fbcon: svgadrmfb (fb0) is primary device
[  175.785208]  sda: sda1 sda2 sda3 sda4 sda5
[  175.790120] sd 32:0:0:0: [sda] Attached SCSI disk
[  175.792436] Console: switching to colour frame buffer device 128x48
pre-trigger:/# [  175.798533] [drm] Initialized vmwgfx 2.15.0 20180704 for 0000:00:0f.0 on minor 0
[ OK ] Found device VMware_Virtual_S 5.
[ OK ] Reached target Initrd Root Device.

pre-trigger:/# ls -l /dev/sda
brw-rw---- 1 root disk 8, 0 Dec 30 09:32 /dev/sda
pre-trigger:/#
pre-trigger:/# ls -l /dev/sda
sda    sda1  sda2  sda3  sda4  sda5
pre-trigger:/# _
```

Figure 7-29. *The pre-trigger hook*

As you can see in Figure 7-29, the sda devices have been created. The same commands will be fired by systemd through systemd-udev-trigger.service, which will discover and create the storage device files under /dev.

 # cat usr/lib/systemd/system/systemd-udev-trigger.service | grep -v '#'

```
[Unit]
Description=udev Coldplug all Devices
Documentation=man:udev(7) man:systemd-udevd.service(8)
DefaultDependencies=no
Wants=systemd-udevd.service
After=systemd-udevd-kernel.socket systemd-udevd-control.socket
Before=sysinit.target
ConditionPathIsReadWrite=/sys

[Service]
Type=oneshot
RemainAfterExit=yes
ExecStart=/usr/bin/udevadm trigger –type=subsystems –action=add
ExecStart=/usr/bin/udevadm trigger –type=devices –action=add
```

But as you can see in Figure 7-30, the same udevadm command will not be successful in the pre-udev hook since the udev environment is missing.

```
pre-udev:/# udevadm trigger --type=subsystems --action=add
pre-udev:/# udevadm trigger --type=devices --action=add
pre-udev:/# ls /dev/sda -l
ls: cannot access '/dev/sda': No such file or directory
```

Figure 7-30. *The udevadm in pre-udev hook*

This is the importance of `dracut-pre-trigger.service` or of the `pre-trigger` hook.

The flowchart given in Figure 7-31 will help you understand the steps so far taken by systemd inside initramfs. The flowchart will be even more understandable after reading Chapter 8. I highly recommend revisiting this chapter after finishing Chapter 8.

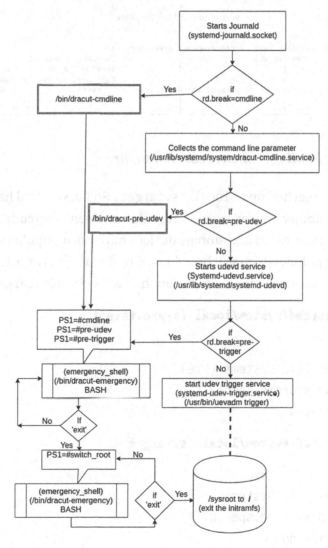

Figure 7-31. *The flowchart*

local-fs.target

As you can see in Figure 7-32, we have reached the local-fs-target stage of booting.

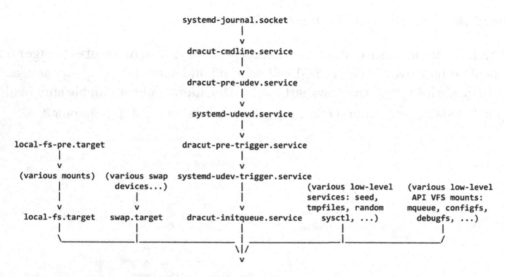

Figure 7-32. *The booting sequence covered so far*

So, systemd has reached up to local-fs.target. So far, systemd has been executing services one after another only because storage devices were not ready. Since the udevadm trigger was successful and storage devices have been populated, it's time to prepare the mount points, which will be achieved by local-fs.target. Before entering into local-fs.target, it will make sure to run the local-fs.pre.target.

cat usr/lib/systemd/system/local-fs-pre.target

```
[Unit]
Description=Local File Systems (Pre)
Documentation=man:systemd.special(7)
RefuseManualStart=yes
```

#**cat usr/lib/systemd/system/local-fs.target**

```
[Unit]
Description=Local File Systems
Documentation=man:systemd.special(7)
DefaultDependencies=no
```

```
Conflicts=shutdown.target
After=local-fs-pre.target
OnFailure=emergency.target
OnFailureJobMode=replace-irreversibly
```

The systemd-fstab-generator will be navigated by local-fs.target.

man page - systemd.special

> *systemd-fstab-generator(3) automatically adds dependencies of type Before= to all mount units that refer to local mount points for this target unit. In addition, it adds dependencies of type Wants= to this target unit for those mounts listed in /etc/fstab that have the auto mount option set.*

The systemd-fstab-generator binary will be called from initramfs.

 # file usr/lib/systemd/system-generators/systemd-fstab-generator

```
usr/lib/systemd/system-generators/systemd-fstab-generator: ELF 64-bit LSB
pie executable, x86-64, version 1 (SYSV), dynamically linked, interpreter /
lib64/ld-linux-x86-64.so.2, BuildID[sha1]=e16e9d4188e2cab491f551b5f703a5caa
645764b, for GNU/Linux 3.2.0, stripped
```

In fact, systemd runs all the generators at an early stage of the booting sequence.

 # ls -l usr/lib/systemd/system-generators

```
total 92
-rwxr-xr-x. 1 root root  3750 Dec 21 12:19 dracut-rootfs-generator
-rwxr-xr-x. 1 root root 45640 Dec 21 12:19 systemd-fstab-generator
-rwxr-xr-x. 1 root root 37032 Dec 21 12:19 systemd-gpt-auto-generator
```

systemd-fstab-generator is one of them. The main task of systemd-fstab-generator is to read the kernel command line and create systemd mount unit files under the /tmp directory or under /run/systemd/generator/ (keep reading, and this all will make sense). As you can see, it's a binary, which means we need to check the C source code of systemd to understand what it does. The systemd-fstab-generator takes either no input or three inputs.

 # usr/lib/systemd/system-generators/systemd-fstab-generator /dev/sda5
This program takes zero or three arguments.

Of course, the three inputs are the root filesystem name, filesystem type, and root filesystem flag. While writing this book, the latest version of systemd is version 244, so we have used this for the explanation here. The previously shown error message comes from src/shared/generator.h.

 # vim systemd-244/src/shared/generator.h

```
57 /* Similar to DEFINE_MAIN_FUNCTION, but initializes logging and assigns
   positional arguments. */
58 #define DEFINE_MAIN_GENERATOR_FUNCTION(impl)                                \
59         _DEFINE_MAIN_FUNCTION(                                               \
60                 ({                                                          \
61                         log_setup_generator();                              \
62                         if (argc > 1 && argc != 4)                          \
63                                 return log_error_errno(SYNTHETIC_
                                           ERRNO(EINVAL), \
64                                                 "This program takes zero
                                                  or three arguments."); \
65                 }),                                                         \
66                 impl(argc > 1 ? argv[1] : "/tmp",                           \
67                      argc > 1 ? argv[2] : "/tmp",                           \
```

The systemd-fstab-generator binary is made from src/fstab-generator/fstab-generator.c.

 # vim systemd-244/src/fstab-generator/fstab-generator.c

```
868 static int run(const char *dest, const char *dest_early, const char
    *dest_late) {
869         int r, r2 = 0, r3 = 0;
870
871         assert_se(arg_dest = dest);
872         assert_se(arg_dest_late = dest_late);
873
874         r = proc_cmdline_parse(parse_proc_cmdline_item, NULL, 0);
875         if (r < 0)
```

```
876              log_warning_errno(r, "Failed to parse kernel command
                 line, ignoring: %m");
877
878        (void) determine_root();
879
880        /* Always honour root= and usr= in the kernel command line if
           we are in an initrd */
881        if (in_initrd()) {
882              r = add_sysroot_mount();
883
884              r2 = add_sysroot_usr_mount();
885
886              r3 = add_volatile_root();
887        } else
888              r = add_volatile_var();
889
890        /* Honour /etc/fstab only when that's enabled */
891        if (arg_fstab_enabled) {
892              /* Parse the local /etc/fstab, possibly from the initrd */
893              r2 = parse_fstab(false);
894
895              /* If running in the initrd also parse the /etc/fstab
                 from the host */
896              if (in_initrd())
897                    r3 = parse_fstab(true);
898              else
899                    r3 = generator_enable_remount_fs_service(arg_dest);
900        }
901
902        return r < 0 ? r : r2 < 0 ? r2 : r3;
903 }
904
905 DEFINE_MAIN_GENERATOR_FUNCTION(run);
```

As you can see, first it parses the command-line parameters through the function proc_cmdline_parse.

```
root        = root filesystem name
rootfstype  = root filesystem type
rootflags   = ro, rw or auto etc.
```

systemd-fstab-generator runs twice: when it is inside of initramfs and when it is outside of initramfs. Once systemd comes out of initramfs (after mounting the user's root filesystem in sysroot), systemd-fstab-generator will collect the command-line parameters for the usr filesystem (if it is a separate partition and if its entry is available in etc/fstab).

```
'usr' filesystem name
'usr' filesystem type
'usr' filesystem flags
```

For ease of understanding, we will consider the following:

Inside of initramfs: Before mounting the user's root filesystem in /sysroot
Outside of initramfs: After mounting the user's root filesystem in /sysroot

So, the systemd-fstab-generator binary will collect the user's root filesystem-related command-line parameters when systemd is running inside initramfs, and it will collect the usr filesystem-related command-line parameters when systemd is running outside of initramfs. systemd is running inside or outside of initramfs will be checked through the in_initrd function. The function is written in the file src/basic/util.c. It's interesting to check how it verifies whether it is inside or outside the initramfs environment.

vim systemd-244/src/basic/util.c
```
54 bool in_initrd(void) {
55         struct statfs s;
56         int r;
57
58         if (saved_in_initrd >= 0)
59                 return saved_in_initrd;
60
```

```
61          /* We make two checks here:
62           *
63           * 1. the flag file /etc/initrd-release must exist
64           * 2. the root file system must be a memory file system
65           *
66           * The second check is extra paranoia, since misdetecting an
67           * initrd can have bad consequences due the initrd
68           * emptying when transititioning to the main systemd.
69           */
70
71          r = getenv_bool_secure("SYSTEMD_IN_INITRD");
72          if (r < 0 && r != -ENXIO)
73                  log_debug_errno(r, "Failed to parse $SYSTEMD_IN_INITRD,
                        ignoring: %m");
74
75          if (r >= 0)
76                  saved_in_initrd = r > 0;
77          else
78                  saved_in_initrd = access("/etc/initrd-release", F_OK)
                        >= 0 &&
79                                  statfs("/", &s) >= 0 &&
80                                  is_temporary_fs(&s);
81
82          return saved_in_initrd;
83 }
```

It checks whether the /etc/initrd-release file is available. If this file is not present, it means we are outside of initramfs. This function then calls the statfs function, which will provide the filesystem details, as shown here:

```
struct statfs {
            __fsword_t f_type;    /* Type of filesystem (see below) */
            __fsword_t f_bsize;   /* Optimal transfer block size */
            fsblkcnt_t f_blocks;  /* Total data blocks in filesystem */
            fsblkcnt_t f_bfree;   /* Free blocks in filesystem */
            fsblkcnt_t f_bavail;  /* Free blocks available to
                                     unprivileged user */
```

```
                fsfilcnt_t f_files;    /* Total file nodes in filesystem */
                fsfilcnt_t f_ffree;    /* Free file nodes in filesystem */
                fsid_t     f_fsid;     /* Filesystem ID */
                __fsword_t f_namelen;  /* Maximum length of filenames */
                __fsword_t f_frsize;   /* Fragment size (since Linux 2.6) */
                __fsword_t f_flags;    /* Mount flags of filesystem
                                         (since Linux 2.6.36) */
                __fsword_t f_spare[xxx];
                            /* Padding bytes reserved for future use */
        };
```

Then it calls the is_temporary_fs() function, which is written inside /src/basic/ stat-util.c.

```
190  bool is_temporary_fs(const struct statfs *s) {
191        return is_fs_type(s, TMPFS_MAGIC) ||
192                is_fs_type(s, RAMFS_MAGIC);
193  }
```

As you can see, it checks whether the root filesystem has a ramfs magic number assigned to it. If yes, then we are inside initramfs. In our case, we are inside the initramfs environment, so this function will return true and will proceed further from src/fstab-generator/fstab-generator.c to create only the root filesystem's -.mount (sysroot. mount) unit files. If we had been outside of initramfs (after mounting sysroot with the user's root filesystem), it would have created a -.mount unit file for the usr filesystem. In short, first it checks if we are inside initramfs. If we are, then it creates the mount unit file for the root filesystem, and if we're outside, then it creates it for the usr (if it is a separate filesystem) filesystem. To see this in action, we will drop ourselves in the switch_root (hook) stage so that we are able to run the systemd-fstab-generator binary manually.

1) First I have deleted the /tmp directory contents. This is because the fstab generator makes the mount unit files inside /tmp.

2) Run the systemd-fstab-generator binary, and as you can see in Figure 7-33, it has created a couple of files in /tmp.

```
switch_root:/# rm -rf /tmp/*
switch_root:/#
switch_root:/# ls /tmp
switch_root:/#
switch_root:/# usr/lib/systemd/system-generators/systemd-fstab-generator
switch_root:/#
switch_root:/# ls /tmp -l
total 8
drwxr-xr-x 2 root root    0 Dec 30 18:55 initrd-root-device.target.d
drwxr-xr-x 2 root root    0 Dec 30 18:55 initrd-root-fs.target.requires
-rw-r--r-- 1 root root 358 Dec 30 18:55 sysroot.mount
-rw-r--r-- 1 root root 632 Dec 30 18:55 systemd-fsck-root.service
switch_root:/#
```

Figure 7-33. *The systemd-fstab-generato0072*

3) It has created a `sysroot.mount` unit file. As the name suggests, it has been created to mount the user's root filesystem. The unit file has been created by reading `/proc/cmdline`. Please refer to Figure 7-34 to see the contents of `sysroot.mount` file.

```
switch_root:/tmp# cat sysroot.mount
# Automatically generated by systemd-fstab-generator

[Unit]
SourcePath=/proc/cmdline
Documentation=man:fstab(5) man:systemd-fstab-generator(8)
DefaultDependencies=no
Before=initrd-root-fs.target
Requires=systemd-fsck-root.service
After=systemd-fsck-root.service

[Mount]
Where=/sysroot
What=/dev/disk/by-uuid/6588b8f1-7f37-4162-968c-8f99eacdf32e
Options=ro
switch_root:/tmp#
switch_root:/tmp# blkid
/dev/sr0: UUID="2019-10-23-23-21-29-00" LABEL="Fedora-WS-Live-31-1-9" TYPE="iso9660" PTUUID="6f869649" PTTYPE="dos"
/dev/sda1: UUID="FBC0-BBD6" TYPE="vfat" PARTLABEL="EFI System Partition" PARTUUID="557553aa-f11f-4d67-a4c9-68944e3d3c33"
/dev/sda2: UUID="cc6a7fe8-d67a-4793-b9b0-21557732cbe8" TYPE="ext4" PARTUUID="b49bd562-70f9-4477-a0d3-0143f07e89e6"
/dev/sda4: UUID="C27C4E0C7C4DFC23" TYPE="ntfs" PARTLABEL="Basic data partition" PARTUUID="be7e9e01-b172-42f5-b95d-6e378e6a2c93"
/dev/sda5: UUID="6588b8f1-7f37-4162-968c-8f99eacdf32e" TYPE="ext4" PARTUUID="a500e83e-8702-4cb6-a80b-85ec28f59f47"
/dev/sda3: PARTLABEL="Microsoft reserved partition" PARTUUID="4fb8ac07-ca42-41c9-910b-e323bcbd82fd"
switch_root:/tmp# _
```

Figure 7-34. *The sysroot.mount file*

The root filesystem will be mounted from sda5 (by using the UUID) to the `sysroot` directory.

4) Check the `requires` section of the `sysroot.mount` unit file. It says `systemd-fsck-root.service` has to be executed first, before mounting the root filesystem. Figure 7-35 shows the `systemd-fsck-root.service` file.

```
switch_root:/tmp# cat systemd-fsck-root.service
# Automatically generated by systemd-fstab-generator

[Unit]
Description=File System Check on /dev/disk/by-uuid/6588b8f1-7f37-4162-968c-8f99eacdf32e
Documentation=man:systemd-fsck-root.service(8)
DefaultDependencies=no
BindsTo=dev-disk-by\x2duuid-6588b8f1\x2d7f37\x2d4162\x2d968c\x2d8f99eacdf32e.device
Conflicts=shutdown.target
After=initrd-root-device.target local-fs-pre.target dev-disk-by\x2duuid-6588b8f1\x2d7f37\x2d4162\x2d968c\x2d8f99eacdf32e.device
Before=shutdown.target

[Service]
Type=oneshot
RemainAfterExit=yes
ExecStart=/usr/lib/systemd/systemd-fsck /dev/disk/by-uuid/6588b8f1-7f37-4162-968c-8f99eacdf32e
TimeoutSec=0
switch_root:/tmp# _
```

Figure 7-35. *The systemd-fsck-root.service file contents*

So while booting, if you are inside initramfs, then systemd-fstab-generator will generate the mount unit files for the user's root filesystem, and the respective fsck service file will also be generated.

At the end of the initramfs booting sequence, systemd will refer to these files from the /tmp directory, will perform the fsck first on a root device, and will mount the root filesystem on sysroot (inside initramfs); eventually switch_root will be performed.

Now you must understand that though the binary name is systemd-fstab-generator, it does not really create the /etc/fstab file. Rather, its job is to create the systemd mount units for root (when inside initramfs) and usr (when outside of initramfs) at /tmp or inside the run/systemd/generator/ directories. This system has only the root mount point, so it created the systemd unit files only for root filesystem. Inside initramfs, it calls add_sysroot_mount for mounting the user's root filesystem. Once it is mounted, the root filesystem systemd calls the add_sysroot_usr_mount function. These functions call the add_mount named function, which in turn makes the systemd mount unit files. The following is a snippet of the add_mount function from src/fstab-generator/fstab-generator.c:

vim systemd-244/src/fstab-generator/fstab-generator.c

```
341      r = unit_name_from_path(where, ".mount", &name);
342          if (r < 0)
343                  return log_error_errno(r, "Failed to generate unit
                     name: %m");
344
345          r = generator_open_unit_file(dest, fstab_path(), name, &f);
346          if (r < 0)
347                  return r;
348
```

```
349          fprintf(f,
350                  "[Unit]\n"
351                  "SourcePath=%s\n"
352                  "Documentation=man:fstab(5) man:systemd-fstab-
                     generator(8)\n",
353                  source);
354
355          /* All mounts under /sysroot need to happen later, at initrd-
                fs.target time. IOW, it's not
356           * technically part of the basic initrd filesystem itself, and
                so shouldn't inherit the default
357           * Before=local-fs.target dependency. */
358          if (in_initrd() && path_startswith(where, "/sysroot"))
359                  fprintf(f, "DefaultDependencies=no\n");
```

The current system has only a root partition. To help you understand this even better, here I have prepared a test system that has root, boot, usr, var, and opt as separate filesystems:

```
UUID = f7ed74b5-9085-4f42-a1c4-a569f790fdad     /       ext4    defaults    1  1
UUID = 06609f65-5818-4aee-a9c5-710b76b36c68     /boot   ext4    defaults    1  2
UUID = 68fa7990-edf9-4a03-9011-21903a676322     /opt    ext4    defaults    1  2
UUID = 6fa78ab3-6c05-4a2f-9907-31be6d2a1071     /usr    ext4    defaults    1  2
UUID = 9c721a59-b62d-4d60-9988-adc8ed9e8770     /var    ext4    defaults    1  2
```

We will drop ourselves in the pre-pivot shell (which we have not discussed yet) of initramfs. Figure 7-36 shows that we have passed the rd.break=pre-pivot command-line parameter to the kernel.

```
load_video
set gfx_payload=keep
insmod gzio
linux ($root)/vmlinuz-5.3.7-301.fc31.x86_64 root=UUID=f7ed74b5-9085-4f42-a1c4-\
a569f790fdad ro rd.break=pre-pivot_
initrd ($root)/initramfs-5.3.7-301.fc31.x86_64.img
```

Figure 7-36. *The kernel command-line parameter*

As you can see in Figure 7-37, in the pre-pivot hook, the root filesystem will be mounted along with the usr filesystem since the pre-pivot hook stops the booting sequence after mounting the user's root filesystem on sysroot. But opt, var, and boot will not be mounted.

```
pre-pivot:/# ls /sysroot/
@System.solv  boot  etc   lib    lost+found  mnt  proc  run   srv  tmp  var
bin           dev   home  lib64  media            opt   root  sbin sys  usr
pre-pivot:/#
pre-pivot:/# ls /tmp -l
total 0
pre-pivot:/#
pre-pivot:/# ls /sysroot/boot/
pre-pivot:/#
pre-pivot:/# ls /sysroot/usr/
bin games include lib lib64 libexec local lost+found sbin share src tmp
pre-pivot:/#
pre-pivot:/# ls /sysroot/opt/
pre-pivot:/#
pre-pivot:/# ls /sysroot/var/
pre-pivot:/#
pre-pivot:/#
```

Figure 7-37. The pre-pivot hook

Even if you run systemd-fstab-generator, you will find that only the usr and root mount unit files will be created. You can see the systemd-fstab-generator output in Figure 7-38.

```
pre-pivot:/# usr/lib/systemd/system-generators/systemd-fstab-generator
pre-pivot:/#
pre-pivot:/# ls /tmp/ -l
total 12
drwxr-xr-x 2 root root   0 Dec 31 04:53 initrd-fs.target.requires
drwxr-xr-x 2 root root   0 Dec 31 04:53 initrd-root-device.target.d
drwxr-xr-x 2 root root   0 Dec 31 04:53 initrd-root-fs.target.requires
-rw-r--r-- 1 root root 515 Dec 31 04:53 sysroot-usr.mount
-rw-r--r-- 1 root root 358 Dec 31 04:53 sysroot.mount
-rw-r--r-- 1 root root 632 Dec 31 04:53 systemd-fsck-root.service
pre-pivot:/#
```

Figure 7-38. The systemd-fstab-generator in pre-pivot hook

This proves that in an initramfs environment, only root and usr will be mounted. The rest of the mount points will be mounted after initramfs or after switching to root. Since the var filesystem is not mounted yet, the journalctl logs will be maintained from the /run filesystem, and as we know, this is a temporary filesystem. This clearly says that inside the initramfs environment, you cannot access the permanent logs of journald, which are at /var/log. Please refer to Figures 7-39, 7-40, and 7-41 to understand this better.

```
pre-pivot:/# ls /sysroot/var/
pre-pivot:/#
pre-pivot:/# ls /run/log/journal/0eeb43ddc61945c0b50c2f15b776f626/system.journal -lh
-rw-r-----+ 1 root systemd-journal 8.0M Dec 31 05:03 /run/log/journal/0eeb43ddc61945c0b50c2f15b776f6
26/system.journal
pre-pivot:/#
pre-pivot:/# journalctl
```

Figure 7-39. *The journalctl command in pre-pivot hook*

```
-- Logs begin at Tue 2019-12-31 05:03:29 UTC, end at Tue 2019-12-31 05:03:31 UTC. --
Dec 31 05:03:29 localhost.localdomain kernel: Linux version 5.3.7-301.fc31.x86_64 (mockbuild@bkerne>
Dec 31 05:03:29 localhost.localdomain kernel: Command line: BOOT_IMAGE=(hd0,msdos1)/vmlinuz-5.3.7-3>
Dec 31 05:03:29 localhost.localdomain kernel: Disabled fast string operations
Dec 31 05:03:29 localhost.localdomain kernel: x86/fpu: Supporting XSAVE feature 0x001: 'x87 floatin>
Dec 31 05:03:29 localhost.localdomain kernel: x86/fpu: Supporting XSAVE feature 0x002: 'SSE registe>
Dec 31 05:03:29 localhost.localdomain kernel: x86/fpu: Supporting XSAVE feature 0x004: 'AVX registe>
Dec 31 05:03:29 localhost.localdomain kernel: x86/fpu: Supporting XSAVE feature 0x008: 'MPX bounds >
Dec 31 05:03:29 localhost.localdomain kernel: x86/fpu: Supporting XSAVE feature 0x010: 'MPX CSR'
Dec 31 05:03:29 localhost.localdomain kernel: x86/fpu: Supporting XSAVE feature 0x020: 'AVX-512 opm>
Dec 31 05:03:29 localhost.localdomain kernel: x86/fpu: Supporting XSAVE feature 0x040: 'AVX-512 Hi2>
Dec 31 05:03:29 localhost.localdomain kernel: x86/fpu: Supporting XSAVE feature 0x080: 'AVX-512 ZMM>
Dec 31 05:03:29 localhost.localdomain kernel: x86/fpu: xstate_offset[2]:  576, xstate_sizes[2]:  256
Dec 31 05:03:29 localhost.localdomain kernel: x86/fpu: xstate_offset[3]:  832, xstate_sizes[3]:   64
Dec 31 05:03:29 localhost.localdomain kernel: x86/fpu: xstate_offset[4]:  896, xstate_sizes[4]:   64
Dec 31 05:03:29 localhost.localdomain kernel: x86/fpu: xstate_offset[5]:  960, xstate_sizes[5]:   64
Dec 31 05:03:29 localhost.localdomain kernel: x86/fpu: xstate_offset[6]: 1024, xstate_sizes[6]:  512
Dec 31 05:03:29 localhost.localdomain kernel: x86/fpu: xstate_offset[7]: 1536, xstate_sizes[7]: 1024
Dec 31 05:03:29 localhost.localdomain kernel: x86/fpu: Enabled xstate features 0xff, context size i>
Dec 31 05:03:29 localhost.localdomain kernel: BIOS-provided physical RAM map:
Dec 31 05:03:29 localhost.localdomain kernel: BIOS-e820: [mem 0x0000000000000000-0x000000000009ebff>
Dec 31 05:03:29 localhost.localdomain kernel: BIOS-e820: [mem 0x000000000009ec00-0x000000000009ffff>
Dec 31 05:03:29 localhost.localdomain kernel: BIOS-e820: [mem 0x00000000000dc000-0x00000000000fffff>
Dec 31 05:03:29 localhost.localdomain kernel: BIOS-e820: [mem 0x0000000000100000-0x00000000bfecffff>
Dec 31 05:03:29 localhost.localdomain kernel: BIOS-e820: [mem 0x00000000bfed0000-0x00000000bfefefff>
Dec 31 05:03:29 localhost.localdomain kernel: BIOS-e820: [mem 0x00000000bfeff000-0x00000000bfefffff>
Dec 31 05:03:29 localhost.localdomain kernel: BIOS-e820: [mem 0x00000000bff00000-0x00000000bfffffff>
Dec 31 05:03:29 localhost.localdomain kernel: BIOS-e820: [mem 0x00000000f0000000-0x00000000f7ffffff>
Dec 31 05:03:29 localhost.localdomain kernel: BIOS-e820: [mem 0x00000000fec00000-0x00000000fec0ffff>
Dec 31 05:03:29 localhost.localdomain kernel: BIOS-e820: [mem 0x00000000fee00000-0x00000000fee00fff>
Dec 31 05:03:29 localhost.localdomain kernel: BIOS-e820: [mem 0x00000000fffe0000-0x00000000ffffffff>
Dec 31 05:03:29 localhost.localdomain kernel: BIOS-e820: [mem 0x0000000100000000-0x00000001dfbfffff>
Dec 31 05:03:29 localhost.localdomain kernel: NX (Execute Disable) protection: active
Dec 31 05:03:29 localhost.localdomain kernel: SMBIOS 2.7 present.
Dec 31 05:03:29 localhost.localdomain kernel: DMI: VMware, Inc. VMware Virtual Platform/440BX Deskt>
Dec 31 05:03:29 localhost.localdomain kernel: Hypervisor detected: VMware
lines 1-36
```

Figure 7-40. *The logs provided by journalctl from /run*

```
pre-pivot:/# rm -rf /run/log/journal/0eeb43ddc61945c0b50c2f15b776f626/system.journal
pre-pivot:/#
pre-pivot:/# journalctl
No journal files were found.
-- No entries --
pre-pivot:/#
```

Figure 7-41. *The journalctl behavior in pre-pivot hook*

Did you notice one thing? The dracut-cmdline service is reading the kernel command-line parameters, and the usr-related command-line parameters are not available in /proc/cmdline. So, how does systemd manage to mount the usr filesystem? Also, at the time of initramfs generation, dracut does not copy the etc/fstab file in it.

lsinitrd | grep -i fstab

```
-rw-r--r--  1 root root         0 Jul 25 03:54 etc/fstab.empty
-rwxr-xr-x  1 root root     45640 Jul 25 03:54 usr/lib/systemd/system-
generators/systemd-fstab-generator
```

lsinitrd -f etc/fstab.empty

```
    <no_output>
```

Then how does systemd manage to mount the usr filesystem inside initramfs when it does not have an entry of it?

When systemd-fstab-generator runs during local-fs.target, it makes the mount unit files only for root; then it continues the booting sequence and mounts the root file system on sysroot. Once the root filesystem is mounted, it reads the usr entry from /etc/sysroot/etc/fstab and makes a usr.mount unit file and at the end mounts it. Let's cross-verify this understanding:

1) Drop in the pre-pivot hook.

2) Delete the /etc/fstab from the mounted /sysroot.

3) Run the systemd-fstab-generator.

4) Refer to Figure 7-42.

Since the root filesystem name will be fetched by dracut-cmdline from proc/cmdline, systemd-fstab-generator will make the sysroot.mount. But since the fstab file is missing inside sysroot, it will consider the usr as an separate partition that is not available, and it will skip creating the usr.mount unit file even though usr is a separate mount point.

```
pre-pivot:/# mv /sysroot/etc/fstab /
pre-pivot:/# ls /tmp/
pre-pivot:/# /usr/lib/systemd/system-generators/systemd-fstab-generator
pre-pivot:/#
pre-pivot:/# ls /tmp/ -l
total 8
drwxr-xr-x 2 root root   0 Dec 31 05:59 initrd-root-device.target.d
drwxr-xr-x 2 root root   0 Dec 31 05:59 initrd-root-fs.target.requires
-rw-r--r-- 1 root root 358 Dec 31 05:59 sysroot.mount
-rw-r--r-- 1 root root 632 Dec 31 05:59 systemd-fsck-root.service
pre-pivot:/#
```

Figure 7-42. *The systemd-fstab-generator behavior*

What if you want to have opt- and var-like separate mount points available inside /sysroot or you want them in an initramfs environment? systemd's man page has an answer for this, shown here:

x-initrd.mount

An additional filesystem to be mounted in the initramfs. See the `initrd-fs.target` description in `systemd.special(7)`.

initrd-fs.target

`systemd-fstab-generator(3)` automatically adds dependencies of type Before= to `sysroot-usr.mount` and all mount points found in `/etc/fstab` that have `x-initrd.mount` and not have the `noauto` mount options set.

So, we need to use the x-initrd.mount [systemd.mount] option in /etc/fstab. For example, here I have enabled the var mount point inside initramfs through the same pre-pivot environment:

pre-pivot:/# **vi /sysroot/etc/fstab**

```
UUID=f7ed74b5-9085-4f42-a1c4-a569f790fdad   /      ext4   defaults   1  1
UUID=06609f65-5818-4aee-a9c5-710b76b36c68   /boot  ext4   defaults   1  2
UUID=68fa7990-edf9-4a03-9011-21903a676322   /opt   ext4   defaults   1  2
UUID=6fa78ab3-6c05-4a2f-9907-31be6d2a1071   /usr   ext4   defaults   1  2
UUID=9c721a59-b62d-4d60-9988-adc8ed9e8770   /var   ext4   defaults,x-initrd.
mount   1  2
```

As you can see in Figure 7-43, the var mount unit file has been created, but fsck is available only for the root filesystem. Please refer to the flowchart in Figure 7-44 to help you understand this better.

```
pre-pivot:/# usr/lib/systemd/system-generators/systemd-fstab-generator
pre-pivot:/#
pre-pivot:/# ls /tmp/ -l
total 16
drwxr-xr-x 2 root root    0 Dec 31 08:14 initrd-fs.target.requires
drwxr-xr-x 2 root root    0 Dec 31 08:14 initrd-root-device.target.d
drwxr-xr-x 2 root root    0 Dec 31 08:14 initrd-root-fs.target.requires
-rw-r--r-- 1 root root 515 Dec 31 08:14 sysroot-usr.mount
-rw-r--r-- 1 root root 547 Dec 31 08:14 sysroot-var.mount
-rw-r--r-- 1 root root 358 Dec 31 08:14 sysroot.mount
-rw-r--r-- 1 root root 632 Dec 31 08:14 systemd-fsck-root.service
pre-pivot:/#
pre-pivot:/# cat /tmp/sysroot-var.mount
# Automatically generated by systemd-fstab-generator

[Unit]
SourcePath=/sysroot/etc/fstab
Documentation=man:fstab(5) man:systemd-fstab-generator(8)
DefaultDependencies=no
Before=initrd-fs.target
Requires=systemd-fsck@dev-disk-by\x2duuid-9c721a59\x2db62d\x2d4d60\x2d9988\x2dadc8ed9e8770.service
After=systemd-fsck@dev-disk-by\x2duuid-9c721a59\x2db62d\x2d4d60\x2d9988\x2dadc8ed9e8770.service

[Mount]
# Canonicalized from /var
Where=/sysroot/var
What=/dev/disk/by-uuid/9c721a59-b62d-4d60-9988-adc8ed9e8770
Type=ext4
Options=defaults,x-initrd.mount
pre-pivot:/# _
```

Figure 7-43. *The working of systemd-fstab-generator*

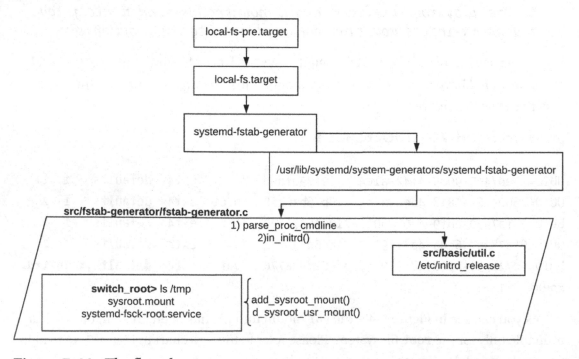

Figure 7-44. *The flowchart*

swap.target

As you can see in Figure 7-45, we have reached the `swap.target` stage of booting.

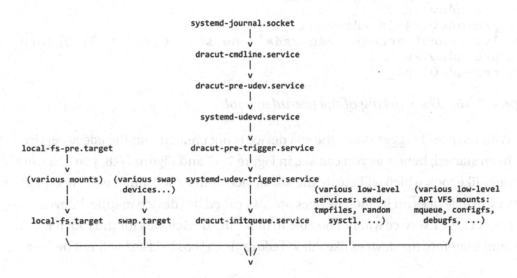

Figure 7-45. *The booting sequence so far*

This will execute parallel to `local-fs.target`. `local-fs-.target` makes the mount points for `root` and `usr`, whereas `swap.target` makes the mount unit files for the swap device. Once the root filesystem mount file is ready, `sysroot` is mounted according to it. `systemd-fstab-generator` will read the `fstab`, and if the swap device entry is present, it will make the `swap.mount` unit file. That means the `swap.mount` file will be created only after switching into the user's root filesystem (`switch_root` into `sysroot`). The `swap.mount` will not be created at this stage.

dracut-initqueue.service

This service creates the actual `root`, `swap`, and `usr` devices. Let's understand this with an example.

With the `pre-udev` hook, we have seen that sda-like devices are not available. Neither `udevadm` command will work as the `udevd` service itself is not started yet. Refer to Figure 7-46.

```
pre-udev:/# ls /dev/sda -l
ls: cannot access '/dev/sda': No such file or directory
pre-udev:/#
pre-udev:/# udevadm trigger
pre-udev:/#
pre-udev:/# ls /dev/sda -l
ls: cannot access '/dev/sda': No such file or directory
pre-udev:/#
pre-udev:/# _
```

Figure 7-46. *The working of the pre-udev hook*

With the pre-trigger hook, the sda device is not created, but the udevd service has been started; hence, as you can see in Figure 7-47 and Figure 7-48, you can use a udevadm-like tool, which will create the sda device under /dev, but it will not create lvm or raid-like devices on it. Such devices are also called dm (device mapper) devices. So, the pre-trigger service will not be able to make the device files for the root if it is on lvm, and therefore the devices like /dev/fedora_localhost-live/ will not be created.

```
          Starting Dracut Emergency Shell...
Warning: /dev/disk/by-uuid/6588b8f1-7f37-4162-968c-8f99eacdf32e does not exist

Generating "/run/initramfs/rdsosreport.txt"


Entering emergency mode. Exit the shell to continue.
Type "journalctl" to view system logs.
You might want to save "/run/initramfs/rdsosreport.txt" to a USB stick or /boot
after mounting them and attach it to a bug report.


pre-trigger:/# ls /dev/sda
ls: cannot access '/dev/sda': No such file or directory
pre-trigger:/#
pre-trigger:/# udevadm trigger --type=subsystems --action=add;
pre-trigger:/#              Mounting Kernel Configuration File System...
[  OK  ] Mounted Kernel Configuration File System.

pre-trigger:/# ls /dev/sda
ls: cannot access '/dev/sda': No such file or directory
pre-trigger:/#
pre-trigger:/# udevadm trigger --type=devices --action=add;
```

Figure 7-47. *The pre-trigger hook*

```
[  175.767498] scsi 32:0:0:0: Direct-Access     VMware,  VMware Virtual S 1.0  P
[  175.769872] sd 32:0:0:0: Attached scsi generic sg1 type 0
[  175.770416] sd 32:0:0:0: [sda] 125829120 512-byte logical blocks: (64.4 GB/60
[  175.771153] e1000e 0000:0b:00.0 ens192: renamed from eth0
[  175.771904] sd 32:0:0:0: [sda] Write Protect is off
[  175.774422] sd 32:0:0:0: [sda] Cache data unavailable
[  175.775519] sd 32:0:0:0: [sda] Assuming drive cache: write through
[  175.777279] fb0: switching to svgadrmfb from EFI VGA
[  175.777911] Console: switching to colour dummy device 80x25
pre-trigger:/# [  175.778142] fbcon: svgadrmfb (fb0) is primary device
[  175.785208]  sda: sda1 sda2 sda3 sda4 sda5
[  175.790120] sd 32:0:0:0: [sda] Attached SCSI disk
[  175.792436] Console: switching to colour frame buffer device 128x48
pre-trigger:/# [  175.798533] [drm] Initialized vmwgfx 2.15.0 20180704 for 0000:00:0f.0 on minor 0
[  OK  ] Found device VMware_Virtual_S 5.
[  OK  ] Reached target Initrd Root Device.

pre-trigger:/# ls -l /dev/sda
brw-rw---- 1 root disk 8, 0 Dec 30 09:32 /dev/sda
pre-trigger:/#
pre-trigger:/# ls -l /dev/sda
sda   sda1 sda2  sda3 sda4  sda5
pre-trigger:/# _
```

Figure 7-48. *The sda devices have been created under the pre-trigger hook*

The service dracut-initqueue.service has not started yet. Let's see first what exactly the unit file says.

cat usr/lib/systemd/system/dracut-initqueue.service | grep -v '#'

```
[Unit]
Description=dracut initqueue hook
Documentation=man:dracut-initqueue.service(8)
DefaultDependencies=no
Before=remote-fs-pre.target
Wants=remote-fs-pre.target
After=systemd-udev-trigger.service
Wants=systemd-udev-trigger.service
ConditionPathExists=/usr/lib/initrd-release
ConditionPathExists=|/lib/dracut/need-initqueue
ConditionKernelCommandLine=|rd.break=initqueue
Conflicts=shutdown.target emergency.target

[Service]
Environment=DRACUT_SYSTEMD=1
Environment=NEWROOT=/sysroot
Type=oneshot
```

ExecStart=-/bin/dracut-initqueue
```
StandardInput=null
StandardOutput=syslog
StandardError=syslog+console
KillMode=process
RemainAfterExit=yes
KillSignal=SIGHUP
```

As you can see, this service is simply starting the /bin/dracut-initqueue script, and if we open this script, you will find it is actually executing the udevadm settle command with a timeout value of 0.

`vim bin/dracut-initqueue`
```
22 while :; do
23
24     check_finished && break
25
26     udevadm settle --exit-if-exists=$hookdir/initqueue/work
27
28     check_finished && break
29
30     if [ -f $hookdir/initqueue/work ]; then
31         rm -f -- "$hookdir/initqueue/work"
32     fi
33
34     for job in $hookdir/initqueue/*.sh; do
35         [ -e "$job" ] || break
36         job=$job . $job
37         check_finished && break 2
38     done
39
40     udevadm settle --timeout=0 >/dev/null 2>&1 || continue
41
42     for job in $hookdir/initqueue/settled/*.sh; do
43         [ -e "$job" ] || break
44         job=$job . $job
```

```
45          check_finished && break 2
46      done
47
48      udevadm settle --timeout=0 >/dev/null 2>&1 || continue
49
50      # no more udev jobs and queues empty.
51      sleep 0.5
```

This will eventually run the lvm_scan command from lib/dracut/hooks/ initqueue/timeout/. Note the root and rd.break kernel command-line parameters that are passed in Figure 7-49.

```
load_video
set gfx_payload=keep
insmod gzio
linux ($root)/vmlinuz-5.3.7-301.fc31.x86_64 root=/dev/mapper/fedora_localhost-\
-live-root ro resume=/dev/mapper/fedora_localhost--live-swap rd.lvm.lv=fedora_\
localhost-live/root rd.lvm.lv=fedora_localhost-live/swap rd.break=initqueue
initrd ($root)/initramfs-5.3.7-301.fc31.x86_64.img
```

Figure 7-49. *The kernel command-line parameters*

As you can see in Figure 7-50, the lvm_scan command is written in one of the files.

```
initqueue:/# cat /lib/dracut/hooks/initqueue/timeout/51-lvm_scan.sh
[ -e "$job" ] && rm -f -- "$job"
/sbin/lvm_scan --partial
initqueue:/#
initqueue:/# cat /lib/dracut/hooks/initqueue/settled/lvm_scan.sh
[ -e "$job" ] && rm -f -- "$job"
/sbin/lvm_scan
initqueue:/#
```

Figure 7-50. *The initqueue hook*

So, here we have two options: either we can just execute /bin/dracut-initqueue or, as shown in Figure 7-51, we can execute the lvm_scan command either from the pre-trigger hook or from the initqueue hook.

```
initqueue:/# ls /dev/sda
sda    sda1  sda2
initqueue:/#
initqueue:/# ls /dev/fedora_localhost-live -l
ls: cannot access '/dev/fedora_localhost-live': No such file or directory
initqueue:/#
initqueue:/# lvm_scan
Scanning devices sda2  for LVM logical volumes fedora_localhost-live/root fedora_localhost-live/swap
inactive '/dev/fedora_localhost-live/swap' [2.20 GiB] inherit
inactive '/dev/fedora_localhost-live/root' [18.79 GiB] inherit
[   57.935898] audit: type=1130 audit(1577811317.568:11): pid=1 uid=0 auid=4294967295 ses=4294967295
 subj=kernel msg='unit=systemd-hibernate-resume@dev-mapper-fedora_localhost\x2d\x2dlive\x2dswap comm
="systemd" exe="/usr/lib/systemd/systemd" hostname=? addr=? terminal=? res=success'
[   57.936063] audit: type=1131 audit(1577811317.568:12): pid=1 uid=0 auid=4294967295 ses=4294967295
 subj=kernel msg='unit=systemd-hibernate-resume@dev-mapper-fedora_localhost\x2d\x2dlive\x2dswap comm
="systemd" exe="/usr/lib/systemd/systemd" hostname=? addr=? terminal=? res=success'
[   57.958510] audit: type=1130 audit(1577811317.591:13): pid=1 uid=0 auid=4294967295 ses=4294967295
 subj=kernel msg='unit=systemd-tmpfiles-setup comm="systemd" exe="/usr/lib/systemd/systemd" hostname
=? addr=? terminal=? res=success'
initqueue:/#
initqueue:/# ls /dev/fedora_localhost-live/ -l
total 0
lrwxrwxrwx 1 root root 7 Dec 31 16:55 root -> ../dm-0
lrwxrwxrwx 1 root root 7 Dec 31 16:55 swap -> ../dm-1
initqueue:/#
```

Figure 7-51. *The lvm_scan command in the initqueue hook*

Since we have discussed up to the LVM part of initramfs, it is the right time to see one of the most common and crucial "can't boot" issue.

"Can't Boot" Issue 7 (systemd + Root LVM)

Issue: We changed the standard root device name from /dev/mapper/fedora_localhost--live-root to /dev/mapper/root_vg-root. We made the appropriate entry in /etc/fstab, but after rebooting, the system is not able to boot. Figure 7-52 shows what is visible on the screen.

```
[    4.185237] [drm] Initialized qxl 0.1.0 20120117 for 0000:00:01.0 on minor 0
[    4.188104] fbcon: qxldrmfb (fb0) is primary device
[    4.193643] Console: switching to colour frame buffer device 128x48
[    4.206916] qxl 0000:00:01.0: fb0: qxldrmfb frame buffer device
[    4.222529] pcieport 0000:00:02.6: pciehp: Failed to check link status
[    5.017631] IPv6: ADDRCONF(NETDEV_CHANGE): enp1s0: link becomes ready
[ TIME ] Timed out waiting for device /dev/mapper/fedora_localhost--live-swap.
[DEPEND] Dependency failed for Resume from hibernation using device /dev/mapper/fedora_localhost--live-swap.
[   93.485153] audit: type=1130 audit(1577942489.698:10): pid=1 uid=0 auid=4294967295 ses=4294967295 subj=kernel msg='unit=syste
md-tmpfiles-setup comm="systemd" exe="/usr/lib/systemd/systemd" hostname=? addr=? terminal=? res=success'
[  OK  ] Reached target Local File Systems (Pre).
[  OK  ] Reached target Local File Systems.
         Starting Create Volatile Files and Directories...
[  OK  ] Started Create Volatile Files and Directories.
[  OK  ] Reached target System Initialization.
[  OK  ] Reached target Basic System.
[  147.238113] dracut-initqueue[449]: Warning: dracut-initqueue timeout - starting timeout scripts
[  148.029437] dracut-initqueue[449]: Warning: dracut-initqueue timeout - starting timeout scripts
[  148.603981] dracut-initqueue[449]: Warning: dracut-initqueue timeout - starting timeout scripts
[  149.163617] dracut-initqueue[449]: Warning: dracut-initqueue timeout - starting timeout scripts
[  149.730411] dracut-initqueue[449]: Warning: dracut-initqueue timeout - starting timeout scripts
[  150.310162] dracut-initqueue[449]: Warning: dracut-initqueue timeout - starting timeout scripts
[  150.919305] dracut-initqueue[449]: Warning: dracut-initqueue timeout - starting timeout scripts
```

Figure 7-52. *The console messages*

Since we have a better understanding of dracut-initqueue now, we can see that the error messages clearly mean systemd is not able to assemble the root lvm device.

1. Let's isolate the issue first by recalling the performed steps. The original root lv name is as follows:

   #cat /etc/fstab

   ```
   /dev/mapper/fedora_localhost--live-root          /
   ext4   defaults 1  1
   UUID=eea3d947-0618-4d8c-b083-87daf15b2679  /boot ext4   defaults 1  2
   /dev/mapper/fedora_localhost--live-
   swap          none    ext4   defaults 0  0
   ```

2. The root volume group name has been changed.

   # vgrename fedora_localhost-live root_vg

   ```
   The volume group Fedora_localhost-live was successfully renamed to
   root_vg.
   ```

3. The /etc/fstab entry of root lvm has been appropriately changed.

   ```
   /dev/mapper/root_vg-root /              ext4     defaults   1 1
   UUID=eea3d947-0618-4d8c-b083-87daf15b2679 /boot ext4   defaults  1 2
   /dev/mapper/root_vg-swap none           swap     defaults      0 0
   ```

But after rebooting, systemd starts throwing dracut-initqueue timeout error messages.

The steps look like they were properly followed, but we need to investigate further to understand why dracut-initqueue is not able to assemble LVMs.

If we wait for some time on the error screen, as shown in Figure 7-53, systemd will automatically drop us on an emergency shell. We will see in detail how systemd drops us in an emergency shell in Chapter 8.

```
[ TIME ] Timed out waiting for device /dev/mapper/fedora_localhost--live-root.
[   13.365127] audit: type=1131 audit(1577942648.552:10): pid=1 uid=0 auid=4294967295 ses=4294967295 subj=kernel msg='unit=dracu
t-pre-udev comm="systemd" exe="/usr/lib/systemd/systemd" hostname=? addr=? terminal=? res=success'
[DEPEND] Dependency failed for Initrd Root Device.
[DEPEND] Dependency failed for /sysroot.
[DEPEND] Dependency failed for Initrd Root File System.
[DEPEND] Dependency failed for Reload Configuration from the Real Root.
[DEPEND] Dependency failed for File System Check on /dev/mapper/fedora_localhost--live-root.
[  OK  ] Reached target Initrd File Systems.
[  OK  ] Stopped dracut pre-udev hook.
[  OK  ] Stopped dracut cmdline hook.
[   13.374194] audit: type=1131 audit(1577942648.553:11): pid=1 uid=0 auid=4294967295 ses=4294967295 subj=kernel msg='unit=dracu
t-cmdline comm="systemd" exe="/usr/lib/systemd/systemd" hostname=? addr=? terminal=? res=success'
         Starting Setup Virtual Console...
[  OK  ] Stopped dracut initqueue hook.
[   13.394183] audit: type=1130 audit(1577942648.582:12): pid=1 uid=0 auid=4294967295 ses=4294967295 subj=kernel msg='unit=dracu
t-initqueue comm="systemd" exe="/usr/lib/systemd/systemd" hostname=? addr=? terminal=? res=success'
[   13.401837] audit: type=1131 audit(1577942648.582:13): pid=1 uid=0 auid=4294967295 ses=4294967295 subj=kernel msg='unit=dracu
t-initqueue comm="systemd" exe="/usr/lib/systemd/systemd" hostname=? addr=? terminal=? res=success'
[  OK  ] Reached target Remote File Systems (Pre).
[  OK  ] Reached target Remote File Systems.
[  OK  ] Started Setup Virtual Console.
[   13.489239] audit: type=1130 audit(1577942648.676:14): pid=1 uid=0 auid=4294967295 ses=4294967295 subj=kernel msg='unit=syste
md-vconsole-setup comm="systemd" exe="/usr/lib/systemd/systemd" hostname=? addr=? terminal=? res=success'
[   13.489246] audit: type=1131 audit(1577942648.676:15): pid=1 uid=0 auid=4294967295 ses=4294967295 subj=kernel msg='unit=syste
md-vconsole-setup comm="systemd" exe="/usr/lib/systemd/systemd" hostname=? addr=? terminal=? res=success'
[   13.502917] audit: type=1130 audit(1577942648.691:16): pid=1 uid=0 auid=4294967295 ses=4294967295 subj=kernel msg='unit=emerg
ency comm="systemd" exe="/usr/lib/systemd/systemd" hostname=? addr=? terminal=? res=success'
[  OK  ] Started Emergency Shell.
[  OK  ] Reached target Emergency Mode.
[   18.538415] audit: type=1131 audit(1577942653.726:17): pid=1 uid=0 auid=4294967295 ses=4294967295 subj=kernel msg='unit=plymo
uth-start comm="systemd" exe="/usr/lib/systemd/systemd" hostname=? addr=? terminal=? res=success'
Warning: /dev/fedora_localhost-live/root does not exist
Warning: /dev/fedora_localhost-live/swap does not exist
Warning: /dev/mapper/fedora_localhost--live-root does not exist

Generating "/run/initramfs/rdsosreport.txt"


Entering emergency mode. Exit the shell to continue.
Type "journalctl" to view system logs.
You might want to save "/run/initramfs/rdsosreport.txt" to a USB stick or /boot
after mounting them and attach it to a bug report.

:/#
```

Figure 7-53. *The emergency shell*

As shown in Figure 7-54, we will scan the currently available LVs and will mount root vg to verify its contents.

```
:/# lvm lvs
  LV   VG       Attr       LSize    Pool Origin Data%  Meta%  Move Log Cpy%Sync Convert
  root root_vg  -wi------- <17.00g
  swap root_vg  -wi-------   2.00g
:/#
:/# lvm vgchange -ay root_vg
  2 logical volume(s) in volume group "root_vg" now active
:/#
:/# blkid
/dev/vda1: UUID="eea3d947-0618-4d8c-b083-87daf15b2679" TYPE="ext4" PARTUUID="6186139e-01"
/dev/vda2: UUID="wQ9sz6-hMUI-uf6N-1Jrn-1CpS-cQd1-CZef4z" TYPE="LVM2_member" PARTUUID="6186139e-02"
/dev/mapper/root_vg-swap: UUID="5ae857b2-aa62-4e4e-8125-00d589f28212" TYPE="swap"
/dev/mapper/root_vg-root: UUID="1e17ecc8-d901-4946-a88e-06215ac6374a" TYPE="ext4"
:/# _
```

Figure 7-54. *Activating the LVs*

As you can see, root_vg (the renamed vg) is available, and we are able to activate it too. It clearly means that the LVM metadata is not corrupted and that the LVM device does not have any integrity issues. As shown in Figure 7-55, we will mount root_vg on a temporary directory and cross-verify its fstab entries from the emergency shell itself.

```
:/# mount /dev/mapper/root_vg-root /tmp/
[  612.217849] EXT4-fs (dm-1): mounted filesystem with ordered data mode. Opts: (null)
:/#
:/# ls /tmp/
@System.solv  boot   etc   lib    lost+found  mnt  proc  run   srv  tmp  var
bin           dev    home  lib64  media       opt  root  sbin  sys  usr
:/#
:/# cat /tmp/etc/fstab

#
# /etc/fstab
# Created by anaconda on Mon Dec  9 10:18:05 2019
#
# Accessible filesystems, by reference, are maintained under '/dev/disk/'.
# See man pages fstab(5), findfs(8), mount(8) and/or blkid(8) for more info.
#
# After editing this file, run 'systemctl daemon-reload' to update systemd
# units generated from this file.
#
/dev/mapper/root_vg-root /                               ext4    defaults        1 1
UUID=eea3d947-0618-4d8c-b083-87daf15b2679 /boot                  ext4    defaults        1 2
/dev/mapper/root_vg-swap none                            swap    defaults        0 0
:/#
```

Figure 7-55. *Mounting the root filesystem*

vg is intact, the fstab entries are correct, and we are able to mount the root vg. What is missing then?

The missing part is that the kernel command-line parameters have not been adjusted in GRUB. See Figure 7-56.

```
dracut:/# cat /proc/cmdline
BOOT_IMAGE=(hd0,msdos1)/vmlinuz-5.3.7-301.fc31.x86_64 root=/dev/mapper/fedora_localhost--live-root ro resume=/dev/mapper/fedora_
localhost--live-swap rd.lvm.lv=fedora_localhost-live/root rd.lvm.lv=fedora_localhost-live/swap console=ttyS0,115200 console=tty0
dracut:/# _
```

Figure 7-56. *The kernel command-line parameters*

To boot, we need to interrupt the GRUB splash screen and need to change the kernel command-line parameters from what's shown in Figure 7-57.

```
load_video
set gfx_payload=keep
insmod gzio
linux ($root)/vmlinuz-5.3.7-301.fc31.x86_64 root=/dev/mapper/fedora_localhost-\
-live-root ro resume=/dev/mapper/fedora_localhost--live-swap rd.lvm.lv=fedora_\
localhost-live/root rd.lvm.lv=fedora_localhost-live/swap console=ttyS0,115200 \
console=tty0
initrd ($root)/initramfs-5.3.7-301.fc31.x86_64.img
```

Figure 7-57. *The old kernel command-line parameters*

See Figure 7-58 for the new ones.

```
load_video
set gfx_payload=keep
insmod gzio
linux ($root)/vmlinuz-5.3.7-301.fc31.x86_64 root=/dev/mapper/root_vg-root ro r\
d.lvm.lv=root_vg/root console=ttyS0,115200 console=tty0
initrd ($root)/initramfs-5.3.7-301.fc31.x86_64.img
```

Figure 7-58. *The new kernel command-line parameters*

Once the system is booted, change /etc/default/grub from this:

 # cat /etc/default/grub

GRUB_TIMEOUT=10

GRUB_DISTRIBUTOR="$(sed 's, release .*$,,g' /etc/system-release)"

GRUB_DEFAULT=saved

GRUB_DISABLE_SUBMENU=true

GRUB_TERMINAL_OUTPUT="console"

GRUB_CMDLINE_LINUX="resume=**/dev/mapper/fedora_localhost--live-swap rd.lvm.
lv=fedora_localhost-live/root rd.lvm.lv=fedora_localhost-live/swap**
console=ttyS0,115200 console=tty0"

GRUB_DISABLE_RECOVERY="true"

GRUB_ENABLE_BLSCFG=true

to the following:

 # cat /etc/default/grub

GRUB_TIMEOUT=10

GRUB_DISTRIBUTOR="$(sed 's, release .*$,,g' /etc/system-release)"

GRUB_DEFAULT=saved

GRUB_DISABLE_SUBMENU=true

GRUB_TERMINAL_OUTPUT="console"

GRUB_CMDLINE_LINUX="resume=**/dev/mapper/root_vg-swap rd.lvm.lv=root_vg/root
rd.lvm.lv=root_vg/swap** console=ttyS0,115200 console=tty0"

GRUB_DISABLE_RECOVERY="true"

GRUB_ENABLE_BLSCFG=true

It is not necessary to change the /etc/default/grub file since Fedora uses the BLS
entries from /boot/loader/entries.

Change /boot/grub2/grubenv from this:

 # cat /boot/grub2/grubenv
saved_entry=2058a9f13f9e489dba29c477a8ae2493-5.3.7-301.fc31.x86_64
menu_auto_hide=1
boot_success=0
kernelopts=**root=/dev/mapper/fedora_localhost--live-root ro resume=/dev/**
mapper/fedora_localhost--live-swap rd.lvm.lv=fedora_localhost-live/root
rd.lvm.lv=fedora_localhost-live/swap console=ttyS0,115200 console=tty0
boot_indeterminate=9

to the following:

 # cat /boot/grub2/grubenv
saved_entry=2058a9f13f9e489dba29c477a8ae2493-5.3.7-301.fc31.x86_64
menu_auto_hide=1
boot_success=0
kernelopts=root=/dev/root_vg/root ro resume=/dev/mapper/root_vg-swap
rd.lvm.lv=root_vg/root rd.lvm.lv=root_vg/swap console=ttyS0,115200
console=tty0
boot_indeterminate=9

This fixes the "can't boot" issue.

plymouth

Now it's time to talk about one interesting service called plymouth. Earlier Linux would show boot messages directly on the console, which was kind of boring for desktop users. Hence, plymouth was introduced, as shown here:

 # cat usr/lib/systemd/system/plymouth-start.service
[Unit]
Description=Show Plymouth Boot Screen
DefaultDependencies=no
Wants=systemd-ask-password-plymouth.path systemd-vconsole-setup.service
After=systemd-vconsole-setup.service **systemd-udev-trigger.service systemd-**
udevd.service
Before=systemd-ask-password-plymouth.service

```
ConditionKernelCommandLine=!plymouth.enable=0
ConditionVirtualization=!container

[Service]
ExecStart=/usr/sbin/plymouthd --mode=boot --pid-file=/var/run/plymouth/pid
--attach-to-session
ExecStartPost=-/usr/bin/plymouth show-splash
Type=forking
KillMode=none
SendSIGKILL=no
```

As you can see, from the /usr/lib/systemd/system/plymouth-start.service unit file, plymouth starts right after systemd-udev-trigger.service and before dracut-initqueue.service, as shown in Figure 7-59.

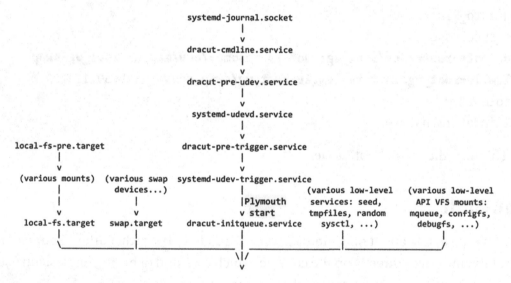

Figure 7-59. *The booting sequence*

As shown in Figure 7-60, plymouth will be active throughout the booting procedure.

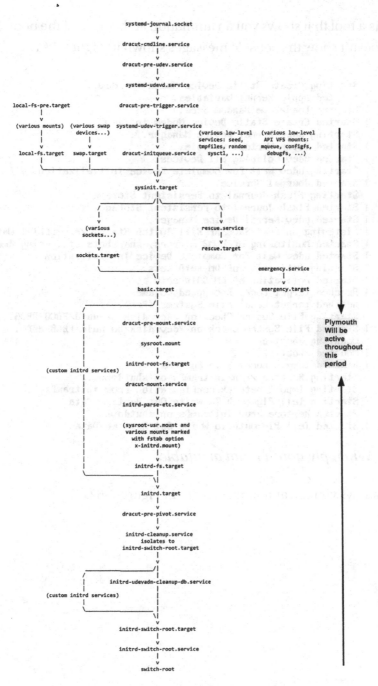

Figure 7-60. *plymouth*

plymouth is a tool that shows you an animation at the time of the boot. For example, in Fedora, it doesn't show the console messages shown in Figure 7-61.

```
                Starting Create Static Device Nodes in /dev...
[  OK  ] Started Apply Kernel Variables.
[  OK  ] Started Load/Save Random Seed.
[  OK  ] Started Create Static Device Nodes in /dev.
                Starting udev Kernel Device Manager...
[  OK  ] Started Setup Virtual Console.
[  OK  ] Started udev Coldplug all Devices.
                Starting udev Wait for Complete Device Initialization...
[  OK  ] Started Journal Service.
                Starting Flush Journal to Persistent Storage...
[  OK  ] Started Flush Journal to Persistent Storage.
[  OK  ] Started udev Kernel Device Manager.
[  OK  ] Listening on Load/Save RF Kill Switch Status /dev/rfkill Watch.
[  OK  ] Started Monitoring of LVM2 mirrors, snapshots etc. using dmeventd
[  OK  ] Started udev Wait for Complete Device Initialization.
                Starting Activation of DM RAID sets...
[  OK  ] Started Activation of DM RAID sets.
[  OK  ] Reached target Local Encrypted Volumes.
[  OK  ] Reached target Local File Systems (Pre).
                Starting File System Check on /dev/disk/by-uuid/FBC0-BBD6...
[  OK  ] Started File System Check on /dev/disk/by-uuid/FBC0-BBD6.
                Mounting /boot/efi...
[  OK  ] Mounted /boot/efi.
[  OK  ] Reached target Local File Systems.
                Starting Restore /run/initramfs on shutdown...
                Starting Import network configuration from initramfs...
                Starting Tell Plymouth To Write Out Runtime Data...
[  OK  ] Started Restore /run/initramfs on shutdown.
[  OK  ] Started Tell Plymouth To Write Out Runtime Data.
```

Figure 7-61. *When plymouth is not available*

plymouth shows you the animation shown in Figure 7-62.

Figure 7-62. *The plymouth screen*

Installing plymouth

If you want to install the different themes of plymouth, then this is what you can do:

1. Download plymouth-theme from gnome-look.org, or you can use
   the following:

   # **dnf install plymouth-theme***

2. Extract the downloaded theme to the following location: `/usr/share/plymouth/themes/`

```
# ls -l /usr/share/plymouth/themes/
total 52
drwxr-xr-x. 2 root root 4096 Apr 26  2019 bgrt
drwxr-xr-x  3 root root 4096 Mar 30 09:15 breeze
drwxr-xr-x  2 root root 4096 Mar 30 09:15 breeze-text
drwxr-xr-x. 2 root root 4096 Mar 30 09:15 charge
drwxr-xr-x. 2 root root 4096 Apr 26  2019 details
drwxr-xr-x  2 root root 4096 Mar 30 09:15 fade-in
drwxr-xr-x  2 root root 4096 Mar 30 09:15 hot-dog
drwxr-xr-x  2 root root 4096 Mar 30 09:15 script
drwxr-xr-x  2 root root 4096 Mar 30 09:15 solar
drwxr-xr-x  2 root root 4096 Mar 30 09:15 spinfinity
drwxr-xr-x. 2 root root 4096 Apr 26  2019 spinner
drwxr-xr-x. 2 root root 4096 Apr 26  2019 text
drwxr-xr-x. 2 root root 4096 Apr 26  2019 tribar
```

3. You need to rebuild initramfs as `plymouth` runs from the initramfs environment. For example, its configuration file has to be updated for the new `plymouth` theme.

```
# cat /etc/plymouth/plymouthd.conf
# Administrator customizations go in this file
#[Daemon]
#Theme=fade-in
[Daemon]
Theme=hot-dog
```

After rebooting, as shown in Figure 7-63, you will see a new `plymouth` theme called `hot-dog`.

Figure 7-63. *The hot-dog plymouth theme*

Managing plymouth

Since plymouth starts at an early stage, dracut does provide some command-line options to manage plymouth's behavior.

plymouth.enable=0
>   disable the plymouth bootsplash completely.

rd.plymouth=0
>   disable the plymouth bootsplash only for the initramfs.

The hot-dog image shown earlier is called a *splash screen*. To see the installed/chosen splash screen, you can use the following:

```
#plymouth --show-splash
```

Another main motive of plymouth is to maintain all the boot-time messages in a simple text file that users can examine after the boot. The logs will be stored at /var/ log/boot.log, but remember that this file is maintained by plymouth. This means you will find the booting messages only after starting plymouth. But at the same time, we need to keep in mind that plymouth does start at an early stage of initramfs (right after udevd kicks in).

less /varlog/boot.log
```
<snip>
------------ Sat Jul 06 01:43:12 IST 2019 ------------
[ESC[0;32m  OK  ESC[0m] Started ESC[0;1;39mShow Plymouth Boot ScreenESC[0m.
[ESC[0;32m  OK  ESC[0m] Reached target ESC[0;1;39mPathsESC[0m.
[ESC[0;32m  OK  ESC[0m] Started ESC[0;1;39mForward Password R...s to
Plymouth Directory WatchESC[0m.
[ESC[0;32m  OK  ESC[0m] Found device ESC[0;1;39m/dev/mapper/fedora_
localhost--live-rootESC[0m.
[ESC[0;32m  OK  ESC[0m] Reached target ESC[0;1;39mInitrd Root DeviceESC[0m.
[ESC[0;32m  OK  ESC[0m] Found device ESC[0;1;39m/dev/mapper/fedora_
localhost--live-swapESC[0m.
        Starting ESC[0;1;39mResume from hiber...fedora_localhost--live-
        swapESC[0m...
[ESC[0;32m  OK  ESC[0m] Started ESC[0;1;39mResume from hibern...r/fedora_
localhost--live-swapESC[0m.
[ESC[0;32m  OK  ESC[0m] Reached target ESC[0;1;39mLocal File Systems (Pre)
ESC[0m.
[ESC[0;32m  OK  ESC[0m] Reached target ESC[0;1;39mLocal File SystemsESC[0m.
        Starting ESC[0;1;39mCreate Volatile Files and DirectoriesESC[0m...
[ESC[0;32m  OK  ESC[0m] Started ESC[0;1;39mCreate Volatile Files and
DirectoriesESC[0m.
[ESC[0;32m  OK  ESC[0m] Reached target ESC[0;1;39mSystem
InitializationESC[0m.
[ESC[0;32m  OK  ESC[0m] Reached target ESC[0;1;39mBasic SystemESC[0m.
[ESC[0;32m  OK  ESC[0m] Started ESC[0;1;39mdracut initqueue hookESC[0m.
[ESC[0;32m  OK  ESC[0m] Reached target ESC[0;1;39mRemote File Systems (Pre)
ESC[0m.
```

```
[ESC[0;32m  OK  ESC[0m] Reached target ESC[0;1;39mRemote File
SystemsESC[0m.
         Starting ESC[0;1;39mFile System Check...fedora_localhost--live-
         rootESC[0m...
[ESC[0;32m  OK  ESC[0m] Started ESC[0;1;39mFile System Check ...r/fedora_
localhost--live-rootESC[0m.
         Mounting ESC[0;1;39m/sysrootESC[0m...
[ESC[0;32m  OK  ESC[0m] Mounted ESC[0;1;39m/sysrootESC[0m.
[ESC[0;32m  OK  ESC[0m] Reached target ESC[0;1;39mInitrd Root File
SystemESC[0m.
         Starting ESC[0;1;39mReload Configuration from the Real
         RootESC[0m...
[ESC[0;32m  OK  ESC[0m] Started ESC[0;1;39mReload Configuration from the
Real RootESC[0m.
[ESC[0;32m  OK  ESC[0m] Reached target ESC[0;1;39mInitrd File
SystemsESC[0m.
[ESC[0;32m  OK  ESC[0m] Reached target ESC[0;1;39mInitrd Default
TargetESC[0m.
         Starting ESC[0;1;39mdracut pre-pivot and cleanup hookESC[0m...
[ESC[0;32m  OK  ESC[0m] Started ESC[0;1;39mdracut pre-pivot and cleanup
hookESC[0m.
         Starting ESC[0;1;39mCleaning Up and Shutting Down DaemonsESC[0m...
[ESC[0;32m  OK  ESC[0m] Stopped target ESC[0;1;39mTimersESC[0m.
[ESC[0;32m  OK  ESC[0m] Stopped target ESC[0;1;39mdracut pre-pivot and cleanup
hookESC[0m.
[ESC[0;32m  OK  ESC[0m] Stopped target ESC[0;1;39mInitrd Default
TargetESC[0m.
[ESC[0;32m  OK  ESC[0m] Stopped target ESC[0;1;39mRemote File
SystemsESC[0m.
[ESC[0;32m  OK  ESC[0m] Stopped target ESC[0;1;39mRemote File Systems (Pre)
ESC[0m.
[ESC[0;32m  OK  ESC[0m] Stopped ESC[0;1;39mdracut initqueue hookESC[0m.
         Starting ESC[0;1;39mPlymouth switch root serviceESC[0m...
[ESC[0;32m  OK  ESC[0m] Stopped target ESC[0;1;39mInitrd Root DeviceESC[0m.
[ESC[0;32m  OK  ESC[0m] Stopped target ESC[0;1;39mBasic SystemESC[0m.
```

```
[ESC[0;32m  OK  ESC[0m] Stopped target ESC[0;1;39mSystem
InitializationESC[0m.
.
.
```

</snip>

Structure

plymouth takes inputs from initramfs/systemd to understand what stage of the booting procedure has been completed (as a percentage of the booting procedure) and accordingly shows the animation or a progress bar on the screen. There are two binaries that take care of the plymouth work.

```
    /bin/plymouth              (Interface to plymouthd)
   /usr/sbin/plymouthd  (main binary which shows splash and logs boot
   messages in boot.log file)
```

There are various plymouth services available inside initramfs on which systemd relies on.

 # ls -l usr/lib/systemd/system/ -l | grep -i plymouth

```
-rw-r--r--. 1 root root  384 Dec 21 12:19 plymouth-halt.service
-rw-r--r--. 1 root root  398 Dec 21 12:19 plymouth-kexec.service
-rw-r--r--. 1 root root  393 Dec 21 12:19 plymouth-poweroff.service
-rw-r--r--. 1 root root  198 Dec 21 12:19 plymouth-quit.service
-rw-r--r--. 1 root root  204 Dec 21 12:19 plymouth-quit-wait.service
-rw-r--r--. 1 root root  386 Dec 21 12:19 plymouth-reboot.service
-rw-r--r--. 1 root root  547 Dec 21 12:19 plymouth-start.service
-rw-r--r--. 1 root root  295 Dec 21 12:19 plymouth-switch-root.service
-rw-r--r--. 1 root root  454 Dec 21 12:19 systemd-ask-password-plymouth.path
-rw-r--r--. 1 root root  435 Dec 21 12:19 systemd-ask-password-plymouth.service
drwxr-xr-x. 2 root root 4096 Dec 21 12:19 systemd-ask-password-plymouth.
service.wants
```

systemd, when running in initramfs, calls these services from time to time during the boot phase. As you can see, every service is calling the plymouthd binary and passing switches accordingly to the current stage of booting. For example, `plymouth-start.service` simply starts the `plymouthd` binary with mode `boot`. There are only two modes; one is `boot`, and another one is `shutdown`.

```
# cat usr/lib/systemd/system/plymouth*  | grep -i execstart
ExecStart=/usr/sbin/plymouthd --mode=shutdown --attach-to-session
ExecStartPost=-/usr/bin/plymouth show-splash
ExecStart=/usr/sbin/plymouthd --mode=shutdown --attach-to-session
ExecStartPost=-/usr/bin/plymouth show-splash
ExecStart=/usr/sbin/plymouthd --mode=shutdown --attach-to-session
ExecStartPost=-/usr/bin/plymouth show-splash
ExecStart=-/usr/bin/plymouth quit                                  <<---
ExecStart=-/usr/bin/plymouth --wait
ExecStart=/usr/sbin/plymouthd --mode=reboot --attach-to-session
ExecStartPost=-/usr/bin/plymouth show-splash
ExecStart=/usr/sbin/plymouthd --mode=boot --pid-file=/var/run/plymouth/pid
--attach-to-session
ExecStartPost=-/usr/bin/plymouth show-splash
ExecStart=-/usr/bin/plymouth update-root-fs --new-root-dir=/sysroot   <<---
```

Another example we can consider is that at the time of the `switch_root`, systemd simply calls `plymouth-switch-root.service`, which in turn runs the `plymouthd` binary with an updated root filesystem as `sysroot`. In other words, you can say along with `switch_root` that `plymouth` changes its root directory from initramfs to the actual root filesystem. Going further, you can see that systemd starts the `plymouth` service in the same way that systemd sends a `quit` message to `plymouthd` at the end of the booting sequence. At the same time, you probably noticed that systemd calls `plymouth` at the time of the reboot or shutdown too. It is not really a big deal since it just calls the same `plymouthd` with the appropriate mode.

Sysinit.target

So, we have reached the `sysinit.target` stage. Figure 7-64 shows the booting sequence we have covered so far.

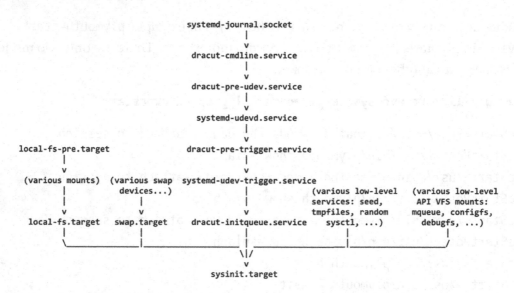

Figure 7-64. *The booting sequence covered so far*

Since this is a `target` unit, its job is to hold or start a bunch of other units (services, sockets, etc.). The list of units will be available in its `wants` directory. As you can see, the available unit files are nothing but symbolic links to the original service unit files.

#ls -l usr/lib/systemd/system/sysinit.target.wants/

```
total 0
kmod-static-nodes.service -> ../kmod-static-nodes.service
plymouth-start.service -> ../plymouth-start.service
systemd-ask-password-console.path -> ../systemd-ask-password-console.path
systemd-journald.service -> ../systemd-journald.service
systemd-modules-load.service -> ../systemd-modules-load.service
systemd-sysctl.service -> ../systemd-sysctl.service
systemd-tmpfiles-setup-dev.service -> ../systemd-tmpfiles-setup-dev.service
systemd-tmpfiles-setup.service -> ../systemd-tmpfiles-setup.service
systemd-udevd.service -> ../systemd-udevd.service
systemd-udev-trigger.service -> ../systemd-udev-trigger.service
```

Most of the services have already been started before we reach `sysinit.target`. For example, `systemd-udevd.service` and `systemd-udev-trigger.service` (after the `pre-trigger` service) have already been started, and we have already seen that `systemd-udevd.service` will execute the `/usr/lib/systemd/systemd-udevd` binary, whereas the systemd-udev-trigger service will execute the udevadm binary. Then why are we starting these services again with sysinit.target? We are not. sysinit.target will start only the services that have not yet started, and it will ignore taking any action on the services that are already started. Let's see the purpose of each of these service unit files.

The kmod-static-nodes systemd unit file executes the kmod binary with the static-nodes switch. We have already seen in Chapter 5 that lsmod, insmod, modinfo, modprobe, depmod, etc., are the symlinks to the kmod binary.

#lsinitrd | grep -i kmod

```
lrwxrwxrwx   1 root   root   11 Jul 25 03:54 usr/sbin/depmod -> ../bin/kmod
lrwxrwxrwx   1 root   root   11 Jul 25 03:54 usr/sbin/insmod -> ../bin/kmod
lrwxrwxrwx   1 root   root   11 Jul 25 03:54 usr/sbin/lsmod -> ../bin/kmod
lrwxrwxrwx   1 root   root   11 Jul 25 03:54 usr/sbin/modinfo -> ../bin/kmod
lrwxrwxrwx   1 root   root   11 Jul 25 03:54 usr/sbin/modprobe -> ../bin/kmod
lrwxrwxrwx   1 root   root   11 Jul 25 03:54 usr/sbin/rmmod -> ../bin/kmod
```

 # cat usr/lib/systemd/system/kmod-static-nodes.service | grep -v '#'
```
[Unit]
Description=Create list of static device nodes for the current kernel
DefaultDependencies=no
Before=sysinit.target systemd-tmpfiles-setup-dev.service
ConditionCapability=CAP_SYS_MODULE
ConditionFileNotEmpty=/lib/modules/%v/modules.devname

[Service]
Type=oneshot
RemainAfterExit=yes
ExecStart=/usr/bin/kmod static-nodes --format=tmpfiles --output=/run/
tmpfiles.d/static-nodes.conf
```

With the static-nodes switch, systemd is just collecting all of the static nodes (devices) present in the system. Why do we need static nodes in the age of dynamic node handling (udev)? There are some modules like fuse or ALSA that need some device files present in /dev, or they might create them. But it could be dangerous since the device files are made by kernel or udev. So, to avoid modules from creating device files, systemd will create static nodes like /dev/fuse or /dev/snd/seq through the kmod-static-nodes.service. The following are the static nodes created by kmod-static-nodes.service on a Fedora system:

 # kmod static-nodes
```
Module: fuse
      Device node: /dev/fuse
              Type: character device
              Major: 10
              Minor: 229
Module: btrfs
      Device node: /dev/btrfs-control
              Type: character device
              Major: 10
              Minor: 234
Module: loop
      Device node: /dev/loop-control
              Type: character device
              Major: 10
              Minor: 237
Module: tun
      Device node: /dev/net/tun
              Type: character device
              Major: 10
              Minor: 200
Module: ppp_generic
      Device node: /dev/ppp
              Type: character device
              Major: 108
              Minor: 0
Module: uinput
      Device node: /dev/uinput
              Type: character device
              Major: 10
              Minor: 223
```

```
Module: uhid
      Device node: /dev/uhid
            Type: character device
            Major: 10
            Minor: 239
Module: vfio
      Device node: /dev/vfio/vfio
            Type: character device
            Major: 10
            Minor: 196
Module: hci_vhci
      Device node: /dev/vhci
            Type: character device
            Major: 10
            Minor: 137
Module: vhost_net
      Device node: /dev/vhost-net
            Type: character device
            Major: 10
            Minor: 238
Module: vhost_vsock
      Device node: /dev/vhost-vsock
            Type: character device
            Major: 10
            Minor: 241
Module: snd_timer
      Device node: /dev/snd/timer
            Type: character device
            Major: 116
            Minor: 33
Module: snd_seq
      Device node: /dev/snd/seq
            Type: character device
            Major: 116
            Minor: 1
```

```
Module: cuse
      Device node: /dev/cuse
            Type: character device
            Major: 10
            Minor: 203
```

Next, we have the plymouth service, which has already been started; then we have systemd-ask-password-console.path, which is a .path unit file.

 # cat usr/lib/systemd/system/systemd-ask-password-console.path | grep -v '#'

```
[Unit]
Description=Dispatch Password Requests to Console Directory Watch
Documentation=man:systemd-ask-password-console.service(8)
DefaultDependencies=no
Conflicts=shutdown.target emergency.service
After=plymouth-start.service
Before=paths.target shutdown.target cryptsetup.target
ConditionPathExists=!/run/plymouth/pid

[Path]
DirectoryNotEmpty=/run/systemd/ask-password
MakeDirectory=yes
```

The .path unit file is for path-based activation, but since we have not encrypted our root disk with LUKS, we do not have the actual service file that will accept the password from the user. If we had configured LUKS, we would have had the /usr/lib/systemd/system/systemd-ask-password-plymouth.service service unit file, as shown here:

 # cat usr/lib/systemd/system/systemd-ask-password-plymouth.service
```
[Unit]
Description=Forward Password Requests to Plymouth
Documentation=http://www.freedesktop.org/wiki/Software/systemd/
PasswordAgents
DefaultDependencies=no
Conflicts=shutdown.target
After=plymouth-start.service
Before=shutdown.target
```

```
ConditionKernelCommandLine=!plymouth.enable=0
ConditionVirtualization=!container
ConditionPathExists=/run/plymouth/pid
```

```
[Service]
ExecStart=/usr/bin/systemd-tty-ask-password-agent --watch --plymouth
```

As you can see, this is executing the systemd-tty-ask-password-agent binary, which will ask for a password with plymouth instead of a TTY. Next, the service unit file is systemd-journald.service, which will start the journald daemon for us. Until this time, all the messages are logged with the journald socket, which systemd started as the first service of the booting sequence. The journald socket is 8 MB in size. If the socket runs out of buffer, then the services will be blocked until the socket becomes available. The 8 MB of buffer space is more than enough for the production systems.

#vim usr/lib/systemd/system/sysinit.target.wants/systemd-journald.service
```
[Unit]
Description=Journal Service
Documentation=man:systemd-journald.service(8) man:journald.conf(5)
DefaultDependencies=no
```
Requires=systemd-journald.socket
After=systemd-journald.socket systemd-journald-dev-log.socket systemd-
journald-audit.socket syslog.socket
Before=sysinit.target

```
[Service]
OOMScoreAdjust=-250
CapabilityBoundingSet=CAP_SYS_ADMIN CAP_DAC_OVERRIDE CAP_SYS_PTRACE CAP_
SYSLOG CAP_AUDIT_CONTROL CAP_AUDIT_READ CAP_CHOWN CAP_DAC_READ_SEARCH CAP_
FOWNER CAP_SETUID CAP_SETGID CAP_MAC_OVERRIDE
DeviceAllow=char-* rw
```
ExecStart=/usr/lib/systemd/systemd-journald
```
FileDescriptorStoreMax=4224
IPAddressDeny=any
LockPersonality=yes
MemoryDenyWriteExecute=yes
```

```
Restart=always
RestartSec=0
RestrictAddressFamilies=AF_UNIX AF_NETLINK
RestrictNamespaces=yes
RestrictRealtime=yes
RestrictSUIDSGID=yes
```
Sockets=systemd-journald.socket systemd-journald-dev-log.socket systemd-journald-audit.socket
```
StandardOutput=null
SystemCallArchitectures=native
SystemCallErrorNumber=EPERM
SystemCallFilter=@system-service
Type=notify
WatchdogSec=3min

LimitNOFILE=524288
```

Next, if you want systemd to load some specific module statically, then you can get some help from our next service, which is systemd-modules-load.service.

 # cat usr/lib/systemd/system/systemd-modules-load.service | grep -v '#'

```
[Unit]
Description=Load Kernel Modules
Documentation=man:systemd-modules-load.service(8) man:modules-load.d(5)
DefaultDependencies=no
Conflicts=shutdown.target
Before=sysinit.target shutdown.target
ConditionCapability=CAP_SYS_MODULE
ConditionDirectoryNotEmpty=|/lib/modules-load.d
ConditionDirectoryNotEmpty=|/usr/lib/modules-load.d
ConditionDirectoryNotEmpty=|/usr/local/lib/modules-load.d
ConditionDirectoryNotEmpty=|/etc/modules-load.d
ConditionDirectoryNotEmpty=|/run/modules-load.d
ConditionKernelCommandLine=|modules-load
ConditionKernelCommandLine=|rd.modules-load
```

```
[Service]
Type=oneshot
RemainAfterExit=yes
ExecStart=/usr/lib/systemd/systemd-modules-load
TimeoutSec=90s
```

The service executes /usr/lib/systemd/systemd-modules-load. The binary understands the two command-line parameters.

- module_load: This is a kernel command-line parameter.

- rd.module_load: This is a dracut command-line parameter.

If you pass a dracut command-line parameter, then systemd-modules-load will statistically load the module in memory, but for that, the module has to be present in initramfs. If it is not present in initramfs, then first it has to be pulled in initramfs. While generating initramfs, dracut reads the <module-name>.conf files from here:

```
/etc/modules-load.d/*.conf
/run/modules-load.d/*.conf
/usr/lib/modules-load.d/*.conf
```

You need to create the *.conf file and need to mention the module name in it, which you want to add in initramfs.

For example, here we have created a new initramfs image that does not have the vfio module in it:

```
# dracut new.img
# lsinitrd | grep -i vfio
  <no_output>
```

To pull the module statistically inside initramfs, here we have created the vfio.conf file:

```
# cat /usr/lib/modules-load.d/vfio.conf
  vfio
```

Here we have rebuilt initramfs:

```
# dracut new.img -f
# lsinitrd new.img | grep -i vfio
```

```
Jul 25 03:54 usr/lib/modules/5.3.16-300.fc31.x86_64/kernel/drivers/vfio
Jul 25 03:54 usr/lib/modules/5.3.16-300.fc31.x86_64/kernel/drivers/vfio/
vfio.ko.xz
Jul 25 03:54 usr/lib/modules-load.d/vfio.conf
```

As you can see, the module has been pulled inside initramfs, and it will be loaded in memory as soon as the service systemd-modules-load.service starts.

Loading modules statistically is not really a good idea. These days, modules are loaded dynamically in memory when it is necessary or on demand, whereas static modules will always be loaded in memory irrespective of need or demand.

Don't get confused with the /etc/modprobe.d directory. Its use is to pass the options to modules. Here's an example:

```
#cat /etc/modprobe.d/lockd.conf
    options lockd nlm_timeout=10
```

nlm_timeour=10 is an option passed to the lockd module. Remember, the .conf file inside /etc/modprobe.d has to be a module name. Through the same conf file, you can set an alias for the module name. Here's an example:

```
"alias my-mod really_long_modulename"
```

Next, systemd will set the sysctl kernel parameters with the help of systemd-sysctl.service.

```
# cat usr/lib/systemd/system/systemd-sysctl.service | grep -v '#'
```

```
[Unit]
Description=Apply Kernel Variables
Documentation=man:systemd-sysctl.service(8) man:sysctl.d(5)
DefaultDependencies=no
Conflicts=shutdown.target
After=systemd-modules-load.service
Before=sysinit.target shutdown.target
ConditionPathIsReadWrite=/proc/sys/net/
```

```
[Service]
Type=oneshot
RemainAfterExit=yes
ExecStart=/usr/lib/systemd/systemd-sysctl
TimeoutSec=90s
```

systemd-sysctl.service will start the /usr/lib/systemd/systemd-sysctl binary, which will set the kernel tuning parameters by reading the *.conf files from three different locations.

```
/etc/sysctl.d/*.conf
    /run/sysctl.d/*.conf
    /usr/lib/sysctl.d/*.conf
```

Here's an example:

sysctl -a | grep -i swappiness
```
    vm.swappiness = 60
```

The default swappiness kernel parameter value is set to 60. If you want to change it to 10 and it has to be permanent across reboots, then add it in /etc/sysctl.d/99-sysctl.conf.

#cat /etc/sysctl.d/99-sysctl.conf

```
    vm.swappiness = 10
```

You can reload and set the sysctl parameters by using this:

sysctl -p
```
vm.swappiness = 10
```

To make these changes in initramfs, you need to regenerate initramfs. At the time of the boot, systemd-sysctl.service will read the swappiness value from the 99-sysctl.conf file and will set it in the initramfs environment.

systemd creates many temporary files for its smooth execution. After setting up the sysctl parameters, it executes the next service, called systemd-tmpfiles-setup-dev.service, which will execute the /usr/bin/systemd-tmpfiles --prefix=/dev --create --boot binary. This will create dev filesystem-related temporary files according to these rules:

```
/etc/tmpfiles.d/*.conf
/run/tmpfiles.d/*.conf
/usr/lib/tmpfiles.d/*.conf
```

After sysinit.target, systemd will verify if the required sockets are created or not through sockets.target.

 # ls usr/lib/systemd/system/sockets.target.wants/ -l
```
total 0
32 Jan  3 18:05 systemd-journald-audit.socket -> ../systemd-journald-audit.
socket
34 Jan  3 18:05 systemd-journald-dev-log.socket -> ../systemd-journald-dev-
log.socket
26 Jan  3 18:05 systemd-journald.socket -> ../systemd-journald.socket
31 Jan  3 18:05 systemd-udevd-control.socket -> ../systemd-udevd-control.
socket
30 Jan  3 18:05 systemd-udevd-kernel.socket -> ../systemd-udevd-kernel.
socket
```

So, our boot process has finished the sequence up to sysinit.target. Refer the flowchart shown in Figure 7-65.

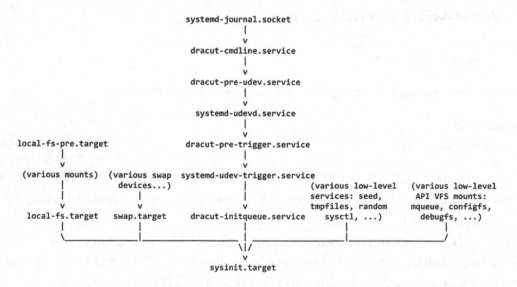

Figure 7-65. *The boot sequence covered so far*

"Can't Boot" Issue 8 (sysctl.conf)

Issue: After rebooting, the kernel is panicking, and the system is not able to boot. This is what is visible on the console:

```
[    4.596220] Mem-Info:
[    4.597455] active_anon:566 inactive_anon:1 isolated_anon:0
[    4.597455]  active_file:0 inactive_file:0 isolated_file:0
[    4.597455]  unevictable:19700 dirty:0 writeback:0 unstable:0
[    4.597455]  slab_reclaimable:2978 slab_unreclaimable:3180
[    4.597455]  mapped:2270 shmem:22 pagetables:42 bounce:0
[    4.597455]  free:23562 free_pcp:1982 free_cma:0
[    4.611930] Node 0 active_anon:2264kB inactive_anon:4kB active_file:0kB
inactive_file:0kB unevictable:78800kB isolated(anon):0kB isolated(file):0kB
mapped:9080kB dirty:0kB writeback:0kB shmem:88kB shmem_thp: 0kB
shmem_pmdmapped: 0kB anon_thp: 0kB writeback_tmp:0kB unstable:0kB all_
unreclaimable? yes
[    4.621748] Node 0 DMA free:15900kB min:216kB low:268kB high:320kB
active_anon:0kB inactive_anon:0kB active_file:0kB inactive_file:0kB
unevictable:0kB writepending:0kB present:15992kB managed:15908kB
mlocked:0kB kernel_stack:0kB pagetables:0kB bounce:0kB free_pcp:0kB local_
pcp:0kB free_cma:0kB
[    4.632561] lowmem_reserve[]: 0 1938 4764 4764 4764
[    4.634609] Node 0 DMA32 free:38516kB min:27404kB low:34252kB
high:41100kB active_anon:0kB inactive_anon:0kB active_file:0kB
inactive_file:0kB unevictable:0kB writepending:0kB present:2080628kB
managed:2015092kB mlocked:0kB kernel_stack:0kB pagetables:0kB bounce:0kB
free_pcp:2304kB local_pcp:0kB free_cma:0kB
[    4.645636] lowmem_reserve[]: 0 0 2826 2826 2826
[    4.647886] Node 0 Normal free:39832kB min:39956kB low:49944kB
high:59932kB active_anon:2264kB inactive_anon:4kB active_file:0kB
inactive_file:0kB unevictable:78800kB writepending:0kB present:3022848kB
managed:2901924kB mlocked:0kB kernel_stack:1776kB pagetables:168kB
bounce:0kB free_pcp:5624kB local_pcp:1444kB free_cma:0kB
[    4.659458] lowmem_reserve[]: 0 0 0 0 0
```

[4.661319] Node 0 DMA: 1*4kB (U) 1*8kB (U) 1*16kB (U) 0*32kB 2*64kB (U) 1*128kB (U) 1*256kB (U) 0*512kB 1*1024kB (U) 1*2048kB (M) 3*4096kB (M) = 15900kB

[4.666730] Node 0 DMA32: 1*4kB (M) 0*8kB 1*16kB (M) 1*32kB (M) 1*64kB (M) 0*128kB 0*256kB 1*512kB (M) 3*1024kB (M) 1*2048kB (M) 8*4096kB (M) = 38516kB

[4.673247] Node 0 Normal: 69*4kB (UME) 16*8kB (M) 10*16kB (UME) 7*32kB (ME) 5*64kB (E) 1*128kB (E) 1*256kB (U) 9*512kB (ME) 9*1024kB (UME) 2*2048kB (ME) 5*4096kB (M) = 39892kB

[4.680399] Node 0 hugepages_total=0 hugepages_free=0 hugepages_surp=0 hugepages_size=1048576kB

[4.683930] Node 0 hugepages_total=2303 hugepages_free=2303 hugepages_surp=0 hugepages_size=2048kB

[4.687749] 19722 total pagecache pages

[4.689841] 0 pages in swap cache

[4.691580] Swap cache stats: add 0, delete 0, find 0/0

[4.694275] Free swap = 0kB

[4.696039] Total swap = 0kB

[4.697617] 1279867 pages RAM

[4.699229] 0 pages HighMem/MovableOnly

[4.700862] 46636 pages reserved

[4.703868] 0 pages cma reserved

[4.705589] 0 pages hwpoisoned

[4.707435] Tasks state (memory values in pages):

[4.709532] [pid]   uid tgid total_vm   rss pgtables_bytes swapents oom_score_adj name

[4.713849] [341]   0   341   5118   1178   77824
0   -1000 (md-udevd)

[4.717805] Out of memory and no killable processes...

[4.719861] Kernel panic - not syncing: System is deadlocked on memory

[4.721926] CPU: 3 PID: 1 Comm: systemd Not tainted 5.3.7-301.fc31. x86_64 #1

[4.724343] Hardware name: QEMU Standard PC (Q35 + ICH9, 2009), BIOS 1.12.0-2.fc30 04/01/2014

[4.727959] Call Trace:

```
[    4.729204]  dump_stack+0x5c/0x80
[    4.730707]  panic+0x101/0x2d7
[    4.747357]  out_of_memory.cold+0x2f/0x88
[    4.749172]  __alloc_pages_slowpath+0xb09/0xe00
[    4.750890]  __alloc_pages_nodemask+0x2ee/0x340
[    4.752452]  alloc_slab_page+0x19f/0x320
[    4.753982]  new_slab+0x44f/0x4d0
[    4.755317]  ? alloc_slab_page+0x194/0x320
[    4.757016]  ___slab_alloc+0x507/0x6a0
[    4.758768]  ? copy_verifier_state+0x1f7/0x270
[    4.760591]  ? ___slab_alloc+0x507/0x6a0
[    4.763266]  __slab_alloc+0x1c/0x30
[    4.764846]  kmem_cache_alloc_trace+0x1ee/0x220
[    4.766418]  ? copy_verifier_state+0x1f7/0x270
[    4.768120]  copy_verifier_state+0x1f7/0x270
[    4.769604]  ? kmem_cache_alloc_trace+0x162/0x220
[    4.771098]  ? push_stack+0x35/0xe0
[    4.772367]  push_stack+0x66/0xe0
[    4.774010]  check_cond_jmp_op+0x1fe/0xe60
[    4.775644]  ? _cond_resched+0x15/0x30
[    4.777524]  ? _cond_resched+0x15/0x30
[    4.779315]  ? kmem_cache_alloc_trace+0x162/0x220
[    4.780916]  ? copy_verifier_state+0x1f7/0x270
[    4.782357]  ? copy_verifier_state+0x16f/0x270
[    4.783785]  do_check+0x1c06/0x24e0
[    4.785218]  bpf_check+0x1aec/0x24d4
[    4.786613]  ? _cond_resched+0x15/0x30
[    4.788073]  ? kmem_cache_alloc_trace+0x162/0x220
[    4.789672]  ? selinux_bpf_prog_alloc+0x1f/0x60
[    4.791564]  bpf_prog_load+0x3a3/0x670
[    4.794915]  ? seq_vprintf+0x30/0x50
[    4.797085]  ? seq_printf+0x53/0x70
[    4.799013]  __do_sys_bpf+0x7e5/0x17d0
[    4.800909]  ? __fput+0x168/0x250
[    4.802352]  do_syscall_64+0x5f/0x1a0
```

```
[    4.803826]  entry_SYSCALL_64_after_hwframe+0x44/0xa9
[    4.805587] RIP: 0033:0x7f471557915d
[    4.807638] Code: 00 c3 66 2e 0f 1f 84 00 00 00 00 00 90 f3 0f 1e fa 48
89 f8 48 89 f7 48 89 d6 48 89 ca 4d 89 c2 4d 89 c8 4c 8b 4c 24 08 0f 05
<48> 3d 01 f0 ff ff 73 01 c3 48 8b 0d fb 5c 0c 00 f7 d8 64 89 01 48
[    4.814732] RSP: 002b:00007fffd36da028 EFLAGS: 00000246 ORIG_RAX:
0000000000000141
[    4.818390] RAX: ffffffffffffffda RBX: 000055fb6ad3add0 RCX:
00007f471557915d
[    4.820448] RDX: 0000000000000070 RSI: 00007fffd36da030 RDI:
0000000000000005
[    4.822536] RBP: 0000000000000002 R08: 0070756f7267632f R09:
000001130000000f
[    4.826605] R10: 0000000000000000 R11: 0000000000000246 R12:
0000000000000000
[    4.829312] R13: 0000000000000006 R14: 000055fb6ad3add0 R15:
00007fffd36da1e0
[    4.831792] Kernel Offset: 0x26000000 from 0xffffffff81000000
(relocation range: 0xffffffff80000000-0xffffffffbfffffff)
[    4.835316] ---[ end Kernel panic - not syncing: System is deadlocked on
memory ]---
```

So, this is a "kernel panic" issue. We need to isolate the issue first since kernel panic can occur due to thousands of situations. If you look at the highlighted messages of kernel panic, it is clear that an "OOM-killer" has been invoked since the system is running out of memory. The kernel tried to free the memory from cache and even tried to use the swap space, but eventually it gave up, and the kernel panicked.

So, we have isolated the issue. We need to concentrate on who is eating the memory. The OS out-of-memory (OOM) mechanism will be invoked when the system has immense memory pressure.

There are three situations when an OOM-killer can be invoked during the boot sequence:

- The system has really low physical memory installed.

- The wrong kernel tuning parameters have been set.

- Some modules have a memory leak.

This system has 4.9 GB of physical memory, which is not big, but it is certainly more than enough for the Linux kernel to finish the booting sequence.

Some modules might have memory leaks, but identifying that will be a difficult task. So, we will verify first whether any memory-related kernel tuning parameters have been set incorrectly.

1. To do that, we will drop ourselves inside initramfs. In Figure 7-66, we have passed rd.break as a kernel command-line parameter.

```
load_video
set gfx_payload=keep
insmod gzio
linux ($root)/vmlinuz-5.3.7-301.fc31.x86_64 root=/dev/mapper/root_vg-root ro r\
esume=/dev/mapper/root_vg-swap rd.lvm.lv=root_vg/root rd.lvm.lv=root_vg/swap c\
onsole=ttyS0,115200 console=tty0 rd.break
initrd ($root)/initramfs-5.3.7-301.fc31.x86_64.img
```

Figure 7-66. *The kernel command-line parameter*

2. We will remount sysroot in read-write mode and verify the sysctl parameters.

   switch_root:/# **cat /proc/sys/vm/nr_hugepages**
                2400

3. The issue is the wrongly reserved number of hugepages. We will disable the setting as per Figure 7-67.

```
switch_root:/# mount -o remount,rw /sysroot/
[  183.088836] EXT4-fs (dm-0): re-mounted. Opts: (null)
switch_root:/#
switch_root:/# cat /sysroot/etc/sysctl.conf
# sysctl settings are defined through files in
# /usr/lib/sysctl.d/, /run/sysctl.d/, and /etc/sysctl.d/.
#
# Vendors settings live in /usr/lib/sysctl.d/.
# To override a whole file, create a new file with the same in
# /etc/sysctl.d/ and put new settings there. To override
# only specific settings, add a file with a lexically later
# name in /etc/sysctl.d/ and put new settings there.
#
# For more information, see sysctl.conf(5) and sysctl.d(5).
#vm.nr_hugepages = 2400
switch_root:/#
switch_root:/# reboot
```

Figure 7-67. *Disabling the hugepage setting*

After rebooting, the system is able to boot successfully. Let's try to understand what went wrong. This system has 4.9 GB of memory, and earlier there were no hugepages reserved.

```
# cat /proc/meminfo | grep -e MemTotal -e HugePages_Total

MemTotal:        4932916 kB
HugePages_Total:       0
```

```
# cat /proc/sys/vm/nr_hugepages
0
```

A normal page is 4 KB in size, whereas a hugepage is 2 MB in size, which is 512 times bigger than a normal page. Hugepage has its own advantages, but at the same time it has its own disadvantages too.

- A hugepage cannot be swapped out.
- The kernel don't use hugepages.
- Only the applications that are hugepage-aware can use the hugepages.

Someone wrongly set the 2,400 hugepages and rebuilt initramfs.

```
# echo "vm.nr_hugepages = 2400" >> /etc/sysctl.conf

    # sysctl -p
            vm.nr_hugepages = 2400

    # dracut /boot/new.img
    # reboot
```

So, 2,400 hugepages = 4.9 GB, which is all the installed main memory, and since the total memory got reserved in hugepages, the kernel cannot use it. So, while booting, when systemd reached the stage of sysinit.target and executed systemd-sysctl.service, the service read the sysctl.conf file from initramfs and reserved 4.9 GB of hugepages, which the kernel cannot use. Therefore, the kernel itself ran out of memory, and the system panicked.

basic.target

So, we have reached `basic.target`. As we know, targets are for synchronizing or grouping the units. `basic.target` is a synchronization point for late boot services.

```
# cat usr/lib/systemd/system/basic.target | grep -v '#'
[Unit]
Description=Basic System
Documentation=man:systemd.special(7)
Requires=sysinit.target
Wants=sockets.target timers.target paths.target slices.target
After=sysinit.target sockets.target paths.target slices.target tmp.mount

RequiresMountsFor=/var /var/tmp
Wants=tmp.mount
```

So, `basic.target` will be successful when all the earlier services' unit files `requires`, `wants`, and `after` phases are successfully started. In fact, almost all of the services have `After=basic.target` added in their unit files.

dracut-pre-mount.service

systemd will execute the `dracut-pre-mount.service` service just before mounting the user's root filesystem inside initramfs. Since it is a dracut service, it will execute only if the user has passed the `rd.break=pre-mount` dracut command-line parameter. Figure 7-68 shows that we have passed `rd.break=pre-mount` as a kernel command-line parameter.

As you can see in Figure 7-69, it has dropped us at the emergency shell, and the user's root filesystem is not mounted at `sysroot`. Yes, I said it has dropped us at the emergency shell, but you will be surprised to see that the emergency shell is nothing but a simple bash shell provided by systemd but at the time when booting is not finished yet. To understand the emergency shell better, we will pause our booting sequence for a while and discuss the debugging shells of initramfs in Chapter 8. We will resume our paused systemd's booting sequence in Chapter 9.

```
load_video
set gfx_payload=keep
insmod gzio
linux ($root)/boot/vmlinuz-5.3.16-300.fc31.x86_64 root=UUID=6588b8f1-7f37-4162\
-968c-8f99eacdf32e ro rd.break=pre-mount_
initrd ($root)/boot/initramfs-5.3.16-300.fc31.x86_64.img
```

Figure 7-68. *The kernel command-line parameter*

```
[  OK  ] Reached target Initrd Root Device.
[    4.822084] audit: type=1130 audit(1578222850.898:9): pid=1 uid=0 auid=4294967295 ses=4294967295 subj=kernel msg='unit=dracut
-initqueue comm="systemd" exe="/usr/lib/systemd/systemd" hostname=? addr=? terminal=? res=success'
[  OK  ] Started dracut initqueue hook.
[  OK  ] Reached target Remote File Systems (Pre).
[  OK  ] Reached target Remote File Systems.
         Starting dracut pre-mount hook...
[    4.829539] dracut-pre-mount[653]: Warning: Break pre-mount
         Starting Setup Virtual Console...
[  OK  ] Started Setup Virtual Console.
[    4.918583] audit: type=1130 audit(1578222850.994:10): pid=1 uid=0 auid=4294967295 ses=4294967295 subj=kernel msg='unit=syste
md-vconsole-setup comm="systemd" exe="/usr/lib/systemd/systemd" hostname=? addr=? terminal=? res=success'
         Starting Dracut Emergency Shell...

Generating "/run/initramfs/rdsosreport.txt"


Entering emergency mode. Exit the shell to continue.
Type "journalctl" to view system logs.
You might want to save "/run/initramfs/rdsosreport.txt" to a USB stick or /boot
after mounting them and attach it to a bug report.


pre-mount:/# ls /sysroot -l
total 0
pre-mount:/#
```

Figure 7-69. *The pre-mount hook*

CHAPTER 8

Debugging Shells

As of now, we know that initramfs has bash built in, and we have used it from time to time through `rd.break` hooks. This chapter's aim is to understand how systemd provides us with a shell inside an initramfs. What are the steps that have to be followed, and how can one use it more effectively? But before that, let's recap what we have learned so far about the debugging and emergency shells of initramfs.

The Shell

rd.break

        drop to a shell at the end

   `rd.break` drops us inside initramfs, and we can explore the initramfs environment through it. This initramfs environment is also called the *emergency mode*. In normal scenarios, we get dropped in emergency mode when initramfs is not able to mount the user's root filesystem. Remember, passing `rd.break` without any parameters will drop us at initramfs after mounting the user's root filesystem under `/sysroot` but before performing `switch_root` on it. You can always find the detailed logs in the `/run/initramfs/rdsosreport.txt` file. Figure 8-1 shows the logs from `rdsosreport.txt`.

© Yogesh Babar 2020
Y. Babar, *Hands-on Booting*, https://doi.org/10.1007/978-1-4842-5890-3_8

```
[   5.021670] localhost.localdomain systemd[1]: Mounting /sysroot...
[   5.037009] localhost.localdomain kernel: EXT4-fs (sda5): mounted filesystem with ordered data mode. Opts: (null)
[   5.036140] localhost.localdomain systemd[1]: Mounted /sysroot.
[   5.036582] localhost.localdomain systemd[1]: Reached target Initrd Root File System.
[   5.039821] localhost.localdomain systemd[1]: Starting Reload Configuration from the Real Root...
[   5.054518] localhost.localdomain systemd[1]: Reloading.
[   5.262476] localhost.localdomain systemd[1]: initrd-parse-etc.service: Succeeded.
[   5.263032] localhost.localdomain systemd[1]: Started Reload Configuration from the Real Root.
[   5.263360] localhost.localdomain audit[1]: SERVICE_START pid=1 uid=0 auid=4294967295 ses=4294967295 subj=kernel msg='unit=in
itrd-parse-etc comm="systemd" exe="/usr/lib/systemd/systemd" hostname=? addr=? terminal=? res=success'
[   5.263442] localhost.localdomain audit[1]: SERVICE_STOP pid=1 uid=0 auid=4294967295 ses=4294967295 subj=kernel msg='unit=ini
trd-parse-etc comm="systemd" exe="/usr/lib/systemd/systemd" hostname=? addr=? terminal=? res=success'
[   5.263488] localhost.localdomain systemd[1]: Reached target Initrd File Systems.
[   5.265162] localhost.localdomain systemd[1]: Reached target Initrd Default Target.
[   5.265567] localhost.localdomain systemd[1]: Condition check resulted in dracut mount hook being skipped.
[   5.267323] localhost.localdomain systemd[1]: Starting dracut pre-pivot and cleanup hook...
[   5.338352] localhost.localdomain dracut-pre-pivot[693]: Warning: Break before switch_root
[   5.379408] localhost.localdomain systemd[1]: Starting Setup Virtual Console...
[   5.441189] localhost.localdomain systemd[1]: systemd-vconsole-setup.service: Succeeded.
[   5.441585] localhost.localdomain systemd[1]: Started Setup Virtual Console.
[   5.441831] localhost.localdomain audit[1]: SERVICE_START pid=1 uid=0 auid=4294967295 ses=4294967295 subj=kernel msg='unit=sy
stemd-vconsole-setup comm="systemd" exe="/usr/lib/systemd/systemd" hostname=? addr=? terminal=? res=success'
[   5.441934] localhost.localdomain audit[1]: SERVICE_STOP pid=1 uid=0 auid=4294967295 ses=4294967295 subj=kernel msg='unit=sys
temd-vconsole-setup comm="systemd" exe="/usr/lib/systemd/systemd" hostname=? addr=? terminal=? res=success'
[   5.443893] localhost.localdomain systemd[1]: Starting Dracut Emergency Shell...
[   5.469385] localhost.localdomain systemd[1]: Received SIGRTMIN+21 from PID 609 (plymouthd).
[   5.479533] localhost.localdomain systemd[1]: Received SIGRTMIN+21 from PID 609 (plymouthd).
[   5.480148] localhost.localdomain systemd[1]: plymouth-start.service: Succeeded.
[   5.480811] localhost.localdomain audit[1]: SERVICE_STOP pid=1 uid=0 auid=4294967295 ses=4294967295 subj=kernel msg='unit=ply
mouth-start comm="systemd" exe="/usr/lib/systemd/systemd" hostname=? addr=? terminal=? res=success'
switch_root:/#
switch_root:/#
switch_root:/#
switch_root:/#
switch_root:/#
switch_root:/#
switch_root:/# exit _
```

Figure 8-1. *The rdsosreport.txt runtime logs*

In the log messages, you can clearly see that it dropped just before performing
pivot_root. pivot_root and switch_root will be discussed in Chapter 9, whereas
chroot will be discussed in Chapter 10. Once you exit from the emergency shell, systemd
will continue the paused booting sequence and will eventually provide the login screen.

Then we discussed how we can use emergency shells to fix some of the "can't boot"
issues. For example, initramfs is as good as the user's root filesystem. So, it does have
lvm, raid, and filesystem-related binaries that we can use to find, assemble, diagnose,
and fix the missing user's root filesystem. Then we discussed how we can mount it under
/sysroot and explore the contents of it to fix grub.cfg's wrong entries, for example.

Likewise, rd.break does provide us with various options to break the booting
sequence at different stages.

> **cmdline**: This hook gets the kernel command-line parameters.
>
> **pre-udev**: This breaks the booting sequence before the udev handler.
>
> **pre-trigger**: You can set udev environment variables with the
> udevadm control or can set --property=KEY=value like parameters
> or control the further execution of udev with udevadm.

pre-mount: This breaks the booting sequence before mounting the user's root filesystem at /sysroot.

mount: This breaks the booting sequence after mounting the root filesystem at /sysroot.

pre-pivot: This breaks the booting sequence just before switching to the actual root filesystem.

Now let's see how exactly systemd manages to provide us with the shells in these various stages.

How Does systemd Drop Us to an Emergency Shell?

Let's consider an example of a pre-mount hook. systemd from initramfs collects the rd.break=pre-mount command-line parameter from dracut-cmdline.service, and it runs the systemd service dracut-pre-mount.service from the initramfs location /usr/lib/systemd/system. The service will run before running initrd-root-fs.target, sysroot.mount, and systemd-fsck-root.service.

 # cat usr/lib/systemd/system/dracut-pre-mount.service | grep -v #'

```
[Unit]
Description=dracut pre-mount hook
Documentation=man:dracut-pre-mount.service(8)
DefaultDependencies=no
Before=initrd-root-fs.target sysroot.mount systemd-fsck-root.service
After=dracut-initqueue.service cryptsetup.target
ConditionPathExists=/usr/lib/initrd-release
ConditionDirectoryNotEmpty=|/lib/dracut/hooks/pre-mount
ConditionKernelCommandLine=|rd.break=pre-mount
Conflicts=shutdown.target emergency.target

[Service]
Environment=DRACUT_SYSTEMD=1
Environment=NEWROOT=/sysroot
Type=oneshot
```
ExecStart=-/bin/dracut-pre-mount

```
StandardInput=null
StandardOutput=syslog
StandardError=syslog+console
KillMode=process
RemainAfterExit=yes

KillSignal=SIGHUP
```

As you can see, it is simply executing the /bin/dracut-pre-mount script from initramfs.

vim bin/dracut-pre-mount

```
 1 #!/usr/bin/sh
 2
 3 export DRACUT_SYSTEMD=1
 4 if [ -f /dracut-state.sh ]; then
 5     . /dracut-state.sh 2>/dev/null
 6 fi
 7 type getarg >/dev/null 2>&1 || . /lib/dracut-lib.sh
 8
 9 source_conf /etc/conf.d
10
11 make_trace_mem "hook pre-mount" '1:shortmem' '2+:mem' '3+:slab'
   '4+:komem'
12 # pre pivot scripts are sourced just before we doing cleanup and switch over
13 # to the new root.
14 getarg 'rd.break=pre-mount' 'rdbreak=pre-mount' && emergency_shell -n
   pre-mount "Break pre-mount"
15 source_hook pre-mount
16
17 export -p > /dracut-state.sh
18
19 exit 0
```

Inside the /bin/dracut-pre-mount script, the most important line is the following:

```
getarg rd.break=pre-mount' rdbreak=pre-mount
    && emergency_shell -n pre-mount "Break pre-mount"
```

We have already discussed the getarg function, which is used to check what parameter has been passed to rd.break=. If rd.break=pre-mount has been passed, then only the emergency-shell() function will be called. The function is defined in /usr/lib/dracut-lib.sh, and it passes pre-mount as a string parameter to it. -n stands for the following:

> [-n STRING] or [STRING]: True if the length of STRING is
> nonzero

The emergency_shell function accepts the _rdshell_name variable's value as pre-mount.

```
if [ "$1" = "-n" ]; then
    _rdshell_name=$2
```

Here, -n is considered as the first argument ($1), and pre-mount is the second argument ($2). So, the value of _rdshell_name becomes pre-mount.

```
#vim /usr/lib/dracut-lib.sh
1123 emergency_shell()
1124 {
1125     local _ctty
1126     set +e
1127     local _rdshell_name="dracut" action="Boot" hook="emergency"
1128     local _emergency_action
1129
1130     if [ "$1" = "-n" ]; then
1131         _rdshell_name=$2
1132         shift 2
1133     elif [ "$1" = "--shutdown" ]; then
1134         _rdshell_name=$2; action="Shutdown"; hook="shutdown-emergency"
1135         if type plymouth >/dev/null 2>&1; then
1136             plymouth --hide-splash
1137         elif [ -x /oldroot/bin/plymouth ]; then
1138             /oldroot/bin/plymouth --hide-splash
1139         fi
1140         shift 2
1141     fi
1142
1143     echo ; echo
```

```
1144    warn "$*"
1145    echo
1146
1147    _emergency_action=$(getarg rd.emergency)
1148    [ -z "$_emergency_action" ] \
1149        && [ -e /run/initramfs/.die ] \
1150        && _emergency_action=halt
1151
1152    if getargbool 1 rd.shell -d -y rdshell || getarg rd.break -d
        rdbreak; then
1153        _emergency_shell $_rdshell_name
1154    else
1155        source_hook "$hook"
1156        warn "$action has failed. To debug this issue add \"rd.shell
            rd.debug\" to the kernel command line."
1157        [ -z "$_emergency_action" ] && _emergency_action=halt
1158    fi
1159
1160    case "$_emergency_action" in
1161        reboot)
1162            reboot || exit 1;;
1163        poweroff)
1164            poweroff || exit 1;;
1165        halt)
1166            halt || exit 1;;
1167    esac
1168 }
```

Then, at the end, it calls another _emergency_shell function from the same file (note the underscore before the function name). As you can see, _rdshell_name is the argument to the _emergency_shell function.

_emergency_shell $_rdshell_name

Inside the _emergency_shell() function, we can see that _name gets the argument, which is pre-mount.

local _name="$1"

#vim usr/lib/dracut-lib.sh

```
1081 _emergency_shell()
1082 {
1083     local _name="$1"
1084     if [ -n "$DRACUT_SYSTEMD" ]; then
1085         > /.console_lock
1086         echo "PS1=\"$_name:\\\${PWD}# \"" >/etc/profile
1087         systemctl start dracut-emergency.service
1088         rm -f -- /etc/profile
1089         rm -f -- /.console_lock
1090     else
1091         debug_off
1092         source_hook "$hook"
1093         echo
1094         /sbin/rdsosreport
1095         echo 'You might want to save "/run/initramfs/rdsosreport.txt" to a
             USB stick or /boot'
1096         echo 'after mounting them and attach it to a bug report.'
1097         if ! RD_DEBUG= getargbool 0 rd.debug -d -y rdinitdebug -d -y
             rdnetdebug; then
1098             echo
1099             echo 'To get more debug information in the report,'
1100             echo 'reboot with "rd.debug" added to the kernel command line.'
1101         fi
1102         echo
1103         echo 'Dropping to debug shell.'
1104         echo
1105         export PS1="$_name:\${PWD}# "
1106         [ -e /.profile ] || >/.profile
1107
1108         _ctty="$(RD_DEBUG= getarg rd.ctty=)" && _ctty="/dev/${_ctty##*/}"
1109         if [ -z "$_ctty" ]; then
1110             _ctty=console
1111             while [ -f /sys/class/tty/$_ctty/active ]; do
1112                 _ctty=$(cat /sys/class/tty/$_ctty/active)
1113                 _ctty=${_ctty##* } # last one in the list
```

```
1114              done
1115              _ctty=/dev/$_ctty
1116         fi
1117         [ -c "$_ctty" ] || _ctty=/dev/tty1
1118         case "$(/usr/bin/setsid --help 2>&1)" in *--ctty*) CTTY="--
             ctty";; esac
1119         setsid $CTTY /bin/sh -i -l 0<>$_ctty 1<>$_ctty 2<>$_ctty
1120      fi
```

The same pre-mount string has been passed to PS1. Let's see first what exactly PS1 is.

PS1 is called a *pseudo* variable. This will be shown by bash when the user has successfully logged in. Here's an example:

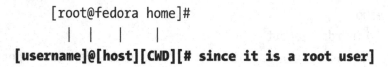

[username]@[host][CWD][# since it is a root user]

The ideal entries accepted by bash are PS1='\u:\w\$'.

> **u** = This is the username.

> **w** = This is the working directory.

> **$** = If UID is 0, then #; otherwise $'.

So, in our case, when we get a emergency shell, PS1 will be printed by the shell as follows:

'pre-mount#'

Next in the source code, you can see that the PS1 variable's new value is also getting added in /etc/profile. The reason is that bash reads this file every time before presenting the shell to the user. At the end, we are simply starting the dracut-emergency service.

systemctl start dracut-emergency.service

The following is the dracut-emergency.service file from usr/lib/systemd/system/ of initramfs:

 # cat usr/lib/systemd/system/dracut-emergency.service | grep -v #'

```
[Unit]
Description=Dracut Emergency Shell
DefaultDependencies=no
After=systemd-vconsole-setup.service
Wants=systemd-vconsole-setup.service
Conflicts=shutdown.target emergency.target

[Service]
Environment=HOME=/
Environment=DRACUT_SYSTEMD=1
Environment=NEWROOT=/sysroot
WorkingDirectory=/
ExecStart=-/bin/dracut-emergency
ExecStopPost=-/bin/rm -f -- /.console_lock
Type=oneshot
StandardInput=tty-force
StandardOutput=inherit
StandardError=inherit
KillMode=process
IgnoreSIGPIPE=no
TasksMax=infinity

KillSignal=SIGHUP
```

The service is simply executing /bin/dracut-emergency. This script first stops the plymouth service.

type plymouth >/dev/null 2>&1 && plymouth quit

This stores the hook variable's value as emergency and calls the source_hook function with the emergency argument.

export _rdshell_name="dracut" action="Boot" hook="emergency"
source_hook "$hook"

 # vim bin/dracut-emergency
```
    1 #!/usr/bin/sh
  2
  3 export DRACUT_SYSTEMD=1
```

```
 4 if [ -f /dracut-state.sh ]; then
 5     . /dracut-state.sh 2>/dev/null
 6 fi
 7 type getarg >/dev/null 2>&1 || . /lib/dracut-lib.sh
 8
 9 source_conf /etc/conf.d
10
11 type plymouth >/dev/null 2>&1 && plymouth quit
12
13 export _rdshell_name="dracut" action="Boot" hook="emergency"
14 _emergency_action=$(getarg rd.emergency)
15
16 if getargbool 1 rd.shell -d -y rdshell || getarg rd.break -d rdbreak; then
17     FSTXT="/run/dracut/fsck/fsck_help_$fstype.txt"
18     source_hook "$hook"
19     echo
20     rdsosreport
21     echo
22     echo
23     echo Entering emergency mode. Exit the shell to continue.'
24     echo Type "journalctl" to view system logs.'
25     echo You might want to save "/run/initramfs/rdsosreport.txt" to a
       USB stick or /boot'
26     echo after mounting them and attach it to a bug report.'
27     echo
28     echo
29     [ -f "$FSTXT" ] && cat "$FSTXT"
30     [ -f /etc/profile ] && . /etc/profile
31     [ -z "$PS1" ] && export PS1="$_name:\${PWD}# "
32     exec sh -i -l
33 else
34     export hook="shutdown-emergency"
35     warn "$action has failed. To debug this issue add \"rd.shell rd.debug\"
       to the kernel command line."
36     source_hook "$hook"
```

```
37     [ -z "$_emergency_action" ] && _emergency_action=halt
38 fi
39
40 /bin/rm -f -- /.console_lock
41
42 case "$_emergency_action" in
43     reboot)
44         reboot || exit 1;;
45     poweroff)
46         poweroff || exit 1;;
47     halt)
48         halt || exit 1;;
49 esac
50
51 exit 0
```

The source_hook function is again defined in usr/lib/dracut-lib.sh.

```
source_hook() {
    local _dir
    _dir=$1; shift
    source_all "/lib/dracut/hooks/$_dir" "$@"
}
```

The _dir variable has captured the hook name, which is emergency. All the hooks are nothing but a bunch of scripts, stored and executed from the /lib/dracut/hooks/ directory of initramfs.

```
# tree usr/lib/dracut/hooks/
usr/lib/dracut/hooks/
├── cleanup
├── cmdline
│   ├── 30-parse-lvm.sh
│   ├── 91-dhcp-root.sh
│   └── 99-nm-config.sh
├── emergency
│   └── 50-plymouth-emergency.sh
```

```
├──── initqueue
│      ├──── finished
│      ├──── online
│      ├──── settled
│      │      └──── 99-nm-run.sh
│      └──── timeout
│             └──── 99-rootfallback.sh
├──── mount
├──── netroot
├──── pre-mount
├──── pre-pivot
│      └──── 85-write-ifcfg.sh
├──── pre-shutdown
├──── pre-trigger
├──── pre-udev
│      └──── 50-ifname-genrules.sh
├──── shutdown
│      └──── 25-dm-shutdown.sh
└──── shutdown-emergency
```

For an emergency hook, it is executing usr/lib/dracut/hooks/emergency/50-plymouth-emergency.sh, which is stopping the plymouth service.

#!/usr/bin/sh
plymouth --hide-splash 2>/dev/null || :

Once the emergency hook is executed and plymouth has been stopped, it will go back to bin/dracut-emergency and print the following banner:

echo Entering emergency mode. Exit the shell to continue.'
echo Type "journalctl" to view system logs.'
echo You might want to save "/run/initramfs/rdsosreport.txt" to a USB stick or /boot'
echo after mounting them and attach it to a bug report.'

So, it does not matter what the rd.break=hook_name user has passed. systemd will execute the emergency hook, and once the banner is printed, it will fetch the /etc/profile directory in which we have added PS1=_rdshell_name/PS1=hook_name, and then we can simply run the bash shell.

exec sh -i -l

When the shell starts running, it will read /etc/profile, and it will find the PS1=hook_
name variable. In this case, hook_name is pre-mount. That is why pre-mount as a prompt
name of bash has been printed. Refer to the flowchart shown in Figure 8-2 for a better
understanding of this.

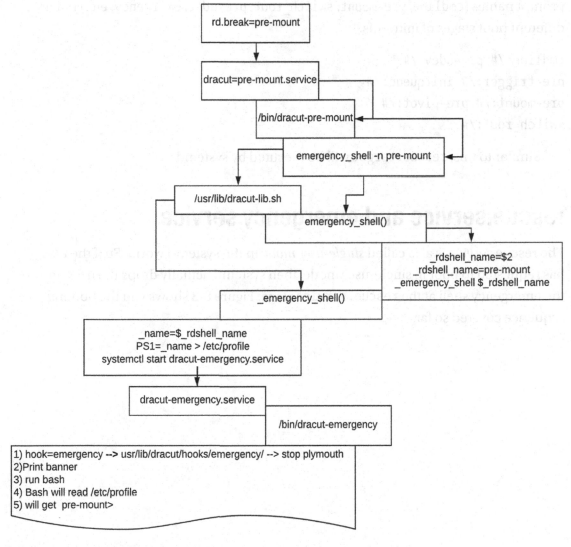

Figure 8-2. *The flowchart*

If a user passes any other parameter to `rd.break`, for example, `initqueue`, then it will be fed into `PS1`, `_rdshell_name`, and hook variables. Later, bash will be called through the emergency service. Bash will read the `PS1` value from the `/etc/profile` file and will show the `initqueue` name in the prompt.

The conclusion is that the same bash shell will be provided to the user under various prompt names (`cmdline`, `pre-mount`, `switch_root`, `pre-udev`, `emergency`, etc.) but at different boot stages of initramfs.

```
cmdline:/# pre-udev:/#
pre-trigger:/# initqueue:/#
pre-mount:/# pre-pivot:/#
switch_root:/#
```

Similar to this, `rescue.target` will be executed by systemd.

rescue.service and emergency.service

The rescue service is also called *single-user mode* in the systemd world. So if the user has requested to boot in single-user mode, then systemd actually drops the user on the emergency shell at the `rescue.service` stage. Figure 8-3 shows you the booting sequence covered so far.

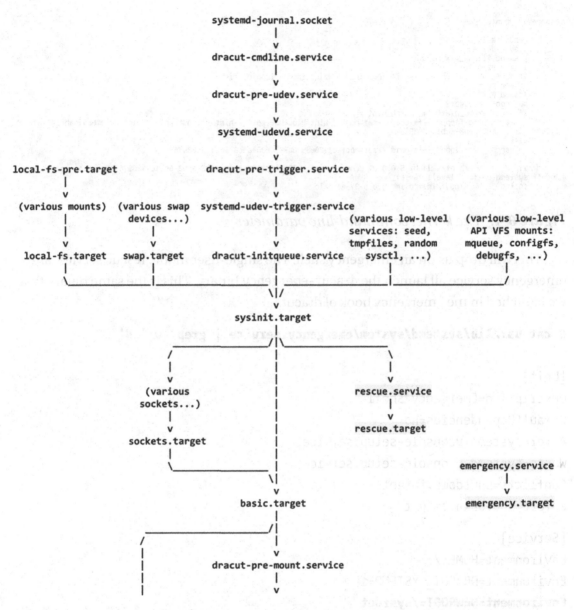

Figure 8-3. *The flowchart of the booting sequence*

You can either pass rescue.target or pass runlevel1.target or emergency. service to systemd.unit to boot in single-user mode. As shown in Figure 8-4, we will use Ubuntu this time to explore the booting stages.

```
setparams 'Ubuntu'

        recordfail
        load_video
        gfxmode $linux_gfx_mode
        insmod gzio
        if [ x$grub_platform = xxen ]; then insmod xzio; insmod lzopio; fi
        insmod part_gpt
        insmod ext2
        set root='hd0,gpt2'
        if [ x$feature_platform_search_hint = xy ]; then
          search --no-floppy --fs-uuid --set=root --hint-bios=hd0,gpt2 --hint-efi=hd0,gpt2 --hint-baremetal=ahci0,gpt2  \
c1420089-3b00-4e83-aeb3-6cb1c7583576
        else
          search --no-floppy --fs-uuid --set=root c1420089-3b00-4e83-aeb3-6cb1c7583576
        fi
        linux       /boot/vmlinuz-5.0.0-37-generic root=UUID=c1420089-3b00-4e83-aeb3-6cb1c7583576 ro  quiet splash $vt_\
handoff systemd.unit=runlevel1.target_
        initrd       /boot/initrd.img-5.0.0-37-generic
```

Figure 8-4. *The kernel command-line parameter*

This will drop us on an emergency shell. The single-user mode, rescue service, and emergency service all launch the dracut-emergency binary. This is the same binary that we launched in the emergency hook of dracut.

 # cat usr/lib/systemd/system/emergency.service | grep -v ' #'

[Unit]
Description=Emergency Shell
DefaultDependencies=no
After=systemd-vconsole-setup.service
Wants=systemd-vconsole-setup.service
Conflicts=shutdown.target
Before=shutdown.target

[Service]
Environment=HOME=/
Environment=DRACUT_SYSTEMD=1
Environment=NEWROOT=/sysroot
WorkingDirectory=/
ExecStart=/bin/dracut-emergency
ExecStopPost=-/usr/bin/systemctl --fail --no-block default
Type=idle
StandardInput=tty-force
StandardOutput=inherit

```
StandardError=inherit
KillMode=process
IgnoreSIGPIPE=no
TasksMax=infinity

KillSignal=SIGHUP
```

 # cat usr/lib/systemd/system/rescue.service | grep -v ' #'

```
[Unit]
Description=Emergency Shell
DefaultDependencies=no
After=systemd-vconsole-setup.service
Wants=systemd-vconsole-setup.service
Conflicts=shutdown.target
Before=shutdown.target

[Service]
Environment=HOME=/
Environment=DRACUT_SYSTEMD=1
Environment=NEWROOT=/sysroot
WorkingDirectory=/
ExecStart=/bin/dracut-emergency
ExecStopPost=-/usr/bin/systemctl --fail --no-block default
Type=idle
StandardInput=tty-force
StandardOutput=inherit
StandardError=inherit
KillMode=process
IgnoreSIGPIPE=no
TasksMax=infinity

KillSignal=SIGHUP
```

And as we all know, the dracut-emergency script executes a bash shell.

vim bin/dracut-emergency

```
 1 #!/usr/bin/sh
 2
 3 export DRACUT_SYSTEMD=1
 4 if [ -f /dracut-state.sh ]; then
 5     . /dracut-state.sh 2>/dev/null
 6 fi
 7 type getarg >/dev/null 2>&1 || . /lib/dracut-lib.sh
 8
 9 source_conf /etc/conf.d
10
11 type plymouth >/dev/null 2>&1 && plymouth quit
12
13 export _rdshell_name="dracut" action="Boot" hook="emergency"
14 _emergency_action=$(getarg rd.emergency)
15
16 if getargbool 1 rd.shell -d -y rdshell || getarg rd.break -d rdbreak; then
17     FSTXT="/run/dracut/fsck/fsck_help_$fstype.txt"
18     source_hook "$hook"
19     echo
20     rdsosreport
21     echo
22     echo
23     echo 'Entering emergency mode. Exit the shell to continue.'
24     echo 'Type "journalctl" to view system logs.'
25     echo 'You might want to save "/run/initramfs/rdsosreport.txt" to a
       USB stick or /boot'
26     echo 'after mounting them and attach it to a bug report.'
27     echo
28     echo
29     [ -f "$FSTXT" ] && cat "$FSTXT"
30     [ -f /etc/profile ] && . /etc/profile
31     [ -z "$PS1" ] && export PS1="$_name:\${PWD}# "
32     exec sh -i -l
33 else
```

```
34     export hook="shutdown-emergency"
35     warn "$action has failed. To debug this issue add \"rd.shell
       rd.debug\" to the kernel command line."
36     source_hook "$hook"
37     [ -z "$_emergency_action" ] && _emergency_action=halt
38 fi
39
40 /bin/rm -f -- /.console_lock
41
42 case "$_emergency_action" in
43     reboot)
44         reboot || exit 1;;
45     poweroff)
46         poweroff || exit 1;;
47     halt)
48         halt || exit 1;;
49 esac
50
51 exit 0
```

```
[    2.749129] Couldn't get size: 0x800000000000000e
[    4.437146] sd 32:0:0:0: [sda] Assuming drive cache: write through
[    5.797837] piix4_smbus 0000:00:07.3: SMBus base address uninitialized - upgr
You are in rescue mode. After logging in, type "journalctl -xb" to view
system logs, "systemctl reboot" to reboot, "systemctl default" or "exit"
to boot into default mode.
Press Enter for maintenance
(or press Control-D to continue):
root@yogesh:~#
root@yogesh:~# ls /
bin   cdrom  etc   initrd.img      lib     lost+found  mnt  proc  run   snap  swapfile  tmp  var
boot  dev    home  initrd.img.old  lib64   media            opt   root  sbin  srv   sys       usr  vmlinuz
root@yogesh:~#
root@yogesh:~# _
```

Figure 8-5. *The emergency shell*

As you can see in Figure 8-5, sysroot is not mounted yet since we have not reached the mounting stage of booting.

I hope you now understand how systemd presents the emergency shell to users at various booting stages. In the next chapter, we will resume our paused systemd's booting sequence.

CHAPTER 9

systemd (Part II)

So far, we have reached the service `dracut.pre-mount.service` where the user's root filesystem is not yet mounted inside initramfs. systemd's next stage of booting will mount the root filesystem on `sysroot`.

sysroot.mount

systemd accepts the `mount` dracut command-line parameter, which will drop us on a mount emergency shell. As you can see in Figure 9-1, we have passed the `rd.break=mount` kernel command-line parameter.

```
load_video
set gfx_payload=keep
insmod gzio
linux ($root)/vmlinuz-5.3.7-301.fc31.x86_64 root=/dev/mapper/root_vg-root ro r\
esume=/dev/mapper/root_vg-swap rd.lvm.lv=root_vg/root rd.lvm.lv=root_vg/swap c\
onsole=ttyS0,115200 console=tty0 rd.break=mount
initrd ($root)/initramfs-5.3.7-301.fc31.x86_64.img
```

Figure 9-1. *The kernel command-line parameter*

As you can see in Figure 9-2, `sysroot` has been mounted with a user's root filesystem in read-only mode.

```
mount:/# ls /sysroot
@System.solv  boot   etc   lib    lost+found  mnt  proc  run   srv  tmp  var
bin           dev    home  lib64  media            opt   root  sbin sys  usr
mount:/#
mount:/# echo qwer >> sysroot/etc/fstab
sh: sysroot/etc/fstab: Read-only file system
mount:/#
mount:/#
```

Figure 9-2. *The mount hook*

© Yogesh Babar 2020
Y. Babar, *Hands-on Booting*, https://doi.org/10.1007/978-1-4842-5890-3_9

The dracut.mount hook (usr/lib/systemd/system/dracut-mount.service) will run the /bin/dracut-mount script from initramfs, which will do the mounting part.

#**vim usr/lib/systemd/system/dracut-mount.service**

As you can see, this is executing the dracut-mount script from initramfs and also exporting the NEWROOT variable with the sysroot value.

Environment=NEWROOT=/sysroot
ExecStart=-/bin/dracut-mount

```
[Unit]
Description=dracut mount hook
Documentation=man:dracut-mount.service(8)
After=initrd-root-fs.target initrd-parse-etc.service
After=dracut-initqueue.service dracut-pre-mount.service
```
ConditionPathExists=/usr/lib/initrd-release
ConditionDirectoryNotEmpty=|/lib/dracut/hooks/mount
ConditionKernelCommandLine=|rd.break=mount
```
DefaultDependencies=no
Conflicts=shutdown.target emergency.target

[Service]
Environment=DRACUT_SYSTEMD=1
```
Environment=NEWROOT=/sysroot
```
Type=oneshot
```
ExecStart=-/bin/dracut-mount
```
StandardInput=null
StandardOutput=syslog
StandardError=syslog+console
KillMode=process
RemainAfterExit=yes

KillSignal=SIGHUP
```
#**vim bin/dracut-mount**
```
  1 #!/usr/bin/sh
  2 export DRACUT_SYSTEMD=1
  3 if [ -f /dracut-state.sh ]; then
```

```
 4     . /dracut-state.sh 2>/dev/null
 5 fi
 6 type getarg >/dev/null 2>&1 || . /lib/dracut-lib.sh
 7
 8 source_conf /etc/conf.d
 9
10 make_trace_mem "hook mount" '1:shortmem' '2+:mem' '3+:slab'
11
12 getarg 'rd.break=mount' -d 'rdbreak=mount' && emergency_shell -n mount
   "Break mount"
13 # mount scripts actually try to mount the root filesystem, and may
14 # be sourced any number of times. As soon as one suceeds, no more are
      sourced.
15 i=0
16 while :; do
17     if ismounted "$NEWROOT"; then
18         usable_root "$NEWROOT" && break;
19         umount "$NEWROOT"
20     fi
21     for f in $hookdir/mount/*.sh; do
22         [ -f "$f" ] && . "$f"
23         if ismounted "$NEWROOT"; then
24             usable_root "$NEWROOT" && break;
25             warn "$NEWROOT has no proper rootfs layout, ignoring and
                 removing offending mount hook"
26             umount "$NEWROOT"
27             rm -f -- "$f"
28         fi
29     done
30
31     i=$(($i+1))
32     [ $i -gt 20 ] && emergency_shell "Can't mount root filesystem"
33 done
34
```

```
35 export -p > /dracut-state.sh
36
37 exit 0
```

We saw in Chapter 8 how exactly it drops us on an emergency shell and the
associated functions of this. Since we stopped the booting sequence after mounting
the user's root filesystem inside initramfs, as you can see in Figure 9-3, the `systemd-
fstab-generator` has already been executed, and the `-mount` unit files have already
been created.

```
mount:/# ls -l /run/systemd/generator/
total 8
drwxr-xr-x 2 root root   60 Jan 10 06:57 'dev-mapper-root_vg\x2droot.device.d'
drwxr-xr-x 2 root root   60 Jan 10 06:57  initrd-root-device.target.d
drwxr-xr-x 2 root root   60 Jan 10 06:57  initrd-root-fs.target.requires
drwxr-xr-x 2 root root   60 Jan 10 06:57  initrd.target.wants
drwxr-xr-x 2 root root   60 Jan 10 06:57  sysinit.target.wants
-rw-r--r-- 1 root root  328 Jan 10 06:57  sysroot.mount
-rw-r--r-- 1 root root  488 Jan 10 06:57  systemd-fsck-root.service
drwxr-xr-x 2 root root   60 Jan 10 06:57 'systemd-fsck@dev-mapper-root_vg\x2droot.service.d'
mount:/#
mount:/# cat /run/systemd/generator/sysroot.mount
# Automatically generated by systemd-fstab-generator

[Unit]
SourcePath=/proc/cmdline
Documentation=man:fstab(5) man:systemd-fstab-generator(8)
DefaultDependencies=no
Before=initrd-root-fs.target
Requires=systemd-fsck-root.service
After=systemd-fsck-root.service

[Mount]
Where=/sysroot
What=/dev/mapper/root_vg-root
Options=ro
mount:/#
```

Figure 9-3. *The systemd-fstab-generator behavior*

Remember, the user's root filesystem name added in `sysroot.mount` has been
taken from the `/proc/cmdline` file. The `sysroot.mount` clearly mentions what has to be
mounted and where it has to be mounted.

initrd.target

As we have said multiple times, the ultimate aim of the booting sequence is to provide the user's root filesystem to the user, and while doing that, the major stages that systemd achieves are as follows:

1) Find the user's root filesystem.

2) Mount the user's root filesystem (we have reached this stage of booting).

3) Find the other necessary filesystems and mount them (usr, var, nfs, cifs, etc.).

4) Switch into the mounted user's root filesystem.

5) Start the user space daemons.

6) Start either multi-user.target or graphical.target (which is outside the scope of this book).

As you can see, as of now, we have reached step 2, which is mounting the user's root filesystem inside initramfs. We all know that systemd has .targets, and target is nothing but a bunch of unit files. The .target can be successfully started only when all of its unit files have been successfully started.

There are many targets in the systemd world, such as basic.target, multi-user.target, graphical.target, default.target, and sysinit.target to name a few. The ultimate aim of initramfs is to achieve the initrd.target. Once the initrd.target is successfully started, then systemd will switch_root into it. So, first, let's look at initrd.target and where it stands in terms of the booting sequence. Please refer to the flowchart shown in Figure 9-4.

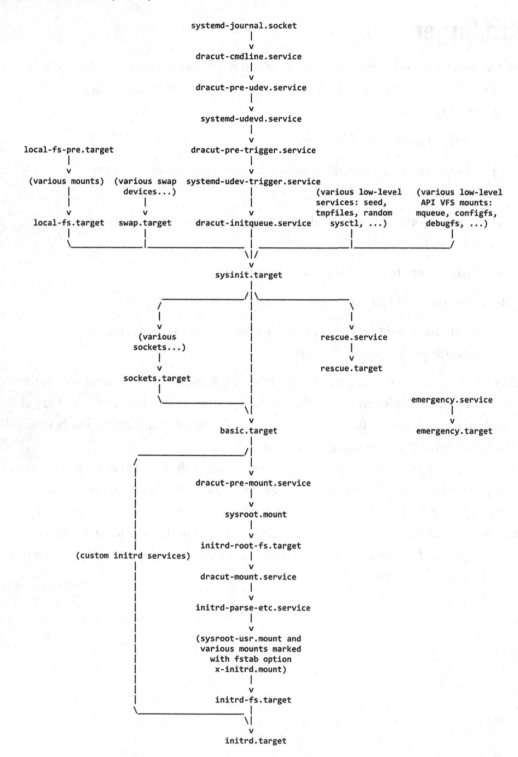

Figure 9-4. *The booting sequence*

When you are outside of initramfs (that means after switch_root), systemd's default.
target will be either multi-user.target or graphical.target, whereas inside initramfs
(that means before switch_root) after basic.target, systemd's default.target will be
initrd.target. So, after successfully completing the sysinit.target and basic.target,
systemd's main task is to achieve the initrd.target. To reach there, systemd will use the
sysroot.mount stage to read the mount unit files created by systemd-fstab-generator. The
service dracut-mount.service will mount the user's root filesystem to /sysroot, and then
systemd will execute the service initrd-parse-etc.service. It will parse the /sysroot/
etc/fstab file and will make the mount unit files for usr or any other mount points that have
the x-initrd.mount option set. This is how the initrd-parse-etc.service works:

 # cat usr/lib/systemd/system/initrd-parse-etc.service | grep -v '#'

```
[Unit]
Description=Reload Configuration from the Real Root
DefaultDependencies=no
```
Requires=initrd-root-fs.target
After=initrd-root-fs.target
```
OnFailure=emergency.target
OnFailureJobMode=replace-irreversibly
ConditionPathExists=/etc/initrd-release

[Service]
Type=oneshot
```
ExecStartPre=-/usr/bin/systemctl daemon-reload
```
ExecStart=-/usr/bin/systemctl --no-block start initrd-fs.target
ExecStart=/usr/bin/systemctl --no-block start initrd-cleanup.service
```

Basically, the service is executing systemctl with a daemon-reload switch. This will
reload the systemd manager configuration. This will rerun all generators, reload all unit
files, and re-create the entire dependency tree. While the daemon is being reloaded, all
sockets that systemd listens to on behalf of the user configuration will stay accessible.
The systemd generators, which will be re-executed, are as follows:

 # ls usr/lib/systemd/system-generators/ -l

```
    total 92
    -rwxr-xr-x. 1 root root  3750 Jan 10 19:18 dracut-rootfs-generator
    -rwxr-xr-x. 1 root root 45640 Dec 21 12:19 systemd-fstab-generator
    -rwxr-xr-x. 1 root root 37032 Dec 21 12:19 systemd-gpt-auto-generator
```

As you can see, it will execute `systemd-fstab-generator`, which will read the `/sysroot/etc/fstab` entries and create the mount unit files for `usr` and for devices that have the `x-initrd.mount` option set. In short, `systemd-fstab-generator` has executed twice.

So, when you drop yourself to the mount shell (`rd.break=mount`), you are actually interrupting the booting sequence after the target `initrd.target`. This target just runs the following services:

 # ls usr/lib/systemd/system/initrd.target.wants/

```
dracut-cmdline-ask.service    dracut-mount.service       dracut-pre-
                                                          trigger.service
dracut-cmdline.service        dracut-pre-mount.service   dracut-pre-udev.
                                                          service
dracut-initqueue.service      dracut-pre-pivot.service
```

Please refer to Figure 9-5 for a better understanding of this.

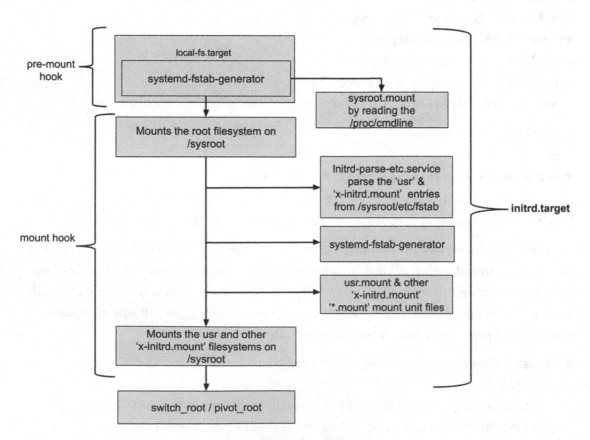

Figure 9-5. *The overall execution of initrd.target*

switch_root/pivot_root

Now we have reached the final stage of systemd's booting, which is switch_root. systemd switches the root filesystem from initramfs (/) to the user's root filesystem (/sysroot). systemd achieves this by taking the following steps:

1. Mounting the new root filesystem (/sysroot)

2. Turning it into the root filesystem (/)

3. Removing all accesses to the old (initramfs) root filesystem

4. Unmounting the initramfs filesystem and de-allocating the ramfs filesystem

There are three major points that will be discussed in this chapter.

- switch_root: We will explain this the old init way.

- pivot_root: We will explain this the systemd way.

- chroot: We will explain this in Chapter 10.

Switching to the New Root Filesystem on an init-Based System

An init-based system uses switch_root to switch to a new root filesystem (sysroot). The purpose of switch_root is explained well on its man page, as shown here:

#man switch_root
NAME
        switch_root - switch to another filesystem as the root of the mount tree
SYNOPSIS
        switch_root [-hV]

        switch_root newroot init [arg...]

DESCRIPTION
        switch_root moves already mounted /proc, /dev, /sys and /run to newroot and makes newroot the new root filesystem and starts init process.

> **WARNING: switch_root removes recursively all files and directories on the current root filesystem.**

OPTIONS

> -h, --help
>> Display help text and exit.
>
> -V, --version
>> Display version information and exit.

RETURN VALUE

> switch_root returns 0 on success and 1 on failure.

NOTES

> switch_root will fail to function if newroot is not the root of a mount. If you want to switch root into a directory that does not meet this requirement then you can first use a bind-mounting trick to turn any directory into a mount point:
>
>> mount --bind $DIR $DIR

So, it switches to a new root filesystem (sysroot), and along with the root, it moves the old root filesystem's virtual file systems (proc, dev, sys, etc.) to the new root. The best feature of switch_root is that after mounting the new root filesystem, it starts the init process on its own. Switching to a new root filesystem takes place in dracut's source code. The latest version of dracut while writing this book was 049. The switch_root function is defined in the dracut-049/modules.d/99base/init.sh file.

```
387 unset PS4
388
389 CAPSH=$(command -v capsh)
390 SWITCH_ROOT=$(command -v switch_root)
391 PATH=$OLDPATH
392 export PATH
393
394 if [ -f /etc/capsdrop ]; then
395     . /etc/capsdrop
396     info "Calling $INIT with capabilities $CAPS_INIT_DROP dropped."
397     unset RD_DEBUG
```

```
398     exec $CAPSH --drop="$CAPS_INIT_DROP" -- \
399         -c "exec switch_root \"$NEWROOT\" \"$INIT\" $initargs" || \
400     {
401         warn "Command:"
402         warn capsh --drop=$CAPS_INIT_DROP -- -c exec switch_root
                "$NEWROOT" "$INIT" $initargs
403         warn "failed."
404         emergency_shell
405     }
406 else
407     unset RD_DEBUG
408     exec $SWITCH_ROOT "$NEWROOT" "$INIT" $initargs || {
409         warn "Something went very badly wrong in the initramfs.  Please "
410         warn "file a bug against dracut."
411         emergency_shell
412     }
413 fi
```

In the previous code, you can see that exec switch_root has been called just like it was described on the man page of switch_root. The defined variable values of NEWROOT and INIT are as follows:

NEWROOT = "/sysroot"
INIT   = 'init' or 'sbin/init'

Just for your information, these days the init file is a symlink to systemd.

 # ls -l sbin/init
```
lrwxrwxrwx. 1 root root 22 Dec 21 12:19 sbin/init -> ../lib/systemd/systemd
```

To successfully switch_root the virtual filesystems, they have to be mounted first. This will be achieved through dracut-049/modules.d/99base/init.sh. These are the steps that will be followed:

1. Mount the proc filesystem.

2. Mount the sys filesystem.

3. Mount the /dev directory with devtmpfs.

4. Create the stdin, stdout, stderr, pts, and shm device files manually.

5. Make the /run mount point with tmpfs in it. (The /run mount point is not available on init-based systems.)

#vim dracut-049/modules.d/99base/init.sh

```
11 NEWROOT="/sysroot"
12 [ -d $NEWROOT ] || mkdir -p -m 0755 $NEWROOT
13
14 OLDPATH=$PATH
15 PATH=/usr/sbin:/usr/bin:/sbin:/bin
16 export PATH
17
18 # mount some important things
19 [ ! -d /proc/self ] && \
20     mount -t proc -o nosuid,noexec,nodev proc /proc >/dev/null
21
22 if [ "$?" != "0" ]; then
23     echo "Cannot mount proc on /proc! Compile the kernel with
       CONFIG_PROC_FS!"
24     exit 1
25 fi
26
27 [ ! -d /sys/kernel ] && \
28     mount -t sysfs -o nosuid,noexec,nodev sysfs /sys >/dev/null
29
30 if [ "$?" != "0" ]; then
31     echo "Cannot mount sysfs on /sys! Compile the kernel with
       CONFIG_SYSFS!"
32     exit 1
33 fi
34
35 RD_DEBUG=""
36 . /lib/dracut-lib.sh
37
```

```
38 setdebug
39
40 if ! ismounted /dev; then
41     mount -t devtmpfs -o mode=0755,noexec,nosuid,strictatime devtmpfs
       /dev >/dev/null
42 fi
43
44 if ! ismounted /dev; then
45     echo "Cannot mount devtmpfs on /dev! Compile the kernel with
       CONFIG_DEVTMPFS!"
46     exit 1
47 fi
48
49 # prepare the /dev directory
50 [ ! -h /dev/fd ] && ln -s /proc/self/fd /dev/fd >/dev/null 2>&1
51 [ ! -h /dev/stdin ] && ln -s /proc/self/fd/0 /dev/stdin >/dev/null 2>&1
52 [ ! -h /dev/stdout ] && ln -s /proc/self/fd/1 /dev/stdout >/dev/null 2>&1
53 [ ! -h /dev/stderr ] && ln -s /proc/self/fd/2 /dev/stderr >/dev/null 2>&1
54
55 if ! ismounted /dev/pts; then
56     mkdir -m 0755 /dev/pts
57     mount -t devpts -o gid=5,mode=620,noexec,nosuid devpts /dev/pts >/
       dev/null
58 fi
59
60 if ! ismounted /dev/shm; then
61     mkdir -m 0755 /dev/shm
62     mount -t tmpfs -o mode=1777,noexec,nosuid,nodev,strictatime tmpfs
       /dev/shm >/dev/null
63 fi
64
65 if ! ismounted /run; then
66     mkdir -m 0755 /newrun
67     if ! str_starts "$(readlink -f /bin/sh)" "/run/"; then
```

```
68          mount -t tmpfs -o mode=0755,noexec,nosuid,nodev,strictatime
            tmpfs /newrun >/dev/null
69      else
70          # the initramfs binaries are located in /run, so don't mount it
              with noexec
71          mount -t tmpfs -o mode=0755,nosuid,nodev,strictatime tmpfs /
            newrun >/dev/null
72      fi
73      cp -a /run/* /newrun >/dev/null 2>&1
74      mount --move /newrun /run
75      rm -fr -- /newrun
76 fi
```

Switching to a New Root Filesystem on a systemd-Based System

The steps are almost similar to what we discussed for an init-based system. The only difference for systemd is a binary made from C code. So, obviously, switching the root will take place in systemd's C source code, as shown here:

src/shared/switch-root.c:

First, consider the following:

new_root = sysroot
old_root = /

This will move the virtual filesystems that are already populated in initramfs' root filesystem; then the path_equal function checks whether the new_root path is available.

```
if (path_equal(new_root, "/"))
    return 0;
```

Later it calls a pivot_root syscall (init uses switch_root) and changes the root from / (the initramfs root filesystem) to sysroot (the user's root filesystem).

```
pivot_root(new_root, resolved_old_root_after) >= 0)
```

Before we go further, we need to understand what pivot_root is and what it does.

 # man pivot_root
NAME
        pivot_root - change the root filesystem

SYNOPSIS
        pivot_root new_root put_old

DESCRIPTION
        pivot_root moves the root file system of the current process to
        the directory put_old and makes new_root the new root file system.
        Since pivot_root(8) simply calls pivot_root(2), we refer to the man
        page of the latter for further details:

Note that, depending on the implementation of pivot_root, root and cwd of the caller may or may not change. The following is a sequence for invoking pivot_root that works in either case, assuming that pivot_root and chroot are in the current PATH:

cd new_root

pivot_root . put_old

exec chroot . command

Note that chroot must be available under the old root and under the new root, because pivot_root may or may not have implicitly changed the root directory of the shell.

Note that exec chroot changes the running executable, which is necessary if the old root directory should be unmounted afterwards. Also note that standard input, output, and error may still point to a device on the old root file system, keeping it busy. They can easily be changed when invoking chroot (see below; note the absence of leading slashes to make it work whether pivot_root has changed the shell's root or not).

pivot_root changes the root filesystem (the initramfs root filesystem) of the current process (systemd) to the new root filesystem (sysroot), and it also changes the running executable (systemd from initramfs) to a new one (systemd from the user's root filesystem).

After pivot_root, it detaches the old root device of initramfs (src/shared/switch-root.c).

vim src/shared/switch-root.c

```
96          /* We first try a pivot_root() so that we can umount the old
               root dir. In many cases (i.e. where rootfs is /),
 97          * that's not possible however, and hence we simply overmount
               root */
 98          if (pivot_root(new_root, resolved_old_root_after) >= 0) {
 99
100                  /* Immediately get rid of the old root, if detach_
                       oldroot is set.
101                   * Since we are running off it we need to do this
                       lazily. */
102                  if (unmount_old_root) {
103                          r = umount_recursive(old_root_after,
                               MNT_DETACH);
104                          if (r < 0)
105                                  log_warning_errno(r, "Failed to unmount
                                       old root directory tree, ignoring: %m");
106                  }
107
108          } else if (mount(new_root, "/", NULL, MS_MOVE, NULL) < 0)
109                  return log_error_errno(errno, "Failed to move %s
                       to /: %m", new_root);
110
```

After a successful pivot_root, this is the current state:

- sysroot has become root (/).

- The current working directory has become root (/).

- chroot will be executed so that bash changes its root directory from the old root (initramfs) to the new (user's) root filesystem. chroot will be discussed in the next chapter.

Finally, delete the old_root device (rm -rf).

```
110
111        if (chroot(".") < 0)
112                return log_error_errno(errno, "Failed to change root: %m");
113
114        if (chdir("/") < 0)
115                return log_error_errno(errno, "Failed to change
                   directory: %m");
116
117        if (old_root_fd >= 0) {
118                struct stat rb;
119
120                if (fstat(old_root_fd, &rb) < 0)
121                        log_warning_errno(errno, "Failed to stat old
                           root directory, leaving: %m");
122                else
123                        (void) rm_rf_children(TAKE_FD(old_root_fd), 0,
                           &rb); /* takes possession of the dir fd, even
                           on failure */
124        }
```

For a better understanding, I highly recommend reading the entire src/shared/
switch-root.c source code shown here:

```
 1 /* SPDX-License-Identifier: LGPL-2.1+ */
 2
 3 #include <errno.h>
 4 #include <fcntl.h>
 5 #include <limits.h>
 6 #include <stdbool.h>
 7 #include <sys/mount.h>
 8 #include <sys/stat.h>
 9 #include <unistd.h>
10
11 #include "base-filesystem.h"
12 #include "fd-util.h"
13 #include "fs-util.h"
```

```
14 #include "log.h"
15 #include "missing_syscall.h"
16 #include "mkdir.h"
17 #include "mount-util.h"
18 #include "mountpoint-util.h"
19 #include "path-util.h"
20 #include "rm-rf.h"
21 #include "stdio-util.h"
22 #include "string-util.h"
23 #include "strv.h"
24 #include "switch-root.h"
25 #include "user-util.h"
26 #include "util.h"
27
28 int switch_root(const char *new_root,
29                 const char *old_root_after, /* path below the new root,
                    where to place the old root after the transition */
30                 bool unmount_old_root,
31                 unsigned long mount_flags) {  /* MS_MOVE or MS_BIND */
32
33         _cleanup_free_ char *resolved_old_root_after = NULL;
34         _cleanup_close_ int old_root_fd = -1;
35         bool old_root_remove;
36         const char *i;
37         int r;
38
39         assert(new_root);
40         assert(old_root_after);
41
42         if (path_equal(new_root, "/"))
43                 return 0;
44
45         /* Check if we shall remove the contents of the old root */
46         old_root_remove = in_initrd();
47         if (old_root_remove) {
```

```
48          old_root_fd = open("/", O_RDONLY|O_NONBLOCK|
            O_CLOEXEC|O_NOCTTY|O_DIRECTORY);
49          if (old_root_fd < 0)
50                  return log_error_errno(errno, "Failed to open
                    root directory: %m");
51      }
52
53      /* Determine where we shall place the old root after the
           transition */
54      r = chase_symlinks(old_root_after, new_root, CHASE_PREFIX_
            ROOT|CHASE_NONEXISTENT, &resolved_old_root_after, NULL);
55      if (r < 0)
56              return log_error_errno(r, "Failed to resolve %s/%s:
                %m", new_root, old_root_after);
57      if (r == 0) /* Doesn't exist yet. Let's create it */
58              (void) mkdir_p_label(resolved_old_root_after, 0755);
59
60      /* Work-around for kernel design: the kernel refuses MS_MOVE if
           any file systems are mounted MS_SHARED. Hence
61       * remount them MS_PRIVATE here as a work-around.
62       *
63       * https://bugzilla.redhat.com/show_bug.cgi?id=847418 */
64      if (mount(NULL, "/", NULL, MS_REC|MS_PRIVATE, NULL) < 0)
65              return log_error_errno(errno, "Failed to set \"/\"
                mount propagation to private: %m");
66
67      FOREACH_STRING(i, "/sys", "/dev", "/run", "/proc") {
68              _cleanup_free_ char *chased = NULL;
69
70              r = chase_symlinks(i, new_root, CHASE_PREFIX_
                    ROOT|CHASE_NONEXISTENT, &chased, NULL);
71              if (r < 0)
72                      return log_error_errno(r, "Failed to resolve
                        %s/%s: %m", new_root, i);
73              if (r > 0) {
```

```
74                        /* Already exists. Let's see if it is a mount
                             point already. */
75                        r = path_is_mount_point(chased, NULL, 0);
76                        if (r < 0)
77                                return log_error_errno(r, "Failed to
                                  determine whether %s is a mount
                                  point: %m", chased);
78                        if (r > 0) /* If it is already mounted, then do
                          nothing */
79                                continue;
80                } else
81                        /* Doesn't exist yet? */
82                        (void) mkdir_p_label(chased, 0755);
83
84                if (mount(i, chased, NULL, mount_flags, NULL) < 0)
85                        return log_error_errno(errno, "Failed to
                          mount %s to %s: %m", i, chased);
86        }
87
88        /* Do not fail if base_filesystem_create() fails. Not all
             switch roots are like base_filesystem_create() wants
89         * them to look like. They might even boot, if they are RO and
             don't have the FS layout. Just ignore the error
90         * and switch_root() nevertheless. */
91        (void) base_filesystem_create(new_root, UID_INVALID,
          GID_INVALID);
92
93        if (chdir(new_root) < 0)
94                return log_error_errno(errno, "Failed to change
                  directory to %s: %m", new_root);
95
96        /* We first try a pivot_root() so that we can umount the old
             root dir. In many cases (i.e. where rootfs is /),
97         * that's not possible however, and hence we simply overmount
             root */
```

```
 98          if (pivot_root(new_root, resolved_old_root_after) >= 0) {
 99
100                  /* Immediately get rid of the old root, if detach_
                        oldroot is set.
101                   * Since we are running off it we need to do this
                        lazily. */
102                  if (unmount_old_root) {
103                          r = umount_recursive(old_root_after, MNT_DETACH);
104                          if (r < 0)
105                                  log_warning_errno(r, "Failed to unmount
                                        old root directory tree, ignoring: %m");
106                  }
107
108          } else if (mount(new_root, "/", NULL, MS_MOVE, NULL) < 0)
109                  return log_error_errno(errno, "Failed to move %s to
                        /: %m", new_root);
110
111          if (chroot(".") < 0)
112                  return log_error_errno(errno, "Failed to change root: %m");
113
114          if (chdir("/") < 0)
115                  return log_error_errno(errno, "Failed to change
                        directory: %m");
116
117          if (old_root_fd >= 0) {
118                  struct stat rb;
119
120                  if (fstat(old_root_fd, &rb) < 0)
121                          log_warning_errno(errno, "Failed to stat old
                                root directory, leaving: %m");
122                  else
123                          (void) rm_rf_children(TAKE_FD(old_root_fd),
                                0, &rb); /* takes possession of the dir fd,
                                even on failure */
124          }
```

```
125
126          return 0;
127 }
```

Here we have successfully switched to the user's root filesystem and left the initramfs environment. Now systemd from the user's root filesystem with PID 1 will start running and take care of the rest of the booting procedure, which is as follows:

- systemd will start the user space services such as httpd, mysql, postfix, network services, etc.

- Ultimately, the goal will be to reach default.target. As we discussed earlier, before switch_root, the target called default.target of systemd will be initrd.target, and after switch_root, it will be either multi-user.target or graphical.target.

But what happens to the existing systemd process, which started from initramfs (the root filesystem)? Is it getting killed after switch_root or pivot_root? Is the new systemd process starting from the user's root filesystem?

The answer is simple.

1) systemd of initramfs creates a pipe.

2) systemd forks.

3) The original PID 1 chroots into /systemd and executes /sysroot/usr/lib/systemd/systemd.

4) The forked systemd serializes its state over the pipe to PID 1 and exits.

5) PID 1 deserializes the data from the pipe and continues with the fresh configuration in / (formerly /sysroot).

I hope you have enjoyed the journey of systemd inside initramfs. As we mentioned earlier, the rest of the systemd booting sequence, which will take place outside of initramfs, will be more or less similar to what we have discussed so far.

How GUI is started is beyond the scope of this book. In our next chapter, we will discuss the live ISO images and about the rescue mode.

CHAPTER 10

Rescue Mode and Live Images

In this final chapter, we'll cover rescue mode and live images. During our rescue mode discussion, we'll cover the rescue initramfs, as well as some "can't boot" issues. The live images discussion covers Squashfs, `rootfs.img`, and the booting sequence of live images.

Rescue Mode

There are two ways to boot in rescue mode.

- Through the built-in GRUB menuentry. Refer to Figure 10-1.

```
CentOS Linux (4.18.0-80.el8.x86_64) 8 (Core)
CentOS Linux (0-rescue-53dc2e297cd34e949a6608ed6f494333) 8 (Core)
```

Figure 10-1. *The rescue mode entry from GRUB*

- Through a live ISO image. Refer to Figure 10-2.

© Yogesh Babar 2020

Y. Babar, *Hands-on Booting*, https://doi.org/10.1007/978-1-4842-5890-3_10

```
                              Troubleshooting

     Install CentOS Linux 8.0.1905 in basic graphics mode
     Rescue a CentOS Linux system
     Run a memory test

     Boot from local drive


     Return to main menu                                        <

       Press Tab for full configuration options on menu items.
                                •
     If the system will not boot, this lets you access files
     and edit config files to try to get it booting again.
```

Figure 10-2. *The rescue mode entry from a live image*

As the name suggests, this mode is designed to rescue the systems that are stuck in "can't boot" issues. Imagine a situation where the system is not able to mount the root filesystem and you are getting this never-ending generic message:

'**dracut-initqueue: warning dracut-initqueue timeout - starting timeout scripts**'

And say you have only one kernel installed, as shown here:

```
<snip>
.

.

[  OK  ] Started Show Plymouth Boot Screen.
[  OK  ] Started Forward Password R...s to Plymouth Directory Watch.
[  OK  ] Reached target Paths.
[  OK  ] Reached target Basic System.
[  145.832487] dracut-initqueue[437]: Warning: dracut-initqueue timeout -
starting timeout scripts
[  146.541525] dracut-initqueue[437]: Warning: dracut-initqueue timeout -
starting timeout scripts
[  147.130873] dracut-initqueue[437]: Warning: dracut-initqueue timeout -
starting timeout scripts
[  147.703069] dracut-initqueue[437]: Warning: dracut-initqueue timeout -
starting timeout scripts
```

```
[  148.267123] dracut-initqueue[437]: Warning: dracut-initqueue timeout -
starting timeout scripts
[  148.852865] dracut-initqueue[437]: Warning: dracut-initqueue timeout -
starting timeout scripts
[  149.430171] dracut-initqueue[437]: Warning: dracut-initqueue timeout -
starting timeout scripts
.

.
</snip>
```

Since this system has only one kernel (which can't boot), how would you fix the "can't boot" issue without an environment? Rescue mode was created for this sole purpose. Let's first choose the default rescue mode, which comes pre-installed with Linux and can be chosen from the GRUB menu. Please see Figure 10-3.

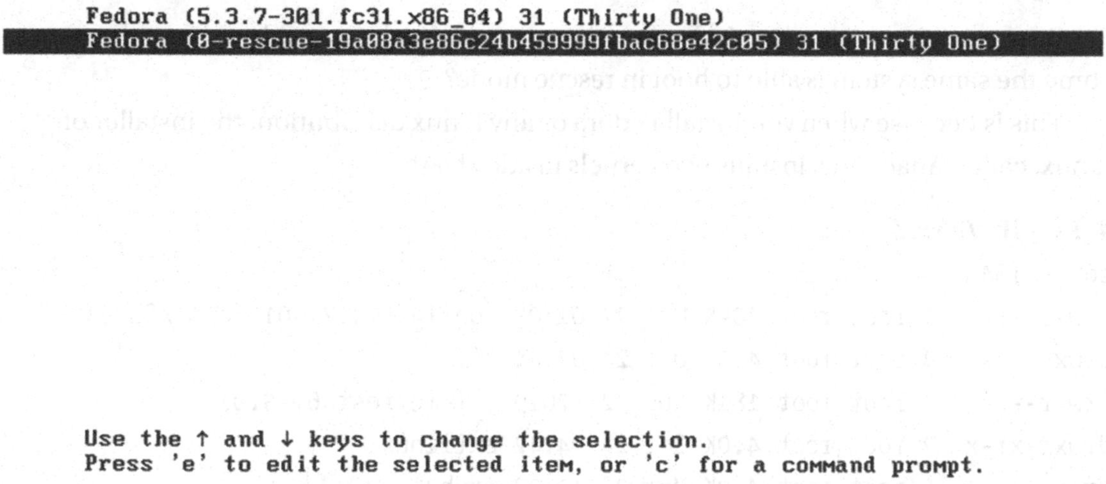

```
Fedora (5.3.7-301.fc31.x86_64) 31 (Thirty One)
Fedora (0-rescue-19a08a3e86c24b459999fbac68e42c05) 31 (Thirty One)




Use the ↑ and ↓ keys to change the selection.
Press 'e' to edit the selected item, or 'c' for a command prompt.
```

Figure 10-3. The GRUB screen

The rescue mode will boot normally, and as you can see in Figure 10-4, if everything is good, it will present the user with its root filesystem.

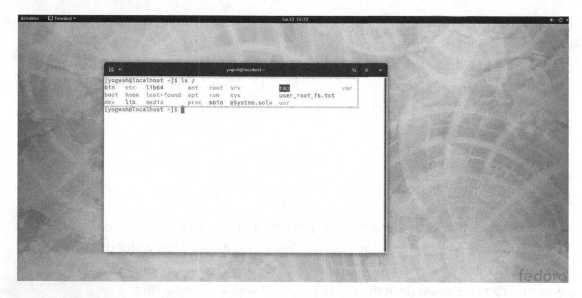

Figure 10-4. *The root filesystem mounted under rescue mode*

But a question comes to mind: when the normal kernel is not able to boot, then how come the same system is able to boot in rescue mode?

This is because when you install Fedora or any Linux distribution, the installer of Linux, called Anaconda, installs two kernels inside /boot.

```
# ls -lh /boot/
total 164M
-rw-r--r--. 1 root root 209K Oct 22 01:03 config-5.3.7-301.fc31.x86_64
drwx------. 4 root root 4.0K Oct 24 04:44 efi
-rw-r--r--. 1 root root 181K Aug  2  2019 elf-memtest86+-5.01
drwxr-xr-x. 2 root root 4.0K Oct 24 04:42 extlinux
drwx------. 5 root root 4.0K Mar 28 13:37 grub2
-rw-------. 1 root root  80M Dec  9 10:18 initramfs-0-rescue-2058a9f13f9e48
                                         9dba29c477a8ae2493.img
-rw-------. 1 root root  32M Dec  9 10:19 initramfs-5.3.7-301.fc31.x86_64.img
drwxr-xr-x. 3 root root 4.0K Dec  9 10:18 loader
drwx------. 2 root root  16K Dec  9 10:12 lost+found
-rw-r--r--. 1 root root 179K Aug  2  2019 memtest86+-5.01
-rw-------. 1 root root  30M Jan  6 09:37 new.img
-rw-------. 1 root root 4.3M Oct 22 01:03 System.map-5.3.7-301.fc31.x86_64
```

```
-rwxr-xr-x. 1 root root 8.9M Dec  9 10:18 vmlinuz-0-rescue-2058a9f13f9e489d
                                                    ba29c477a8ae2493
-rwxr-xr-x. 1 root root 8.9M Oct 22 01:04 vmlinuz-5.3.7-301.fc31.x86_64
```

As you can see, vmlinuz-5.3.7-301.fc31.x86_64 is a normal kernel, whereas
vmlinuz-0-rescue-19a08a3e86c24b459999fbac68e42c05 is the rescue kernel, which is a
separate kernel with its own initramfs file, called initramfs-0-rescue-19a08a3e86c24b
459999fbac68e42c05.img.

Let's say you installed a new package (.rpm or .deb) provided by nvidia, which
has new graphics drivers in it. Since the graphics drivers have to be added in initramfs,
the nvidia package rebuilt the original kernel initramfs (initramfs-5.3.7-301.fc31.
x86_64.img). So, the original kernel has the newly added graphics driver, but the rescue
initramfs does not have that driver added. When the user tries to boot, the system fails
to boot with the original kernel (vmlinuz-5.3.7-301.fc31.x86_64) since the installed
graphics driver is not compatible with the attached graphics card, but at the same time
the system will successfully boot with the rescue mode because the noncompatible
drivers are not present in the rescue initramfs. The rescue mode kernel will have the
same command-line parameters as the normal kernel has, and therefore the installed
rescue kernel knows the name of the user's root filesystem.

Figure 10-5 shows the normal kernel's command-line parameters.

```
load_video
set gfx_payload=keep
insmod gzio
linux ($root)/vmlinuz-5.3.16-300.fc31.x86_64 root=UUID=f7ed74b5-9085-4f42-a1c4\
-a569f790fdad ro rhgb quiet
initrd ($root)/initramfs-5.3.16-300.fc31.x86_64.img
```

Figure 10-5. *The normal kernel's command-line parameters*

Figure 10-6 shows the rescue kernel's command-line parameters.

```
load_video
set gfx_payload=keep
insmod gzio
linux ($root)/vmlinuz-0-rescue-0eeb43ddc61945c0b50c2f15b776f626 root=UUID=f7ed\
74b5-9085-4f42-a1c4-a569f790fdad ro rhgb quiet
initrd ($root)/initramfs-0-rescue-0eeb43ddc61945c0b50c2f15b776f626.img
```

Figure 10-6. *The rescue kernel's command-line parameters*

439

Rescue Mode initramfs

The rescue mode initramfs (initramfs-0-rescue-2058a9f13f9e489dba29c
477a8ae2493.img) is much bigger in size than the original kernel's initramfs
(initramfs-5.3.7-301.fc31.x86_64.img).

```
# ls -lh /boot/
total 164M
-rw-r--r--. 1 root root 209K Oct 22 01:03 config-5.3.7-301.fc31.x86_64
drwx------. 4 root root 4.0K Oct 24 04:44 efi
-rw-r--r--. 1 root root 181K Aug  2  2019 elf-memtest86+-5.01
drwxr-xr-x. 2 root root 4.0K Oct 24 04:42 extlinux
drwx------. 5 root root 4.0K Mar 28 13:37 grub2
-rw-------. 1 root root  80M Dec  9 10:18 initramfs-0-rescue-2058a9f13f9e48
                                         9dba29c477a8ae2493.img
-rw-------. 1 root root  32M Dec  9 10:19 initramfs-5.3.7-301.fc31.x86_64.img
drwxr-xr-x. 3 root root 4.0K Dec  9 10:18 loader
drwx------. 2 root root  16K Dec  9 10:12 lost+found
-rw-r--r--. 1 root root 179K Aug  2  2019 memtest86+-5.01
-rw-------. 1 root root  30M Jan  6 09:37 new.img
-rw-------. 1 root root 4.3M Oct 22 01:03 System.map-5.3.7-301.fc31.x86_64
-rwxr-xr-x. 1 root root 8.9M Dec  9 10:18 vmlinuz-0-rescue-2058a9f13f9e489d
ba29c477a8ae2493
-rwxr-xr-x. 1 root root 8.9M Oct 22 01:04 vmlinuz-5.3.7-301.fc31.x86_64
```

Why is this? It's because the rescue initramfs is not host-specific the way a normal
kernel's initramfs is. The rescue initramfs is a generic initramfs that is prepared by
considering all the possible devices on which a user can create a root filesystem. Let's
compare both the initramfs systems.

```
# tree
.
├── normal_kernel
│   └── initramfs-5.3.7-301.fc31.x86_64.img
└── rescue_kernel
    └── initramfs-0-rescue-2058a9f13f9e489dba29c477a8ae2493.img

2 directories, 2 files
```

We will extract them in their respective directories.

#/usr/lib/dracut/skipcpio
   initramfs-5.3.7-301.fc31.x86_64.img | gunzip -c | cpio -idv

#/usr/lib/dracut/skipcpio
   initramfs-0-rescue-2058a9f13f9e489dba29c477a8ae2493.img | gunzip -c |
   cpio -idv

We will make the list of files from the extracted initramfs.

 # tree normal_kernel/ > normal.txt
 # tree rescue_kernel/ > rescue.txt

The following are the differences among both the initramfs systems. The rescue initramfs system has almost 2,189 extra files compared to the normal initramfs. Also, almost 719 extra modules have been added in the rescue initramfs.

 # diff -yt rescue.txt normal.txt | grep '<' | wc -l
   2186
 # diff -yt rescue.txt normal.txt | grep '<' | grep -i '.ko' | wc -l
   719

```
<skip>
.
.
|   |   |---- lspci                            <
|   |   |---- mdadm                            <
|   |   |---- mdmon                            <
|   |   |---- mdraid-cleanup                   <
|   |   |---- mdraid_start                     <
|   |   |---- mount.cifs                       <
|   |   |---- mount.nfs                        <
|   |   |---- mount.nfs4 -> mount.nfs          <
|   |   |---- mpathpersist                     <
|   |   |---- multipath                        <
|   |   |---- multipathd                       <
|   |   |---- nfsroot                          <
|   |   |---- partx                            <
```

441

```
|   |     ├── pdata_tools                                      <
|   |     ├── ping -> ../bin/ping                              <
|   |     ├── ping6 -> ../bin/ping                             <
|   |     ├── rpcbind -> ../bin/rpcbind                        <
|   |     ├── rpc.idmapd                                       <
|   |     ├── rpcinfo -> ../bin/rpcinfo                        <
|   |     ├── rpc.statd                                        <
|   |     ├── setpci                                           <
|   |     ├── showmount                                        <
|   |     ├── thin_check -> pdata_tools                        <
|   |     ├── thin_dump -> pdata_tools                         <
|   |     ├── thin_repair -> pdata_tools                       <
|   |     ├── thin_restore -> pdata_tools                      <
|   |     ├── xfs_db                                           <
|   |     ├── xfs_metadump                                     <
|   |     └── xfs_repair                                       <
├── lib                                                        <
|   ├── iscsi                                                  <
|   ├── lldpad                                                 <
|   ├── nfs                                                    <
|   |   ├── rpc_pipefs                                         <
|   |   └── statd                                              <
|   |       └── sm                                             <
</skip>
```

The rescue initramfs will have almost all the modules and supported files for the device on which the user can make a root filesystem, whereas the normal initramfs will be host-specific. It will have only those modules and supported files of the device on which the user has made the root filesystem. If you want to make a rescue initramfs on your own, then you can install a dracut-config-generic package on Fedora-based systems. The package provides only one file, and it has the configuration to turn off the host-specific initramfs generation.

 # rpm -ql dracut-config-generic
```
    /usr/lib/dracut/dracut.conf.d/02-generic-image.conf
```

```
# cat /usr/lib/dracut/dracut.conf.d/02-generic-image.conf
    hostonly="no"
```

As you can see, the file will restrict dracut from creating a host-specific initramfs.

"Can't Boot" Issue 9 (chroot)

Issue: Both the normal and rescue kernels are failing to boot. Figure 10-7 shows the normal kernel panic messages.

```
Press any key to continue...
[    2.050006] Kernel panic - not syncing: VFS: Unable to mount root fs on unkno
wn-block(0,0)
[    2.050145] CPU: 2 PID: 1 Comm: swapper/0 Not tainted 5.3.7-301.fc31.x86_64 #
1
[    2.050248] Hardware name: VMware, Inc. VMware Virtual Platform/440BX Desk::op
 Reference Platform, BIOS 6.00 07/29/2019
[    2.050340] Call Trace:
[    2.050373]  dump_stack+0x5c/0x80
[    2.050407]  panic+0x101/0x2d7
[    2.050440]  mount_block_root+0x25b/0x306
[    2.050477]  prepare_namespace+0x13b/0x171
[    2.050514]  kernel_init_freeable+0x220/0x248
[    2.050554]  ? rest_init+0xaa/0xaa
[    2.050586]  kernel_init+0xa/0x106
[    2.050619]  ret_from_fork+0x35/0x40
[    2.051027] Kernel Offset: 0x21000000 from 0xffffffff81000000 (relocation ran
ge: 0xffffffff80000000-0xffffffffbfffffff)
[    2.051149] ---[ end Kernel panic - not syncing: VFS: Unable to mount root fs
 on unknown-block(0,0) ]---
_
```

Figure 10-7. *The kernel panic messages*

The thrown kernel panic messages are complaining that the kernel is not able to mount the root filesystem. We saw earlier that whenever the kernel is not able to mount the user's root filesystem, it throws the dracut-initqueue timeout messages.

'dracut-initqueue: warning dracut-initqueue timeout - starting timeout scripts'

However, this time, the panic messages are different. So, it looks like the issue is not related to the user's root filesystem. One more clue is that it mentions the VFS filesystem; VFS stands for "virtual file system," so this indicates that the panic messages are not able to mount the root filesystem from initramfs. Based on these clues, I guess we have isolated the issue, and we should concentrate on initramfs of both the kernels.

As you can see in Figure 10-8, the rescue mode kernel panic messages are also similar.

```
Press any key to continue...
[    1.992168] Kernel panic - not syncing: VFS: Unable to mount root fs on unkno
wn-block(0.0)
[    1.992271] CPU: 3 PID: 1 Comm: swapper/0 Not tainted 5.3.7-301.fc31.x86_64 #
1
[    1.992341] Hardware name: VMware, Inc. VMware Virtual Platform/440BX Desktop
 Reference Platform, BIOS 6.00 07/29/2019
[    1.992412] Call Trace:
[    1.992437]  dump_stack+0x5c/0x80
[    1.992463]  panic+0x101/0x2d7
[    1.992488]  mount_block_root+0x25b/0x306
[    1.992516]  prepare_namespace+0x13b/0x171
[    1.992544]  kernel_init_freeable+0x220/0x248
[    1.992575]  ? rest_init+0xaa/0xaa
[    1.992610]  kernel_init+0xa/0x106
[    1.992636]  ret_from_fork+0x35/0x40
[    1.992992] Kernel Offset: 0x2e000000 from 0xffffffff81000000 (relocation ran
ge: 0xffffffff80000000-0xffffffffbfffffff)
[    1.993092] ---[ end Kernel panic - not syncing: VFS: Unable to mount root fs
 on unknown-block(0,0) ]---
```

Figure 10-8. *The rescue mode kernel panic messages*

Resolution: Here are the steps to resolve the issue:

1) Since the installed rescue kernel is also panicking, we need to use the live image of Fedora or of any Linux distribution to boot. As shown in Figure 10-9 and Figure 10-10, we are using a live image of Fedora.

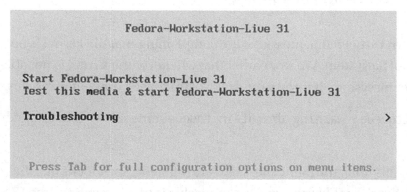

Figure 10-9. *The live image welcome screen*

```
                        Troubleshooting

    Start Fedora-Workstation-Live 31 in basic graphics mode
    Run a memory test

    Boot from local drive


    Return to main menu                                      <


      Press Tab for full configuration options on menu items.

    Try this option out if you're having trouble starting
    Fedora-Workstation-Live 31.
```

Figure 10-10. *Booting with a live image*

2) The system has booted in rescue mode. The live image booting sequence will be discussed in the "Live Images" section of this chapter. Let's become a sudo user first.

   ```
   $ sudo su
   ```

   ```
   We trust you have received the usual lecture from your local
   system administrator. It usually boils down to these three things:
   ```

   ```
   #1) Respect the privacy of others.
   #2) Think before you type.
   #3) With great power comes great responsibility.
   ```

   ```
   [root@localhost-live liveuser] #
   ```

3) The root directory that we are seeing here is from a live image. Since the live image kernel does not know the name of the user's root filesystem, it cannot mount it like a rescue kernel.

   ```
   [root@localhost-live liveuser]# ls /
        bin boot dev etc home lib lib64 lost+found media mnt
        opt proc root run sbin srv sys tmp usr var
   ```

4) Let's find out what is wrong with the initramfs of the normal and rescue kernels. To do that, we need to mount the user's root filesystem first.

```
# vgscan -v
    Found volume group "fedora_localhost-live" using metadata type lvm2

# lvscan -v
    ACTIVE        '/dev/fedora_localhost-live/swap' [2.20 GiB] inherit
    ACTIVE        '/dev/fedora_localhost-live/root' [18.79 GiB]
inherit

# pvscan -v
    PV /dev/sda2  VG fedora_localhost-live  lvm2 [<21.00 GiB / 0  free]
    Total: 1 [<21.00 GiB] / in use: 1 [<21.00 GiB] / in no VG: 0 [0 ]
```

As you can see, this system has a user's root filesystem based on LVM. The physical volume is on the sda device. Next we will mount the user's root filesystem on a temporary directory.

```
# mkdir temp_root
# mount /dev/fedora_localhost-live/root temp_root/
# ls temp_root/
    bin   dev  home  lib64  media  opt    root  sbin  sys
    tmp usr boot  etc  lib    lost+found  mnt        proc  run
    srv   @System.solv  user_root_fs.txt  var
```

5) Let's check the initramfs file's status.

```
# ls temp_root/boot/ -l
    total 0
```

The boot directory of the user's root filesystem is empty. That is because on this system, the boot is a separate partition.

```
# mount /dev/sda1 temp_root/boot/
#ls temp_root/boot/
Config-5.3.7-301.fc31.x86_64  efi elf-memtest86+-5.01
extlinux grub2 loader lost+found
Memtest86+-5.01 System.map-5.3.7-301.fc31.x86_64
vmlinuz-0-rescue-19a08a3e86c24b459999fbac68e42c05
vmlinuz-5.3.7-301.fc31.x86_64
```

Surprisingly, as you can see, there are no initramfs files available on the user's root filesystem, and this is the reason why both the kernels were panicking.

So, the issue has been identified, and we need to regenerate the initramfs. To make the new initramfs, we need to use the dracut command, but there are some problems.

- Whichever binary or command we execute, that binary will be from the live image root filesystem. For example, the dracut command will run from /usr/bin/dracut, whereas the user's root filesystem's binary is in temp_root/usr/bin/dracut.

- To run any binary, it needs supporting libraries like libc.so, which will again be used from the root filesystem of a live image. This means the entire environment that we are using now is from the live image, and it can create serious issues. For example, we can install any package, and it will be installed in the live image root filesystem, not in the user's root filesystem.

In short, we need to change our current root (/) from the live image root filesystem to the user's root filesystem (temp_root). chroot is the command that we need to use for this.

6) The name itself suggests it will change the root of bash from the current root to the new root. chroot will be successful only if the virtual filesystems are already mounted on the new root.

```
root@localhost-live liveuser]# ls /
    bin  boot  dev  etc  home  lib  lib64  lost+found  media  mnt
    opt  proc  root  run  sbin  srv  sys  tmp  usr  var
```

Our current root is the live image root filesystem. Before chroot, we will mount the proc, dev, devpts, sys, and run virtual filesystems.

```
# mount -v --bind /dev/ temp_root/dev
mount: /dev bound on /home/liveuser/temp_root/dev.

# mount -vt devpts devpts temp_root/dev/pts -o gid=5,mode=620
mount: devpts mounted on /home/liveuser/temp_root/dev/pts.

# mount -vt proc proc temp_root/proc
mount: proc mounted on /home/liveuser/temp_root/proc.

# mount -vt sysfs sysfs temp_root/sys
mount: sysfs mounted on /home/liveuser/temp_root/sys.
```

```
# mount -vt tmpfs tmpfs temp_root/run
mount: tmpfs mounted on /home/liveuser/temp_root/run.
```

7)   We are all set to chroot into a user's root filesystem.

```
# chroot temp_root/
# ls
        bin    dev  home  lib64
media  opt    root  sbin  sys    tmp
        usr boot  etc  lib    lost+found  mnt      proc  run    srv
        @System.solv  user_root_fs.txt  var
```

So, temp_root became the root filesystem of bash now. If you exit from this shell, bash will change its root directory from the user's root filesystem to a live image root filesystem. So, as long as we are in the same shell instance, our root directory is temp_root. Now, no matter what command or binary we execute, it will run inside the user's root filesystem environment. Hence, it is completely safe to execute the processes in this environment now.

8)   To fix this "can't boot" issue, we need to regenerate initramfs.

```
root@localhost-live /]# ls /lib/modules
5.3.7-301.fc31.x86_64
```

```
[root@localhost-live /]# cd /boot/
```

```
[root@localhost-live boot]# rpm -qa | grep -i 'kernel-5'
kernel-5.3.7-301.fc31.x86_64
```

```
[root@localhost-live boot]# dracut initramfs-5.3.7-301.fc31.
x86_64.img  5.3.7-301.fc31.x86_64
```

9)   If you want to regenerate the rescue kernel initramfs, then you need to install a dracut-config-generic package.

10)   After rebooting, the system is able to boot, and the "can't boot" issue has been fixed.

Rescue Mode of Enterprise Linux Distributions

In some of the Linux distributions such as CentOS, the rescue image approach is a bit different. The enterprise edition of Linux will try to find the user's root filesystem on its own. Let's see this in action. Figure 10-11 and Figure 10-12 show the rescue mode selection procedure of CentOS.

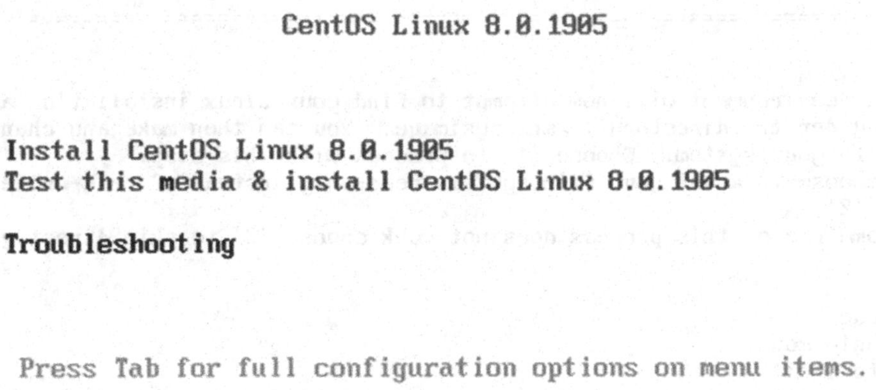

```
                  CentOS Linux 8.0.1905


   Install CentOS Linux 8.0.1905
   Test this media & install CentOS Linux 8.0.1905

   Troubleshooting                                              >



   Press Tab for full configuration options on menu items.
```

Figure 10-11. *The CentOS welcome screen*

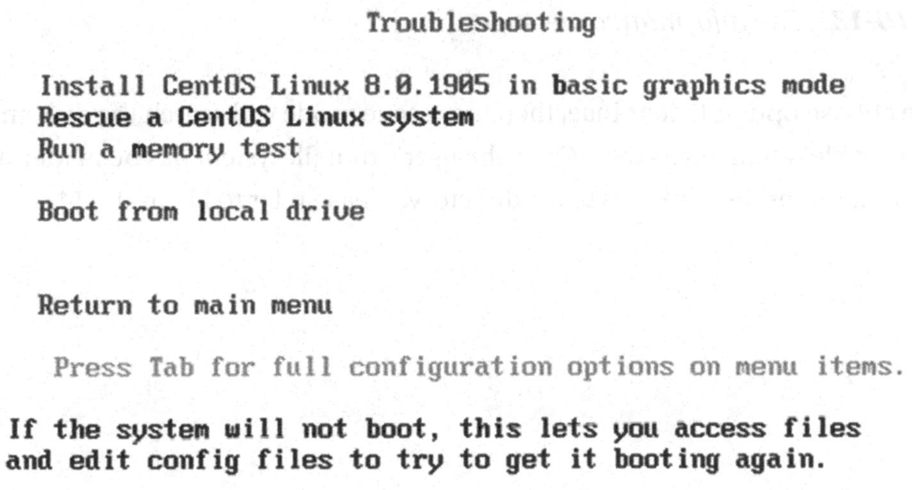

```
                     Troubleshooting

     Install CentOS Linux 8.0.1905 in basic graphics mode
     Rescue a CentOS Linux system
     Run a memory test

     Boot from local drive


     Return to main menu

      Press Tab for full configuration options on menu items.

    If the system will not boot, this lets you access files
    and edit config files to try to get it booting again.
```

Figure 10-12. *The rescue mode selection*

It will boot, and as you can see in Figure 10-13, it will display some messages on the screen.

```
Starting installer, one moment...
anaconda 29.19.0.40-1.el8 for CentOS Linux 8.0.1905 started.
 * installation log files are stored in /tmp during the installation
 * shell is available on TTY2
 * when reporting a bug add logs from /tmp as separate text/plain attachments
===============================================================================
===============================================================================
Rescue

The rescue environment will now attempt to find your Linux installation and
mount it under the directory : /mnt/sysimage.  You can then make any changes
required to your system.  Choose '1' to proceed with this step.
You can choose to mount your file systems read-only instead of read-write by
choosing '2'.
If for some reason this process does not work choose '3' to skip directly to a
shell.

1) Continue
2) Read-only mount
3) Skip to shell
4) Quit (Reboot)

Please make a selection from the above: 1
```

Figure 10-13. *The informative message*

If we choose option 1, continue, then the rescue mode will search the disk and will find the root filesystem on its own. Once the user's root filesystem has been identified, it will mount it under the /mnt/sysimage directory. Please refer to Figure 10-14.

```
1) Continue
2) Read-only mount
3) Skip to shell
4) Quit (Reboot)

Please make a selection from the above: 1
===============================================================================
===============================================================================
Rescue Shell

Your system has been mounted under /mnt/sysimage.

If you would like to make the root of your system the root of the active system,
run the command:

        chroot /mnt/sysimage
When finished, please exit from the shell and your system will reboot.
Please press ENTER to get a shell:
sh-4.4#
sh-4.4#
sh-4.4#
sh-4.4#
[anaconda]1:main* 2:shell  3:log  4:storage-log  5:program-log        Switch tab: Alt
```

Figure 10-14. *The root filesystem is mounted under /mnt/sysimage*

As you can see, it has mounted the user's root filesystem in /mnt/sysimage; we just
need to chroot into it. But the beauty is we don't need to mount the virtual filesystems
beforehand. This is because, as you can see in Figure 10-15, the chroot binary used in
CentOS has been customized, and it will mount the virtual filesystems on its own.

```
sh-4.4#
sh-4.4#
sh-4.4#
sh-4.4# ls /mnt/sysimage/
bin   dev  home  lib64  mnt   proc  run   srv   tmp  var
boot  etc  lib   media  opt   root  sbin  sys   usr
sh-4.4#
sh-4.4# chroot  /mnt/sysimage/
bash-4.4#
bash-4.4# ls /
bin   dev  home  lib64  mnt   proc  run   srv   tmp  var
boot  etc  lib   media  opt   root  sbin  sys   usr
bash-4.4#
bash-4.4#
[anaconda]1:main* 2:shell  3:log  4:storage-log  5:program-log
```

Figure 10-15. *chroot*

If we had chosen option 2, Read-Only Mount, then the rescue scripts would have mounted the user's root filesystem in read-only mode but in /mnt/sysimage. If we had chosen the third option of Skip, the rescue system would not have attempted to find and mount the user's root filesystem on its own; it would have simply provided us with a shell.

But how does it manage to find out the root filesystem when the rescue kernel of the CentOS ISO does not have a user's root filesystem name with it?

There is no trick here that Anaconda can do to find out the user's root filesystem name. Anaconda will mount each and every disk connected to the system and check whether /etc/fstab is present on it or not. If /etc/fstab is found, then it will fetch the user's root filesystem name from it. If your system has a huge number of disks attached, then there is a high chance that Anaconda might take a long time to mount the user's root filesystem. It is better to manually mount the user's root filesystem in such a scenario. The source code to find the user's root filesystem is present in Anaconda's source tarball, as shown here:

#vim pyanaconda/storage/root.py

```
 91 def _find_existing_installations(devicetree):
 92     """Find existing GNU/Linux installations on devices from the
            device tree.
 93
 94     :param devicetree: a device tree to find existing installations in
 95     :return: roots of all found installations
 96     """
 97     if not os.path.exists(conf.target.physical_root):
 98         blivet_util.makedirs(conf.target.physical_root)
 99
100     sysroot = conf.target.physical_root
101     roots = []
102     direct_devices = (dev for dev in devicetree.devices if dev.direct)
103     for device in direct_devices:
104         if not device.format.linux_native or not device.format.
                mountable or \
105             not device.controllable or not device.format.exists:
106               continue
```

```
107
108        try:
109            device.setup()
110        except Exception:  # pylint: disable=broad-except
111            log_exception_info(log.warning, "setup of %s failed",
                   [device.name])
112            continue
113
114        options = device.format.options + ",ro"
115        try:
116            device.format.mount(options=options, mountpoint=sysroot)
117        except Exception:  # pylint: disable=broad-except
118            log_exception_info(log.warning, "mount of %s as %s failed",
                   [device.name, device.format.type])
119            blivet_util.umount(mountpoint=sysroot)
120            continue
121
122        if not os.access(sysroot + "/etc/fstab", os.R_OK):
123            blivet_util.umount(mountpoint=sysroot)
124            device.teardown()
125            continue
126
127        try:
128            (architecture, product, version) = get_release_
                   string(chroot=sysroot)
129        except ValueError:
130            name = _("Linux on %s") % device.name
131        else:
132            # I'd like to make this finer grained, but it'd be very
                   difficult
133            # to translate.
134            if not product or not version or not architecture:
135                name = _("Unknown Linux")
136            elif "linux" in product.lower():
137                name = _("%(product)s %(version)s for %(arch)s") % \
```

```
138                        {"product": product, "version": version, "arch":
                           architecture}
139          else:
140              name = _("%(product)s Linux %(version)s for %(arch)s") % \
141                        {"product": product, "version": version, "arch":
                           architecture}
142
143      (mounts, swaps) = _parse_fstab(devicetree, chroot=sysroot)
144      blivet_util.umount(mountpoint=sysroot)
145      if not mounts and not swaps:
146          # empty /etc/fstab. weird, but I've seen it happen.
147          continue
148      roots.append(Root(mounts=mounts, swaps=swaps, name=name))
149
```

Live Images

Live images are one of the best features of Linux systems. This book wouldn't be complete if we just stuck to the normal hard disk booting part. Let's see how a live image of Linux boots. First let's mount the ISO image and see what it holds.

```
# mkdir live_image
# mount /dev/cdrom live_image/
mount: /home/yogesh/live_image: WARNING: device write-protected, mounted
read-only.
```

```
# tree live_image/
live_image/
├── EFI
│   └── BOOT
│       ├── BOOT.conf
│       ├── BOOTIA32.EFI
│       ├── BOOTX64.EFI
│       ├── fonts
│       │   └── unicode.pf2
│       ├── grub.cfg
```

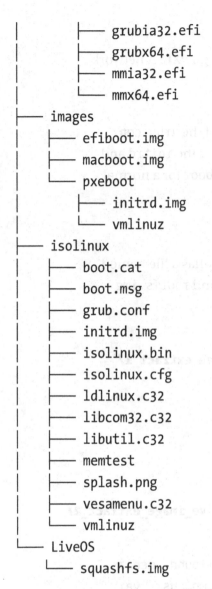

```
│       ├── grubia32.efi
│       ├── grubx64.efi
│       ├── mmia32.efi
│       └── mmx64.efi
├── images
│   ├── efiboot.img
│   ├── macboot.img
│   └── pxeboot
│       ├── initrd.img
│       └── vmlinuz
├── isolinux
│   ├── boot.cat
│   ├── boot.msg
│   ├── grub.conf
│   ├── initrd.img
│   ├── isolinux.bin
│   ├── isolinux.cfg
│   ├── ldlinux.c32
│   ├── libcom32.c32
│   ├── libutil.c32
│   ├── memtest
│   ├── splash.png
│   ├── vesamenu.c32
│   └── vmlinuz
└── LiveOS
    └── squashfs.img
```

The live image is divided into four directories: EFI, images, isolinux, and LiveOS.

- **EFI:**

  We have already discussed this directory when talking about the bootloader. The UEFI firmware will jump into this directory and will run the grubx64.efi file. The grubx64.efi file will read the grub.cfg file and will pull the initrd.img and vmlinuz files from the isolinux directory.

- **images:**

  This will be used mainly if we are booting through PXE. A network boot is out of the scope of this book.

- **isolinux:**

  If UEFI is booting the BIOS way, then it will read the grub.conf file from here. This directory is mainly for storing the initrd and vmlinuz files. In other words, this directory is /boot for a normal root filesystem.

- **liveOS:**

  This is where the magic happens. This directory has a file named squashfs.img. Once you mount that, you will find rootfs.img in it.

```
# mkdir live_image_extract_1
# mount live_image/LiveOS/squashfs.img  live_image_extract_1/

# ls live_image_extract_1/
    LiveOS
# ls live_image_extract_1/LiveOS/
    rootfs.img

# mkdir live_image_extract_2
# mount live_image_extract_1/LiveOS/rootfs.img live_image_extract_2/

# ls live_image_extract_2/
    bin   boot  dev  etc  home  lib  lib64  lost+found  media
    mnt  opt  proc  root  run  sbin  srv  sys  tmp  usr  var
```

SquashFS

Squashfs is a small, compressed, read-only filesystem. This filesystem is generally used for embedded systems where every byte of storage is precious. Squashfs gives us more flexibility and performance over tarball archives. Squashfs stores a live Fedora's root filesystem (rootfs.img) in it, and it will be mounted as read-only.

 # mount | grep -i rootfs
/home/yogesh/live_image_extract_1/LiveOS/rootfs.img on /home/yogesh/
live_image_extract_2 type ext4 (ro,relatime,seclabel)

You can use the mksquashfs command provided by squashfs-tool to make the Squashfs image/archive.

rootfs.img

rootfs.img is an ext4 filesystem with a typical root filesystem in it. Some distros create a guest user or a user named live for a live image, but in Fedora it's the root user who does everything.

 # file live_image_extract_1/LiveOS/rootfs.img
live_image_extract_1/LiveOS/rootfs.img: Linux rev 1.0 **ext4 filesystem data**,
UUID=849bdfdc-c8a9-4fed-a727-de52e24d981f, volume name "Anaconda" (extents)
(64bit) (large files) (huge files)

Booting Sequence of a Live Image

Here is the sequence:

1) The firmware will call the bootloader (grubx64.efi). It will read the grub.cfg file and copy the vmlinuz and initrd files from the isolinux directory.

2) The kernel will extract itself at a specific location and will extract initramfs at any available location.

3) systemd, started from initramfs, will extract the rootfs.img file to the device-mapper target device at /dev/mapper/live-rw, mount it on the root (/) filesystem, and switch_root into it.

4) Once the root filesystem is available, you can consider it as a normal operating that is installed in a CD, DVD, or .iso file.

Also, it is obvious that the live-image initramfs will be much bigger in size compared to the host-specific initramfs.

Index

© Yogesh Babar 2020
Y. Babar, *Hands-on Booting*, https://doi.org/10.1007/978-1-4842-5890-3

Printed in the United States
By Bookmasters